PRAISE FOR
HARRY POTTER AND THE ART OF SPYING
YOUNG AGENT EDITION

"A truly imaginative romp through much of the spycraft I tried
to teach Harry—almost as pleasant as lemon drops!"
– ALBUS DUMBLEDORE

"Harry finally figured everything out—thanks to me. Maybe
he wouldn't have been so slow if he had this wonderful book."
– SEVERUS SNAPE

"A truly intellectual book to teach the younger reader
much of what we—well, at least what I—learned roaming
the stacks in the library."
– HERMIONE GRANGER

"A real giant of a book! But the *Monster Book of
Monsters* 'tweer better."
– RUBEUS HAGRID

UNAUTHORIZED
HARRY POTTER
AND THE ART OF SPYING

LYNN BOUGHEY
AUTHOR OF THE SPY NOVEL, *MISSION TO CHARA*

PETER EARNEST
EXECUTIVE DIRECTOR, INTERNATIONAL SPY MUSEUM

WISE
CREATIVE • PUBLISHING
Ink

ISBN 13: 978-1-940014-14-2

Library of Congress Catalog Number: 2014936945

Printed in the United States of America
Third Printing: 2017
20   19   18   17   6   5   4   3

Cover and Interior design and typesetting by James Monroe Design LLC.

Wise Ink, Inc.
837 Glenwood Avenue
Minneapolis, MN 55408
www.wiseinkpub.com
To order, visit www.itascabooks.com or call 1-800-901-3480.
Reseller discounts available.

CONTENTS

PART 1
SPY CRAFT IN *HARRY POTTER AND THE ORDER OF THE PHOENIX*: A CHAPTER·BY·CHAPTER REVIEW

iii

HARRY POTTER AND THE ART OF SPYING

CONTENTS

PART 2
THE ART OF SPYING IN THE WIZARDING AND MUGGLE WORLDS

CONTENTS

ACKNOWLEDGMENTS

Lynn received great assistance with talking through some of the more esoteric aspects of the Potter series from his many fellow Harry Potter fans. Much of the book was typed up by Courtney Klein of Minot and Nichole Ellis of Red Lodge, both of whom know the Potter series so well that they added their own insights, discussed the most subtle nuances, and made necessary corrections. Nichole also found each and every page reference so the readers can go straight to the source if they so desire! Thank you to Adam Files of New York City for the preliminary draft of the book cover, Jay of James Monroe Design for the final book cover, and Amy Quale of Wise Ink Creative Publishing for all her assistance. Kellie Hultgren of KMH Editing provided literally thousands of suggestions and edits, which were gladly received and incorporated into this book. Kellie also took on the task of transforming this book into a children's or young adult version, which will be coming out in the near future. The team of Amy, Kellie, and Jay made our final product so much better, and we thank all three not only for this assistance and professionalism, but also for making the project fun and even the editing process enjoyable.

We also acknowledge the assistance of Allison Bishop and Jackie Eyl at the International Spy Museum and their insights about children's books and book selling in general, and Peter's assistant, Mary Henderson, for arranging meetings at the International Spy Museum. We also thank David Major for reviewing the Hanssen information.

I thank my twin daughters, Miranda and Sophia, who found enjoyment in the stories first when they were read to them and then on their own. Like their father, they are avid Harry Potter fans.

—Lynn

To my wife Karen, for her humor, imagination and boundless support, and my daughters Nancy, Sheila, Patricia, and Carol whose childhoods kept the magic alive.

—Peter

ABBREVIATIONS

Throughout this book we provide page references so the reader can review what was said or what happened in the original book. In part one, which focuses almost exclusively on book 5, *Harry Potter and the Order of the Phoenix*, we provide the page numbers alone. When discussing other books in part one, and throughout part two, we use the following abbreviations:

Book 1   SS—*Harry Potter and the Sorcerer's Stone*

Book 2   CS—*Harry Potter and the Chamber of Secrets*

Book 3   PA—*Harry Potter and the Prisoner of Azkaban*

Book 4   GF—*Harry Potter and the Goblet of Fire*

Book 5   OP—*Harry Potter and the Order of the Phoenix*

Book 6   HBP—*Harry Potter and the Half-Blood Prince*

Book 7   DH—*Harry Potter and the Deathly Hallows*

Page references to these books appear in parentheses. These refer to the first US hardcover printing.

Words contained in the glossary are shown in bold at first use.

INTRODUCTION

There have been many books and articles written about the Harry Potter series, using the wonderful world created by J. K. Rowling as a means to discuss history, psychology, law, philosophy, and even cooking! But no one, until now, has reviewed the many elements of spy craft and the art of spying that exists throughout the Potter series.

Each of the Potter books contains numerous elements of spying: use of codes (62442), covert observations (often using the invisibility cloak), science and technology (extendable ears), secret messages (letters to "Snuffles"), psychological warfare ("Weasley Is Our King"), misdirection (Snape—need we say more?), the use of elucidation and interrogation (Harry's trial before the Wizengamot), and even the creation of subversive organizations (Dumbledore's Army)!

The books of the Potter series provide numerous hidden clues and require the careful reader to repeatedly apply critical thinking and analysis.

In our view, this is no mere set of kids' books, but a complex, multifaceted, superb primer on spying and spy craft!

Peter, with his thirty-six years at the CIA primarily in covert operations, and Lynn, with his background as a spy novelist and research using spying methods, try to bring all these facets together in a fun-filled romp through the Potter series with special emphasis on book five, *Harry Potter and the Order of the Phoenix*, a book that superbly describes the art of spying.

HARRY POTTER AND THE ART OF SPYING

Although some Potterphiles consider *Order of the Phoenix* to be one of the lesser books in the series, we heartily disagree. This book is Harry's true coming-of-age story, alongside his best friends Hermione and Ron. With little to no help from the adults, the famous triad rebels against authority, organizes a **subversive organization**, and takes matters into its own hands! The fact that the kids must do this in secret allows them to develop important skills not only in magic, but in spy craft as well.

We hope you join up and come along for the ride!

Lynn Boughey & Peter Earnest

This book is for those young men and women who choose to serve their country in any way—particularly those who decide to join the CIA or other intelligence organizations. The world is indeed worth saving, and only the best and the brightest, imbued with a thorough understanding of politics and the human condition, have a chance to steer the course of destiny toward an ideal worthy of the effort. It is always better to preserve peace through the wise use of information and knowledge—or even covert action—than to be forced to wage a war.

PART 1

SPY CRAFT IN
HARRY POTTER AND THE ORDER
OF THE PHOENIX:
A CHAPTER·BY·CHAPTER REVIEW

1

SAVING PRIVATE DUDLEY—
THE SPIES AMONG US

In chapter 1 of *Harry Potter and the Order of the Phoenix*, "Dudley Demented," secrecy and spying are everywhere. The adventure begins, as usual, on Privet Drive. We find Harry hiding in the bushes, trying to listen to the news (*OP* 1). There's a short reference to that batty neighbor Mrs. Figg, Harry's unpleasant old babysitter (2). (Of course we soon find out that there's a lot more to Mrs. Figg!) Harry is interested in the news because he hopes that the Muggle world may, in some way, report on the return of Lord Voldemort through "an unexplained disappearance, perhaps, or some strange accident" (3).

In the **spy** business, news is a form of what we call **open-source** intelligence. This merely means that a good spy, or **intelligence officer**, is able to learn much from public sources. These include newspapers, webpages, and, yes indeed, those bothersome people on the nightly news who jabber on and on about which country is doing this and which candidate is saying that and the usual nonsense of Muggles who have no clue that a war is brewing right under their noses!

One of Harry's concerns—indeed, a *negative* observation—is

the lack of any real information in the owls from his friends. We all know that wizards use owls as couriers for **secure communications**—although sometimes they are not so secure. (Who could forget that scene in the first book when hundreds upon hundreds of owls bombarded the Dursleys' home with Harry's first letter from Hogwarts?) But the notes this summer from his friends and his godfather Sirius have instead been filled with statements like "can't say much," "have been told not to say anything important in case our letters go astray," and "can't give you any details here" (8–9). Letters going astray?

ANALYSIS: *Why are Harry's friends refusing to say much in their letters to Harry?* They fear that their letters may be intercepted!

When someone other than the person to whom a message is addressed reads or overhears the message, we call it a **communication interception** or a **compromised communication**. We find out later in this book that there have indeed been attempts to intercept owls. Once Harry understands what's going on, he starts writing his messages in a way that only the recipient (for example, Sirius) will understand.

~~~~~~

SHERLOCK HOLMES AND THE DOG THAT DIDN'T BARK

Sometimes what is *not* said or what does *not* happen is an important clue. After learning that a watchdog failed to bark at an intruder, Sherlock Holmes suspected that it didn't bark because the person committing the crime was the dog's owner! This is a negative **observation**.

~~~~~~

Now, a word about communication: **COMMUNICATION!**
Throughout the seven books we find references to the Wizarding world's inability to understand the telephone, which seems quite

strange given their superb intelligence in so many other areas. Every spy must understand technology and how to use it. Mr. Weasley, whose job deals entirely with Muggle artifacts, has asked Harry on several occasions how the phone works, and when wizards attempt to use the phone in the series, it seems to be very problematic—and of course quite humorous (*PA* 4)!

Anyway, back to the owls and communication. We've always wondered throughout our reading of the series whether Dumbledore was able to turn himself into an owl, just as Professor McGonagall can turn herself into a cat! What a wonderful **disguise**! This would certainly explain the owls appearing throughout the book! Is the owl flying through these scenes Professor Dumbledore checking on Harry? It's something to think about!

We will never know for certain—unless, of course, our good friend J. K. Rowling decides to publish what has been termed *The 8th Book*: an encyclopedia of all the bits and pieces untold in the Harry Potter series. According to some press reports, Rowling has a box of notes that she created while writing the series—notes that provide substantial details about the backgrounds of many of the characters, including plot lines involving Lee Jordan and Seamus Finnigan that were cut from the books.

But we digress: time to get back to the story!

So here we have Harry underneath the window, waiting for the news. He suddenly hears a noise that sounds like an Apparation (or is it a Disapparation?), that is, the sound a wizard makes when disappearing from one location and appearing in another.

HERMIONE'S TIME-TURNER AND CATHOLIC BELIEF IN BILOCATION

According to Catholic beliefs, some of the saints, such as Padre Pio the Mystic, were able to be in two locations at once, a capability called *bilocation*. This gift is always used for acts of mercy or benevolence. Perhaps such legends served as a basis for Hermione's Time-Turner, which allowed Harry and Hermione to save Buckbeak and rescue Sirius by being in two places at once in book 3, *Harry Potter and the Prisoner of Azkaban*!

~~~~~~~~~~~~~~~~

Apparating and Disapparating: what a wonderful way to get from one place to another! So, Harry hears a CRACK! After what happened at the cemetery in the previous book, Harry immediately has his wand at the ready, as he should (4)!

ANALYSIS: *Why did Harry go into defensive mode?* By now Harry is well aware that a certain portion of the Wizarding world wants him dead—or at least captured. However, the cracking sound occurs when someone Apparates—*or Disapparates*. Thus, is it possible that somebody has just *arrived*, but it is *equally possible* that somebody has just *left*!

Unfortunately for our young spy, Harry does *not* control his movements or consider his present surroundings fully. When Harry hears what he thinks is someone Apparating, he jumps up and hits his head on the open window—and is of course discovered by his uncle, Vernon Dursley (4).

NOTE TO SELF: *A good spy can control his or her actions—and reactions!*

Moments later, as Harry is being throttled by Uncle Vernon, his forehead hurts (5). This reminds us of the rather unique **communication device** or method that only Harry has: his scar. Harry, as we all know, has the ability—perhaps some would say the *misfortune*—of being able to read Voldemort's thoughts, and sometimes see what Voldemort sees, and apparently what the snake Nagini sees as well.

How can this be? (We find out at the end, of course—something about Horcruxes and a rebounding, lethal Avada Kedavra Curse and the only living thing left in the room [*DH* 686]). In any event, Harry can indeed "read" Voldemort's mind and perceive Voldemort's emotions. Wouldn't every spy want to be able to read the mind of the enemy?

~~~~~~

READING MINDS

The **intelligence community** spent substantial time and money trying to develop "distant viewing" or "remote viewing," which is the ability to visualize places and things from far away. Whether people have or are truly able to use these powers is a matter of great controversy.

~~~~~~

Although reading Voldemort's mind isn't *fun* for Harry, it is a wonderful tool. Harry uses it to great advantage in book 7, *Harry Potter and the Deathly Hallows*, when he needs to find out where Voldemort is meeting with Snape (*DH* 641).

In the first few pages of *Order of the Phoenix*, secrecy and spying are everywhere. Harry is spying on his aunt and uncle. As soon as the neighbors come out, Harry puts his wand away so that no one sees his Wizarding tool. (Statute of Secrecy, you know!)

As Harry leaves the Dursleys' home, we see an example of **counter surveillance**: Harry turns around quickly, sensing that perhaps he is being followed (7). Counter surveillance is merely the act of seeing if you are being spied upon, and Harry knows enough to do just that! And although Harry has been listening to the news for small tidbits that might indicate that something major is happening, he has merely been glancing at the headlines of the *Daily Prophet*. Harry knows that when the "idiots" running the paper finally realize Voldemort is back it will be headline news (8). He has, in other words, concluded that as a source of information, the *Daily Prophet* is not to be trusted: it is filled with lies and indeed is to be *ignored*.

This is a mistake, as Harry finds out soon enough. *Reading even the garbage put out by the enemy is more than a good idea!* It tells you what they are thinking. It tells you what lies are being spread. And it tells you whether—just maybe—the Ministry might be spreading lies about you, Harry Potter!

We further observe two mistakes in spy craft that Harry makes by leaving the Dursleys' and heading to the playground. First, he leaves his **safe house**. Second, he follows a **routine**, in this case a familiar path to his normal haunt. By not changing the pattern of his movements, he makes it quite easy for someone to intercept or capture him (9).

If you are trying to avoid discovery or capture, routine is your enemy. If you are attempting to hide in plain sight, however, routine can be your friend: everyone is used to seeing you at the same times, in the same places. You no longer surprise someone by appearing at a location.

Once on his way, Harry improves his spylike behavior and **observes** the various streets he's on (9). This too is open-source intelligence: information sitting out in the open for anyone to observe. Such observations might at first appear mundane, but in reality, knowing the streets and being able to create a map is essential not only to getting yourself around, but also to telling others how to get where you have gone or where you are going!

And although Harry does not quite understand this yet, number four, Privet Drive, is indeed Harry's safe house: a place where Voldemort and his minions are unable to attack him due to the bond that he has with his mother's remaining family member, Aunt Petunia (836).

We must also mention Harry's **cover story**: the false background created by the Dursleys to explain Harry's presence in their home and, later, his disappearance during the school year. The Dursleys had previously told Harry that his parents had died in a car crash (*SS* 20), which Harry discovered was not true in book 1 (*SS* 53). The Dursleys then created another cover story for Harry, claiming that he attends school at St. Brutus's Secure Center for Incurably Criminal Boys (11), which obviously has a poor reputation.

CHAPTER 1

An important part of the spy business is assessing the psychological makeup of other people—those you want to recruit, the leaders of foreign countries, and especially your sources. This aspect of the spy world is called **psychological assessment.** This, then, is our psychological assessment of Harry.

It is clear that Harry is a natural at spying and the use of spy craft, and with each year Harry becomes more adept at these skills. We personally believe that Harry is a "natural," based on the sudden loss of his parents and the circumstances of his upbringing. The loss of even one parent at an early age tends to make a person mature faster. (Peter, who lost his father when he was twelve years old, knows this all too well.) You realize that you are alone and have to find your own way in many regards. You tend to look for parental figures in other adults, including coaches, teachers, uncles, and aunts.

However, Harry was thrust into an oppressive situation in the Dursley household. This forced Harry to develop a **heightened awareness** of the people and circumstances around him. He learns to "read" people because he is apprehensive about what might happen to him almost moment to moment. As he ages and is bullied by Dudley and his gang, his sensitivity increases. He grows up very aware of his surroundings, always looking for ways to manipulate the people around him—that is, to stop them from causing him hurt. His survival instincts are stronger than average.

~~~~~~~~~~~~~~~~~~~~~~~~~~~~~~~~~

UNDERSTANDING HEIGHTENED AWARENESS

In the military, the ability to perceive the important things all around you is called *situational awareness*. Pilots are trained to have such awareness at all times for very good reason: so they don't run into each other when flying at Mach 2 or in close formation. Spies are provided similar "denied area training" in which they are taught to be especially aware of their surroundings while in an area (or even country) where spying is illegal—that is, denied to them. While in a denied area, the covert operative must assume at all times that he or she is being watched and act accordingly.

A good spy is attuned to everything around him or her. In the spy world this is called *heightened awareness*. If someone walks up to you, you need to recognize their presence; if somebody is following you from behind, you need to be aware of it—but not necessarily by turning around and looking. Windows, mirrors, even hubcaps can be used to "see" as if you have eyes in the back of your head (just like Mad-Eye Moody!).

But let's return to the story, shall we?

~~~~~~

Harry sits on a swing at the playground, apparently unnoticed, hiding in plain sight (9). **Concealment** can be achieved by means other than a disguise—it can also be attained by *blending in*. Harry is just another kid at the playground. Harry sees the other boys but, demonstrating his growing maturity, does not yell at or taunt them and chooses not to start a fight (11).

Staying cool—keeping your wits about you—is a spy's most important tool. We call this *equanimity*. It is the ability to act (or not act) under stress, that famous *grace under pressure* that sets the best spies apart.

~~~~~~

KEEPING YOUR COOL IN THE COLD WAR

A superb example of equanimity is Colonel Ryszard Kuklinski, a Polish officer who spied for the CIA from 1972 to 1981. Kuklinski's superiors learned that some of the information to which Kuklinski had **access** was known to the CIA, including the Soviet master plans for instituting martial law. Kuklinski knew that the original sat in his safe and only two or three other officers had access to that information. On November 2, 1981, all of those officers, including Kuklinski, were called into a room by their superiors and accused of stealing it. The first two officers rightfully claimed their innocence, and so did Kuklinski, who remained calm and shifted the blame to another group that had access to the plans. Despite his equanimity, Kuklinski felt an inexplicable urge to confess—but he was interrupted by the superior officer, who declared they had work to do and finding the thief would be left to the Polish **counterintelligence** unit.

A short time later, the CIA helped Kuklinski and his family leave Poland. For a retelling of this very interesting true spy story, we recommend *A Secret Life: The Polish Officer, His Covert Mission, and the Price He Paid to Save His Country,* by Benjamin Weiser. The moment when Kuklinski almost confessed appears on pages 265 to 267. Peter served as the principal researcher for this fine book.

~~~~~~~~~~~~~~~~~~~~~~~~~~~~~~~~~~~

But Harry is still a young man and cannot stop himself from taunting Dudley until he does something stupid (13). **Baiting the enemy** is a very old trick, used by every brother and sister in every land! Dudley taunts Harry right back, mocking his nightmares about Cedric's death (15).

Harry loses his temper and pulls out his wand. While it's foolish of Harry to lose his temper, in a sense it's also lucky, because the Dementors attack at that moment (17). Harry rises to the challenge, saving himself and Dudley by performing a Patronus Charm while under enormous pressure (18).

The Dementors flee, and who shows up next but Mrs. Figg! As Harry begins to put away his wand, she shrieks, shockingly, "Don't put it away, idiot boy! What if there are more of them around?" (19).

Mrs. Figg, it seems, is *not* what she seems.

BEING NOT WHAT ONE SEEMS

"Not what she seems" is a phrase used in Shakespeare's play *Othello*, in which the villain Iago says, "Men should be what they seem; Or those that be not, would they seem none!" (Act III, scene iii, lines 139–140). Perhaps the greatest study of manipulation is Iago's successful attempt to turn Othello from a loving husband to a man ready to murder his wife in just that one scene!

In the spy world, you should always be asking whether what seems to be the truth is truly so. Trusting in appearances can cause an operation to go very bad, very quickly—as Harry will learn by the end of book 5!

Mrs. Figg—"a batty, cat-loving old lady" who had been asking Harry to come by for tea whenever he ran into her—is of course an *undercover* **operative** (or **mole**, or **sleeper agent**), sent by Dumbledore to keep an eye on Harry for all these years!

AGENT VS. INTELLIGENCE OFFICER/OPERATIVE

Generally speaking, members of spy agencies do not refer to *themselves* as agents. "Agents" are the people they recruit or run. Unlike the FBI—where, by the way, every agent is a *special* agent—members of the intelligence community generally refer to themselves as **intelligence officers, operatives,** or **case officers**. Thus, the term *agent* in the intelligence world usually refers not to someone who is a member of the intelligence agency, but rather to someone recruited by that agency.

CHAPTER 1

Mrs. Figg has presumably been a mole or sleeper agent since Harry arrived at the Dursleys' doorstep. In a sense, she is manning an **observation post** on behalf of Dumbledore. If only the Dursleys knew!

2

HOW TO SUCCEED IN GETTING IN TROUBLE USING MAGIC WITHOUT REALLY TRYING, OR, I RAISE YOU ONE OWL AND SEE YOU ANOTHER

We find out quite quickly in chapter 2, "A Peck of Owls," that Harry was being spied upon by none other than Mundungus Fletcher and Mr. Tibbles, one of Mrs. Figg's cats! The crack that Harry identified as someone Apparating was actually Mundungus *Disapparating*—leaving despite the fact that the Order of the Phoenix had ordered him to watch over and protect Harry (20). As we find out later in the series, Mundungus is *not* the most reliable person to assist Harry (*DH* 78)!

ANALYSIS: *Why would the order select Mundungus to watch over Harry Potter?* Perhaps now is a good time to discuss *assignments*, or more accurately, the selection of the person most appropriate for the task. The distribution of tasks is one of the most important duties of people in leadership positions in the intelligence community. In order to properly assign a person to a specific task in the field, the senior intelligence officer needs to understand not only the task and its risks, but also the nature and capabilities of the people being assigned.

Perhaps all the other members of the Order of the Phoenix were busy with other things—maybe guarding something really important called a prophecy?—and Mundungus was one of the few members available for the mission. In theory, it is a rather safe assignment: Harry is automatically protected by *staying put* in the Dursleys' house; Mrs. Figg is near; and the Dementors are safely tucked away in Azkaban, obedient to the orders of the Ministry. *What, pray tell, could possibly go wrong?*

When Mundungus left his post, Mr. Tibbles, who was watching from underneath the car, alerted Mrs. Figg that Harry had left the safe house (20). Mrs. Figg now tells Harry to ignore the Statute of Secrecy, explaining that there are certain exceptions to it—and defending yourself from Dementors is certainly one of those exceptions (21)!

We also learn that Mundungus has an Invisibility Cloak—though we wonder if it is as good as Harry's, or if indeed it *could be Harry's,* since he never uses it at Privet Drive (22). (Perhaps use of the Invisibility Cloak would result in a nasty letter from the Ministry of Magic for underage use of magic, and use of magic in the Muggle world.)

When Mundungus returns from his "very good business opportunity," he bears the wrath of Mrs. Figg and then Disapparates, supposedly to tell Dumbledore what has happened, at Mrs. Figg's direction (23).

Harry drags a demented Dudley Dursley into number four, Privet Drive (24). Uncle Vernon and Aunt Petunia are understandably shocked that their most perfect son has been attacked and believe Dudley when he indicates that it is Harry's fault—which it is, when you think about it! The Dementors were no doubt after Harry, and Dudley happened to get in the way. (Oh well, these things do happen—at least to Harry Potter!)

Uncle Vernon understandably wants information and tries to

acquire it by questioning Harry (26). Indeed, one would more properly call this an **interrogation**, as a lengthy questioning of a person, usually by an authoritarian figure such as a police officer or detective . . . or an enraged uncle.

There are many *types* of interrogations. Some are the pleasant "please sit down and have a cup of coffee and tell me your story," and others are the "good cop, bad cop" type, where one questioner plays your friend and the other plays the tough interrogator. And of course there are interrogations in which the normal rules of civility do not apply and *force* is used on the subject, sometimes by means of *fear* alone, and sometimes through **torture**. (Cruciatus Curse, here we come!)

In this case, Uncle Vernon's interrogation is certainly not pleasant, but he does *not* step over the bounds of law or improper duress.

We now return to one of the Wizarding world's wonderful forms of **communication**: owls, bearing an old-fashioned thing called a letter. When was the last time you wrote somebody a letter? No, not a text! Not an email! A *real* letter! Not so many years ago, vast amounts of information traveled mainly on paper, through the post office. Although we didn't use owls, letters for the most part arrived safely in the hands of those to whom they were sent. But just as Harry is learning, most forms of communication can be intercepted by a careful opponent!

THINGS COME IN THREES

Isn't it wonderful that J. K. Rowling does so many things by threes? It reminds us of the three witches in *Macbeth* chanting, "Double, double toil and trouble. Fire burn, and cauldron bubble!" Shakespeare is an old dude who wrote *really good plays*, unless you buy into the movie *Anonymous* or other drivel that fails to acknowledge that William Shakespeare actually wrote all his plays and sonnets and

CHAPTER 2

just happens to be **THE GREATEST WRITER OF OUR TIME!**

What are some examples of threes in the Harry Potter series? How about the three friends, Harry, Ron, and Hermione? Or the three schools that participate in the Triwizard Tournament? Or, perhaps, a three-headed dog named Fluffy?

~~~~~~

The first owl is from the Ministry (the Improper Use of Magic Office, of course), which monitors magic use and is immediately alerted when an underage wizard uses magic outside of Hogwarts (26). Do note, however, that the Ministry can't actually detect *who* performed the magic, just where the magic was performed. That fact was hinted at in *Chamber of Secrets,* when Harry was blamed for the Hover Charm that Dobby the house-elf performed in the Dursleys' kitchen (*CS* 19), and is confirmed in book 6, *Harry Potter and the Half-Blood Prince* (*HBP* 368). This seems unfair, considering that people could get blamed for magic they didn't do. It also means that children born of magical families won't get in trouble for underage magic because the Ministry assumes that magic was performed by their parents (or at least under their supervision).

The first owl is the owl of the *law,* the messenger of civil authority from the Ministry of Magic itself. In this case, the law is clear: use of magic by a minor outside of Hogwarts is illegal, and the penalty is quite severe—expulsion from Hogwarts and destruction of the offender's wand (27)!

What could be worse for a young wizard or witch than that? You are sent away from your friends, banned from the Wizarding world, and left defenseless! Uncle Vernon is thrilled by this prospect, of course, but Harry's reaction is quite different.

Harry reads the letter through twice. The Ministry is on its way to the Dursleys' to destroy his wand! There is only one thing to do: *Escape*! Run for it! Keep your wand! Without it, he is defenseless (27–28).

19

PART 1

NOTE TO SELF: *Never look away when someone is planning to take your weapon!*

And then owl number two arrives with a message from a friend, Mr. Weasley. He tells Harry to stay where he is, do no more magic, and *not* surrender his wand (28). Whew! But how did he know? News travels fast in the Wizarding world, we guess.

ANALYSIS: *How did Mr. Weasley know? What is happening behind the scenes?* Mr. Weasley either had inside knowledge of the first owl and its message, or he simply realized how the Ministry would respond to Harry's use of (underage) magic. In addition, Mr. Weasley immediately understood what Harry's reaction would be to the first message. He knows Harry. He knows the Ministry. He knows what to tell Harry to do. Mr. Weasley would be a very good chief: he understands the bureaucracy and "his" man.

Now for the third owl—again from the Ministry—bearing a message about the missive sent twenty-two minutes earlier. We find out that the Ministry has "revised" its decision to destroy Harry's wand "forthwith," but he is still required to attend a disciplinary hearing (an official process led by a judge, less formal than a trial but more formal than a talk with your parents). In addition, the Headmaster of Hogwarts will be consulted about possible expulsion, which will be decided during the hearing (32–33).

ANALYSIS: *Why the change of decision by the Ministry as indicated through the third owl?* Dumbledore clearly intervened! He prevented the orderly administration of stupidity by the Ministry and demanded a hearing before any punishment took place. (It reminds us of the "Sentence first! Verdict afterwards!" actions of the Queen of Hearts in *Alice in Wonderland*.) Expulsion from Hogwarts is in Dumbledore's

CHAPTER 2

domain and *his domain only*. Can you imagine the conversation he had with the Ministry officials? Had we only been there to watch . . . though we think we can all imagine it quite well, thank you.

Finally, a fourth owl arrives, this time from Sirius. News does indeed travel fast in the Wizarding world! Harry's godfather—perhaps unnecessarily, and *perhaps* not—tells him, "Don't leave the house again, whatever you do" (35). Perhaps Sirius thought that Harry might be as rash or impetuous as he is!

IT IS NOW TIME TO DISCUSS THE LAW.

Society, we are told, must have **laws** in order to function. In his poem "Law Like Love," W. H. Auden wrote:

Law is as I've told you before,

Law is as you know I suppose,

Law is but let me explain it once more,

Law is The Law.

Some laws are *prohibitive*: that is, they prohibit something. The things they prohibit can be crimes (defined in *criminal* law) that result in penalties, such as fines, imprisonment, or even a sentence to death. Other laws are *civil*, meaning that you could be sued in court and penalized for doing something wrong, such as damaging someone's fence while trying to escape from a Dementor, or, dare we say it, inappropriately blowing up your Aunt Marge into a very large balloon (*PA* 29)!

As we all know, wizards decided long ago to adopt the International Statute of Secrecy, thereby keeping their existence secret from the Muggle world while living among Muggles. A violation of this law, by a minor or an adult, is a serious offense indeed. If Muggles knew there were wizards about, they would be asking for gifts and requesting magical help with everything, which of course would give the wizards no time to do what wizards normally do! Hagrid tells Harry exactly this in book 1, *Harry Potter and the Sorcerer's Stone,* when Harry asks,

> "But what does a Ministry of Magic do?"
>
> "Well, their main job is to keep it from the Muggles that there's still witches an' wizards up an' down the country."
>
> "Why?"
>
> "Why? Blimey, Harry, everyone'd be wantin' magic solutions to their problems. Nah, we're best left alone"

(*SS* 65).

It is also important to notice that the Wizarding world has not only laws, but also a *process* that must be followed. In our modern society, we call this **due process** *of law.* You cannot be punished or have property taken away from you without due process, which normally means that you have a right to a hearing or trial, and that you have notice of when that hearing will occur, time to prepare for the hearing, the opportunity to attend the hearing and to object to the evidence as well as cross-examine those who are testifying against you, and the right to present your own evidence in your defense.

The concept of "innocent until proven guilty" applies in the Wizarding world. In *Chamber of Secrets,* when Snape argued for Harry's punishment after Filch's cat, Mrs. Norris, was petrified, Dumbledore refused: "Innocent until proven guilty, Severus," he said (*CS* 144). We note that the same application of the law did *not* apply to Hagrid, however, when he was suspected by the Ministry of Magic of reopening the Chamber of Secrets; Cornelius Fudge sent Hagrid to Azkaban, telling him, "Not a punishment, Hagrid, more a precaution. If someone else is caught, you'll be let out with a full apology" (*CS* 261).

Have we had enough owls yet? Of course not!

The fifth and final owl bears a Howler for Aunt Petunia,

which inevitably yells out its contents: "REMEMBER MY LAST, PETUNIA" (40).

ANALYSIS: *Why would Aunt Petunia receive a Howler?* We now realize, or at least *Harry* does, that Aunt Petunia is well aware of the Wizarding world. *Someone* sent her a Howler, and she is abiding by what it said. Very interesting!

Harry does his *own* **analysis** after each owl arrives. He does indeed think of escape and is prepared to run, but he wisely follows Mr. Weasley's and Sirius's advice instead (27–29). Harry's analysis shows his maturity as both a young man and an intelligence officer. Harry is taking facts he has observed and analyzing them logically and methodically. He is also dutifully following instructions.

THE TYPES OF SPIES—HUMANS VS. TECHNOLOGY

There are of course many types of spies. Spies who work in the field, like James Bond, are called *operatives*. But we often forget that the majority of spies are *not* gallivanting around the world, but are instead sitting at desks, using computers to analyze information. Sometimes it is the very secret information obtained by the operatives, and sometimes it is obtained by pulling together bits and pieces of public and confidential information and determining the truth. The truth might concern the **plans, capabilities, and intentions** of adversaries, the truth about a country's financial or scientific prowess or weaknesses, or the truth about some weapon system—the newest submarine or rocket or bomb—that needs to be discovered and analyzed. These "desk spies" are called *analysts*.

The world of espionage has shifted its focus—perhaps too much—away from *human* spies (**HUMINT**) and toward *spy satellites* (taking pictures from orbit) and computer espionage known as **cyber warfare**.

According to various articles and books, the United States (in conjunction with Israel) inserted at least three computer viruses into the computer programs that controlled the centrifuges at the Natanz facility in Iran. These centrifuges were enriching uranium to be used to build a nuclear bomb. The operation's **code name** was *Olympic Games*. The viruses—the first and most famous was named Stuxnet—shut down the centrifuges and destroyed their ability to function. Although they were replaced, the destruction of these centrifuges put Iran's nuclear program back years. Unfortunately, the virus escaped from the Iranian stand-alone computer system and "went public."

For an overview of Operation Olympic Games, we suggest David E. Sanger's *Confront and Conceal: Obama's Secret Wars and Surprising Use of American Power* (Crown, 2012), especially pages ix through xiii and 188 through 225. Sanger also discusses the use of unmanned drones armed with missiles in Afghanistan and other countries of the Middle East. These robot drones are flown by pilots located in the United States.

The world of espionage involves more than simply one spy putting himself or herself at risk, but we still need people on the ground—the operatives who find out what can't be seen by satellites!

3

HOSTAGE RESCUE—FROM SAFE HOUSE NUMBER 1 TO SAFE HOUSE NUMBER 2

Chapter 3, "The Advance Guard," is full of adventure and disclosures. Harry escapes from the Dursleys (47) and learns that the adults have not just been twiddling their thumbs. They have actively organized a **headquarters** (49) and reinstituted the Order of the Phoenix (58)—though Harry does not yet know what the Order is.

Harry reunites with Hermione and Ron. He is disappointed to find that the children have been intentionally left out of the adults' plans, but at least they now have proof that the adults they love are *actively engaged* in spying and spy craft, all for the purpose of tracking and defeating Voldemort.

(Interesting point: This rescue foreshadows Harry's rescue in book 7, *Harry Potter and the Deathly Hallows*—although that escapade tragically results in the death of Mad-Eye Moody [*DH* 78], the loss of Hedwig [*DH* 56], and serious injury to George Weasley [*DH* 69]).

Chapter 3 also makes a good point about why it might be best *not* to use an owl for communication. At the very beginning, Hedwig has been gone for four days (44). Harry desperately wants information

25

about what is going on, but no news comes.

ANALYSIS: *Why hasn't Hedwig returned? Why stop using owls?*
We know you know the answer, so we won't bother telling
you. (OK, we'll tell: Owls can be intercepted and therefore
are *not* a secure form of communication! The members of
the Order know this and do not allow Hedwig to return a
message to Harry.)

Harry is understandably upset and cannot understand why
nobody will tell him what is going on. You may recall a previous year
in which this happened: Remember the summer between Harry's
first and second years, when he heard nothing from Ron and Hermione? . . . Bad Dobby! Bad Dobby!—Dobby had been intercepting
his mail (*CS* 18)!

All spies have to deal with lack of information about what is
really happening. Often a spy out in the field knows little or nothing
about what's going on and must therefore be patient and trust that
others are working on his or her behalf. This is particularly difficult
when the spy is in danger or needs to be extracted from a thorny
situation.

In other words, operatives and their agents can be *left in the dark*
for days. But they know that this is just part of being a spy.

ANALYSIS: *What would happen to Harry if he was expelled?*
Before Harry is rescued from number four, Privet Drive,
he does his own analysis of the situation. Where would he
live? He certainly wouldn't stay with the Dursleys, would
he (42–43)?

Harry realizes that his real family is now the Wizarding world,
especially his godfather, Sirius. If he were expelled from that world,
what would he do? We suppose he would just move from place to
place, hiding in forests and cold ocean cliff-sides, still trying to defeat
Voldemort.

Oh, wait a minute! That is *exactly* what he does after leaving Hogwarts . . . but of course that's not until book 7!

ANALYSIS: *Why are the Dursleys removed from their home before Harry's rescue?* It is interesting that the Dursleys leave their home *before* the rescue occurs (45). Is this for their safety, or just so they don't get in the way? One suspects a little bit of both.

So there sits Harry, locked in his room, a true captive. He hears something downstairs and then the key being turned at his door; it's followed by a **security question**, something that only Harry will know (45–48).

If you have ever needed to retrieve a forgotten password for an important account, you know what a security question is. When you set up an online account at your bank, for instance, it offers you a whole list: Who was the best man at your wedding? What was the name of your elementary school? Who was your favorite teacher? Where was your oldest child born? So, what is Harry's security question?

What form does your Patronus take? (45).

ANALYSIS: *Is this a good security question?* Maybe not! The Dementors just witnessed Harry's stag defending Harry and Dudley. Wouldn't they tell whoever it was that sent them? Even worse, Harry's enemies, Malfoy, Crabbe, and Goyle, know what form his Patronus takes quite well, having seen it up close and personal after they disguised themselves as Dementors to scare Harry in book 3. Oh well, that's the question the rescuers use!

And who are Harry's rescuers? Mad-Eye Moody, Remus Lupin, Nymphadora Tonks, Kingsley Shacklebolt, Elphias Doge, Dedalus Diggle, Emmeline Vance, Sturgis Podmore, and Hestia Jones (49). Many of these members of the Order will appear again: they will serve as the **security detail** (or **protective detail**) assigned to protect Harry. A good spy must remember names and other details about people—and whose side they are on. CONSTANT VIGILANCE! as Mad-Eye Moody always says (*GF* 213, 217, 571).

Harry still wants to know what's going on, but Mad-Eye Moody won't allow any discussion about what is going on or where they are going. This is because the discussion is taking place at the Dursleys' home, an obviously **unsecured location** where others might be observing or **eavesdropping**. Moody says, gruffly, "We're not discussing anything here, it's too risky" (50).

EAVESDROPPING THROUGH THE AGES

The word *eavesdropping* comes from the historical spying practice of hanging from somebody's eaves and listening at their window, an old English tradition. With the development of electronics, the term now relates to much more sophisticated means, such as hidden microphones, laser microphones that can "hear" conversations inside the building through the vibrations of the windowpanes, and good old-fashioned wiretapping, whether on the wires of landline phones or, more recently, the interception of electronic cell phone signals. Such eavesdropping is one of the important functions of the **National Security Agency (NSA)**, known early on as "No Such Agency" because of the great secrecy of its work.

This is not the first time that Harry is assigned a security detail, but he hasn't always had one. In Harry's first year, Hagrid left him with a ticket, and the Dursleys simply dumped him and his bags at King's Cross Station (*SS* 87, 90–91). In the second year, Harry was staying at the Burrow—in the wake of the Dobby incident and his rescue by the Weasleys in the Flying Ford Anglia—and was transported to King's Cross by the Weasley family. A security detail might have helped at that point, given that Dobby prevented Harry and Ron from getting through the barrier, forcing them to fly to Hogwarts in Mr. Weasley's flying car—to somewhat disastrous results (*CS* 66–67, 68, 70–76)!

In the third year, when Sirius Black was on the loose and supposedly after Harry, the Ministry of Magic provided a very professional security detail. Harry and the Weasleys traveled in "two old-fashioned dark green cars, each of which was driven by a furtive-looking wizard wearing a suit of emerald velvet" (*PA* 70). Once the detail found trolleys, unloaded their trunks, and saluted Mr. Weasley with a touch of their hats, Mr. Weasley took over, keeping very close to Harry's elbow until they had crossed through the barrier covertly and in unison (*PA* 71).

And finally, in the fourth year—following the mayhem at the Quidditch World Cup—Harry and the Weasleys merely took Muggle taxis to the train station (*GF* 162).

The selection of a type of **transportation** is often very important to a spy. After the Dementor attack, Harry's rescuers use brooms (51), even though they could use the Floo Network, Portkeys, or perhaps even another bewitched Muggle vehicle on loan from Mr. Weasley!

Moody selects the simplest form of Wizarding transportation, brooms, because the other means of transportation might be under observation. This is true for all spies: the more complicated way of doing things often has more risks, depending on the technology involved. In our view, the more sophisticated the technology, the better chance of it being defeated or compromised (weakened).

We find out later that the Floo Network *is* being controlled and observed by the Ministry, and apparently Portkeys have the same problem. Harry is not old enough yet to Apparate, nor has he been taught to do so, so that is not a useful alternative. (In the next book we learn that you can Apparate while holding onto someone else's arm, as Harry Apparates with Dumbledore (*HBP* 58), but perhaps the Ministry of Magic might identify that as use of magic by an underage Wizard?)

In any event, brooms seem to be the right answer, and Harry is adept at using them. When transportation is necessary but possibly dangerous, go with your skills—just as Harry did when fighting the dragon during the Triwizard Tournament (*GF* 345)—and if necessary, take longer to use a safer means of travel.

As an added precaution, Moody puts a Disillusionment Charm on Harry, making him a "human Chameleon (54)."

Ever the optimist, Mad-Eye informs everyone that if anyone should get killed, "keep flying, don't stop, don't break ranks" (55).

Meanwhile, another spy tool has been used to entice the Dursleys to leave their home: **disinformation**, also known as a *subterfuge*, made them believe that they were receiving an award for the All-England Best-Kept Suburban Lawn Competition at a dinner held in their honor. Quite simply, they were told a lie (48).

MISINFORMATION VS. DISINFORMATION

Operatives appreciate the subtle differences between *mis*information and *dis*information.

*Mis*information is simply information that is incorrect. It may be incorrect for many reasons, even innocent ones, such as someone drawing the wrong conclusion.

*Dis*information, on the other hand, is a fact or belief that is known *not* to be true, usually distributed for the purpose of confusing or misdirecting the recipient.

J. K. Rowling's critics have sometimes claimed that the books teach children how to lie. What rubbish! Children already know *how* to lie. Part of growing up is learning that lying is usually bad and has unpleasant consequences for the liar. The characters who lie in the Harry Potter series are almost always bad people, and more often than not they come to *great* misfortune as a result. Harry tells a few lies, but almost always to protect himself or his friends—deciding who needs to know what, we suppose—and he knows it's not the best choice. And if you look closely, he almost always ends up coming clean about his lies, doesn't he?

Be that as it may, lying is an art form and comes as easily to spies as tying their shoes! But, as any spy knows, it's best to *tell the truth if at all possible*—that way you don't have to remember which things you've said that are *different* from what you said *previously*. Make up a good story, but the closer it is to something true, the better your chance of not slipping up on an inconsistency when you have to remember it later.

Some would say that being a spy is by definition *living a lie*—even if it's directed only at those against whom you are spying. But you must not become *too* good at lying. Remember that you are lying for a purpose: which side you are on, and why you are there and not on the other side. Spies have a *code of ethics*, which we will investigate in chapter 52.

Harry knows very well which side he is on. In the film adaptation of *Order of the Phoenix*, Harry says that they have something Voldemort doesn't have. A weapon? No. More age and experience? No. What is it? "Something worth fighting for."

And now, a word about weapons: **WEAPONS!** (Sorry, couldn't help it.)

The weapon of choice for a wizard or witch is a wand. They must be able to properly use a wand and diligently follow the rules of safety for wands (and *all* other weapons). Moody gives a great example:

> "Don't put your wand there, boy! What if it
> ignited? Better wizards than you have lost buttocks, you
> know! . . . Elementary wand safety, nobody bothers with it
> anymore" (48).

How true! A loaded weapon is dangerous in the Muggle world; just think about how dangerous a wand in your pocket could be!

By the same token, it is best to keep your weapon and other protective devices close by. Harry has a lot to learn about this. He leaves his Invisibility Cloak on Hagrid's table when he follows the spiders into the Forbidden Forest (*CS* 271) and at the top of the Astronomy Tower when Dumbledore is killed (*HBP* 630), despite the Headmaster's earlier warning that Harry should keep the cloak with him at all times, even at Hogwarts (*HBP* 79).

Before the security detail spirits Harry away, they also attend to communications, awaiting a **signal**—"*the all clear*"—before they leave the Dursleys' house (49). The signal they selected ahead of time is a shower of wand sparks (55). The rescue team is obviously using **look-outs** to assist in the exfiltration—perhaps Mundungus Fletcher will actually stay at his post this time!

EXFILTRATION AND THE MOVIE ARGO

The 2012 movie *Argo* portrays the *exfiltration,* or removal, of several State Department employees from Iran in 1979. In the film, a CIA operative goes to Iran soon after the takeover of the United States Embassy by militant "students." In reality, the embassy was invaded, and *two* **operations officers** made the trip, intending to rescue six foreign service officers who had been working next door to the embassy but were not captured. The operatives and the six employees escaped Iran by posing as a scouting crew for a fake science-fiction movie.

In this chapter, Harry also meets Tonks, a Metamorphmagus (52). She can change her looks at will, which is handy for a spy! Instead of donning a disguise, a la Sherlock Holmes, Tonks merely *thinks* of a disguise and becomes that person.

It is interesting that so few people use this power in the Harry Potter series. Perhaps it is because the Ministry of Magic's Aurors can see through such disguises. Nevertheless, being a Metamorphmagus certainly beats drinking the obnoxious and foul-smelling Polyjuice Potion (*CS* 216, *DH* 51)!

CHAPTER 3

~~~~~~~~~~~~~~~~~~~~~~~~~~~~~~~~~~~~

AURORS—THE MINISTRY'S INTELLIGENCE AGENCY?

A career as an Auror involves an extensive amount of spy craft. There is mention of a class in Concealment and Disguise, the ability to change one's appearance with wands, potions, and other such methods. There is even a reference to stealth and tracking as a course that Aurors could take, which would be interesting indeed (52)! We will get to those lessons later, after our review of this book.

~~~~~~~~~~~~~~~~~~~~~~~~~~~~~~~~~~~~

Taken together, all of these **security** measures suggest that Harry is considered a **high-value asset**. Protection surrounds important assets all the time: just look at the security around the President of the United States. The **Secret Service** knows exactly where the president is at all times. He or she is surrounded by several layers of protection: when traveling, he or she has an escort, and he or she is protected at close range by Secret Service agents even in one-on-one meetings. In much the same way, Harry is here surrounded by a **security team** that keeps him protected all the time.

In chapter 1 we discussed Harry's development of heightened awareness or situational awareness. Part of awareness is the method you use for observation. Security teams differentiate between two kinds of observation: *linear* observation and *three-dimensional* observation.

Many people, if not most, think in linear terms. That is, they think in a flat, point-to-point manner. Your GPS screen in your car is a good example of this. When people travel from point A to point B, most of them worry about looking straight ahead and to the left and right, with occasional glances in the rearview mirror. This is a *big* mistake in the security world!

Things happen in three dimensions, which means that operatives must observe not just forward, backward, left, and right, but also *up* and *down* and *all around*. Proper security includes not only a 360-degree circle around you, but also a full sphere including *above and below* you. Think of your asset as standing in the middle of that sphere. You need to be observant of the *entire sphere* to know whether there is any risk.

In the film adaptation of Tom Clancy's *Clear and Present Danger*, there is a scene in which the US ambassador to a South American city picks up the director of the FBI in a car and drives through the crowded streets. The tragedy that follows is sadly predictable if you observe the actions of the ambassador's security detail—they look to the left and right at the streets, but *nobody looks up at the roof,* where the enemy just happens to be aiming an RPG (rocket-propelled grenade) at their vehicle!

~~~~~~~~~~~~~~~~~~~~

PETER AND *PATRIOT GAMES* WITH HARRISON FORD

Fun Author Fact: While Peter was serving as the director of media relations for the CIA, he arranged for the filming of a portion of *Patriot Games* at CIA headquarters at Langley. He was invited to appear in the film as one of the people at the security station when Jack Ryan, played by Harrison Ford, was being checked in. Unfortunately, Peter's portion of the scene ended up on the cutting room floor.

~~~~~~~~~~~~~~~~~~~~

During the escape from Privet Drive, Moody mentions a *secondary* layer of protection and observation: the *rear guard.* Whoever these people are, they will step in if anything happens to Harry's security team.

Once the coast is clear, they also have to worry about **navigation**. Many people have the ability to "see" direction—to sense which way is north or south at any time, or to create a map in their head as easily as drawing a simple flower. Those of us who have this sense of direction are rarely lost and can always get back to a place we've visited, even years later.

Harry and his security team are now heading south on their

brooms. A **team leader** has been selected: Mad-Eye Moody. He takes this role *very* seriously, just as we would expect, even though the others seem not *quite* as serious.

At one point Moody considers **doubling back,** to turn around and go past a spot where they had just been (57). Why would he do this? To make sure they're not being followed! Doubling back is done by all spies. The real problem occurs when you double back and find yourself face-to-face with whoever is trying to follow you!

Our fine friends make it to the headquarters of the Order of the Phoenix at number twelve, Grimmauld Place (58). But headquarters looks nothing like a headquarters. It's a *secret* headquarters, so naturally it must look like something else. Indeed, not only does it look like something else, it doesn't look like anything at all! The average person can't even see number twelve, Grimmauld Place. Only those who learn its location from the Secret Keeper can make it appear in-between two other buildings.

THE CIA IS "TECHNICALLY" NEVER OVERSEAS

Just as Muggles and those without permission from the Secret Keeper cannot see headquarters, operatives with missions on foreign soil are not technically there. The covert agent acts under cover, using a cover **legend** (cover story) and usually a specific job title and assignment. The operative is under cover and thus not "visible" to the enemy or the foreign government.

In the movie version of *Order of the Phoenix,* the apartments on each side of number twelve, Grimmauld Place rock wildly and make a great deal of noise, but their inhabitants don't notice. We have to assume that some form of Memory Charm or other device prevents these Muggles from realizing that they are being shoved ten to twenty-five feet to one side or the other as people come and go from the Order's headquarters.

PART 1

Of course, this type of magic appears throughout the entire series. A phone booth that descends into the Ministry of Magic (125); small tents that have as much room as a large home (*GF* 80); cars that have space for more luggage than they should hold (*CS* 70); and of course Hermione's famous purse, which seems capable of carrying half the world, along with all of her books and any other supplies, even a tent (*DH* 162)! Magic is indeed a wonderful thing!

4

HEADQUARTERS: A PLACE THAT GROWS ON YOU, EXCEPT FOR ALL THAT SCREAMING

Now let's get back to headquarters and the security that prohibits the other members of the Wizarding world from getting into or even seeing number twelve, Grimmauld Place. In the Muggle world we call these **passwords**. Chapter 4, entitled "Number Twelve, Grimmauld Place," shows us the ultimate safe house.

For the first level of security, the Order of the Phoenix has used the Fidelius Charm to hide the location of its headquarters with a Secret Keeper. Only that person can relay that location to someone who has been brought into the fold. We first assume (58) and then confirm that Dumbledore is the Secret Keeper of number twelve, Grimmauld Place.

Harry found out all about Secret Keepers in book 3, *Harry Potter and the Prisoner of Azkaban*, while hiding under a table at the Three Broomsticks in Hogsmeade and eavesdropping on Madam Rosemerta, Professor McGonagall, Professor Flitwick, Hagrid, and Minister of Magic Cornelius Fudge (*PA* 205). At that time, everyone thought that Sirius Black had betrayed James and Lily Potter, when in truth it was Peter Pettigrew (374)! As the Secret Keeper for James and Lily Potter, Peter was able to disclose the location of their home in Godric's Hollow. This led to their great misfortune and their death at the hands (er, wand) of Voldemort (365).

As Secret Keeper, Dumbledore conveys the address of the Order's headquarters to Harry not by saying it out loud, but instead by writing it on a slip of paper. Harry memorizes the address and destroys the paper (58–59). Harry is now a member of that special group. We call such a nonverbal transfer of information **"eyes-only" communication**.

Standing outside number twelve, Grimmauld Place, for the first time, Harry and his security detail are careful about communication and security. While they're outside, they do not speak because it's not a **secure** place. They do not know whether someone might be observing or eavesdropping on them. And they are not being too careful, either! Later on, the Order's enemies in the Wizarding world determine the location of its headquarters, but they still cannot *see* it. They therefore put the area under **surveillance**, standing guard nearby, waiting for Harry, Hermione, or Ron to make a mistake and show up outside the illusion that protects number twelve, Grimmauld Place (*DH* 201).

THE BIGOT LIST—A LIST OF WHO KNOWS A PARTICULAR SECRET

The fewer the people who know a secret, the less likely it is to be exposed. Knowledge of the location of the Order's headquarters and access to it are limited strictly to those who have a need to know. A list of people who have been given such highly secret information is called a **bigot list**. The term comes from World War II, when the British armed forces created a top-secret plan to attack the German forces occupying France: a **B**ritish **I**nvasion of **G**erman **O**ccupied **T**erritory. The few English and American officers who had access to and knowledge of the date and location of the Normandy Invasion were thus on the BIGOT list.

INVISIBLE INK, FLASH PAPER, AND LYNN'S CELL PHONE NUMBER

Lynn here: I jokingly tell anyone who has my cell phone number that once they have used it, they must either burn or eat the piece of paper so that the number does not get out to anybody else. In theory, it also means the caller will use it only that one time. Spies still use invisible ink, as well as water-soluble paper that "melts" when put in water, and flash paper that disappears completely when ignited, leaving no ashes.

There are only a few *truly* important secrets in the world: the codes used to launch nuclear missiles; what really exists at Area 51; where Elvis is presently living; and *my cell number.*

Once we get inside headquarters, we discover that the Order of the Phoenix exists and its meetings are carefully restricted to those who are *members* of the Order of the Phoenix (61). In other words, access is allowed only to the individuals who have the proper **security clearance**.

In the world of espionage (and in the military), the type of clearance you have is essential to determine what information you are allowed to get. The most basic clearance is **Confidential**. The next is **Secret**. Next is **Top Secret**. When Top Secret information is placed in special compartments—boxed up, if you will, in a location to which only a select few people have access—it is called **Sensitive Compartmented Information**, or **SCI**.

Generally speaking, only people who have a "need to know"

can access Sensitive Compartmented Information. It often has a one-or two-word code name (such as "Snuffles"?), currently selected by a computer to make sure that it is purely random—and therefore hardest to guess.

THE CORONA PROJECT—IT HAS SOMETHING TO DO WITH A MEXICAN BEER, RIGHT?

Lynn here again: I once listened to a briefing from someone who worked on the *Corona* program, which was the name of one of the first spy satellite programs. Many years later, after the *Corona* program had been replaced by other more sophisticated programs, the code name *Corona* was finally declassified and my acquaintance was finally able to tell his older teenage children what program he had been working. His teenage daughter was thrilled to find out that her father had secretly been working for a Mexican beer manufacturer all these many years!

When Harry first enters headquarters, he looks past Mrs. Weasley to a room filled with members of the Order of the Phoenix . . . but she tells him to go upstairs and visit with Ron and Hermione (61). Harry feels disappointed and monumentally angry about being **left in the dark**. The other students try to make it up to him by sharing the history of the Order of the Phoenix and discussing what they know about the **assignments** that have been handed out and what **spying** is presently being done by the members of the Order (67).

We find out that the members of the Order are following Death Eaters to find out Voldemort's plans, trying to **recruit** more members, and standing guard over something (67–68)—but that something is a big mystery!

CHAPTER 4

ANALYSIS: *Why are the members of the Order of the Phoenix standing guard? What or who are they guarding?* Ron states that some of the members "are standing guard over something" and that they are "always talking about guard duty" (68). Harry, using good analysis, points out something that is obvious to him, having just been rescued by the Order: "Couldn't have been me, could it?" "Oh yeah," replies Ron, with a look of dawning comprehension (68).

But is Harry only half right? Is there something else the Order is guarding? We wonder. . . .

OK, OK, I'll talk! They *are* standing guard over something else. But we won't learn what that is for a while yet. . . .

Fred and George are not quite old enough to be in the Order of the Phoenix, though they *are* old enough to Apparate, and they passed their tests. Therefore, they Disapparate and Apparate to and from each room, causing great consternation, surprise, and always—with the twins—laughter (68). Scientists at heart, the twins are always inventing new items, including one of our favorites: the Extendable Ears (67). What better way to eavesdrop than to literally drop ears into a conversation?

So what about the Extendable Ears? And how are they defeated? When Molly Weasley catches the twins eavesdropping, she implements **counter measures**. She uses a counter-jinx, the Imperturbable Charm, to block the twins' attempt to listen in on the Order's plans (69). (Don't you just love J. K. Rowling's use of the English language? This charm is imperturbable: extremely calm and steady, do not disturb!)

This is just another part of **counter surveillance**. In order to stop somebody from spying on you, you have to know what technology the other side is using and then defeat that technology.

REAL-WORLD DISCUSSIONS WITH CIA SCIENTISTS—OR, HOW TO DEFEAT A LASER MIC

Lynn here: I recall vividly a discussion at the NSA Museum with a former scientist of the CIA's **Directorate of Science and Technology** about how to defeat a laser microphone if it were directed at my cabin window in Montana. A laser mic perceives the vibrations of people's voices in a window or other reflective surface and converts them to audio signal for eavesdroppers.

The scientist and I concluded that you could defeat the microphone by surrounding the window with copper wiring (at a cost of hundreds of thousands of dollars), but a cheaper and easier solution would be a motorized device that taps at the window at about 1,000 beats per second. The motorized tapping would superimpose a new vibration pattern on the windows and interrupt any vibrations created by people talking inside the house! (I am pleased to tell you that I had come up with that solution earlier, before talking to my friends.)

But Ginny is becoming a spy too! She gets Tonks to tell her how to determine if a door has an Imperturbable Charm on it. You throw something at the door and observe whether it hits the door or bounces away before actually touching the door, as though hitting a force field (69). What is the object of choice that Ginny uses to see if Mrs. Weasley has placed counter measures on the door? Dungbombs, of course!

We next find out something *very* important: one of the members of the Order is—you guessed it—*Snape* (69)! Of course, the kids are just *thrilled* to find out that they will be seeing Snape on a regular basis. They assume, as they do throughout the whole series, that Snape is a villain and an enemy, despite Dumbledore's trust in him.

Snape is at headquarters to deliver a top-secret report to the Order. Fred calls Snape as a "git," but Hermione—no real fan of Snape herself—nonetheless argues that Snape's "on our side now." Ron retorts, "Doesn't stop him being a git" (69). Yeah, Ron! (We will save our detailed discussion on Snape, his role as a **double agent**, and his bravery and brilliance—making him perhaps the perfect spy—for one of the final chapters in this book.)

The friends also learn that both of the older Weasley brothers, Bill and Charlie, are in the Order (70). It is no wonder that Molly is worried about losing some members of her family (175): just about *every* member of her family is in the Order! Her personal prophecy and vivid nightmare (in the form of the boggart) will, unfortunately, be partially true in the end (*DH* 637). Percy, however, is *not* in the Order. He has left the Weasleys' home so the Ministry would know where his loyalties lie: if his mom and dad wanted to become traitors, he was going to make sure that everyone knew he wasn't part of the Weasley family anymore (72).

Percy has been promoted at the Ministry, and the Weasleys wonder whether his bosses hope to put Percy in a position to spy on his family (71). This is another way of thinking like a spy: when someone with little experience or talent receives honors, promotions, or access to the higher reaches of government, you wonder why. To help them? To sing their praises? *To spy on their family and friends?*

Of course, if Percy *did* want to spy on behalf of the Ministry, it would have been a much better idea to *pretend* to be close to his family. As a true double agent, he might find out something of value for the Ministry. Fortunately for his family, perhaps, he is merely a Ministry sycophant—in other words, an obnoxious brownnoser!

(Percy eventually realizes his mistake and confesses in the final book that he had been a fool, an idiot, and a pompous prat [*DH* 605–6]. But in this book and a few more, he has not yet reached this epiphany and remains a total dweeb.)

Percy's promotion can also be considered an attack by J. K. Rowling on **bureaucrats** in general. In a complicated system, such as government, mediocre people are sometimes promoted to higher levels, just to get them out of the way of the people who are actually doing the work. We know it's hard to believe, but it is true! The question is, *who* can operate more easily with that person out of the way?

Consider Percy, who, just a year earlier, did not realize that his boss was acting strangely (indeed, he was insane) and failed to report it because he was too enthralled with being the person wielding the power (71). As Percy told his father during their row, his loyalty lies with the Ministry (72). He even went so far as to espouse the Ministry's **party line** and question whether Voldemort is back, asserting that the only evidence is Harry's word—and Harry's word is not good enough for Percy (73).

~~~

THE PARTY LINE

The collection of facts that those in charge want you to believe is often called the *party line*. By definition, anyone who deviates from the party line becomes, in a sense, an enemy of the party. Much of current intelligence analysis involves the explicit assumption that one must question the party line, question what we think we know, and develop a rigorous debate about not only issues of policy, but also issues of fact. For intelligence agencies to work well, they must question themselves and their assumptions regularly, even to the point of developing competing centers of analysis.

~~~

In any event, Percy has been promoted, despite his failings of last year. Thus, the old saying: If they screw up, they send them up!

~~~

WHEN A PROMOTION ISN'T REALLY A PROMOTION

Promotions can also be used to get someone suspected of spying out of a position with access to the secret

information that has been compromised. Both Robert
Hanssen and Aldrich Ames, once they were suspected
of being double agents, were "promoted" and sent to
different areas.

~~~~~~

It's obvious that **politics** is in effect at the Ministry, and we
must now, unfortunately, discuss that word. POLITICS! Not a nice
word, in our view, because many of those engaged in it care more
for themselves than for anyone else—which makes our point exactly.
The process of fighting for power and influence is complicated and
unpredictable, and a smart operative always knows *who* wants *what*
power and *why*. Much of spying involves analyzing who is in power,
what their objectives are, and how to influence those individuals. The
Order of the Phoenix is concerned not only about what Voldemort is
up to, but also what is going on in the Ministry of Magic, partly due
to the realization that Voldemort, through his minions, is using the
Ministry of Magic to fulfill his own goals.

According to Fudge (and the Ministry), if you take Dumbledore's
side, then you are a traitor, guilty of treason (71). In other words, the
Ministry of Magic has developed a party line—and if you don't toe
that line, then you are considered an enemy and not to be trusted.

So much for **intellectual freedom** and **intellectual debate**!

One of the best things about people who work in **intelligence
analysis** is that they are trained to *question everything*, to *look at all
sides*, and to *be a devil's advocate*. They are not afraid to ask any question, even if it might make important people look bad, in search of the
truth. The mantra of the intelligence community is "Speaking truth
to power." Indeed, the following quotation from the Bible is chiseled
into the marble at the entry to CIA headquarters for all to see:

AND YE SHALL KNOW THE TRUTH AND
THE TRUTH SHALL MAKE YOU FREE.
JOHN VIII–XXXII

PART 1

Dissent is one of the essential building blocks of intelligence work. Just as Supreme Court justices issue dissenting opinions when they are in the minority, the intelligence community intentionally fosters and encourages dissent.

When CIA Director Stansfield Turner appeared before the Senate Intelligence Oversight Committee to discuss a covert operation under consideration, he was asked, "Do all your officers agree with you on this?" Director Turner replied, "No. Would you like to read their written dissents?" And when Peter himself, as a young acting station chief, disagreed with certain planned activities, his superiors considered and discussed his concerns without punishing him for disagreeing.

Unfortunately, the Ministry of Magic has no such respect for the positive power of dissent, and instead chooses to punish those who ask inconvenient questions. Restricting freedom of thought, especially unfettered intellectual analysis of a situation, *prevents* the discovery of truth and often results in huge mistakes, sometimes with dire consequences. Things certainly aren't going to go well for Fudge, Percy, and the rest of the Ministry in this book!

NOTE TO SELF: *An open mind can see in all directions; a closed mind cannot see out of the box it has created around itself.*

Harry and his friends know far too much to toe the Ministry's party line. They retreat to a bedroom and discuss Harry's upcoming trial. Everyone seems to agree that, according to the details of the Statute of Secrecy regarding self-defense, there is no case against Harry "if they abide by their own laws," because there is an *exception* and it applies to Harry (75). When one is in mortal danger, the general law about concealing magic use does not apply, and of course that is what happened when Harry protected himself and Dudley from the Dementors (148).

In other words, there is a Wizarding right to **self-defense** based on an understanding that one has the right to protect oneself when in imminent danger, even to the point of breaking other, more minor laws.

We also learn that the *Daily Prophet* has been publishing nasty untruths about Harry over the summer (73–74). (Perhaps *Prophet* should be spelled *Profit* instead?) The *Daily Prophet* has thus subjected Harry to a **disinformation campaign**. In the Muggle world, if one person dislikes what another person is saying, instead of countering the argument, they might attack that person directly, questioning his or her credibility, experience, intelligence, or even loyalty. This is called **argument ad hominem**, or argument "to the person," because it appeals to emotions or prejudices rather than facts and logic.

As has been shown in dictatorships all around the world, unscrupulous leaders can **bribe** or force the press to misinform their citizens and tell them what to believe. The Ministry of Magic isn't a dictatorship, but it isn't above using ad hominem attacks in the press to make "disloyal" dissenters like Harry and Professor Dumbledore look bad. The *Daily Prophet*'s disinformation campaign against Harry has been quite successful, as we see by the students' reactions when Harry returns to Hogwarts (184).

Harry is not the least bit prepared for the effects of this disinformation, for even though he has been receiving the *Daily Prophet*, he has not been reading it *thoroughly*, to Hermione's great chagrin. "Not cover to cover," Harry admits (73). Unfortunately, there isn't much that he can do about a slippery collection of rude questions and rumors.

NOTE TO SELF: *Read the enemy's press thoroughly so you pick up all clues that may be there.*

It is said that the first casualty of war is the truth. It has also been said that a lie told often enough *becomes* the truth.

In the United States, we enjoy what is called **freedom of the press**. Journalists and other media professionals enjoy certain protections so they can do their jobs, including the freedom to report on mistakes that the government may have made. Only through a free and unfettered press can the people have a chance to know the truth.

As a side effect, however, people as famous as Harry have to develop a thick skin, because press protection extends to writers who spread gossip for entertainment. It is very hard to sue a newspaper in the United States for libel because you have to prove that the information it printed was not only false, but also circulated maliciously or with a reckless disregard for the truth. Harry's case is particularly frustrating, though, because all that "gossip" is actually disinformation that lets Voldemort do what he likes!

Despite the bothersome nature of the junk we see on TV and read in the tabloids, our laws allow for the *marketplace of ideas*. In that marketplace, as long as ideas can be presented by anyone and be heard by the public at large, the truth will *eventually* come out—though not always quickly or without damage to the truth and those speaking it! Harry breathes a relieved sigh when the *Daily Prophet* is eventually sidelined by Hermione's and Luna's clever appeal to Xenophilius Lovegood's paper, *The Quibbler* (578–80). Sadly, Mr. Lovegood finds out the cost of going against Voldemort and the Ministry of Magic (and its view of the world) when his daughter Luna is kidnapped and thrown into the Malfoy dungeon. Thus, he is forced—indeed, **blackmailed** and coerced—to turn against Harry in book 7 (*DH* 419).

Enough, we think, of POLITICS and the press!

With all that unpleasantness revealed, it's a bit of a relief for Harry when talk turns to S.P.E.W. (the Society for Promotion of Elfish Welfare), and Hermione's determination to stand up for the rights of the house-elves . . . even those as unpleasant as Kreacher, the elderly Black family elf. His devious loyalty will soon give her a lot to think about!

In order to understand another country or political system, spies have to have a good understanding of politics, justice, and how to develop organizations to change the present system or any perceived wrongs. Which brings us to the mention of Hermione's project, S.P.E.W. (Society for Promotion of Elfish Welfare) (76). Once again we are reminded of the maturity and intelligence of this young woman, Hermione. She perceives an injustice and wants to develop an organization—which she created in Book 4, *Harry Potter and the*

CHAPTER 4

Goblet of Fire (*GF* 224)—to change that injustice.

In many ways, Hermione's attempt to help the house-elves through organization and convincing others of what needs to be done serves as a prototype to another new organization at Hogwarts: Dumbledore's Army! And of course Hermione's concern about elves is not at all subtle or without comparison in the real world.

One hundred and seventy years ago slavery existed in the United States. Sixty years ago blacks in America were relegated to inferior status and denied the right to vote—they even had to drink out of *separate* water fountains. (And yes, in some forms today, slavery exists in the transportation and trading of people, usually young women brought in from foreign countries, called human trafficking.)

Hermione's concern and empathy draws upon all that unfortunate history and is being applied in the Wizarding world not only to humans but to some other creatures in that world, the elves. It is said that you can judge a society by the manner in which it takes care of its least fortunate. Hermione is an advocate of such a benevolent concept, and more power to her!

The kids have even more to discuss about Snape and his past as a Death Eater (69). This is of course a curse and a blessing for Snape. His status as a previous Death Eater allows him access to existing Death Eaters *and* to Voldemort himself. Indeed, Voldemort believes that he has sent Snape to spy on Dumbledore and the Order—though of course we realize at the end of this story that Voldemort is wrong. We will discuss Severus Snape's outstanding spy craft in detail in chapter 53, but for now we will simply say that, in our view, he is one of the best double agents ever described in any work of fiction.

Soon Harry's attempts to catch up on a whole summer's worth of information are interrupted by the call to dinner. But before they can get to the table, Tonks trips over an umbrella stand, and Harry meets (the portrait of) Sirius's loud, angry, insulting mother.

It's now time to have a serious talk about Tonks.

Have you ever met somebody who is always tripping, dropping things, or spilling cups of coffee or water? Waking up Sirius's mother is perhaps the worst thing you could do when entering number twelve, Grimmauld Place, and Tonks seems to do that quite regularly! Indeed, Tonks told Harry when they first met that she "nearly failed Stealth and Tracking" in her Auror schooling, admitting, "I'm dead clumsy" (52).

She's not the first bumbler in Harry's saga, either. In book 1, when we first meet Neville Longbottom, numerous minor misfortunes befall him:

- Losing his toad (again) at the train station and on the train (*SS* 94, 104)

- Falling over on the way to the stool during the sorting ceremony (*SS* 120)

- Running to his table after being sorted with the Sorting Hat still on his head (*SS* 120)

- Attracting the ire of Peeves, who drops walking sticks on his head (*SS* 129)

- Melting Seamus's caldron into a blob (*SS* 139)

- Falling off his broom and breaking his wrist at the first broom lesson (*SS* 146–47)

- Forgetting the Gryffindor password and having to sleep on the floor outside the door (*SS* 156)

- Tripping and running into a suit of armor while trying to avoid Filch (*SS* 157)

At one point in the film version of *Harry Potter and the Chamber of Secrets,* poor Neville asks, "Why does it always happen to me?" And yet it is Neville who is brave enough to try to stop his friends from leaving the dorm room at night (*SS* 272), and it is Neville who will, in the last book, kill Voldemort's snake, Nagini, with the Sword of Gryffindor (*DH* 733).

Tonks and Neville are not the only fumbling people, either. Remember Professor Quirrell in book 1? His constant nervousness, his mumbling, his fainting (*SS* 69–70, 172, 177, 225–26)? *All of it* was a superb act to make sure no one would suspect that he was sharing his turban with Voldemort throughout Harry's first year at Hogwarts!

And what was Quirrell's cover story? According to Hagrid, "he met vampires in the Black Forest, and there was a nasty bit o' trouble with a hag—never been the same since. Scared of the students, scared of his own subject" (*SS* 71). As Quirrell himself said when he finally confronted Harry, "who would suspect p-p-poor, st-stuttering P-Professor Quirrell?" (*SS* 288). He looks helpless, even pathetic, but of course Voldemort is "running" Quirrell, using him as a *penetration agent* or mole: a long-term undercover spy.

Being a bumbler can be both a disguise and a work of art. Think of Clark Kent, Superman's klutzy alter ego. Better yet, look at Inspector Clouseau of the Pink Panther films: although a bumbler, he always gets his man—or woman!

Our point is this: sometimes the most brilliant people appear to be bumblers, and sometimes the most perfect bumblers show us the truth. Many are very worthy of our respect. You never know if a bumbler is the most brilliant person you have met, or the dumbest. Nor do you know whether they are harmless or powerful, and in whose aid. In other words, judge people carefully, and take care to determine whether a bumbler is merely putting on an act.

NOTE TO SELF: *Judge not too quickly, or you will be fooled.*

5

LET HISTORY BE YOUR GUIDE—THE HISTORY OF THE ORDER OF THE PHOENIX

In chapter 5, "The Order of the Phoenix," Harry and his friends (and we readers, too!) find out very important **background information** about Voldemort, his rise to power, and the role of the Order of the Phoenix in his first defeat.

The kids have already learned a lot, but all of it *against* the wishes of the adults. When they are finally allowed to enter the kitchen and discuss recent events, they learn even more (79). (Kind of like being asked to sit at the grown-ups' table, don't you think?)

"KIM'S GAME"

Another excellent story about an orphan boy who learns spy craft is Rudyard Kipling's *Kim* (1901). Growing up in British-ruled India in the nineteenth century, Kim befriends a spy and trains in secret to become a British operative. One of his teachers sharpens his powers of observation by showing him a tray of jewels and other objects and then covering the tray with paper. Kim must then make a list of everything on the tray. Later, the teacher would add or remove objects from the tray, and Kim would list what had changed. This method of developing powers of observation is still known as "Kim's Game."

~~~~~~

Even so, the adults aren't willing to share everything. As the kids enter the room, they notice on the table a parchment with plans of a building (80). The plans are **classified material**. Anyone who has been inside a classified facility knows that no one is let into a **secured area** without the proper **clearance**. If there is a visitor, that person is not let in until an alert has been sounded and *all* classified materials have been put away. Indeed, some facilities actually use special lights on the doors and walls of each room that indicate whether the room is secured, whether there is somebody without proper clearance in the building or area, and whether there is an emergency and all sensitive material must be secured or even destroyed.

Simply put, the **classified material** sitting on the table should have been put away *before* the kids were allowed to enter the room (just as Mrs. Weasley indignantly points out)—and Bill Weasley promptly uses the Vanishing Spell to whisk them out of sight.

Harry later correctly surmises that the plans are for the Ministry of Magic. He is becoming adept at quick observation and analysis—two *very* important traits of a good spy!

Of course, studying people can tell us just as much as studying books. Let's observe the *personalities* of certain members of the Order while the kids are present: Tonks continues to be clumsy, and Mundungus seems to have slept through the meeting (81).

ANALYSIS: *Is Mundungus really sleeping?* Is he just faking sleep? Knowing him, he's probably asleep!

Sirius is no longer able to go out as a dog because Wormtail has

53

undoubtedly disclosed his secret—that Sirius is an Animagus able to transform into a black dog—to Voldemort (82). (Note that the constellation Sirius is a dog! Coincidence? We think not!)

Sirius is obviously frustrated with being stuck at his family home and unable to be out and about as an operative in the fight against Voldemort (82). However, Sirius is still an outlaw in the eyes of the Ministry. If captured, he would be sent to Azkaban, so the Order's decision to keep him at headquarters makes sense.

Unfortunately, the fact that Sirius *should* stay put does not prevent Snape from throwing a few verbal jabs at him, even though they are both members of the Order (85). Remember our discussion about *baiting the enemy*? And the need for *equanimity*? Well, let's be frank: these two just don't get along, and Sirius loses his cool pretty quickly where Snape is concerned!

The reality is that in any organization there will be people who do not get along. You still have to work together as a team and accomplish your tasks, no matter how hard it is to set aside your feelings. If you find yourself tempted to bait the people you're supposed to be working with, think about the weakness that Snape and Sirius's rivalry created in the Order of the Phoenix!

While the plans are off the table, the adults discuss a few things in front of the kids. First is the matter of **recruitment** of additional members, or at least associates, to the Order of the Phoenix. We find out that the goblins are "not giving anything away yet" (85), though they might be taking a neutral stance to see who wins—hedging their bets, if you will. Besides, it makes sense that they wouldn't be giving anything away. After all, banks *keep* money!

ANALYSIS: *Which side will the goblins join?* In analyzing which direction the goblins may go, the members of the Order comment on Voldemort's earlier murder of a goblin family, but still suggest that the goblins may choose a side depending on what they are offered (85).

Compensation applies as a recruitment incentive for spies, too.

A recruiter must ask, What are the individual motives of the person or persons that I'm trying to recruit? Do they have a vendetta against me or my enemy? Have they indicated which side they are on? If they decide to remain neutral, can I still use them in some manner? A spy might work in return for money, or revenge, or to serve a cause.

OF MICE AND MEN—THE FOUR INCENTIVES TO SPY

In the spy world, we use the acronym MICE to list the four most common reasons to spy:

Money—Ideology—Coercion—Ego

The adults do note that the goblins want the "freedoms we've been denying them for centuries" (85). What *exactly* are those freedoms? Are they something that the Order can guarantee them in return for their help? Perhaps the goblins consider the war to be a foolish endeavor. If they see little advantage to getting involved, can they at least be convinced not to help the other side?

RECRUITING THE GOBLINS TO JOIN THE WAR

There is an old saying that applies to the Cold War and the Non-Super Powers: "Whether the elephants fight or make love, the grass suffers."

We find out later that the goblins are in control of much more than just money and gold. There are *very* important treasures hidden deep in the vaults of Gringotts, including a sword (or perhaps a copy of a sword!) with magical power and a certain goblet that contains a piece of Voldemort's soul! And we also learn that negotiating with goblins is a tricky business. In addition to thinking of what your recruit wants out of a deal, remember to ask for *everything* that you want out of it. Otherwise, like Harry in his dealings with Griphook in book 7, you might get exactly what you bargained for—*and nothing else!*

Now, let's get back to Mundungus. Our not-so-brave friend apparently "missed a few crucial lessons" in the realm of **ethics** and right and wrong (86). Mundungus is a thief, and later—right after Sirius's death—he gladly grabs as much of Sirius's property as he can and sells it on the street like a panhandling pawnbroker (191).

ANALYSIS: *Why in the world would the Order allow such a man as Mundungus to be one of its members?* It is obvious. In order to properly spy, one must recruit all types of people, some good and some not so good. But more often than not, the person being recruited is willing to spy for good or at least valid reasons, and often very ethical reasons.

TRAITOR OR HERO?

Colonel Kuklinski, the Polish officer who provided the Soviet battle plans to the United States, did so because he realized that the very nature of the plans—with the Soviet forces initiating a first strike against the West by traveling through Poland—made his home country the target of any nuclear exchange between the two superpowers. He became a spy to save his country.

It took over a decade for Poland to decide whether he was a traitor or a hero.

We are told that Mundungus is willing to help because Dumbledore helped him out of a tight spot once (86). Odds are, that "tight spot" involved something illegal! However ethical his other activities, Mundungus is working for the Order. As Sirius notes, one of the values of having a crook in your midst is that he knows *all* the other crooks and "hears things we don't" (86–87).

It doesn't help that the adults disagree on how much Harry should know. The Order is clearly using a **need-to-know** standard, but Harry is a *very* essential part of the puzzle of Voldemort, and indeed, it is Harry that Voldemort is attempting to find and kill (87–90)!

For that reason alone they decide that Harry should receive more information than the other fifteen-year-olds. To Harry's credit, he informs the adults that he will share anything they tell him with Ron and Hermione anyway, so his two friends are allowed to stay in the room. Character and honesty, not bad traits! Ginny, however, is forced to leave, to her great dismay (91).

"NEED-TO-KNOW" BECOMES "NEED-TO-SHARE"

Prior to 9/11, the rule of thumb in the intelligence world was need-to-know. Afterward, the various agencies evaluated what was missed and focused on the problem of one agency having information that the other agencies did not. Based on these concerns, the new mantra became "need-to-share."

Sirius and Lupin admit that they have a shrewd idea of Voldemort's plans and that the Order "knows more than he thinks we do anyway" (91). We learn that Voldemort's return was supposed to be a secret known only by his followers and that Harry (like Cedric) was not supposed to survive and bear witness to Voldemort's return at the gravesite (92). (Which means that Voldemort believes the best way to make sure someone keeps a secret is to kill them!) Thus, we can conclude that the Order of the Phoenix has a mole in Voldemort's organization—how else would they know this?

We also find out that the Order of the Phoenix was brought back into existence within *an hour* after Voldemort returned (92). It doesn't take much analysis to conclude that the Order's reactivation was Dumbledore's work, undertaken as soon as Harry informed Dumbledore of what had happened at the graveyard when he returned with Cedric's body. Dumbledore is also identified as the founder of the Order of the Phoenix (67). No surprise there!

The Order next analyzes what the enemy is planning. Intelligence officers deal every day with the plans, capabilities, and intentions of the enemy. Voldemort's plan is to rebuild his army, recruit more Death Eaters, and to attempt to recruit the giants (93).

The Order, on the other hand, plans to convince everyone that Voldemort is back, put people back on their guard, and get them ready for the upcoming battle. This decision to alert and train people—that is, to provide *education* and to begin *preparation*—is easier said than done. On the one hand, telling the truth is difficult, given the Ministry's use (and misuse) of the press (94). On the other hand, Harry finds out that telling the truth and being believed is no easy task.

Indeed, the *Daily Prophet* has become a true instrument of **propaganda**, presenting the government's view to the public through means of newspapers, pamphlets, or other means of communication.

THE TYPES OF PROPAGANDA

Propaganda is information, often false ideas or statements, spread to support a particular cause. Generally speaking, we in the spy world classify propaganda as white, gray, or black. *White propaganda* comes from an openly identified source; *black propaganda* lists a source, but the information is derived from some other source; and for *gray propaganda* no source is listed or offered.

One of the most successful campaigns of this sort was the Soviet Union's campaign in the late 1960s and early 1970s spreading rumors that J. Edgar Hoover wore dresses. The evidence is quite clear that the KGB actively spread these rumors and the press in the West printed them. In fact, this disinformation was blindly and eagerly accepted by media outlets hungry for a juicy story. Although there is no evidence to prove or disprove this allegation about Hoover, it is clear that the KGB's disinformation campaign worked wonderfully.

~~~~~~

~~~~~~

MODERN PROPAGANDA AND GOVERNMENTAL RESTRICTIONS ON ACCESS TO INFORMATION

Many countries use state-run television stations and government-authorized newspapers to distribute the government's views, and *only* the government's views. However, with the rise of the Internet and smartphones (which are in many ways very small computers), it is possible to obtain information quickly on almost any subject, and it has become very hard indeed to limit distribution of information. People are now able to investigate an issue and determine the truth very quickly— and, more importantly, are able to communicate to large masses of people in an instant. This has been shown to be true in the Arab Spring that began in 2010, and later in Turkey and Brazil. Faced with such startling uses of communications power, some countries—such as China— actively prevent the unfettered use of Internet by their people.

~~~~~~

When the people hear only one side of a story, they have no ability to question it. One might wonder how the Ministry could be so stupid, but the description of the Minister of Magic, Cornelius Fudge, and his politics makes it quite clear (93–94). He harbors petty jealousies and thinks that Dumbledore wants to take over the Ministry of Magic. Fudge's myopic viewpoint prevents him from seeing the truth (94). In our opinion, Fudge's lack of **objectivity** is based in no small part on *fear* (of Dumbledore) and *bias* (against Harry).

PART 1

Bias is a tendency to believe that certain ideas, beliefs, or even people are inherently better than others, and people without these traits are inherently inferior. The Ministry of Magic throughout the *Order of the Phoenix* has shown bias against Harry, both in its actions and in the pages of the *Daily Prophet*. Note also that bias can be helpful—think of all the times Harry avoids getting expelled because the professors like him—but more often it leads to someone being treated unfairly.

J. K. Rowling tells us something quite profound when she explains that *Fudge's bias is preventing him from seeing the truth*. Think of the bias that many people have against Hagrid: he is described by the Malfoys as an oaf; many suspect him to be a half-giant and therefore unstable; and of course there are still odious rumors about how and why he was kicked out of Hogwarts all those years ago (though we now know that Tom Riddle framed him for opening the Chamber of Secrets). In addition, Hagrid tends to let information slip out that he shouldn't, and he cares for animals that you and the authors of this book would probably not keep as pets (not to mention befriending an Acromantula, known to us all as Aragog)!

But Hagrid is not the only one subject to prejudice in the Wizarding world. We all know the term *Mudblood*, which is used to insult Hermione and other Muggle-born witches and wizards by the worst of the worst in the Wizarding world (*CS* 112, 115, 139; *DH* 197, 452, 460, 465). Rowling rightfully reminds us of how foolish prejudice leads to disaster and injustice—just one of the many ethical points that she makes so well in her wonderful series.

The Order's discussion of Cornelius Fudge is another example of a psychological assessment: taking what they know about Fudge, particularly his personality and psychological makeup, and trying to determine how he would react in a certain situation. Psychological assessments can also help spies to determine how to use a person, or how to get that person to do something they want done, or what that person will do in the future.

Although much has been written recently about **psychological profiling** (the term used by the FBI) of criminals and people who have committed crimes but not yet been caught, psychological assessment is as old as history itself. Analyzing what your enemy will do is part of every battle ever planned.

Understandably, **psychological assessment** can be conducted on any important persons or persons of interest, including world leaders. Through the use of psychological assessments, a reader is able to better understand the person and to some extent predict what that person will do when confronted with certain situations or proposals.

In providing a psychological assessment of Cornelius Fudge, the Order accurately describes his petty jealousies, his fear of Dumbledore, and his desire to retain power. Ironically, they decide that Fudge is unwilling to believe that Voldemort is back because it's easier to believe in a plot to get rid of himself (94)!

The Order realizes that it's hard to convince people who do not want to believe a bad thing. People still remember what Voldemort did, and many would rather stick their heads in the sand and refuse to believe he's back than accept the alternative, which is to live in fear and await the worst (94).

The Order admits the brilliance, if you will, of Voldemort's decision to remain in hiding (92). Yes, one may respect or even compliment an enemy or his or her traits. You must *fully* understand your enemy—positive and negative attributes, strengths and weaknesses, use of intelligence, strategy, and yes, even the use of people.

So, let's do an assessment on Harry's enemy, Voldemort. What is he good at? He's highly intelligent, has superb magical skills, and is excellent at manipulating people, fostering loyalty, using deception, using people, and hiding. What are his weaknesses? He's egotistical and unable to understand love or mercy. Voldemort's talent for using and discarding people appears throughout the series: Voldemort used Quirrell and left him to die in book 1, showing, as Dumbledore put it, "just as little mercy to his followers as his enemies" (*SS* 298). He demands complete loyalty and obedience from the Death Eaters and kills any who stray. Even Voldemort himself, through Tom Riddle's diary, admits, "I've always been able to charm the people I needed" (*CS* 310).

PART 1

The lack of knowledge in the Wizarding world about Voldemort's return makes wizards easy targets for the Death Eaters using the Imperius Curse (94). Voldemort can gain power from the outside without having to show himself or his true nature—or his real intentions. Just as the Order has spies in the Ministry, you can bet that Voldemort has spies there too (95)!

The Order next discusses the Ministry's use of argument ad hominem by recognizing that the Ministry is discrediting people with views contrary to its own views, and thus attempting to discredit Dumbledore and take away his honors and offices because he asserts that Voldemort is back. Meanwhile, Tonks and Arthur—who both work at the Ministry—are keeping their mouths shut so that they don't get fired (95).

Ironically, the Auror Kingsley Shacklebolt, who is in charge of the hunt for Sirius, is himself a member of the Order and knows *exactly* where Sirius is (95)! While he is supposedly searching for Sirius, he is really acting as a mole inside the Ministry of Magic—spying on behalf of the Order of the Phoenix, and, of course, Dumbledore.

Speaking of Dumbledore, everyone seems certain that Voldemort has to act cautiously as long as Dumbledore is around. If Dumbledore disappeared, Voldemort would "have a clear field" (95).

In this discussion at number twelve, Grimmauld Place, we also learn that Voldemort is a very good spy and spy master: the Order discusses Voldemort's ability to work covertly and his use of tricks, jinxes, and blackmails. According to this description, Voldemort is skilled at operating in secrecy (96).

Finally, Harry analyzes everything he has learned and concludes that Voldemort has plans other than recruitment. He is after a *weapon,* operating with great stealth—something, Harry realizes, that he did not have last time (96).

Thus, the stage is set for the quest to find the prophecy. Voldemort is already ahead of them on this question, and soon he'll have Harry Potter's personal assistance!

6

THE HOUSE OF BLACK, KREACHER, AND THE ORDER'S COMINGS AND GOINGS

In Chapter 6, "The Noble and Most Ancient House of Black," we find out a few more interesting facts about Kreacher, the value of poisons, and why Kreacher is allowed to remain at the Black house even though he poses a potential threat.

After the meeting has concluded, the children discuss what type of weapon Voldemort is looking for. The twins point out that size is not an issue, using Ginny as an example of something small but exceedingly powerful (100).

NOTE TO SELF: *Never underestimate the power of someone small!*

Meanwhile, there are many comings and goings at headquarters. Kingsley mentions being relieved by Hestia (Sound familiar? It's the name of a Greek goddess of home and hearth) and that he is using Moody's cloak (103). We see Professor McGonagall disguised as a Muggle (118). And we observe Mundungus with stolen cauldrons (106–7). Tonks continues to be clumsy—no surprise there (118)! We find out that Dumbledore is indeed thoroughly involved in the Order's activities when Kingsley mentions that he is on his way to give a report to Dumbledore.

Harry also makes his first substantial observation of Kreacher, who is muttering and stating his prejudice against Mudbloods, his view that the members of the Order are enemies inside the house, and the fact that he must follow his master's orders (107–10). Kreacher is, from the perspective of the Death Eaters, the perfect recruit: someone who has motive *and* access. But because Kreacher cannot leave the house unless ordered to do so by Sirius, everything is just perfect, isn't it?

Not exactly. When Sirius gives Kreacher a direct order to "go away" (110), unfortunately, he hasn't thought about the precise wording of his order. We find out later where Kreacher goes and what the results are: although he can't disclose the location of headquarters, Kreacher is providing Narcissa, sister of Bellatrix and wife of Lucius Malfoy, important information about Harry. Voldemort subsequently uses that information, particularly about his strong connection to Sirius and his willingness to take risks to save someone (830–31).

There is a lesson here. Take great care in framing any orders or instructions *given* and properly interpreting any instructions *received*. Think out orders or directions thoroughly, write them down carefully, and check and double-check that they do not have a possible secondary meaning. Simply put, a poorly drafted or misinterpreted order can lose a battle!

Communication is a two-way street that requires the person drafting the communication to understand how words can be misinterpreted and to prevent any such misinterpretation by selecting precise and clear words. Someone issuing orders must be sure to provide clear direction, all the while understanding how the person reading the order may understand it.

CHAPTER 6

DEAD DROPS AND BRUSH CONTACTS

Precise communication is particularly important when a case officer employs impersonal communication techniques to deliver orders. One such technique is a **dead drop**, where the orders are hidden in an agreed-upon location for later pickup. Another is **brush contacts**, covert agents who pass information in what appears to any observer to be a chance encounter. In such situations, the sender and the recipient do not have an opportunity to discuss any nuances or answer any questions. The information exchanged must be clear and subject to one interpretation only.

Even though the adults are trying *not* to communicate clearly, our favorite triad learns much at headquarters. They find out what it means to be a Death Eater, like Regulus Black, including the wonderful vacation plan and pension benefits: "It's a lifetime of service or death" (112). Nice career, eh? A case in point: Regulus Black had become a Death Eater and tried to get out, and as a result everyone assumes that he was killed by Voldemort or his followers (112). But of course, we find out differently in Book 7, *Harry Potter and the Deathly Hallows*, when Kreacher tells his tale: Regulus had Kreacher take him to the cave, switched the locket, left the other one with a note from R.A.B., and was dragged into the water, where he met his death (DH 193–97).

They also learn more about security at Grimmauld Place, and that Sirius's father had already put "every security measure known to Wizard-kind" before Dumbledore added *his* protection.

And finally, they learn that the twins are gathering poisons, notably the snuffbox filled with wartcap powder and the paralyzed doxy and doxy eggs (104–5, 116), all of which they are planning to put to good use. The Weasley twins' many questionable but humorous products will come in useful later on (104, 116).

PART 1

On the surface, number twelve, Grimmauld Place, seems to be the perfect place to hide and the ideal headquarters. However, we must ask a few questions about whether it is *really* the most appropriate place.

ANALYSIS: *Why have headquarters at the family home of Sirius, the man everyone is looking for?* Everyone knows that Sirius Black is on the loose and evading capture. Wouldn't it make sense for him to return to his family home and hide there?

In addition, we all know full well where Kreacher's loyalties lie. Surely, sharing your secret headquarters with somebody who completely disagrees with you and is able to observe all your actions is *not* the best idea, regardless of whether Kreacher is securely bound by his master, Sirius. As suspected, Hermione's suggestion to set Kreacher free is rejected because "he knows too much about the Order" (110).

ANALYSIS AGAIN, PLEASE: *Why didn't Sirius simply tell Kreacher—before the Order got there—to go somewhere else while they were using Grimmauld Place as the headquarters?* Why not do this *before* they started using it as the headquarters? They didn't, and as a result, they have a traitor in their midst—or, at the very least, someone *willing* to be a traitor.

THE SAD HISTORY OF DEHUMANIZATION OF THE ENEMY—AND ITS DANGERS

Let's take a moment to think about the name of the Black family's house-elf: Kreacher. *Creature.* This is *not* an accident. Rowling named him after a term we use for a living thing we need not care about, like an ant we might step on as we walk on the sidewalk. His name has *meaning*, as do most of the names Rowling uses.

His behavior is truly awful, but we have to wonder: if Sirius and the Order had had more respect for Kreacher's intelligence and motivations—if they hadn't treated him as worthless and therefore powerless—could they have prevented him from causing so much harm?

In human history, the first step in many evil deeds is the **dehumanization** of a person or group of people: during World War II alone, Hitler promoted the idea that Jews and other groups of people were less than human, and the US government used similar reasoning to justify the imprisonment of more than 120,000 Japanese Americans in internment camps. When those in power portray a person or group of people as less than human, it is easier for the majority to accept it when those people are treated unfairly. In the twenty-first century, bias against those of Muslim faith, including broad assumptions that all Muslims are security risks or even terrorists, have led to claims that torture is an acceptable technique—as long as those tortured are somehow less human than others.

On this point, it's worth a look ahead: Kreacher becomes a friend to Harry (and *his* friends Hermione and Ron) because Harry finally treats him with dignity and gives him a gift that is important to him (*DH* 225), much as Harry befriended Dobby by treating him well (*CS* 15, 337). In these books supposedly written for children, Rowling asks important questions indeed.

7

HARRY ENTERS THE LION'S DEN, WHERE THE TRUTH (AND PROFESSOR DUMBLEDORE) EVENTUALLY SETS HIM FREE

In Chapter 7, "The Ministry of Magic," we get a description of the Wizarding world's legal system, a lecture on how Harry should testify, a description of entering the Ministry of Magic, the security at the Ministry of Magic, how information is sent back and forth in the Ministry, and observation of a double agent hard at work, pretending to search for Sirius when in reality he is concealing him! Observing such a great variety of information is an important part of spying.

From our standpoint, it is especially gratifying to see that Harry is developing into quite a spy—he carefully *observes* and *remembers* important things. He is beginning to *analyze* what he observes and put it into context. He may not like observing planets and tea leaves in Divination, but he is developing the traits of a good spy! So let's get back to the story, shall we?

Lupin tells Harry on the morning of the hearing that the law is on his side. Other members of the Order explain how he should testify, and they remind him not to lose his temper and to stick to

CHAPTER 7

the facts. Because there is an exception for his use of magic in self-defense, the law is on his side. They also reassure him that the judge is Amelia Bones, who has a reputation for being fair (123). (Of course, that doesn't turn out to be entirely true. More about Amelia later!)

Harry and Mr. Weasley enter the Ministry of Magic through a red telephone box that descends into the Ministry of Magic once the "cool female voice" identifies the visitors and the nature of their business in the Ministry (125–26). (Shades of *Dr. Who!*) Harry's observations here pay off later:

> "Mr. Weasley, I think this might be out of order too," Harry said.
>
> "No, no, I'm sure it's fine," said Mr. Weasley, holding the receiver above his head and peering at the dial. "Let's see . . . six . . ." he dialed the number, "two . . . four . . . and another four . . . and another two . . ." (125).

ANALYSIS: *The number that Mr. Weasley dials is 6–2–4–4–2. Can you break this code and tell us what 6–2–4–4–2 stands for?* (Don't worry, we'll tell you later when we discuss code breaking!)

Anyone who has visited a military base knows that you go first to the visitor's center, usually at the main gate just outside of the base itself. There you are required to show ID and asked what your business is on base and who will be vouching for you. (That person will most likely be required to escort you on the base as well.) Here, Mr. Weasley is Harry's escort into the Ministry of Magic.

When Harry enters the Ministry of Magic, he is surprised by its size as well as the level of organization (127). Harry has already provided his name and purpose, and he receives a badge stating both. He is accompanied (perhaps because he's a minor, or because of his lack of clearance) by an adult wizard. Harry and Mr. Weasley check in at a **security station**, where a guard reviews and registers Harry's wand before giving it back to him (128).

PART 1

Visitors to secured areas in the real world are often required to wear badges indicating who they are and the fact that they are visiting. This is particularly true in highly secured areas, such as the White House, the National Security Agency, and CIA Headquarters. You might wonder whether the new badges used in Muggle high-security areas have signaling devices so that the security officers can track where you are at all times, just like a real Marauder's Map! Mischief managed, we'd say!

Another similarity with real-world security is the checking of Harry's wand. This might also be necessary because he is a minor, but it is *implied* that the rule applies equally to adults—why else would they staff a security station? (Kids wouldn't be common visitors, we think—except maybe on Bring Your Child to Work Day!) It could also be due to the fact that Harry has been charged with a crime and is there for a hearing. It is standard procedure in our Muggle world to take weapons away from anyone who might enter a courtroom. And yet Harry gets his wand *back*, so it seems that visitors' wands aren't security's main concern!

As we have discovered throughout the series, and as we see particularly in the final book, losing or giving up your wand is an act that any wizard would find absolutely revolting. Because wands actually *choose* the wizard or witch (according to Mr. Ollivander), we could assume that the wand finds it just as revolting. (The one exception might be the Elder Wand, which was constantly being traded from person to person, usually via the killing of the prior owner by the new one—so we can assume that it is used to change!)

We readers know that Harry will, later in the book, enter the Ministry of Magic with his wand and perform significant acts of magic. In book 7 he does it again, using a Patronus Charm to protect Mrs. Cattermole from Dementors as he and Hermione escape Dolores Umbridge's grasp with the Horcrux in hand (*DH* 262). But on each of these occasions, Harry has entered the Ministry of Magic *illegally* and therefore did *not* go through security and give anyone a chance to take his wand from him.

Once in the Ministry of Magic, Harry and Mr. Weasley take an elevator to Mr. Weasley's office to await the hearing. Mr. Weasley has purposely come early for the hearing and plans to wait with Harry in his office until it is time to go to the office of Amelia Bones (129), who is supposed to be the sole hearing officer for Harry's case.

We will now have another word about communication: COMMUNICATION!

(Okay, enough of that!)

As we find out, **internal communication** at the Ministry of Magic is handled by paper airplanes that magically catch the elevator to the correct floor and fly to the intended recipient (130). You'd think that such messages would be easily intercepted, since the security surrounding these internal memos is quite lax. Mr. Weasley says that the Ministry *used* to use owls, but "the mess was unbelievable"—as one can imagine (130)! Just imagine how many people at the Ministry would have to be assigned to owl-droppings clean-up duty! Ew!

Once on Mr. Weasley's floor, Harry gets a glimpse of what work is like for Kingsley, as the person in charge of locating Sirius Black (131–32). Kingsley is working for one entity while spying for the opposition or some other entity—that is, he is a mole.

Kingsley, as a trained Auror, is perfectly suited to this task. Only the most superb wizards and witches can become Aurors, so we know he is very skilled at magic. He is also in a position to obtain information that others do not have access to, including **inside information** on what the Ministry knows about Sirius Black, Voldemort, and his followers.

Kingsley is also privy to the Ministry's information about the Order of the Phoenix, its presumed whereabouts, the actions of its members, and its organization. In other words, Kingsley—as a member of the Order of the Phoenix—is in a position to inform the other members of the Order if they are in any danger and to share what the Ministry of Magic actually knows or plans to do. A well-placed mole is a wonderful thing for any intelligence officer. They are essential to organizations that want to spy on an opposing organization. Just a word to the wise: don't get caught!

PART 1

Perhaps now is a good time to discuss double agents, loyalty, and "the greater good." A mole is employed by one entity—here the Ministry of Magic—but is really working for another entity—in this case, the Order of the Phoenix. So, Kingsley is a traitor to the Ministry.

But is this *really* the case? *Shouldn't the Ministry of Magic have the same goals as the Order of the Phoenix?* There's the rub!

The Ministry of Magic, just like the Minister Cornelius Fudge himself, is refusing to see the truth or even *consider* that Voldemort is back. The Ministry is making a huge mistake, as we all know, particularly those of us on Harry's side. If Fudge wasn't such an idiot, and if the other witches and wizards who worship the Ministry of Magic (or "THE LAW") weren't so docile, the Ministry would have the *same* goals as the Order of the Phoenix: that is, getting ready for the return of Voldemort and preparing to defeat him.

ANALYSIS: *Is Kingsley a traitor or not?* It all depends on who you think is *right*.

This is equally true in the Muggle world. Many moles or double agents become agents for the other side precisely *because* they believe the entity they are working for has lost its way, is doing something inappropriate, or is in reality "one of the bad guys."

Except for spies who work for money (we will discuss this in Part 2 when we look at types of spies and recruiting), many spies, including some double agents, believe that they are being perfectly loyal, but to a *higher cause* or to *a cause that is more worthy*.

Determining whether a person's actions are justified requires not only an evaluation of the individual's motives, but also a more complete overview of the circumstances at hand, including whether the government or directing entity is truly worthy of that person's support. Just as a good wizard or witch must be ready at a moment's notice to counter an Imperius Curse, it is imperative for witch, wizard, and Muggle alike to evaluate the actions of their employer or leader.

Although this may sound difficult, it isn't that hard at all! In the

CHAPTER 7

Harry Potter series, which side is Muggle-baiting? Which side takes great pleasure in torturing Muggles and wizards, and in creating as much havoc as possible in the Wizarding and Muggle worlds? Which side enjoys taunting defenseless individuals?

It is said that the truth will set you free, and that is true. But it is also true, as discussed above, that the way society treats its most unfortunate tells us a lot about the society itself. Loyalty based on sound principles and the actual implementation of those principles (and not just talking about them) usually results in strong dedication to an organization. Loyalty based on fear—especially the fear of death once you take a particular side (just as Regulus Black found out)—is rarely a good means of obtaining someone's dedication. (Unless you happen to be Voldemort, perhaps the most powerful wizard in the world, who has absolutely no problem with feeding traitors to Nagini!)

ANALYSIS: *Is the Ministry evil? As bad as Voldemort?* Of course not. We can all see that Voldemort and his followers are bad people. But that is not the point. The Ministry knows that Voldemort and his followers are bad. The problem is that the Ministry refuses to believe that he is back. Does this make the Ministry as bad as Voldemort? Certainly not. It is just misinformed, deluded, and stupid—and refusing to see what *should* be obvious.

Before we head down to the trial that awaits Harry Potter, we should talk a little bit about the *greater good*.

The concept of the greater good is quite old, and is usually assigned to the modern—or at least somewhat modern—philosopher John Stuart Mills, the most famous proponent of **utilitarianism**, the system of ethics based on it. Originally proposed by another philosopher, Jeremy Bentham, utilitarianism's goal is *to promote the greatest happiness for the greatest number*. Thus, according to this philosophy, society should base *all* of its decisions on a sort of mathematical formula in which we determine which policy or decision results in the greatest number of people benefiting from it.

The weakness of utilitarianism is that it fails to consider important aspects of society other than happiness, including individual freedom, dignity, or fairness. So utilitarianism could justify, for example, enslaving 10 percent of our population in order to provide a "greater good" to the other 90 percent of society. This concept can be particularly dangerous if we divide society into subgroups by gender, race, or even by those who have magical powers!

Still, the greater good is a very enticing principle, so enticing that it resulted in our dear and wonderful young Dumbledore agreeing to do things that perhaps he would not have otherwise done (*DH* 353–59). Dumbledore and his new friend Grindelwald seriously considered a world in which wizards were supreme and Muggles would be used, without their consent, as providers or servants—and therefore slaves—for the Wizarding world! Young Dumbledore said it best himself in a letter to Grindelwald:

> Your point about Wizard dominance being FOR THE MUGGLES' OWN GOOD—this, I think, is the crucial point. Yes, we have been given power and yes, that power gives us the right to rule, but it also gives us responsibilities over the ruled (*DH* 357).

Perhaps young Dumbledore thought that by taking all this power he would be in a position to be quite fair to the Muggles under his dominion. But such a view is nothing more than a rationalization or excuse to take freedom away from others.

REMEMBERING HISTORY SO IT DOES NOT REPEAT ITSELF

Powerful individuals have often deprived large groups of people of their rights in the Muggle world. History gives us many examples of people subjected to misery, forced servitude, and exclusion from society.

CHAPTER 7

In the early twentieth century, the Soviet Union forced hundreds of thousands of people to build a railroad all the way from Moscow to the Pacific and to dig a canal from the Baltic Sea to the White Sea. The government claimed that the work was for the greater good, because it improved the nation's economic growth. Meanwhile, thousands of those workers died from abuse, illness, and inhumane conditions.

Also in the twentieth century, the Nazi Party gained solid political support in *democratically elected* government bodies based on promises to improve the German economy after the ravages of World War I and the Great Depression, and it continued to claim service to the greater good even after Hitler seized control. It served the happiness of one group at the cost of untold misery to millions of others.

The United States is not immune to such travesties of justice, as is clearly shown by the many years that slavery existed in this country, the many justifications offered for it, and the violent resistance to ending it. Were such unethical acts ever supported by the concept of the greater good?

Now that we feel morally superior and realize that we readers would never be tempted to impose such injustices, we should perhaps get back to the story!

~~~~~~~~~~~~~~~~~~~~~~~~

When Mr. Weasley and Harry run into Kingsley, Harry does not immediately realize that it is important for him to be quiet and to *pretend* that he doesn't know him. Mr. Weasley reminds him with a subtle (or perhaps not-so-subtle) sign—standing on his foot (131)! Second only to loyalty, **discretion** is a spy's most valuable asset. A good operative is discreet in all things: observing much but saying little, knowing when not to say a thing, knowing when to appear ignorant, and knowing when to keep a secret, regardless of the dangers or consequences.

Suddenly, Harry and Mr. Weasley find out from Mr. Weasley's coworker Perkins that the hearing time and location have been changed (134)! A good intelligence officer would consider two possibilities: first, that the *initial* time was disinformation, and second, the *new* time is disinformation.

A good intelligence officer would also take the time to analyze not only *how* this change occurred, but *why* it might have occurred. But Mr. Weasley rushes Harry down to his hearing, having no time to analyze how such a change might have happened.

The law is a wonderful thing, unless you are subjected to it against your will!

A STUDY OF THE PROPER AND FAIR APPLICATION OF LAWS— IN OUR WORLD AND IN THE WORLD OF HARRY POTTER

A good society has laws that are applied fairly and equally to all. It provides fair notice and due process, and it requires that decisions be made by well-qualified and unbiased judges. It allows the accused to question the accusers and to present evidence on his or her own behalf. It does not allow witnesses to be tainted by fear or subjected to torture. And finally, for those who are found guilty within a proper criminal system, it imposes sentences that are fair, proportionate to the crime, and not cruel or unusual.

If you are interested in a detailed analysis of the legal aspects of the Wizarding world, we direct you to a wonderful law review article entitled "Harry Potter and the Law," written by several legal scholars and published in the *Texas Wesleyan Law Review* in 2006. You may download and read the complete text at: **http://papers.ssrn.com/ sol3/papers.cfm?abstract_id=829344**

CHAPTER 7

Based on this unpleasant surprise, we can guess just how much of the process and legal protections that should normally apply to a defendant in a fair legal system will *actually* be applied to Harry Potter at his hearing.

Which gets us to chapter 8!

8

THE MINISTRY OF MAGIC AS THE QUEEN OF HEARTS: SENTENCE FIRST, TRIAL AFTER—THEN OFF WITH THEIR HEADS!

Chapter 8 is entitled "The Hearing." When Harry reaches the courtroom, he is required to enter alone, without Mr. Weasley. He immediately recognizes the Wizarding courtroom from his previous use of the Pensieve in book 4, *Harry Potter and the Goblet of Fire* (137), when he observed the questioning of Karkaroff (*GF* 584–91). Harry also realizes that this must *not* be a simple hearing, such as going to the principal's office! He is being subjected to *a full-blown trial before the Wizengamot*, with three interrogators in addition to the fifty council members deciding his fate (138).

First we have the disinformation and trickery of the correct time and location of the hearing, and now we find out that the *type* of hearing is entirely different than expected—or at least from what Mr. Weasley was told, that is, a single administrator with a reputation for being fair.

It is unclear why Mr. Weasley was not allowed to enter into the courtroom. You would think that all courtrooms are open to the public, even in the Wizarding world. It certainly has a dramatic effect on Harry, facing such adversity alone—that is, until Professor Dumbledore arrives, immediately taking the position as defense counsel on his behalf (139).

ANALYSIS: *Why the change in time and location of the trial?*
Clearly the Ministry, and particularly Cornelius Fudge, wanted to prevent Dumbledore from interceding on behalf of his young ward. Although Dumbledore apparently did not receive the second owl (supposedly sent to tell him the new time), he "luckily" found out on his own—or perhaps Mr. Weasley informed him of the change in time and location (a good reason for him to remain outside the courtroom!)—and immediately came to Harry's aid.

And who are the three interrogators they face? "Cornelius Oswald Fudge, Minister of Magic; Amelia Susan Bones, Head of the Department of Magical Law Enforcement; Dolores Jane Umbridge, Senior Undersecretary to the Minister" (138–39).

We find out next—after Dumbledore conjures a chair for himself out of thin air—that there are indeed specific laws that provide legal rights and certain elements of due process in the Wizarding world. They include the reading of the charges, identification of the accused, confirmation that the person before the Wizengamot is *indeed* the accused, and a rather cursory attempt (through interrogation) to confirm the essential elements of the crime. Notice that Cornelius Fudge gets the young and inexperienced Harry to admit to all of the essential elements of the crime charged (140): he used magic, underage, outside of school, in the presence of a Muggle.

One should note first of all that Harry was never offered the right to remain silent, one of the major due process rights guaranteed in both the English and American legal systems. Second, instead of having a jury of peers or a selection of the jury, it appears that the jury is the Wizengamot itself—certainly not the group of impartial equals assumed in US law (except perhaps in that everyone is either a witch or wizard). Third, instead of a prosecutor, three interrogators have the authority to ask questions of Harry, the accused, as well as other witnesses.

Fourth, Harry is in fact being interrogated, or being asked formal questions. As discussed previously, there are many forms of interrogation, and there are many forms of questions. The questions asked by Fudge at the beginning of the trial are delivered by a person who is an *opponent* to Harry, and the purpose of those questions is to obtain answers that will be *used against Harry,* to prove that he is guilty of the crime (140–41). Some of the questions are *direct questions*, which generally start with the words such as *who, what,* and *where.* Direct questions do not include the answer itself within the question. *Direct questions* are fairer, considering that they allow the witness to actually answer the question and expound on that answer if need be.

However, Fudge is asking another type of question, *leading questions*, in which the person asking places the answer he or she wants *inside* the question itself. Fudge uses leading questions to get the specific admissions he wants from Harry:

- "You are Harry James Potter, of number four, Privet Drive, Little Whinging, Surrey?"
  Instead of, WHAT is your name? Purpose of question: identification of the accused.

- "You received an official warning from the Ministry for using illegal magic three years ago did you not?"
  Instead of, HAVE you ever received a warning? Purpose of question: establish knowledge of the law that prohibits use of magic *by a minor.*

- "And yet you conjured a Patronus on the night of the second of August?"
  Instead of, WHAT happened on August 2nd? Purpose of question: admission of the crime of *using magic,* by a minor.

- "Knowing that you are not permitted to use magic outside school while you are under the age of seventeen?"
  Instead of, ARE you aware that you are not permitted to use magic outside school when you are under the age of seventeen? Purpose of question: establish knowledge of restriction against using magic *outside of school,* an exception that does not apply.

- "Knowing that you were in an area full of Muggles?"
  Purpose of question: establish knowledge that use of magic would violate the Statute of Secrecy, and all that . . .

- "Fully aware that you were in close proximity to a Muggle [Dudley] at the time?"
  Purpose of question: establish likelihood of Muggle observing use of magic (140).

Fudge's questions are clearly *adversarial* questions, asked by an enemy. Fudge's plan and strategy are clear to all, particularly Dumbledore—but Dumbledore does *not* yet intercede, which is interesting but dramatically more powerful. After all, it *appears*, from Harry's own answers, that he has just admitted fully to the crime! Quick side note: Ever notice the definition of the word *fudge* includes stretching the truth or even the act of lying? Kind of like Kreacher and *creature*, don't you think?

Fudge then moves on to Harry's prior record—including prior infractions for which he was never charged or convicted—and demands only yes or no answers, providing no opportunity for Harry to explain. As is clear to everyone, particularly Professor Dumbledore, Fudge is railroading Harry into a conviction, for unknown reasons except perhaps to gain a conviction and prove to the Wizarding world that anything Harry Potter says is untrue (140). Fudge is also asking about Harry's prior record to determine the appropriate sanction or punishment—and, we imagine, to make sure that it is even more severe!

Thus, through the use of leading questions and the intentional limiting of Harry's answers, Fudge has elicited all the facts necessary to obtain a conviction.

He has demonstrated that Harry was well aware of the law as it applies to him—that is, that he had prior notice that his actions were illegal and violated the law. Fudge has proved that Harry had *prior warnings* of the applicable law, and that he had *full knowledge* that he was in an area full of Muggles and in proximity of a Muggle. Fudge has also confirmed that Harry is under the age of seventeen and therefore, by definition, *was a minor using magic outside of Hogwarts and in the presence of a Muggle* (140).

SOVIET SHOW TRIALS AND COMMITMENT TO A MENTAL INSTITUTION

Harry's trial up to this point is reminiscent of the Soviet show trials of the 1940s and 1950s, in which Soviet citizens who were not guilty were placed on trial and found guilty, and then often placed or committed to a psychological ward, never to be seen again.

But then the tide at Harry's trial is quickly turned. Someone *other than Fudge* changes the flow of questioning by asking Harry about the Patronus. Take careful note of *who* asks this question: *Amelia Susan Bones*!

Madam Bones, the gray-haired witch with a monocle, asks Harry, "You produced a fully-fledged Patronus?" (141).

ANALYSIS: *Is this a friendly question from Madam Bones or an adversarial question?* It seems to us that this is a friendly question because when she gets the answer, she is impressed. Harry confirms that he is able to produce a Patronus and that he had first done so over a year earlier (141). The other wizards are similarly impressed that this young man can create a corporeal Patronus (though we wonder about this

amazement when we think of Harry's history and his reputation as The Boy Who Lived!).

This strategically positioned question allows Harry to move
from *whether* he had used magic to *why* he had used magic. (Note
that Madam Bones's niece, Susan Bones, asks the same question at
a strategic point in the first organizational meeting of their secret
Defense Against the Dark Arts study group at the Hog's Head Inn
later on [342].)

Fudge, of course, just claims that Harry's answer proves his case;
it doesn't matter how impressive it is that Harry performed a Patronus
Charm. But Madam Bones's question allows a pause in the action,
which gives Harry an opportunity—*finally*—to state the truth: "'I
did it because of the Dementors!' he said loudly, before anyone could
interrupt him again" (141).

Fudge then claims that Harry has had time to think of an excuse
and develop a cover story. He assumes, since Muggles cannot see
Dementors, and no one from the Wizarding world was around to see
the event, that Harry will not be able to provide a witness to prove
that there truly were Dementors at the scene of the alleged crime.
"Muggles can't see Dementors, can they, boy?" he says. "Highly
convenient, highly convenient . . . so it's just your word and no
witnesses . . ." (142). Fudge thus attacks Harry's credibility, discrediting the person giving the testimony instead of attempting to find
out the truth!

It is here that Fudge falls into Dumbledore's trap, and we
understand exactly why Professor Dumbledore remained quiet until
they got to this point. At a simple clearing of his throat, the entire
room reverts to silence, and Dumbledore states, matter-of-factly,
"We do, in fact, have a witness to the presence of Dementors in that
alleyway . . . other than Dudley Dursley, I mean" (142).

When Fudge tries to prevent Dumbledore from calling witnesses
on Harry's behalf (asserting that they do not have time for such
nonsense), Dumbledore refers to the Wizengamot Charter of Rights,
which includes the right to call witnesses (142–43). Dumbledore

confirms this right to present witnesses through Madam Bones, who is the head of the Department of Magical Law Enforcement, and Fudge begrudgingly accedes because the law, as they say, is THE LAW. Dumbledore therefore calls Mrs. Figg (143).

This is a *great* surprise to Cornelius Fudge, who was convinced that no witch or wizard was around Harry at the time he produced a Patronus. Madam Bones confirms that Fudge was not the only one to think so:

> "We have no record of any witch or wizard living in Little Whinging other than Harry Potter," said Madam Bones at once. "That situation has always been closely monitored, given . . . given past events" (143).

Apparently there are ways of tracking the whereabouts of all witches and wizards—but it appears to work only on those witches and wizards who have *magical powers*. The Ministry of Magic and Fudge did not know about Mrs. Figg's whereabouts because she is a Squib, a person who has no magical powers but comes from a Wizarding family (143). It appears that Dumbledore's placement of Mrs. Figg as his *own* spy on Privet Drive was a wonderful decision indeed!

We note that Mrs. Figg's testimony, as well as Harry's interrogation by Fudge, should be required reading for anyone foolish enough to want to be a lawyer.

Mrs. Figg, who is not the brightest bulb on the tree, is seeking to expose the truth. Ever so slowly, and with some humorous moments, she finally gets exactly to that truth: she confirms that Dementors were indeed attacking Harry and his cousin, that Harry produced his wand to protect himself and Dudley, that he did indeed perform a Patronus Charm and produce a corporeal Patronus that chased away the Dementors and saved both his cousin Dudley's life and his own (144–45).

One would think that the trial would be over at this point, but it is not—and with good reason! It is now Professor Dumbledore's

CHAPTER 8

chance to speak the truth and aim accusations where they should be directed—at the Ministry!

Fudge, perhaps only slightly brighter than Mrs. Figg, steps easily and woefully into Dumbledore's trap. Once again exhibiting no understanding of logic, Cornelius Fudge grasps at what seems to be a self-evident point: that Dementors could not have attacked Harry *because the Dementors are under the control of the Ministry* and are exactly where they belong, in Azkaban (146).

Over the next five pages, Professor Dumbledore exhibits wonderful use of logic, taking this one simple "fact" and following the logic of that assumption to its eventual end. Once Fudge has asserted and confirmed that the Dementors are under the full control of the Ministry, Dumbledore has him! Fudge's win turns to a loss before his very eyes.

WORDS AS TOOLS—LEARNING FROM THE MERCHANT OF VENICE

In the Ministry courtroom, the tide turns in a way quite similar to the trial in Shakespeare's *The Merchant of Venice*. Portia turns Shylock's demand for a strict interpretation of the law (a pound of flesh) on its head when she strictly interprets the law in a way that causes Shylock to lose not only the case, but half his fortune *and* his daughter as well!

ANALYSIS: *How did Dumbledore trap Fudge?* By pure logic! Fudge claimed that the Dementors could not have been at Little Whinging because they are under the Ministry's control. But if the Dementors were indeed near Privet Drive—as testified by both Harry and Mrs. Figg—then, according to Dumbledore, there are only two possibilities: someone *in the Ministry* sent them there (and the Ministry remains in control of the Dementors), OR the Dementors are *not* under the full control of the Ministry!

Fudge asserts that the Dementors are indeed under the full control of the Ministry, so someone from the Ministry *must have* sent them. Dumbledore then states that an investigation must be undertaken to determine *who* in the Ministry sent the Dementors to attack Harry.

Intelligence analysts have to use similar logic every day. Their job is to take facts, assumed or proven, and expand upon them to find out where they may ultimately lead.

(Those of us who have read the rest of the book find it hard not to point at the froglike lady in pink, Dolores Umbridge, who did in fact send the Dementors to silence Harry [746]. Of course, we don't find this out for quite a while, so . . . back to the trial!)

The trial has now clearly shown that Dementors *did* attack Harry and that while he did use magic underage, he used it to defend himself. Which gets us precisely to the *exception* to the Decree for the Reasonable Restriction of Underage Sorcery, found at clause 7: the use of magic *is* allowed, even by minors and in the presence of Muggles, in exceptional circumstances, such as saving your life or the life of your cousin Dudley (*CS* 69; *OP* 147, 148)!

Fudge, knowing full well that he has lost the case, tries once more to resurrect all the bad things that he knows about Harry. He attacks Harry's credibility and Harry himself, a clear attempt to use the fallacious argument ad hominem and irrelevant information to convict Harry (148–49). He lists all of Harry's prior "bad acts" as a basis for conviction, despite his clear innocence (148–49). In the Muggle world, we do not allow somebody to be convicted because of their prior acts. A person's prior acts, even acts *similar* to the criminal act for which they are standing trial, are generally *not* allowed to become part of the evidence against the accused. The fact that someone did something wrong before, indeed even did *the exact same thing* before, does not prove that they did it *this* time! (There are exceptions to this rule, too. What did we tell you about wanting to become a lawyer, again?)

Thus, Fudge's attempt to bring into evidence certain actions at Harry's home—such as blowing up his aunt and the Hover Charm for which he received a warning—is not relevant to the crime being charged *now*. Indeed, Dumbledore goes further than that: when Harry advises Fudge that the person who actually performed the Hover Charm at his home was a house-elf (Dobby), Dumbledore offers to summon the "house-elf in question" to appear at the trial (148).

Fudge, of course, declines this opportunity to allow Dumbledore to firmly and finally disprove Harry's prior "bad" acts. Additionally, Dumbledore points out that no charges were brought against Harry in the prior situation with his aunt, and because he has not been convicted of this act it would be inappropriate for the court to consider such evidence in any event (149).

Grasping at straws, Fudge then tries to bring in evidence of Harry's "bad" actions at Hogwarts—and we all have to admit, he has broken a rule or two. Dumbledore applies his own counter-jinx, if you will, stating that Harry's actions at Hogwarts are under the exclusive purview and jurisdiction of Dumbledore as Headmaster of Hogwarts (149). In other words, anything that occurs at Hogwarts stays at Hogwarts!

Of course, the exclusive jurisdiction of the Headmaster can be changed, as we soon find out. But for now, whatever Harry has done at Hogwarts cannot be used against him at this trial.

Dumbledore, realizing that he has won the case, demands that a verdict be rendered at this time. The vote is taken, and Harry is cleared of all charges. Dumbledore leaves as quickly as he arrived, and Harry is once again alone, wondering what in the world just happened (150)!

But before we leave this chapter we must return to Amelia Bones.

ANALYSIS: *How could the members of the Order be so sure about Amelia Bones? Why wasn't she Harry's sole interviewer, instead of the three he faced?* As we learn after the hearing, when Mad-Eye shows Harry a picture of the original Order of the Phoenix, Edgar Bones, Amelia's brother, was a founding member of the Order, but "they got him, and his family too" (174). With such connections, she sounds like the perfect person to decide Harry's fate. But she doesn't! And why not? The answer is both unfortunate and enlightening: because Fudge took over and appointed himself and Dolores Umbridge as the co-interrogators (138–39).

And why did Fudge do this?

It seems likely that he wanted to personally ensure that Harry was convicted of and punished for a crime, in order to damage his reputation in a very public fashion. He probably knew that Madam Bones lost loved ones to You-Know-Who and suspected that she might be too easy on Harry, who stopped her brother's murderer (Voldemort). To provide the appearance of fairness, he appointed a third person who had no personal connections to Harry—though, of course, Dolores Umbridge just happens to be exceptionally loyal to the Ministry. He could count on her to support his arguments, no matter how weak! If Madam Bones disagreed, it would be two opinions against her one. Together, they could also prevent any lenient treatment of Harry, should he, for instance, be so *irresponsible* and *disrespectful* as to turn up late for the hearing after they moved the time and place with barely any warning!

9

LIFE AT HEADQUARTERS:
BORING, BORING, BORING

The next chapter, "The Woes of Mrs. Weasley," describes perfectly the real-world experience of spying. First, spying is often exciting, but it is just as often mundane and boring, especially when one is at headquarters. Second, it also subjects those involved to great danger and risk, even death.

The chapter begins, however, with a demonstration of the usefulness of being an *observant* spy. Harry observes several interesting tidbits, some of which are important, and some of which *could* be important. We have already identified loyalty and discretion as two of a spy's most important tools. If we had to choose a third, it would be observational and analytical skill. Each is dependent on the other, and so we combine them in a single tool.

What are some of the tidbits Harry and his best friends learn? Both before and after the hearing, Mr. Weasley mentions having to deal with toilets—*regurgitating* toilets, to be specific. Apparently, some wizards think that toilets that flush up instead of down are a fun trick to play on Muggles.

As funny as this may seem, especially if you're the sort who likes to play tricks on your friends (or perhaps your enemies!), Mr. Weasley sees them as a sign of something more serious: Muggle-hating or Muggle-bashing. Have you ever seen someone play a trick on a dog by pretending to throw a ball, but really holding on to it? The trick is quite a mean one: the dog, who trusts humans totally, is confused and cannot understand what has happened. The trick lets the person who plays it feel more powerful than whoever it's played upon. If Harry's story teaches us anything, it is that being mean, particularly to those who cannot defend themselves, is a great moral wrong that harms the mean person's soul as well as the target.

Mr. Weasley is sharing a very important moral lesson with Harry. While people might describe these "tricks" as harmless, they are—especially when done by a person in a position of power—a *misuse and abuse of power.*

Targeting a particular group of people for such misconduct based on their traits (such as not being able to perform magic, or perhaps being from the "wrong" part of town, or perhaps having the "wrong" color of skin) shows not only meanness, but also *prejudice.* J. K. Rowling, through Mr. Weasley, wants to be sure that we understand this important point.

Now, back to an observation that Harry made while standing outside the courtroom with Mr. Weasley after the hearing. Harry sees Lucius Malfoy talking with the Minister of Magic (153–54).

ANALYSIS: *Why is Lucius Malfoy at the Ministry?* Mr. Weasley knows full well that Lucius Malfoy has a history of supporting the Dark Arts, and Voldemort in particular. So, when Harry wonders why Lucius Malfoy was at the Ministry and talking to Fudge, Mr. Weasley immediately provides his explanation and analysis: "Gold, I expect" (155). Mr. Weasley also informs Harry that the Malfoys have a substantial amount of money and are more than willing to use it to increase their influence, delay the enactment of laws, and obtain connections (155).

CHAPTER 9

NOTE TO SELF: *Money is indeed power.*

Money gets you into places that you would never reach without it. It supplies more than just fancy restaurants or private schools; money, in the Wizarding and Muggle worlds alike, allows a person access to the individuals who make decisions and affect how the world works. And access means *influence*, from subtle influence, such as convincing someone (say, Cornelius Fudge) that Harry Potter is lying and can't be trusted, to less subtle forms of influence (perhaps the power to order Dementors on a mission outside Azkaban?).

We think it would be rather hard to place an Imperius Curse on somebody from a hundred miles or even a hundred blocks away. But if Voldemort intends to take control of the Ministry of Magic (which we all know he does), he will need to have *insiders* in the building with access not only to knowledge about what is going on, but also the ability to direct what happens, either through general influence or by the implementation of a well-aimed Imperius Curse. From his observations, Harry can reasonably guess that Lucius Malfoy is trading gold for some kind of *access*.

In the Muggle world, money is just as influential. While we aren't too worried about someone putting an Imperius Curse on our politicians, it's pretty clear that providing the right politician with a stack of Ben Franklins or Andrew Jacksons (legally, of course!) can have much the same effect. Such influence can be acquired under the table as well.

Those willing to stoop as low as Nagini slithers are more than willing to bribe someone, or better yet, threaten or *exploit* them.

It's possible to influence others not only with money, but also with information. Many a person agreed to spy because of the *fear of exposure* of some fact that they want to remain hidden. The Imperius Curse is powerful, but the fear that some private act will become public can be just as powerful—in the Wizarding world as well as in the Muggle world.

This is known as blackmail, a term that might derive from the sending of an all-black envelope, without a return address, containing information that the recipient does not want exposed. Blackmail can get somebody to begin spying, and also to get them to continue it!

For example, once a blackmailer has paid a person to spy, if that person has second thoughts and wants to quit spying, the blackmailer will threaten to expose this fact to the authorities, thus using the threat of the spy's own legal system against him or her.

Whatever his plan, Lucius Malfoy is certainly up to no good! But before Harry and Mr. Weasley can discuss the matter further, they enter the elevator with other people. They choose *not* to talk about the issue in a place where they could be overheard (155). This use of discretion is basic spy craft. Communication—all communication—must be secure. Talking in the presence of outsiders with unknown loyalties would not be a good thing, and Mr. Weasley and Harry know it.

When Harry returns to headquarters, he finds out that Sirius had been thinking that if the trial went badly, and Harry was expelled from Hogwarts, Harry could live with him at Grimmauld Place (158). A good student of people will jump on this chance to make psychological assessments of both Harry and Sirius. Harry is thrilled to have the chance to live with his godfather in a home where he is liked and loved. He does not yet understand the importance of going back to number four, Privet Drive, every summer. And Sirius wants to do more than simply hide at his family home; having a "mission" to protect and care for Harry would give him a purpose and a sense of belonging.

In **analyzing** people—whether they be witches, wizards, or Muggles—it is always important to take into account not only the person's motives, but also their strongest desires and dreams.

GETTING TO KNOW A NEW ACQUAINTANCE—LET PERSONAL INTERESTS BE YOUR GUIDE

Whether you're spying on someone or just making friends, ask new acquaintances about their hobbies. What people do in their spare time, outside of work or family responsibilities, often tells you much about them. It also helps you connect with them, to get a better understanding of them, and perhaps even befriend them.

Hobbies often reflect a person's dreams or true passion, something that you can use to build a friendship or to gather information for a spy mission. Hermione's true passion is righting a wrong, as shown by her development of S.P.E.W. The fact that Abraham Lincoln read Shakespeare more than any other author tells us much about the man; not only did he like great literature, but he had a love for language and a desire to fully understand the foibles of man—and ironically, an understanding of the tragedies.

~~~~~~~~~~~~~~~~~~~~~~~~~~~~~~~~~~~~~

Hermione's hobby is developing and organizing S.P.E.W., her house-elf rights group. And despite Harry and Ron's lack of real interest in the organization, they're Hermione's friends and thus have already joined it (159).

Hermione's dedication to this organization, which she founded in the previous book, tells us much about her: she empathizes with others, particularly those who need and deserve protection. Hermione is indeed the smartest witch of her time, and certainly of her age. We could all learn a lot from her!

With all that in mind, let's get back to the two major points this chapter makes about spying. The life of a spy can be dangerous, and it can also be quite boring.

Harry finds out rather quickly that life at headquarters can be quite mundane, especially if you are given the task of cleaning up number twelve, Grimmauld Place (160)! But it also gives Harry the chance to look back at history when Mad-Eye shows him the picture of the original Order of the Phoenix. Many of its members have died, including both of his parents. It reminds him of how risky it is to be a member of an Order that is trying to defeat an evil and powerful wizard. It shows him that he is part of that history, but he can still analyze it and learn from it. He and the present Order of the Phoenix are still pursuing the same goal, although many of the players have changed (173–74).

LEARNING FROM HISTORY: ANALYZING A MISSION

Following a spying mission, the organizing agency usually conducts an analysis called an *after-action report (AAR)*. The analysis asks three big questions: What went right? What went wrong? What can be improved? You can use these questions to perform an analysis of almost anything—a meeting, a sports game, a test—and figure out how you can do it better the next time.

Faced with all this history and a lot of boring time at headquarters, what can Harry do? Analysis, of course!

ANALYSIS: *What worked last time, and what didn't?* Harry needs to ask, What happened in the last war? What lessons can we learn from it? What steps did the previous Order take? Were those steps successful? Or was the previous Order close to defeat until Voldemort happened to aim his wand at young Harry Potter and have his Avada Kedavra Curse rebound back at him?

More importantly, Harry is The Boy Who Lived. Why did he live? What weapon is Voldemort looking for? Why can Harry see what Voldemort is doing? Why can Harry feel Voldemort's anger and rage? All these questions—or, more accurately, the answers to all these questions—are necessary to destroy Voldemort. By the end we'll know all the answers, but at this point in the story our fellow spies can only analyze the situation based on the knowledge they presently have.

CHAPTER 9

Spies and intelligence analysts almost always have incomplete knowledge: that is the nature of the business. But they must determine what they can from the knowledge they do have and act on it as intelligently as possible.

And then there's the risk inherent in spying. If Harry did not understand the danger he was in when he saw the old photo of the Order, he certainly understands it when Molly Weasley notes—after her encounter with the boggart—that one-half of the Weasley family is in the Order and states, quite truly, "it will be a miracle if we all come through this" (177)!

10

STRANGERS IN A STRANGE LAND—
AN INTRODUCTION TO LUNA LOVEGOOD

At first glance, the next chapter, "Luna Lovegood," does not seem to have much to do with spying. However, our introduction to the strange Luna Lovegood demonstrates that friends can be found in many places, and they can be quite different from you. Indeed, we learn to accept people who appear (and indeed, are!) strange and that it is our differences that sometimes makes us more appreciative of our friendships.

Little did we know, at Luna's first appearance, that she would become such a major player, one of the most essential members of Dumbledore's Army, and—at certain very important points in the plot—would provide understanding (particularly for Harry), great humor, and the ability to state a profound truth simply.

But before we can meet Luna, we must first make it to the Hogwarts Express! Notice the extensive security in place to get Harry to the train platform (180). Notice also that one of the escorts, Sturgis Podmore, is missing!

CHAPTER 10

ANALYSIS: *Why is Sturgis Podmore missing?* At this point, all Harry knows is that nobody seems too worried about it. However, we find out later that Sturgis has been captured at the Ministry of Magic and sent to Azkaban (287). Was he guarding the corridors of the Department of Mysteries on behalf of the Order? If so, then he will soon be replaced by Mr. Weasley, resulting in his serious injury. In any case, they continue with the plan, despite a missing person, showing another great tool of spy craft, *flexibility.*

When we look at the enhanced security, we wonder whether it is intended to protect Harry from Voldemort and his minions, or instead from the Ministry itself! Sirius insists on coming along, albeit as a dog (181). We find out soon enough that by doing so Sirius has blown his cover!

ANALYSIS: *Why does Sirius come when he is a wanted man (or dog, as the case may be)?* Is this an example of Sirius being protective of his godson, or instead of Sirius's known proclivity to rash behavior and risk-taking? The answer seems to lie in the responses of the other members of the Order. Several seem to be upset, or at least worried, by Sirius's insistence on coming along.

When Harry gets to the train station, his security guards say their good-byes. Moody reminds everyone to be "careful of what you put in writing. If in doubt, don't put it in a letter at all" (182). In two words: secure communication.

Or, to put it in a way that Moody would: **CONSTANT VIGILANCE!** (*GF* 213, 217, 571).

ANALYSIS: *Again, we have to wonder, who is the real enemy?* Who is it that might be intercepting messages? And to what use would they be putting that information? Again, is the Order protecting Harry from the Ministry, or from

PART 1

Voldemort and his followers? Serious (Sirius?) questions indeed. The old rule is, *Know thy enemy.* But the problem here is, *Which enemy is your enemy?* Or have they become one and the same?

But enough of that—for now, anyway. Back to the story, we think!

Once on the train, we finally meet Luna (185). As mentioned before, it is hard to believe that Luna will become such a major character in the book. Or is it? Think about it. The chapter is named after her. How often does J. K. Rowling name a chapter after a character? Not very often.

OK, OK, we'll tell you exactly how often! Of the 199 chapters in the entire series (including the prologue), Rowling uses the name of a person for the name of the chapter only nine times:

Nicholas Flamel . . . . Book 1, chapter 13
Gildaroy Lockhart . . . . Book 2, chapter 6
Cornelius Fudge . . . . Book 2, chapter 14
Mad-Eye Moody . . . . Book 4, chapter 13
Luna Lovegood. . . . . Book 5, chapter 10
Professor Umbridge . . . . Book 5, chapter 12
Grawp. . . . . Book 5, chapter 30
Horace Slughorn . . . . Book 6, chapter 4
Xenophilius Lovegood . . . . Book 7, chapter 20

Thus, a careful reader can tell by the title of the chapter alone that Luna is indeed an important character and will have great impact as the story progresses.

Harry makes several *significant observations* in this chapter as they head back to Hogwarts on the Hogwarts Express.

First Observation: Harry observes that in five consecutive carriages on the train, he himself is observed and stared at, and people nudge each other and point him out (184).

Why is everyone staring? Harry correctly surmises that,

unfortunately, many of his classmates have bought into the false information printed in the *Daily Prophet* about Harry being a liar and a showoff (184).

Second Observation: There is only one place left to sit on the train, and that is the last carriage. A disheveled Neville Longbottom informs the others that *all* the carriages are full, and Ginny forcefully informs Neville that he is wrong, and there *is* room in the last compartment (185). (We're beginning to like the new, more forceful Ginny quite a lot. Harry, it turns out, will eventually reach this same conclusion, but first there is the matter of Cho—best deal with that topic later, don't you think?)

The compartment that was supposedly unavailable has only one person in it: "Loony" Lovegood. Neville asserts that he doesn't want to disturb anyone, but the reality is probably that Neville has made the same mistake that the other students are making about Harry this very moment: that Luna is strange and should be avoided (185).

Third Observation: Ginny is coming of age, with a mind of her own and a newfound assertiveness. She has no problem joining Luna and kindly laughs at Neville, telling him not to be silly and stating matter-of-factly, "she's all right" (185). Ginny enters the compartment—and Harry and Neville follow. (Good job, Ginny!) Ginny politely asks Luna if they can sit there, and Luna agrees with a simple nod (185).

Ginny, it seems, couldn't care less if somebody seems a little strange, and J. K. Rowling is clearly indicating that *all* of us should emulate Ginny's actions and willingness to include others.

Fourth Observation: Luna does indeed look and act strange. She has long, untidy hair, huge eyes, and a strange necklace, and she is reading a magazine upside down. Strange indeed! And Harry, we are told, knew immediately why Neville had decided to pass this compartment (185).

After a few brief words with Ginny about their summer, Luna states, "*You're* Harry Potter." Harry replies, "I know I am," which results in laughter from Neville. Luna, totally unperturbed, informs Neville that she does not know who he is. Neville quickly responds,

PART 1

"I'm nobody" (185–86).

Fifth Observation: Neville considers himself a nobody. *What does this tell us about Neville and what he thinks of himself?* He might not think much of himself, but someone thinks otherwise and speaks up!

Ginny says, "No you're not," and introduces Neville Longbottom to *his future wife*, Luna Lovegood (186).

(What is that, you ask? Is that true? Does Neville really marry Luna? Those of you who are sticklers for details know that we are not told this fact in the final chapter of Book 7, *Harry Potter and the Deathly Hallows*. But according to press reports, J. K. Rowling approved all changes and additions in the final movie. And in that final film, Neville claims his love for Luna during the Battle of Hogwarts, and at the very end they are seated together. So we have taken Neville's words and their being together at the end of the final movie as a strong indication that they end up getting married. But no, Luna, we later find out, marries Rolf Scamander, Newt's grandson.)

OK, OK. Back to the story! The third couple who will later marry, Ron and Hermione, shows up about an hour later, and we now have the six most important characters all in one compartment, once again heading to Hogwarts for another year (188)! Wouldn't you have loved to be sitting in there with them? What fun that would be!

The usual camaraderie follows, including Ron, a new prefect, imitating Malfoy's good friend, Goyle. Everybody has a good laugh, but the person who laughs harder than anyone is Luna Lovegood. Harry notices this too. Luna is becoming part of this gang—through humor and her unique personality (189–90).

NOTE TO SELF: *Being nice to people is a good idea, not to get something out of it (necessarily), but because it is the right thing to do!*

In the spy world, this is an important point: friends are often made this easily, and if anyone needed a friend at this point it was certainly Luna (not to mention Neville!). Sometime much later, in a book not so far off, Harry, Hermione, and Ron have an opportunity to see Luna's bedroom and the beautiful drawings that she has made of her friends, connected by a ribbon shaping the word *friends* (*DH* 417). Luna's loyalty to Harry and the gang never wavers after she has befriended them—unlike her father, although we must admit he was being blackmailed at the time (*DH* 418–19)!

Sixth Observation: We are also introduced to a magazine called *The Quibbler*, published of course by Luna's father (193). Although described as an "alternative" paper, to put it somewhat nicely, it is clear by the stories in the paper that we in the United States would call it a rag. Nonetheless, as we all know, *The Quibbler* will be very important during the upcoming year as the publication that finally gets the truth out about Harry, how Cedric Diggory died, and *who* has returned (578–79).

We have already discussed the power of mass publications (especially when controlled by those in power) and the distribution of the party line through the government's official press, such as *The Daily Worker* in Russia. But we should also consider the power of a small press. The smallest of newspapers can have a huge impact, just like pamphlets and other forms of distribution.

NOTE TO SELF: *Often the truth is found on the side roads instead of the major highways.*

Seventh Observation: Another important observation comes when Malfoy makes a comment, possibly about a dog: "Well, just watch yourself, Potter, because I will be *dogging* your footsteps in case you step out of line" (194).

Harry understands this comment immediately as a warning and a hint at the possibility that Malfoy recognized Sirius as a dog and will pass on that information to his father and the Ministry. The problem with any disguise is that once it is discovered, it will no longer work. However, Sirius has no other disguise to use. His decision to see Harry off at the train station might indeed have been very rash (194–95)!

Eighth Observation (or lack thereof): Next we need to discuss the Thestrals, the horse-like creatures with wings that Harry and Luna can see and the others cannot (197–99). Harry and Luna have observed and experienced death and therefore can see the Thestrals. Once again, some people are able to perceive what is there, and some are not—which is why you need the perspective of *several* people when you analyze intelligence!

Many observations are dependent on the perception, intelligence, and experience of the observer. Good spies are able to see things that others do not perceive, if they are well trained and are able to remember what they observe.

NOTE TO SELF: *Prior experiences allow some people to observe things that others may miss. A smart spy listens to others' observations too.*

FURTHER NOTE TO SELF: *A trained observer sees much that others are unable to see.*

Modern technology has allowed observation to be done secretly and on a profound scale. Modern drones have become like movie cameras, capable of observing and recording thousands of images. But the most essential observations are of invisible things: if only a human could observe (as easily as through a telescope) the subtleties of friendship, the nascent connections that develop through shared humor, and the strong bonds that develop when a group of people are endeavoring toward a common purpose! (Or, for that matter, the existence of a love so powerful that it will protect your son, even after your death!)

11

LISTENING CAREFULLY TO AN OLD HAT
AND A NEW PINK LADY

The next chapter, "The Sorting Hat's New Song," provides us a glimpse into the past and present. The past is prologue, as Shakespeare wrote: it can tell us what has already happened and give us perspective on what *will* happen or what needs to be done. Rowling knows her Hogwarts history to a T, obviously, since she wrote it; in fact, she spent five years figuring out the complete history of Hogwarts and of all her characters, and after finishing the second book she plotted out the remaining books in detail. That is truly good planning!

The chapter begins with Harry observing a new person at the professor's table, a toad-like woman wearing pink. Gee, who could she be?

ANALYSIS: *Before she even says a word, what does Harry surmise about their new professor, the woman in pink?* Harry, in a quick and accurate analysis, determines that her presence is *not good*. Harry rightly recalls that she assisted Cornelius Fudge at his hearing and was clearly on the Ministry's side.

PART 1

Harry realizes that this does not bode well for Hogwarts, but he does not realize how badly it bodes for him—yet.

Next, let us look carefully at the Sorting Hat's new song.

In previous books, the Sorting Hat merely sings a song about the qualities each house is looking for and its job in sorting them. But it is different this year. The Sorting Hat's song is different because the situation is different. The Hat *knows*, just as Harry and Dumbledore know, that a battle is coming—perhaps the most important battle in Wizarding history. (Including, yes, even Dumbledore's defeat of Grindelwald.) This new battle is even more important!

In this surprisingly long song, the Sorting Hat provides historic narrative and **historical analysis**. But there is more to it than just the telling of history: those of us who use intelligence analysis and critical thinking can figure out exactly what the hat is trying to say and what its warning entails!

Such a major change in the content of the Sorting Hat's song is certainly newsworthy. If the *Daily Prophet* was not otherwise engaged in attacking Harry on a daily basis, you'd think that this strange new song would be published word-for-word so the entire Wizarding world would know about it! And if Fudge was not in charge, we could expect this new song to be distributed widely. Still, all of the students and the professors have heard it. Dumbledore or one of the other professors, or even some bright individual student, might jot down exactly what the Hat said and distribute it by other means, whether by pamphlets, owl, or even *The Quibbler* (though that fine journal has not yet started supporting Harry).

The Sorting Hat's new song would be prime material for open-source intelligence gathering—*if* it was transcribed and shared with the public. It would become, in spy terms, an open source, available to all with the intelligence and drive to use it. However, because the *Daily Prophet* refuses to cover the news, the source is restricted only to those who happened to be there.

CHAPTER 11

~~~~~~

THE SORTING HAT AS OPEN-SOURCE INFORMATION AND IMPARTING THE MOOD OF A COUNTRY: THE ARAB SPRING OR ARAB AWAKENING

Spies must "discover" secrets won by stealth and risk, but they must also locate and unearth "non-secrets" that are *equally important and valuable.* This includes open-source analysis, statements by the leaders of a country or group, and information about military capabilities, as well as the cultural landscape of a society.

In 2011, a revolt in Tunisia spread to other Arab countries: it has been called the Arab Spring or Arab Awakening. It resulted in the replacement of numerous leaders throughout the Middle East, something that has not happened in dozens of years. Many intelligence agencies, including the CIA, received criticism for not predicting these various revolts that occurred throughout the Middle East. In hindsight, some were able to "look back" at the patterns of unrest, the many comments made in the press and opposition writings, and even the posts found in numerous social media platforms to discern what was coming. But those signs, seen after the fact, did not appear significant to those on the ground at the time, or in the alternative, those perceptions relayed to headquarters were not understood or properly relayed to the persons actually making decisions or relaying prediction to those making decision. Understanding the mood of a country, or even the mood of the Sorting Hat, can be very important indeed!

This same type of revolution occurred in the 1840s throughout Europe and in certain parts of South America. Social movements can change not only society, but also governments and the people in charge of those governments. Never underestimate the power of the people!

~~~~~~

The Sorting Hat's message is loud and clear: an old threat (Voldemort, of course) is trying to split and weaken Wizarding society using fear and disinformation. And the ploy is working, just as the lies told about Harry in the *Daily Prophet* have a chilling effect on the other students. But in the Wizarding world, the press has a huge audience, while the Hat reaches only a few listeners (though some of them are quite powerful!).

The effect of information (and disinformation) distributed by the press is subtle but profound. A spy can use it to judge the mood of the populace, an important factor in predicting what is likely to happen in the short run. Combined with historical analysis, this information helps a spy know whether it's time to dig for more intel, pressure inside sources, or even break cover and run for home.

So, what does the Sorting Hat tell us about the past, the future, and the present mood of the Wizarding world, and what needs to be done?

The Sorting Hat begins by describing a school founded in unity, all four founders working together: they "Thought never to be parted"; "never did they dream that they / Might someday be divided . . . how could it have gone so wrong?" (204). The wise hat goes on, saying it was there and witnessed it all. Slytherin wanted purity and demanded only purebloods in his house; Ravenclaw wanted intelligence and sought only the bright; Gryffindor wanted the brave; and Hufflepuff welcomed the rest (204–5).

This resolution worked for a while, as "Hogwarts worked in harmony / For several happy years" (205). But the seeds of discontent were planted—for division begets pride and difference, which begets animosity and, if left unchecked, hatred and then terrible misdeeds.

And so it was at Hogwarts. The Sorting Hat tells its listeners that "discord crept among us / Feeding on our faults and fears," and the houses "turned upon each other." Following a "clash of friend on friend," Slytherin departed (206). And although the Sorting Hat will continue to do its duty and sort the new students into houses, it reflects that maybe this division is wrong and that now, *particularly now*, *it is time to unite*:

Oh, know the perils, read the signs,

The warning history shows,

For our Hogwarts is in danger

From external, deadly foes

And we must unite inside her

Or we'll crumble from within.

I have told you, I have warned you. . . .

Let the Sorting now begin (206).

In these last eight lines of the new song, the Hat says quite specifically that there are "external dangers" and that the four houses need to unite, lest all come tumbling down.

THE SORTING HAT'S CLARION CALL TO UNITE— HISTORIC ANALOGIES

The song's warning reminds us of what Patrick Henry said in 1799: "United we stand. Divided we fall." The phrase actually has a biblical basis: "A house divided against itself cannot stand," reads Mark 3:25. In one of Abraham Lincoln's most famous pre-election speeches, known as the "House Divided Speech" (1858), he quotes the Bible word-for-word: "A house divided against itself cannot stand."

PART 1

The Sorting Hat is clearly referring to Voldemort and his followers as the external dangers, and at the same time warning the Wizarding world to unite. More literally, the houses of Hogwarts must pull together—as a united team—to assist in defeating Voldemort.

Interestingly, we find out much later that four of the Horcruxes relate to three of the four Hogwarts' houses: the ring, the locket, the cup, and the diadem (Slytherin, Slytherin, Hufflepuff, Ravenclaw). (The diary did not relate to any specific house, and the Sword of Gryffindor was used to destroy Horcruxes.)

Hogwarts does indeed unite in the end, although many of its inhabitants evacuate before the battle.

~~~~~~~~~~~~~~~~~~~~~~~~~~~~~~~~~~~~~

THE ARMED SERVICES, CAMARADERIE, AND THE INTELLIGENCE COMMUNITY

Anyone who has dealt with the four branches of the military knows that there is a general camaraderie among soldiers, but also competitiveness between the four branches of the service. This is also true, to a lesser degree, with the intelligence agencies. Many people incorrectly believe that the **CIA** is the only US intelligence agency (perhaps because it is the one that we hear the most about), but the biggest intelligence agency by numbers in the United States is the **Defense Intelligence Agency**. In total, sixteen agencies report to the Director of National Intelligence: Air Force Intelligence, Surveillance and Reconnaissance Agency (AF ISRA); Army Intelligence and Security Command (G-3); Central Intelligence Agency (CIA); Coast Guard Intelligence (CGI); Defense Intelligence Agency (DIA); Department of Energy's Office of Intelligence and Counterintelligence (DOE OIC); Department of Homeland Security's Office of Intelligence and Analysis (DHS OIA); Department of State's Bureau of Intelligence and Research (INR); Department of the Treasury's Office of Intelligence and Analysis (OIA); Drug Enforcement Administration's Office of National Security Intelligence (ONSI); Federal Bureau of Investigation (FBI); Marine Corps Intelligence (MCI); National Geospatial-Intelligence Agency (NGA); National Reconnaissance Office (NRO); National Security Agency/Central Security Service (NSA); Office of Naval Intelligence (ONI). This command structure for intelligence changed somewhat after 9/11 in that we now have an intelligence "czar" called the Director of Intelligence. But we digress, so let's get back to the story!

Nearly Headless Nick also provides important information. We must remember that the ghosts of the castle have corporate knowledge of what has happened all the years they have been living—or at least existing—at Hogwarts.

NOTE TO SELF: *You can get information from many sources, even dead ones.*

When the children question Nick about whether the Sorting Hat has given warnings before, he confirms that this is the case (207) and further notes that the Sorting Hat lives (hangs around?—sorry, couldn't resist) in Dumbledore's office, stating, "It picks up things up there" (209).

The three basic rules of real estate apply to spying as well: LOCATION, LOCATION, LOCATION! You need to be in the right place to get the right information. And if you can't be in the right place, find someone who is!

Harry learns this quite powerfully in book 7 when he gets a *very* important bit of information from Ravenclaw's ghost, the Gray Lady (*DH* 616–17), about a certain diadem, who owned it, and to whom she told where she had hidden it inside a hollow tree in Albania (Tom Riddle). When you think about it, there are quite a few sources in the castle that have corporate knowledge of what has occurred: the ghosts, the headmasters in the portraits, and all of the various individuals in the portraits throughout the halls of Hogwarts!

After the Sorting Hat's dire warning, the now-Professor Umbridge has her say in a speech filled with vagaries, contradictions, and inane shibboleths, "The Ministry of Magic," she drones, "has always considered the education of young witches and wizards to be of vital importance. . . . our tried and tested traditions often require no tinkering. . . . Let us move forward, then, into a new era of openness, effectiveness, and accountability, intent on preserving what ought to be preserved, perfecting what needs to be perfected, and pruning wherever we find practices that ought to be prohibited" (212–14).

A careful observer would understand, from her sleep-inducing speech, that the Ministry is definitely inserting itself into the running of Hogwarts. Harry fails at his observational task, but fortunately, Hermione (and a few other interested parties) haven't drifted off. To those who apply careful analysis, the speech is "most illuminating" (214).

12

PROFESSOR UMBRIDGE—
LIAR, TRAITOR, SOLDIER, SPY

In chapter 12, "Professor Umbridge," we find out exactly what type of person she is.

The day begins with Harry coming down from his dormitory and once again crossing paths with those who do not believe him, especially Seamus Finnigan and Lavender Brown. We find out that Hermione has been sticking up for Harry—she even finds it necessary to tell *Harry* that she is on his side and that he shouldn't be biting her (or Ron's) head off (222–23)!

We also find out that the Weasley twins are starting to recruit their schoolmates for their experiments. Hermione mentions to Ron that they will have to do something about that—and when Ron asks why, Hermione reminds him that, as prefects, it is their responsibility to intervene (222). Ron, as we find throughout this chapter, is not thrilled about accosting or reprimanding his two older brothers.

A quick note about **internal control**: giving students authority over other students allows professors to spend less time dealing with small disciplinary matters. This is efficient use of the students' talents and helps the prefects to develop leadership skills.

PART 1

At breakfast we find out that Hermione is still receiving the *Daily Prophet*—to the surprise of Harry and Ron. Hermione, quite wisely, states, "It's best to know what the enemy is saying" (225).

The twins are already evaluating their products from a business standpoint, working to find out which of their products fit the demand. They understand not only that they must perform experiments and *document the results*—thus applying basic scientific method in their investigations—but also that the *selection of the products* should be based on what customers need or want to buy. In other words, they're after *confirmation* and *competition*.

~~~~~~

DEVELOPING COMPETING TEAMS TO ANALYZE INTELLIGENCE

Those who work in the spy world always need to obtain confirmation of their findings. Thanks to some recent **intelligence failures**, many spy organizations have set up separate teams that compete against each other to achieve confirmation first. Some organizations use a second team devoted to questioning the assumptions or conclusions of the first team. Hermione and Ron sometimes play this role for Harry, questioning the things that he knows (or wants to believe) must be right.

We'll take a deeper look at these practices later, in the chapter on intelligence analysis.

~~~~~~

Now a few words about *financing*: it's hard to tackle any big project without money. The twins, when asked how they plan to fund a joke shop, say, "Ask us no questions and we'll tell you no lies" (227).

When Hermione wonders how Fred and George got the money to start their business, Harry immediately steers the conversation away from "dangerous waters" (228). As you will recall, Harry gave Fred and George his winnings from the Triwizard Tournament to start their shop (*GF* 733). Harry smartly creates a **diversion** by changing the topic. Pretty good **trade craft**, when you think about it!

NOTE TO SELF: *You do not have to answer every question posed— and the best way not to have to lie is to keep your mouth shut!*

Now, two words about history and historical analysis: *It's important!*

Professor Snape continues to be unfair to Harry in his class. Hermione mentions that she thought things would be better with him this year because Snape is in the Order. Although the boys trust Dumbledore in all other matters, they still cannot accept Dumbledore's trust in Snape; Ron notes that "poisonous toadstools don't change their spots" (235). The boys have a bias against Snape— and of course, he has a bias against Harry. It just goes to show how much trouble an unexamined bias can cause, even for the "good guys"!

When our heroes attend Professor Umbridge's first class, they find out that she will be teaching a "Ministry-approved curriculum" (239). This is a clear indication that the Ministry is taking charge, and there will be little or even no intellectual freedom in many subjects or discussions. Professor Umbridge orders the students to put their wands away, and Harry and his peers discover, to their horror, that their textbooks teach only *theory*, not *practice* (239–42).

When Harry objects, Umbridge tells him he must learn to raise his hand—and then turns away from him. When questioned by other students, Professor Umbridge sarcastically asks whether they expect to be attacked in class. Harry and Hermione find out quite quickly that Umbridge is adamant that Voldemort has *not* come back (the party line) and that whoever is spreading these rumors is a liar. Harry can't help contradicting this, to the point where he gets detention (244–45).

To analyze this situation, let us review *what* was said, and by *whom*, noting carefully how Umbridge baits Harry into blowing up while at the same time "teaching" the class her viewpoint and the consequences of refusing to accept it:

"So we're not supposed to be prepared for what's waiting out there?"

"There is nothing waiting out there, Mr. Potter."

"Oh yeah?" said Harry. . . .

"Who do you imagine wants to attack children like yourselves?" inquired Professor Umbridge in a horribly honeyed voice.

"Hmm, let's think . . ." said Harry in a mock thoughtful voice, "maybe Lord Voldemort?" . . . .

"As I was saying, you have been informed that a certain Dark wizard is at large once again. This is a lie."

"It is NOT a lie!" said Harry. "I saw him, I fought him!"

"Detention, Mr. Potter!" said Professor Umbridge triumphantly (244–45).

Professor Umbridge not only calls Harry a liar, but also requests that the other students act as snitches and tell her if anyone is spreading such lies (245). This form of internal control will undoubtedly create a *chilling effect* on the students discussing these issues among themselves. When Professor McGonagall finds out that Harry has detention, she is extremely disappointed in him and warns him to be careful with Professor Umbridge. Professor McGonagall specifically tells him that Professor Umbridge is a spy for the Ministry: "You know where she comes from, you must know to whom she is reporting" (248).

Everybody now understands that Professor Umbridge is the enemy, there to spy on behalf of the Ministry. Professor McGonagall tells Harry to keep his head down and control his temper. In other words, he should act with *equanimity, caution*, and if possible *subtlety*—in other words, employ spy craft! But Harry isn't doing so well at gathering intelligence now. When Professor McGonagall asks Harry about the meaning of Professor Umbridge's speech and he gives the correct answer, Professor McGonagall correctly surmises that it was Hermione that figured it out, *not* Harry (249).

CHAPTER 12

It is important to understand subtleties.

NOTE TO SELF: *A good spy carefully analyzes all that is said—and also things left unsaid.*

It is often the subtlest things that yield great information. Words deliver meaning, but so do the tone and tenor in which they are spoken, the specific words selected, and the reactions of the listeners. For the modern scholar and intelligence analyst, a person's *words* are the tea leaves of modern divination; a person's *expressions and demeanor* are often a mirror of the soul; and for the most part, a person's *actions* constitute confirmation of intent and motive, credibility, and substance.

One can discern from Professor Umbridge's first words in the Great Hall and then in her first class that, through her, the Ministry of Magic intends to meddle in what is being taught at Hogwarts. Although Professor Umbridge's initially pleasant facial expressions seem friendly, her words and actions indicate otherwise; she is the proverbial wolf in sheep's clothing. In her first class she demonstrates her willingness to use her power over the students maliciously by calling Harry a liar and asking the students to tell on each other.

One need not be a celebrated professor of Divination to understand that Umbridge is a very evil woman—even *before* she tortures Harry with a pen that is as mighty as a sword.

13

CRUEL AND UNUSUAL PUNISHMENT, OR, GETTING TO THE POINT ABOUT LYING

The personal war between Harry and Umbridge, begun when the professor called Harry a liar, is truly on in the next chapter, "Detention with Dolores." The conflict is in full force once Umbridge sadistically **tortures** Harry, who refuses to give her the pleasure of any reaction. Although he clearly has grounds to turn Umbridge in, he does not, because to him this is a war of wills. He keeps this little battle to himself. Perhaps Harry realizes that if he can't stand up to Umbridge, he will have little chance against Voldemort. Or perhaps it is pride? Not wanting to ask for help? Whatever the reason, he is resolute in resisting her demands.

ENHANCED INTERROGATION—TORTURE OR GOOD INFORMATION GATHERING?

A great debate has taken place in the last ten years about the use of enhanced interrogation techniques, particularly waterboarding. That debate has come to focus on whether any useful information has been derived from such activities, and whether we should engage in such activities at all. Throughout the series, Harry and his friends face the threat of torture at the hands of Voldemort and his Death Eaters, who will stop at nothing to get what they want. They also face the temptation to use the same Dark spells to get what they want. Harry's experience with Professor Umbridge's sadistic methods will shape many of his decisions later in the series, and also, we think, his decision not to use Dark methods to get what *he* wants.

~~~~~~

ANALYSIS: *Why are Harry's (true!) claims about Voldemort not believed?* Unfortunately, the only *proof* of Voldemort's return is the word of Harry Potter. As Hermione points out, when Harry returned at the end of the Triwizard Tournament with Cedric's dead body, all anyone saw was Harry returning with the body. *Nobody saw what happened in the maze or in the graveyard* except Harry and the Death Eaters—and the latter certainly won't be admitting to it! Only Harry personally observed Voldemort and communicated that information when he returned to Hogwarts (251).

Since the truth is known by only one person, the **credibility** of that person is essential. Dumbledore knows Harry is right and therefore presents that same view to others. Some believe Dumbledore, but many do not. And, more to the point, the citizens of the Wizarding world must choose whether or not the sole observer of Voldemort's return—Harry Potter—is a **credible source**. Faced with a decision between comforting untruths and terrifying reality, it is no surprise that the *Daily Prophet* has chosen to cast doubt on Harry's credibility.

Now a word about credibility: **CREDIBILITY**!

In order to be believed, a spy or agent must be credible. Often we speak of the agent's *bona fides*, that person's record or reputation for honesty. Credibility is based on a person's history of telling the truth, observing things accurately, and relaying that information effectively. By the same token, those who analyze information received from the field must take into account not only the information received, but also the *source* of that information and any indications that the source and the information might be unreliable.

Obviously it is best to have at least two sources for any significant fact. Confirmation through a secondary source is called **corroboration.** In determining the reliability of an **informant**, spy, or witness, it is important to look at the facts surrounding the observation and the person observing the fact at issue: was the individual providing the information actually *at a location* where the information could be observed? Did the informant have *access* to the information? Is the informant able to provide *other details* indicating that the fact was actually observed?

These same types of standards are used to determine how to analyze information provided to a judge or magistrate who is being asked to issue a search warrant. In doing so, the judge applies **analysis**. If a police officer provides information supplied by a *confidential informant* or an *anonymous informant*, it is important that *other facts* be provided that give the judge or magistrate some level of certainty that the individual can be believed. Again, this may come in the form of details about that person's credibility and history of providing good information, or proof that the person has inside information that could be known *only* by a person who was, literally, inside that location. Establishing credibility is thus important throughout the Muggle world and not just for spies and the information they obtain in the field.

As already noted above, Professor Umbridge is actually recruiting her own spies by asking students to tell her if anyone is talking about Voldemort's return (245).

At one point, the students ask themselves what Dumbledore was thinking in hiring Dolores Umbridge to teach the Dark Arts (252). We later find out the answer: the Ministry passed a decree stating that if the Headmaster could not find somebody to teach a class, *the Ministry* would appoint somebody to do so (307–8). And once again, it is Hermione who figures it out immediately: Umbridge is there "to spy on us all" (252).

Balancing these dire revelations, we now discover that the twins are paying their younger schoolmates to be guinea pigs in their experiments (253–54). This takes us on a short but informative digression about getting others to do what you want. Now, experimenting on human subjects is a complicated area of ethics. Most research institutions, particularly colleges and universities, have very specific, detailed rules requiring that researchers obtain *informed consent* from the research subject showing that they understand and agree to any risks before the experiment is conducted. Researchers must also follow specific protective guidelines and standards. Obviously Fred and George have *not* obtained permission to conduct these experiments, and indeed, they could not even get proper consent because their test subjects are underage.

Hermione firmly objects to their experiments, but she realizes that pressing the issue as a prefect would do little to hinder the twins' work. She therefore brings out her own secret weapon: she threatens to *tell their mother* what they are doing. Now this is a real threat! As we all know, the Weasley children rightfully fear the wrath of their mother. Fred and George take Hermione's threat seriously and amend their behavior accordingly (254).

NOTE TO SELF: *For a threat to work, it must be a viable threat and produce real fear.*

Hermione has also decided that house-elves should be allowed to be free and therefore has been knitting hats and other clothing for the elves to pick up, with the supposed result that the house-elves— being presented with clothes—would immediately become free (255).

Not all plans are successful, even those devised by the smartest people we know. We find out later in the story that Hermione's attempts to "free" the house-elves don't have the desired effect. When the house-elves realize what is happening they refuse to clean the Gryffindor common room any longer. Dobby—a free elf—is the only elf that cleans it and therefore acquired all the clothing for himself and Winky, the other freed house-elf at Hogwarts (385).

ANALYSIS: We should analyze Hermione's actions from the standpoint or perspective of the house-elves: *Do the house-elves really want to be free?* Think of Dobby's friend, Winky, who did not want to be free but was presented with clothes as a form of punishment (*GF* 138). In addition, is it appropriate for Hermione to hide the items under things so that the elves *accidently* receive the clothing and then become free (255)? At what point do people—and house-elves—have the right to choose their own destiny?

THE CONCEPT OF SELF-DETERMINATION AND OTHER PHILOSOPHICAL TENANTS

The issue of self-determination reminds us of a famous saying that was quoted by AP correspondent Peter Arnett during the Vietnam War by an officer who was justifying the bombing of the village of Bến Tre even though there were civilian casualties: "We had to destroy the village in order to save it."

Can freedom be or become a form of slavery? Or exchanged for a different form of subordination? We could perhaps ask you to look to American history, the freeing of slaves, and what occurred from 1865 to 1965. Or on a literary front, we could refer you to Orwell's *1984* ("WAR IS PEACE," "FREEDOM IS SLAVERY," "IGNORANCE IS STRENGTH") or to even the great song by *The Who* where they exclaim in "We Won't Get Fooled Again" (1971) the following: "Meet the new boss/ Same as the old boss."

CHAPTER 13

NOTE TO SELF: *Freedom is filled with ironies, and the path to freedom sometimes begets less freedom than what was previously allowed.*

We next find out that Draco Malfoy seems to have some inside information on Hagrid. Draco refers to Hagrid messing around with something that's too big for him—quite literally too big, as we can tell when we find out he is dealing with the giants. How does Malfoy know this? Undoubtedly through his father (260).

Harry *should* react by ignoring Malfoy; Hermione herself tells Harry *not* to react, or Malfoy will know they don't know what's really going on (260). Once again, a good spy must have equanimity and not react to information or situations in a way that gives information to the enemy.

Quick side note: It is interesting that Hermione says Luna will only believe in things *as long as there is no proof at all* (262). What an interesting twist of logic! (Or, if you want to be more scientific, what a wonderful way to turn empiricism on its head!) However, we suggest that you *not* follow Luna's unique path!

ANALYSIS: *What is Ron really concerned about at this point?* It's interesting to note that Ron mentions that it looks like it might rain. We find out later that his primary concern at this moment is practicing for Keeper tryouts (264).

NOTE TO SELF: *When people make comments about something that seems unrelated or innocuous, they are often commenting about what is presently on their minds or subtly calling attention to what concerns them greatly at the moment.*

Once Harry drags Ron's attention back to matters of life and death, the trio has a detailed discussion about torture and Professor Umbridge's inappropriate use of it on Harry. Ron believes that Harry should tell Dumbledore about what is going on, an understandable relay of information up to the senior leadership. Harry, however, refuses. Is this because of his personal war against Umbridge (272–73) or because kids don't generally trust adults? Or a certain frustration with being left out of the loop, perhaps?

Harry finally settles on writing to Sirius for help, but Hermione reminds him that his letters could be intercepted (278). Harry believes that he must nonetheless find another way to evaluate his findings, either through a second opinion of a trusted friend (like his godfather) or some other form of collaboration. And quite soon in the next chapter, Harry figures out how to write to Sirius in a way that conveys the information he wants to relay and asks the questions he needs to ask, but without allowing any "outsider" to understand what is really being said.

14

MESSAGES WITHOUT MEANING—PREDICTIONS BY PERCY "THE INSIDER"—A SPY'S LIFE OF SOLITUDE AND CALCULATED RISK

As chapter 14, "Percy and Padfoot," opens, Harry is carefully drafting a letter to Sirius. Well aware that the letter could be intercepted, Harry carefully drafts a message that only he and Sirius can understand (280).

Now a word about saying *something* while seemingly saying *nothing*: **SOMETHING → NOTHING!**

Ok, maybe that's really two words.

Yes, you can use *regular* words to send a **coded message,** which is actually called an **open code**. And that is *exactly* what Harry does.

Harry is attempting to turn an otherwise **unsecure communication** into a secure communication by using references that *only he and Sirius would understand*. This is spy craft at its best. Harry is learning how to become a spy!

Harry spends a lot of time considering how he will convey the essential information to Sirius without giving anything away—just in case somebody else should read it. He begins the letter by addressing it to Snuffles, the nickname for Sirius. No one knows who Snuffles is except Harry, his two best friends, and Sirius himself (280).

Harry describes Professor Umbridge negatively, but does so in a way that no one but he and Sirius would understand: she is "nearly as nice as your mum" (280). Next Harry tells Sirius that "that thing that I wrote to you about last summer happened again last night," meaning his scar was hurting without Voldemort being near (280). He next says that he's missing "our biggest friend," a clear reference to Hagrid—who is not back yet from his mission for the Order (280).

As Harry discovers, it takes a long time to write such a short letter because every word must be carefully chosen. Each phrase is crafted with long thought about how another person (either the recipient or someone who intercepts the letter) will understand it or *not* understand it (281)!

This reminds us of the old Mark Twain adage, included in a letter to a friend in 1871. The great American humorist apologized for the length of the letter because *he did not have time to write a short one*!

NOTE TO SELF: *Being concise takes time and is hard work.*

Now let's talk again about our favorite open source, the *Daily Prophet*!

Thanks to Hermione's subscription, the trio catches a reference in its pages to Sirius supposedly being in London. Perhaps this is an indication that Sirius was *indeed* seen as a dog at the train station (286–87). Whoops!

There is also an announcement that Sturgis Podmore was arrested while trying to get through a door at the Ministry of Magic. As we readers know, Sturgis Podmore is a member of the Order, and we can guess that he was trying to protect whatever the Order is guarding (287–88).

Meanwhile, the members of Slytherin are writing insulting chants and generally harassing Harry and the rest of the Gryffindor Quidditch team. In the spy world, of course, this is an example of baiting the enemy; in the military, it is called **PSYOPS** or **psychological operations** (290–93).

CHAPTER 14

NOTE TO SELF: *Insulting or taunting an enemy often causes the enemy to focus on the insult instead of the operation.*

While Harry and Ron are doing their homework (which, naturally, should have been done earlier in the week), Percy's owl shows up with a letter to Ron (296).

As we all know, Percy works at the Ministry—and automatically takes its side. Ron is reluctant to open it, but the trio agrees that Percy's letter, which is both condescending and offensive, should be carefully read and considered because it contains important information, even though it is from someone who is technically an enemy (296–98).

NOTE TO SELF: *The comments or views of an enemy, even when distasteful, may contain important information.*

So what does Ron's older brother have to say? Percy attempts to get Ron to stay away from Harry Potter (aka Ron's best friend) because the Minister of Magic thinks Harry is a bad person (297). In addition, Percy states that although Harry Potter is a favorite of Dumbledore, *Dumbledore may not remain in charge at Hogwarts* (297–98).

This is a very important revelation indeed! The Ministry is focusing not only on Harry as an enemy, but also on Dumbledore—and if the Ministry was to replace Dumbledore, it would undoubtedly be with somebody of their liking (which, as we all know, eventually does happen).

Percy goes on to say that the "people who count" have a different view of Dumbledore, which obviously gets into the *politics* of the situation. According to Percy's definition, the people who "count" are the people who are *in charge* at the Ministry (297).

NOTE TO SELF: *Blind loyalty is a wonderful thing; it allows that person to justify all actions and not have to think for him-or herself!*

PART 1

Politics can indeed be a nasty business, and many politicians are not to be trusted. But there are good people in politics—which is, after all, a necessary evil and the only way you can get your budget approved!

NOTE TO SELF: *The trouble with politics is it matters.*

If politics was just some fun parlor game that didn't negatively (or positively) affect people, it would be much more fun! Kind of like gossip—fun to hear, as long as it isn't about you!

What? We digress?

Okay, back to the story!

Amazingly, Percy goes so far as to suggest that Ron should *spy on Harry* and tell the one person who can be truly trusted (Dolores Umbridge) what Harry is up to (297). Next, Percy mentions that the *Daily Prophet* will have something in the morning that will give Ron a better idea of the way the "wind is blowing" (297).

What an idiot!

ANALYSIS: *Why is Percy agreeing with the Ministry of Magic and disregarding his family's views?* Yes, yes, we think we know this already: because he is a twit!

But there is more to it than that. We need to do more than just call him a name or diagnose him as lacking intelligence. As *spies*, we need to understand him, his motivation, and the rationale he is accepting and employing! So let's spend a bit of time thinking about these issues, shall we?

Notice that Percy demonstrates perfectly (as the prefect he was) that he has totally accepted the party line. He cares more about power than about his family (or Harry), and he is absolutely thrilled to be "in the know" and close to those who run the world (or at least those who think they do!). Yes, he is an egotistical git! But his motives are pure: he has *unquestioningly* adopted the Ministry's "patriotic" party line.

CHAPTER 14

NOTE TO SELF: *The beauty of someone unquestioningly accepting a certain position is that, once the correct facts or the mistaken analysis underlying that position are conveyed to that person, they often will be willing to reject their original position and adopt another one—preferably yours!*

THE DANGER OF A PARTY LINE WHEN DISCOVERED TO BE UNTRUE

One of the problems with a government putting out a party line is that, should the citizens find out that it is not true, they will become disenchanted and possibly investigate whether the government is lying in other areas, or decide that it is unworthy of their commitment or loyalty. Throughout the last books in the series, we see many vehement reactions to revelations of the Ministry's lies.

Ron's loyalty is to Harry, and he would never consider following Percy's suggestions *for even a moment*! Therefore he takes the letter, tears it up, and throws it into the fire (298).

Soon Sirius shows up in the very same fire, as he did the previous year. Sirius informs Harry that he decided to use the fire because he didn't want to use a code: codes are breakable (301). Sirius provides a psychological assessment of Fudge's paranoia about Dumbledore setting up an army (303). (Ironically, this comment eventually results in the creation of Dumbledore's Army!) Sirius also mentions that Dumbledore might be arrested on some "trumped up" criminal charges (303). This is also an important issue. *Criminal laws* can be used to silence individuals, imprison them, or have them removed from leadership or other positions of power.

THE USE OF THE LAW AND THE CRIMINAL SYSTEM TO SUPPORT THE PARTY LINE

Sirius is rightfully concerned that Dumbledore might be set up or that the Ministry would press some bogus charges against him. People in positions of authority tend to be more than willing to use that authority, in any way they think is necessary, to reach the ends they desire.

One of the reasons the United States and other countries have an independent judiciary is to create **checks and balances** for the people in power. Thus, at least in theory, unaffiliated judges independently prevent misuses of power.

Unfortunately, many judges just toe the party line and fail in their role as the last bastion of protecting freedom. Think of how Harry's trial might have gone, had Dumbledore not appeared. Ask anyone wrongfully convicted of a crime (especially after serving twenty years in prison) what they think of the system or judges who "protected" their rights! What's that, you say? We digress again? OK! OK! Back to the story!

Chapter 14 ends with a discussion of two important aspects of spying. The first is the problem of being separated from your supporting team or from contact with headquarters (and your friends and other operatives). The second relates to risks that operatives take.

Throughout the first portion of the book, Harry and his friends are understandably concerned that Hagrid has not yet returned to his teaching post. At the end of this chapter, we hear that he has been separated from his partner (Olympe) and that there has been a lack of communication between Hagrid and anyone else in the Order (304). How could they have become separated, and why is it taking him so long to return? Since the trio knows that Hagrid is gone at

Dumbledore's request, they assume he is on a secret mission—and that assumption is correct (304). Hermione, once again the brightest witch in her class, has already surmised that Hagrid is on a mission that relates to the *giants*; she surmises that Hagrid is *recruiting* the giants to assist Dumbledore (and everyone else) in the upcoming battle against Voldemort (422–23). And, once again, she is correct!

Just as it is difficult for operatives in the field when they are unable to communicate with headquarters, it is also difficult for those back home who are worried about covert operatives who for some reason have gone incommunicado. When an agent *intentionally* fails to communicate, he or she is incommunicado. When an agent is left without any instructions, he or she is said to be "out in the cold." And when they are once again provided with information, agents are "brought in from the cold."

Lack of communication might also be part of the plan. Some officers are placed in **deep cover**, where they are so deep into their fabricated identity that communications back to headquarters may be nonexistent, even for years at a time.

NOTE TO SELF: *Silence is not always golden when the agent doesn't report—or headquarters doesn't tell the agent what is going on!*

In addition, some agents can be sleeper agents—agents who continue their normal day-to-day activities as if they were "asleep" and have nothing to do with spying at all. Such agents are activated only when a certain event occurs or when they are instructed to become activated. The best way for **deep cover agents** and sleeper agents to stay protected is to have *no communication whatsoever* with headquarters—so there is no chance of their discovery.

~~~~~~

REAL DEEP-COVER AGENTS FOUND IN UNITED STATES IN 2010

In 2010, ten Russian sleeper agents were discovered in the United States. These individuals had lived here for years and had started families. What a shock it must have been for the children to discover that their parents were Russian spies, and they now had to return with them back to Russia, a place they had never known!

~~~~~~

~~~~~~

USING THE SIGN OF LIFE TO RECONNECT WITH AN AGENT

If for some reason a case officer has lost contact with one of his or her agents in the field, he or she will employ a sign-of-life technique. The agent has been provided a very specific date, time, and site to "appear" at so the case officer can be assured that the agent is OK. Often this is something as simple as going to a particular store or facility on the third Thursday at 7 p.m.

~~~~~~

There is also such a thing as a **rogue agent**—an agent who was initially on your side and sent out on your behalf, but who is now *on his or her own*, answering to no one. Rogue agents are especially dangerous not only because they were trained by you and know everything that you know, but also because they are capable of going over to the other side as a double agent, of playing one side against the other (often for money), or of creating general havoc with the information they know.

Thus, a missing agent can mean a lot of different things. In Hagrid's case, we find out soon that he has simply been making his way back home. (With, we later discover, his twenty-five-foot-tall half-brother—who, by the way, has "anger-management issues" and knows little to no English [690]!)

Now, a few words about risk: **DON'T TAKE ANY!**

Actually, that was a little joke there. Obviously, spies have to take risks—but they do so with an understanding of *which* risks are appropriate to take and which risks should be *avoided*.

People who become spies generally like to take risks. However, a good spy knows *when* to take a risk and when *not* to. Every risk must be analyzed in light of what would be gained—and what could be lost.

Some people are *risk averse*, which means that they prefer *not* to take risks unless absolutely necessary. Other people are *risk takers* who are more than happy to risk themselves or others, sometimes even when they shouldn't! Somewhere in the middle is the person who takes a risk only when it is appropriate and necessary to the goal at hand.

~~~~~~~~~~~~~~~~~~~~~~~~~~

RISK TAKERS VS. THRILL SEEKERS

In his book *Business Confidential*, Peter wrote, "In the intelligence community, the agency looks for people with solid egos, but not arrogance that would somehow shade what they're doing. The agency wants risk takers, but not thrill seekers or daredevils—people who know how to take intelligent risks, which involves evaluating options, mitigating danger, and seizing opportunity when it presents itself" (42).

It is important to note that the best spies do not take risks every day, but instead figure out how it is possible *not* to have to take a risk. Although it might be fun, there is no reason to scale a four-story building, enter through the skylight, hack all the security codes, break into the safe, retrieve the information in the safe, and make a clean exit—not when you can easily obtain the information by bribing somebody who has access to the safe or by some other, less risky means.

~~~~~~~~~~~~~~~~~~~~~~~~~~~~~~

NOTE TO SELF: *If you can get someone else to get you the information you need, without risk to yourself, why not?*

Let's talk about how Harry and Sirius perceive risk.

Harry and Sirius have quite a conversation while Sirius is visiting in the fire, though it is important to note that the conversation is *not* very friendly. This is, in a way, Harry and Sirius's first fight (304–5).

When Sirius mentions that he might want to meet them at Hogsmeade as a dog, Harry and Hermione together shout "NO!" Sirius—not happy—states that he gets the point and just wanted a chance to get together. *Psychological assessment:* Sirius is using guilt to get what he wants—he feels sorry for himself and is taking it out on Harry. Harry mentions that he would like to get together too, but would not like to see his godfather "chucked back in Azkaban!" (304–5) Sirius reacts negatively, delivering the ultimate insult to Harry: "You're less like your father than I thought. . . . The risk would have been what made it fun for James" (305). Sirius adds further insult by stating that he will write and tell Harry a time to talk again by fire, "If you can stand to risk it?" (305).

Harry is greatly affronted by this statement, and it bothers him for a long time. Indeed, Harry recalls it when he decides to take the risk and use Umbridge's fireplace to communicate with Sirius (667)— and gets caught!

But we're not there yet! We are merely at the end of chapter 14.

15

THE ASSUMPTION OF LEADERSHIP—PROFESSOR DOLORES UMBRIDGE AND HARRY POTTER

Chapter 15, "The Hogwarts High Inquisitor," provides perfect examples of the assumption of leadership, leadership styles, and how new leaders deal with those who may resist or want to thwart them. We also discover the importance of a new leader's underlying purpose or goal in assembling a team that supports his or her leadership. The chapter begins with the power of the press, as the *Daily Prophet* brings news of Dolores Umbridge's appointment as the first-ever Hogwarts High Inquisitor (306).

Let's take a moment to discuss the power of the government and of people in the government who wield it.

Most heads of state and heads of government have **appointment power**, that is, the power to appoint high officials, such as cabinet officers. But these leaders also hold power over people who may someday *want* an appointment.

NOTE TO SELF: *One's self is the most important thing to understand; power is the next most important thing to understand.*

PART 1

The power of appointment gives the leader not only the chance to give important positions to his or her friends or supporters, but also a more subtle influence, because anyone who wants to move up in government will want to support the person who has appointment power. Thus, the act of appointing someone to a post is a *direct* use of power; the realization that others will adhere to your wishes because they want you to appoint them someday is an *indirect* power.

NOTE TO SELF: *Power can be direct or indirect, and you must appreciate and understand both types to analyze properly the motives and actions of others.*

We need think only of Percy to be confident that there are ambitious people in the world, and many of them have the unstated and sometimes clear goal of moving up in the government.

Another aspect of government power is the issuance of **administrative orders**, **executive orders**, and, in the case of the Ministry of Magic, **decrees**. By this point, Harry and his friends all have clear evidence that the Ministry is looking closely at Hogwarts and using legal means—that is, educational decrees—to make changes at the school.

The first administrative action was the appointment of Dolores Umbridge as the Defense Against the Dark Arts professor. We find out in this chapter that the Minister of Magic was able to appoint Dolores Umbridge because of Educational Decree Number 22, which allowed the Ministry to appoint a professor *if* the Headmaster was unable to fill a vacancy (307). (We have to wonder whether Dumbledore was given much of a chance to fill the position. . . .) We should also discuss J. K. Rowling's use of the term *inquisitor.* Historically, particularly in Europe, the position of inquisitor was held by members of the government or the church. These people had significant control over the investigation of persons deemed "questionable" by those in power. Their investigations, or "inquisitions," were first employed in twelfth-century France as a way to prevent heresy (failure to comply with the rules of the Catholic faith or belief in views not accepted by it) and often involved the use of torture to obtain confessions. Inquisitors used their power to support various party lines in Europe for more than four hundred years, from the 1200s until the 1850s. The Catholic Inquisition had a staff of several inquisitors, headed by the Grand Inquisitor.

Thus, J. K. Rowling's use of the term *inquisitor* is intended to taint the position of Hogwarts High Inquisitor with its sordid and draconian history while impugning both Professor Umbridge and the position itself!

NOTE TO SELF: *If you understand history, you will understand subtleties and nuances that others do not understand.*

The job of an inquisitor is to investigate and to question those over whom the inquisitor has power. Dolores Umbridge does so with great zeal. She now has the *power* to inspect her fellow educators. She has been instructed to provide the Minister with "on-the-ground feedback of what's really happening at Hogwarts" (307). In other words, Professor Umbridge is now an "open spy" at Hogwarts.

CHECKS AND BALANCES (AND OVERSIGHT) IN THE SPY WORLD

Not all government investigations are automatically bad things. Almost all government agencies have an **Inspector General** tasked with ensuring that no wrongdoing occurs in that organization or department.

By the same token, in the United States' system of separation of powers, we have a judiciary branch, executive branch, and legislative branch. These three branches of government were instituted in our Constitution to provide checks and balances for each other.

The US executive branch is in charge of the CIA and all the other intelligence agencies. Its checks and balances are provided through the legislative branch (Congress), which monitors the executive branch (the president). Congress assigns to specific committees the task of providing oversight to all intelligence agencies and reviewing any covert actions taken by the executive branch (President of the United States, CIA, DIA, etc.).

The individual members of Congress selected to serve on this committee by the Senate or House leadership are considered the most honest and capable members of Congress. They are obligated to keep what they learn secret from the rest of Congress—and Congress relies on these individuals to make sure that the intelligence community, as well as the president, complies with all the rules and regulations applicable to intelligence gathering and the use of intelligence, as well as covert actions. The other members of Congress rely on these committees to provide proper oversight, even though they may not know the exact information shared on those committees.

The judicial branch, by the same token, can decide that certain activities of the executive branch are beyond its power or illegal. In addition, a special court called the FISA court reviews requests for wiretaps through the issuance of warrants.

~~~~~~

According to the *Daily Prophet* and Percy Weasley, Umbridge has been "an immediate success." This is, obviously, in the students' view, disinformation—if not a bold-faced lie (307)! The word *propaganda* comes to mind!

But in the *Ministry of Magic's* view, Umbridge has *indeed* been an immediate success. She is now in a position to spy very effectively for the Ministry and Cornelius Fudge. However, the *Prophet's* article goes on to assert that Dolores Umbridge is a gifted and wonderful teacher, totally revamping the way in which the Defense Against the Dark Arts is being taught (307). The children, of course, know a lie when they see one, and this one is a whopper!

It is also interesting to see whom the *Daily Prophet* chooses to quote about the *wonderful* job Professor Umbridge is doing: Lucius Malfoy, someone with an obvious bias against Dumbledore. So much for an independent press!

Lucius Malfoy refers to the concerns of parents about "some of Dumbledore's eccentric decisions in the last few years" (307–8). The reporter then discloses and discusses some of those "eccentric decisions": controversial staff appointments such as the hiring of the werewolf Remus Lupin, the half-giant Rubeus Hagrid, and Mad-Eye Moody, a delusional ex-Auror (308).

It is clear that the Ministry has moved away from attacking Harry Potter and has turned its guns on Dumbledore himself. If there is any doubt about the paper's intentions in going after Dumbledore, it is erased when we learn that the Ministry's actions have been cast as *the first step toward ensuring confidence in the Headmaster* (308), which really means the first step toward the *removal* of Professor Dumbledore.

The newspaper continues to show its bias by pretending to present an alternative view—and then immediately attacking the person who gave that alternative view. Madame Marchbanks, who is quoted in support of Dumbledore, is then subjected to an ad hominem attack via a related article on her "alleged links to subversive goblin groups" (308).

Hermione, always thinking, comes alive after reading this issue of the *Daily Prophet*. At the next Defense Against the Dark Arts class, Hermione's personal battle with Professor Umbridge begins in earnest. She questions the textbook's conclusions and is of course immediately shut down by Professor Umbridge (316–17).

A classroom is *supposed* to be a place of learning, but Professor Umbridge silences Hermione's questions and takes five points from Gryffindor house for "disrupting my class with pointless interruptions." Professor Umbridge continues on, explaining that she is there "to teach you using a Ministry-approved method that does not include inviting students to give their opinions on matters about which they understand very little" (317).

So much for learning anything of value!

NOTE TO SELF: *Teachers who don't want questions from their students or cannot countenance a contrary view should find another profession!*

We also observe Professor Umbridge examining her fellow teachers, starting with Professor Trelawney—who understandably reacts to the High Inquisitor's presence with trembling hands (312). Through Professor Umbridge's questioning we learn that Professor Dumbledore was indeed the person who appointed Professor Trelawney. Which makes us wonder: how is it that Umbridge was able to convince Dumbledore to allow her to teach at Hogwarts?

ANALYSIS: *Why in the world would Professor Dumbledore, who seems to hold supreme power at Hogwarts, allow Umbridge to be appointed to teach the class on Defense Against the Dark Arts?* This is really a question of timing. Was he persuaded to take her on, was she really the only teacher available for the "cursed" subject . . . or was Educational Decree 22— enabling the Minister of Magic to fill teaching positions if the Headmaster is not able to do so—issued just for this purpose?

We're not sure of the exact timing, but we are sure that Dumbledore had little to no choice in the matter; the only question is whether he accepted it graciously or had it forced down his throat!

In any event, Professor Umbridge asks Professor Trelawney to predict something for her. Professor Trelawney's incompetence (or, more accurately, *erratic* ability) is unfortunately obvious, and the best she can do is claim that Professor Umbridge is in *grave* danger (315). Hem, hem, we say!

We also observe Professor Umbridge interrogating Professor Grubbly-Plank and putting a fair amount of effort into determining, through the interrogation, where Hagrid is and how she came to substitute in Hagrid's classes. Professor Umbridge determines that Professor Grubbly-Plank knows what she's doing and, more importantly, knows nothing about where Hagrid may be (322–23).

The chapter ends with Hermione's brilliant idea for dealing with Professor Umbridge and learning Defense Against the Dark Arts by themselves (325). When she first suggests that the Hogwarts students should "learn Defense Against the Dark Arts ourselves," Ron immediately reacts negatively, decrying, "You want us to do extra work?" Hermione's response is most telling: "this is much more important than homework!" (325).

What is this? *Hermione*, stating something is *more important than homework*? Wow!

Ron's reaction is also predictable: "I didn't think there was anything in the universe more important than homework." Hermione wisely tells her two best friends, "It's about preparing ourselves. . . . We need a teacher, a proper one . . . who can show us how to use the spells and correct us if we are going wrong" (325). She then announces that the teacher she is talking about is *none other than Harry*!

Thus begins the idea of going *underground* and gathering a secret group of fellow students. Dumbledore's Army (though it doesn't have that name yet) has been born.

Although Harry is shocked by the idea, Ron quickly agrees. Hermione and Ron—in order to convince Harry—describe all the things Harry has done over the years:

> The first year, keeping the Sorcerer's Stone from You-Know-Who, which Harry claims was luck, not skill.
> The second year, killing the basilisk and destroying Riddle; Harry claims that Fawkes saved him.
> The third year, fighting off about a hundred Dementors at once, though Harry asserts it was a fluke and that the Time-Turner had assisted him.
> And, of course, the fourth year, fighting off Lord

PART 1

Voldemort again after Cedric was killed, and Harry asserts that "all that stuff was luck—I didn't know what I was doing half the time, I didn't plan any of it, I just did whatever I could think of, and I nearly always had help" (327).

Harry's statements are true, but the points Ron and Hermione make are equally true. Harry did indeed have skill—and luck. But often you do not get the opportunity to use luck unless you already have great skills.

NOTE TO SELF: *You can take advantage of luck only if you are good enough to get to a position in which luck can be used!*

Harry finally blows up, yelling, "You don't know what it's like . . . Like you can think straight when you know you're about a second away from being murdered, or tortured, or watching your friends die!" (327–28).

Hermione again saves the day and tells Harry this is *exactly* why he is needed. Nobody else has survived facing Voldemort, so nobody knows what it's like (328). As we know, this is the first time Hermione has ever said Voldemort's name. This fact alone calms Harry and brings the discussion back to the point at hand.

Harry promises to think about it—and think about it he does.

16

HARRY TAKES THE LEAD—A NOT·SO·SECRET MEETING—WE BAND OF BROTHERS (AND SISTERS)

In chapter 16, "In the Hog's Head," Harry finally assumes a leadership role. Doing so involves organization, recruitment, the selection of an appropriate place to meet in secret, and the germination and growth of an idea—the creation of a subversive organization—into a reality.

The chapter begins with a reference to chapter 14, when Filch said that he had been tipped off about Harry trying to get Dungbombs via the owl post and attempted to intercept Harry's owl. Harry thinks very little of Filch's attempt to intercept his message, but Hermione thinks it's very strange and, indeed, instructive—and again she is right (334).

ANALYSIS: *Where did Filch get his information?* It is very easy for the powers that be to create a pretext for searching for something, and you'd think it would be simple for Professor Umbridge to "disclose" to Filch that Harry is attempting to order Dungbombs so that Filch would try to intercept Harry's communications. We put our money on Umbridge!

NOTE TO SELF: *Sometimes a coincidence is not a coincidence! Think about everything that happens and take the time to discern whether a "coincidence" could be something else.*

As our three friends enter the Hog's Head, they discuss the fact that the meeting point is a less crowded place, which means there is less of a chance of being overheard by an eavesdropper (335). (As Sirius notes later, this is a mistake: you're less likely to be overheard at a place that is *more* crowded [370]—but we'll will get to that in a moment.)

As they look around the Hog's Head, Harry, Ron, and Hermione see several unsavory characters, including a witch whose face is hidden behind a veil and thus seems like an obvious spy (336). We find out later that this is Mundungus Fletcher, who is wearing a disguise because he was kicked out of the Hog's Head twenty years ago and—we are told by Sirius—the bartender has a very good memory (370). There is also "a man at the bar whose whole head was wrapped in dirty gray bandages" (336), "two figures shrouded in hoods . . . at a table in one of the windows" speaking with Yorkshire accents, and the barman—"a grumpy-looking old man with a great deal of long gray hair and beard" who looks vaguely familiar to Harry (a little like Albus Dumbledore, perhaps?).

So, upon consideration, perhaps *not* the best place for a secret meeting where you don't want to be overheard—what do you think?

Anyway, the trio discusses whether what they are doing is legal or against the rules, and Hermione matter-of-factly (and correctly) states that there is no rule against study groups—at least, NOT YET (336)!

Still, the students meet in secret for obvious reasons: they all realize that Professor Umbridge would object to what they are doing (336).

Now, a word about loyalty: **LOYALTY.**

Of the twenty-four or so people who are there, only one appears not to want to be there: Cho's friend. Note the importance of observation and what conclusions the new organization's leaders draw from them (338, 347)!

~~~~~~

THE RISKS INHERENT IN RECRUITING—IS SHE A POTENTIAL MARIETTA?

In any organization you have to be able to trust the people that you recruit. However, you will never have a 100 percent guarantee that the person recruited is trustworthy. In fact, if such certainty was required, we would rarely be able to recruit anyone! There are risks in spying, and there is of course risk in recruitment. The intelligence communities do their best to do thorough **background checks** on the people they recruit, in hopes of finding any indications or warnings about those who should *not* be admitted into the fold.

~~~~~~

The meeting at the Hog's Head is indeed an interesting one. Harry is shocked when so many people show up, but he stays nonetheless. Hermione takes charge, since she is the one who organized the meeting, and describes the purpose of their group: to learn real spells and to practice Defense Against the Dark Arts (339).

When someone asks about Cedric's death, Harry suddenly realizes that many of the people might be there because they want to find out the details about how Cedric died (340). In other words, Harry is analyzing the **motivations** of his fellow students, as he should.

ANALYSIS: *What does Harry conclude about the motives of those who came?* Harry has the insight that some of the people came because they are curious about something only Harry can describe.

PART 1

Harry has no intention of going into the details of Cedric's death (although he does so later, when he is interviewed by Rita Skeeter), and shuts down that issue quite quickly [340–41]. This decisive action on Harry's part, you will note, indicates good leadership abilities. A good leader can quickly analyze a situation and the motivations of those around him or her, and use those observations to make a quick but well-thought-out decision.

ANALYSIS: *Is the location where they are meeting really secure?* There are several indications that it is not. The bartender is listening, washing the same glass (with a very dirty rag) for a long time (341). The "witch" is also shifting slightly in her seat (342). Harry notices these things but does nothing about them.

NOTE TO SELF: *Switching gender or race serves you well when you are in disguise.*

We find out much later that Willy Widdershins, who was heavily bandaged at the time, just "happened" to be at the Hog's Head—as a spy (and a **floater**) for the Ministry or Professor Umbridge—and heard everything that Harry had said. When the meeting breaks up, he will go directly to the school and tell Umbridge (613).

The meeting continues, despite clear signs they are being overheard and should move elsewhere. The students discuss the creation of the subversive organization, how often to meet, and where. The Ministry's fear of Dumbledore developing a private army eventually inspires the name of their new group: Dumbledore's Army (343–45, 392). They will also need a secret place to meet, though no one knows yet what place will serve (346).

Harry's assumption of **leadership** occurs as he answers various questions from those who will become part of Dumbledore's Army. Through these questions, all of the students are in a position to find out all the different things that Harry has done that prove his *abilities* and *experiences*—indeed, his *qualifications* to teach them Defense Against the Dark Arts. One of his questioners turns out to be Susan

Bones, the niece of the judge at Harry's hearing. Susan asks whether it's true that Harry can produce a Patronus—a stag Patronus, no less (341–42) (proving once again that Mad-Eye chose a pretty weak security question for Harry!).

Everyone agrees to begin a Defense Against the Dark Arts study group, and each of the students signs his or her name on the list (though Cho's friend, Marietta, is clearly reluctant to do so). Several of the students are concerned—rightly so!—that the list should not be "left lying around" (in spy terms, they are concerned about **document security**). Hermione explains that she certainly would not let that happen (346–47). In other words, the list itself is **classified material** and should be protected.

Many of the people felt that, in signing their names to the list of members, they were signing "some kind of contract"; unbeknownst to them, this was *exactly* the case because Hermione had jinxed the document (354). If any of the signers broke their vow to keep the organization a secret, he or she would break out with terrible boils and acne forming the word *sneak* across their face (612)!

SIGNING YOUR LIFE AWAY—AND THE DECLARATION OF INDEPENDENCE

The founding members of Dumbledore's Army knew that they were taking a serious risk in defying authority. The signers of the Declaration of Independence felt the same way, joking as they signed that they were signing their own death warrants. John Hancock supposedly signed in large letters so King George could read his name more easily, and one delegate supposedly said that, by signing, "we shall all hang together."

As Dumbledore's Army gets going, the members develop not only camaraderie but also a true sense of loyalty, for they shall soon join in battle—first against Umbridge, but later against Lord

Voldemort. And after the final battle is over, they too can speak those happy words delivered before the battle in act IV, scene iii, of Shakespeare's *Henry V*: "We few, we happy few, we band of brothers [and sisters]."

SECRECY CONTRACTS: SECURITY CLEARANCES AND THE NEED TO KEEP SECRETS SECRET

In many ways, the students are indeed signing a contract, an agreement to *keep something secret*, to *keep the secret among themselves*, and to *have loyalty to each other*. This is true in the real world as well, where individuals with a security clearance sign a contract acknowledging that they have a certain clearance and that it is a federal crime to improperly disclose any of the information obtained as a result of that clearance. You are also obligated to obtain permission to print anything relating to the clearance you have or have had—even if you were a participant on something as secret and successful as the mission to kill Osama bin Laden!

Because I had previously had a security clearance, I was required to submit the manuscript for my spy novel *Mission to Chara* to the Department of Defense for review. I had to be able to indicate an open-source basis for every fact or detail that could be possibly derived from classified material or from things that I had observed or learned in a classified briefing or at a classified location. The same is true of everything Peter has published, including this book. Everyone who has had a security clearance knows this simple fact—and anyone who fails to comply with this legal obligation is most likely going to be prosecuted and forced to give up any proceeds from the publication.

Those of us who have been privileged to see classified information have an obligation to the government and our country to keep such secrets secret and disclose them only as allowed by the government. That is the deal we made when we signed the agreement, and we are honor-bound to keep our word.

—Lynn Boughey

~~~~~~~~~~~~~~~~~~~~~~~~

When the meeting is over at The Hog's Head, the students leave by "twos and threes" (347): while they don't seem to have decided on this plan, they do so anyway, presumably so it will be less obvious that they had met. The children are well aware that what they are doing is at the very least *suspect* and has *an element of risk*, and they act accordingly. They are, in fact, taking their first steps toward becoming spies! The young students who are applying trade craft have both common sense and the intelligence to use it!

Let's pause here to compare Harry's way of assuming leadership and Umbridge's assumption of leadership at Hogwarts. Where Professor Umbridge uses *fear and intimidation* to control teachers and students, Harry develops **camaraderie** and *friendships* based on trust with his fellow students.

Professor Umbridge's purpose is to *prevent* the children from learning Defense Against the Dark Arts and to toe the Ministry's line that Voldemort is not back. She wants the children to *remain ignorant* and not ask questions or develop any type of intellectual freedom. Harry's goal is to *teach* his fellow students Defense Against the Dark Arts for the purpose of preparing for the inevitable battle against Voldemort. He wants his fellow students to *learn* from his hard-won knowledge and to use both curiosity and *intellectual freedom*. (True, he refuses to discuss the details of Cedric's death in the Hog's Head, in part because it is morbid and in part because doing so might hurt Cedric's former girlfriend, Cho. But we're not quite there yet.)

Overall, Professor Umbridge leads by threatening those who oppose her and bribing her followers with promises of advancement, all the while reinforcing and defending her own position of power. She divides those she is supposed to lead and sets them against each

other. Harry, in contrast, encourages his followers to build friendships and work together. He has patience for those who are doubtful
or frightened and shows compassion when he takes Cho's feelings
into consideration.

ASSUMPTION OF LEADERSHIP IN THE MUGGLE WORLD: LYNDON BAINES JOHNSON AND THE US PRESIDENCY

On November 22, 1963, the Muggle leader of the
United States government, President John F. Kennedy,
was assassinated while traveling in a motorcade through
Dallas, Texas. In the hours that followed, Vice President
Lyndon B. Johnson made many calm, well-reasoned
decisions that made his assumption of leadership both
organized and politic. While doctors attempted to save
the president's life, Johnson refused to flee to safety as the
Secret Service requested. Instead, he stood by his president
and First Lady Jackie Kennedy until all hope was gone.
When the terrible news came down, he again refused to
flee, waiting respectfully for the release of Kennedy's body
and refusing to leave Jackie Kennedy behind.

However, he used this time to make many decisions crucial
to a smooth and organized transition of authority. He
considered when and where he should take the oath of
office and what support he would need to do so. He called
US Attorney General Bobby Kennedy, the nation's head
lawyer and the president's brother, to offer condolences
and consult about the legal necessities of the transition. He
met with two of President Kennedy's closest advisers and
friends, Larry O'Brian and Ken O'Donnell, and humbly
asked them to stay on at the White House because, as the
new president, he had so much to learn.

Like Harry, Lyndon Johnson had been having a rough
time of it. Although he had been a popular and respected

member of the US Senate, the press was now running wild with accusations of alleged financial improprieties in Johnson's campaigns. As vice president, he seemed to have been relegated to following the president around at parties, holding little power. He feared that Kennedy himself was losing trust in him and that he would be dropped from the campaign. But when tragedy struck and the nation needed a leader, Lyndon B. Johnson's thoughtful and determined assumption of leadership made all the difference. Too bad that Harry isn't taking Muggle Studies!

If you have further interest in reading about Lyndon B. Johnson's assumption of the presidency, we direct you to an article published in *The New Yorker* on April 2, 2012, by Robert A. Caro, entitled "Annals of History: The Transition—Lyndon Johnson and the Events in Dallas."

~~~~~~~~~~

Just as President Johnson was able to convince a plane full of grieving Americans that he was up to the task, Harry Potter was able to convince twenty-four of his fellow students that preparing for the final battle against Lord Voldemort was worthwhile and that *he* had the experience and knowledge to be their teacher.

Perhaps even more important than his magical abilities was Harry's humility and genuine belief that luck and help from others had played a part in surviving his many exploits (341–43). Harry's honesty and lack of pride no doubt played a large role in convincing the others to become members of Dumbledore's Army.

NOTE TO SELF: *When trying to convince others to join you in an endeavor, setting aside your ego, being yourself, and displaying humility are often essential to success.*

FURTHER NOTE TO SELF: *One can accomplish a lot when there is a common goal, common friends, and a need for action against a common enemy.*

17

EDUCATIONAL DECREE NO. 24—LEAKS OTHER THAN THE LEAKY CAULDRON, IDEAS SUPPRESSED AND ASSOCIATIONS THWARTED

A repressive regime fears two things more than anything else: **outside influence** and inside subversive organizations of any type. People, when properly organized, have been known to overthrow dictatorial governments. Repressing freedoms and preventing mass organization—or even *small-scale* organization—are the tools used by those in power to continue that power.

Freedom, as we hope you all know by now, is a very dangerous thing!

In a free society, people can actually exchange ideas, organize behind a cause, attempt to change their government, and indeed replace one government with another! It is said that the pen is mightier than the sword. Ideas are powerful weapons indeed! Albert Einstein had the idea that great power could be released through nuclear fission and was most certainly correct. (He was also correct in warning all of us about the *ways* in which that power could be used—and *misused*!)

We have already seen Professor Umbridge's reactions to students who dared question the Ministry, the Ministry's selected textbook on Defense Against the Dark Arts, or worse yet, the Ministry's view that Voldemort is *not* back, despite any *lies* distributed by that attention-seeking boy, Harry Potter!

Once the members of the fledgling Defense Against the Dark Arts study group read Educational Decree No. 24 (which also happens to be the title of the chapter), they immediately assume that they have a traitor among them (352). This is not necessarily so; somebody could have overheard them, or Professor Umbridge could have simply been advised that more than twenty students had met at the Hog's Head—with Harry Potter being one of them. This seems to be the more likely scenario, given that nobody has tripped Hermione's brilliant curse (354).

Professor Umbridge seems to know about the meeting at The Hog's Head and that the students have a plan to begin their own Defense Against the Dark Arts training. We learn just how later in the story, but for now the students easily guess that somebody in The Hog's Head relayed the information to Professor Umbridge, or perhaps to Filch (352–53).

ANALYSIS: *Is there indeed a spy in their midst?* Not at this time. As they learn later, an eavesdropper, Willy Widdershins, relayed the information to Professor Umbridge (613). But at this point, the students' only reassurance of their secrecy is the fact that no one has the word *SNEAK* blazoned on their forehead (at least, not yet!).

In any event, Umbridge knows that the students have attempted to organize, and she therefore issues Educational Decree No. 24 to prevent any such organizations from forming and to stop any meetings of three or more students (351). She has, in other words, outlawed **freedom of association**.

PART 1

FREEDOM OF SPEECH AND FREEDOM OF ASSOCIATION— TWO IMPORTANT RIGHTS

Two of the rights guaranteed under the **First Amendment** of the United States Constitution are **freedom of speech** and **freedom of association**. Freedom of speech allows people to say what they want to say, as long as it does not create a danger to others, such as yelling "Fire!" in a crowded theater. Freedom of association allows people to organize in groups, associate with each other, and work together on common goals. Of course, Professor Umbridge wants none of that!

Importantly, you will note that all of the students wanted to continue meeting, *despite* Educational Decree No. 24. The battle against Professor Umbridge has begun in earnest, and in breaking the rules, the students are demonstrating true bravery against great odds and powerful adult enemies (354). (Professor Dumbledore must have been proud indeed when Mundungus reported to him what they were doing and the name selected for this subversive organization by his most gifted students!)

We next find Harry in Professor Binns's History of Magic class, bored out of his mind. However, that boredom is quickly replaced by curiosity when Hedwig shows up at the window (356).

Professor Binns, oblivious as always, fails to notice as Harry crouches down and goes over to the window, opens it, and brings Hedwig back to his desk. Harry soon realizes that Hedwig has been injured and asks Professor Binns if he may leave because he's not feeling well (357).

This was, of course, a lie, or in spy terminology, disinformation, a **deception,** or a **diversionary tactic**. In any event, Harry is allowed to leave with the injured Hedwig and attempts to get treatment for his bird. Since Hagrid is gone, he tries to locate Professor Grubbly-Plank, who is in the staff room with Professor McGonagall (357–58).

CHAPTER 17

ANALYSIS: *How and why was Hedwig injured?* Harry and the others immediately realize that Hedwig would not normally deliver a message while the children are in class—messages normally arrive in the morning while everyone is eating breakfast. This fact alone indicates that whoever sent the message to Harry did not want anyone to observe the message coming to him. In addition, by arranging delivery at a different time and place, the sender of Hedwig was attempting to *lessen* the risk of the owl being intercepted. Thirdly, the injury to Hedwig clearly demonstrates that someone is indeed trying to intercept messages sent to Harry. And fourthly, Hedwig was late because she was injured!

Professor Grubbly-Plank immediately takes control of the situation. Professor McGonagall, when inquiring of Harry as to where the bird came from (a seemingly innocent question, but actually one filled with purpose!), is informed obliquely that the owl came "from London" (358).

Professor McGonagall immediately realizes that "from London" most likely means from headquarters and from Sirius himself. McGonagall rightfully warns Harry of what he is probably already beginning to understand: "Bear in mind . . . that channels of communication in and out of Hogwarts may be being watched, won't you?" As Professor Grubbly-Plank walks away with the injured Hedwig, Professor McGonagall once again saves the day by ensuring that Harry doesn't forget his letter, which Hedwig still has (359)!

You can just hear Mad-Eye Moody yelling, "Wake up, boy! CONSTANT VIGILANCE! Keep your head about you!"

CONSTANT VIGILANCE! We might have heard that admonition a few times in book 4 (*GF* 213, 217, 571), as we recall.

The message from Sirius to Harry—just like the letter Harry had sent to Sirius—provided information that would be understood *only* by someone with the essential inside information to properly interpret the message. In other words, an open code.

PART 1

Sirius's message, "today, same time, same place," is clearly a secure way of providing the information to the individual who already knows the time and place. Importantly, the message is unsigned (359).

Once again, we learn from Harry Potter and his godfather ways in which you can communicate securely, even when you are being watched! And as we all know, secure communication is essential to spying without being caught.

Harry next considers whether to reply to Sirius.

ANALYSIS: *Should Harry respond to Sirius's note and inform him about the attempted interception of Hedwig?* Harry, Hermione, and Ron discuss whether or not they should send a reply with the news about the owl being injured and perhaps intercepted. They correctly decide *not* to respond, for several reasons.

First, they realize (without explicitly stating this fact) that sending an owl back might simply make it possible for somebody to follow Hedwig and see exactly where Sirius—and thus headquarters—is located. In addition, Sirius probably already knows of the attempt to intercept communications, just as Professor McGonagall said. Concerning whether anyone has been able to intercept or read the message, Hermione correctly notes that many wizards have the ability to open and reseal a message, and the fact that it does not look tampered with does not mean it hasn't been (360)!

So, back to the story!

Educational Decree No. 24, by restricting associations and meetings of three or more students, also forces the Gryffindor Quidditch team to seek approval from *none other than* Professor Umbridge!

Draco Malfoy provides us an example of baiting—or perhaps psychological operations—by his comments that the Slytherin Quidditch team was immediately reauthorized. Draco flaunts his father's influence, openly asserting that the team was reinstated quickly through Lucius Malfoy's involvement and noting that Lucius knows Dolores Umbridge (360–61).

Draco is attempting to rub it in and get Ron and Harry worried, if not confused, about what Draco actually knows. Draco goes on to assert as fact that Mr. Weasley is going to be sacked from the Ministry of Magic and that Harry will be sent to Saint Mungo's, the hospital for the magically injured and psychologically damaged wizards (361).

SENDING HARRY TO SAINT MUNGO'S— AN HISTORIC BASIS

Sending somebody to be committed in a psychological ward because you don't like what they're saying is a clear *abuse of power*, but at this point it doesn't seem to be beneath the Ministry of Magic. The Soviet Union often used this tactic to silence dissidents. Doing so is an extreme use of argument ad hominem. Instead of countering a person's viewpoint with proper argument or logic, you instead attack the person's mental health, even to the extent of having them put into a treatment program or secured hospital, where they cannot be seen or heard and are presumed to be insane—incapable of rational thought.

We should also note Neville Longbottom's reaction to Draco's mention of St. Mungo's. Without warning, Neville Longbottom attacks—or at least *attempts* to attack—Draco, but is held back by Harry and Ron. Of the students witnessing this event, only Harry understands the significance of St. Mungo's to Neville Longbottom (361). And Harry keeps the fact that he knows secret—even from Neville. Harry promised Dumbledore that he would not disclose what happened to Neville's parents, and he abides by that promise (362).

PART 1

KEEPING PERSONAL SECRETS, AND THE USE OF DISCRETION

Often in life, we find out interesting or important information about others. In some professions, such as law or medicine, and in the priesthood, there are rules and laws requiring that information received in confidence stay confidential and not be shared under any circumstances.

But one need not have specific laws or even obligations to decide to keep a secret. Again, we all find out things that would be considered confidential or at least embarrassing to another person. Discretion, once again, is an important aspect of getting along with people. Knowing when to keep your mouth shut can help a spy gain allies—and while it might be tempting to blackmail someone with the secrets you know, a bond of friendship can be much more reliable.

The physician's first rule is to do no harm. If only that same rule could be followed by all people, wizards and Muggles alike!

NOTE TO SELF: *Never disclose something that could be harmful to another person unless absolutely necessary, and for a very good reason.*

We next get the opportunity to watch Professor Umbridge interrogate Professor Snape about his history as a professor at Hogwarts. Significantly, Harry observes that when Snape is questioned by Umbridge, "His expression was unfathomable" (363).

Once again, we see Professor Snape's skill in Occlumency as well as in not disclosing his innermost thoughts accidentally or inadvertently. This is a man who is in full control of his emotions and able to keep his thoughts secure from outsiders (363–64)—including, dare we say the name? Voldemort!

Harry understands that Umbridge is holding her control of the Gryffindor Quidditch team's fate over his head and that of everyone else in Gryffindor. This too is a use of power and, we would assert, a *misuse* of power. Umbridge immediately approved the Slytherin team but not the other teams. Harry, who is clearly developing sophisticated forms of analysis, understands why Professor Umbridge has not yet approved the Gryffindor Quidditch team and correctly guesses the reasons behind her decision—or lack of decision—to approve the team (367).

Harry, Hermione, and Ron are anxious to speak with Sirius at the same bat-time and same bat-station (a la the old Batman TV series), so let's now say a word about scheduling: **SCHEDULING!**

One of their main topics of conversation is determining an appropriate meeting site for Harry's Defense Against the Dark Arts classes. Sirius is of course *thrilled* that the children are organizing themselves, but he nonetheless feels obligated to relay Molly Weasley's instructions forbidding Ron's participation in such a group (370–72). Sirius also has some criticism about their plans, especially their selection of The Hog's Head as the place for their meeting. Sirius confirms that The Three Broomsticks would have been better because it's harder to hear when there are more people around (369–71).

From the standpoint of spying, the selection of a **secure meeting place** where you can't be overheard is important. Obviously, a place where you cannot be heard *at all* is your best option, and one where you cannot be heard *or seen* is even better! Thus, in the spy world, many secure conversations are held in vehicles or pre-selected rooms that are known to be secure.

If it is necessary to hold a meeting in a public place, Sirius has a good point: the louder the place, the less likely it is that somebody could overhear you. The Hog's Head was empty except for a few patrons and the bartender, and those patrons could easily overhear what was being said, identify quite easily where the students were from (Hogwarts School), and potentially identify them individually.

Sirius tells the trio that Mundungus was the Order's spy that day, and that he was there to try to protect Harry while he was in Hogsmeade. He also explains that Mundungus was in costume—under the veil as a witch—because he had once been thrown out of The Hog's Head, and the bartender has a very long memory (370).

We also find out from Sirius that Sturgis Podmore had lost the Invisibility Cloak when he was arrested. Sturgis is a member of the Order of the Phoenix (something Harry knew already), but more importantly, Harry is able to conclude that the Order of the Phoenix is attempting to break into the Ministry of Magic. Why could this be? To find something, or to *protect* something? Unfortunately for Sturgis, he was caught and sent to Azkaban (287).

Have we mentioned yet the risks that spies take—for God or country?

Speaking of risk, our good friends properly analyze the situation and conclude that secretly developing a Defense Against the Dark Arts class is worth the risk of being caught.

NOTE TO SELF: *Risk must always be analyzed by considering both what is being done and the importance of what is at stake.*

ANALYSIS: *Why take such a risk and create your own Defense Against the Dark Arts class?* The previous year, our three friends knew that there was someone who wanted to kill Harry; this year they now know that there's somebody who wants to kill "all of us"—meaning, we think, anyone willing to stand up to the Dark Lord. The danger is now more real and substantial, and as such the risks are justified (371).

Their new conclusion is based on the new information obtained through **intelligence**, observation, and analysis. Again, *you must always analyze and reanalyze risk at each step of any mission or plan.* Risk is inherent to any operation, and you must determine how to lessen that risk and whether the risk is appropriate based on the necessity of the situation. Thus, the case officer must conduct a cost–benefit analysis to determine the appropriate risk, based on the importance of obtaining the information.

The risk under discussion by Harry and his friends is how to meet in secret. Where could Harry teach his classes? Harry, Ron, and Hermione consider the Shrieking Shack, but of course there are too many people to practice in such a small place. They discuss a certain passageway, but it turns out to have been blocked (372).

But before any further discussion can be had, Sirius realizes that his cover has been blown, that he is no longer secure—and disappears. Moments later, the children see Umbridge's toadlike hand reaching through the fire, trying to grab Sirius (373)!

Obviously *this* method of communication has been discovered by Professor Umbridge and is no longer secure!

18

THE DEVELOPMENT OF DUMBLEDORE'S ARMY: ORGANIZATION, COMMUNICATION, SECRECY, AND FINDING THE PERFECT MEETING PLACE

Chapter 18, "Dumbledore's Army," centers on secure communications, a secure meeting place, organization, and leadership. Each of these issues is an important facet of being a spy or running a spy organization.

The chapter begins, not surprisingly, with the discussion of how Professor Umbridge knew about the meeting with Sirius, and how *secure* their communications are (374–75).

ANALYSIS: *How did Umbridge find out about the meeting with Sirius?* Since the meeting was set up via a letter from Sirius, the first issue of analysis is whether or not the mail is being intercepted. The children conclude, probably quite correctly, that the mail has indeed been intercepted by Professor Umbridge or someone reporting to her. The injury to Harry's owl is a clear indicator that this is happening—or at least that someone has attempted to intercept the owl post! Our friends consider Filch's earlier attempt to intercept Harry's owl under the accusation that Harry had been ordering Dungbombs (374–75).

FURTHER ANALYSIS: *What is the basis for Filch's assertion that Harry is ordering Dungbombs?* As mentioned above, this assertion is most likely a pretext for reading Harry's mail (374–75).

You'd assume that Harry has better things to do than order Dungbombs by post. (On the other hand, if you had told us that the Weasley twins were doing so, we would whole-heartedly agree!) In analyzing Filch's assertion, we should consider two possibilities. Number one, that Filch honestly believes that Harry is ordering Dungbombs, and we personally would place money on Professor Umbridge as the purveyor of this information! Number two, that *no one* believes that Harry could be ordering Dungbombs by mail, and the assertion is *merely* for the purpose of justifying the search of Harry's mail (375).

THE GOVERNMENT'S USE OF PRETEXT— FINDING AN EXCUSE TO STOP YOU

A reason made up to justify an activity is called a *pretext*. It is unfortunately very easy to cast aspersions about illegal activities and then use that made-up information to obtain a warrant or create the basis for stopping or searching someone. It is also possible to use a *minor infraction* to look for a *serious infraction*.

A good example of a pretextual stop and search would be a police officer pulling over a car because the license tags are expired. Although it is lawful to do so, pulling over the vehicle because of an expired license tag is often a pretext for stopping the car, and talking to the driver, and looking inside the car to see if there is anything illegal going on.

There is a substantial area of law relating to stop and frisk—where a police officer perceives the possibility that a crime is afoot and inquires of the person what he or she is doing there. If the officer perceives danger, he or she may touch or pat down the person to see if he or she has a weapon, and if something is felt that could possibly be a weapon, the officer is allowed to delve further and extract the potentially offending item. If all of the preconditions are met, this whole process would be authorized by the law, *without* a search warrant.

Of course, a police officer would NEVER *assume* that the object being felt is a weapon even if it is too small to be a weapon of any kind—nor would a police officer be willing to "assume" that the object (a small round cylinder) holds drugs.

Perhaps we digress. But you get the point: it is easy for the government and its agents to find a pretext to search someone—all perfectly legally. In the world of law enforcement, as well as in the spy world, pretext is a wonderful tool for searching where you would not be otherwise able to snoop. And it is one that your enemies will be quite happy to use on you as well!

In the spy world, a less formal pretextual "stop" would include the spy asking a stranger if he or she knows the time. Spies often gain access to businesses or even people's homes by using a pretext. The pretext can be an honest one, such as "May I use your restroom?" at a business, or a sophisticated sting operation in which a spy impersonates a phone repairman or a cable TV installer assigned to fix a problem. Once inside, the spy is in a position to search for information or to hook up a bug or other electrical device that allows the spy (or his or her organization) to monitor the business or home.

CHAPTER 18

PEOPLE ARE MORE THAN HAPPY TO TELL YOU LOTS!

It really is amazing how friendly and cooperative people are willing to be! I remember one occasion when my brother Don dropped by my new home in Bismarck while I was in Montana. My brother asked the neighbor whether that was our house, and the neighbor was happy not only to confirm that it was our house, but also to tell him that I was out of town in Red Lodge, Montana, for the next few weeks. Had that been somebody wanting to rob our home, the neighbor would just have indicated that we were out of town, and please feel free to rob the place at your leisure!

—Lynn Boughey

The trio next discusses whether or not they should warn Sirius that he had almost been caught. They correctly surmise that Sirius already knows and that sending a message just for that purpose would be more of a risk than it's worth (375). Again, a **risk analysis** needs to be conducted for everything done on a regular basis, and preferably *each* time something new is being planned or something planned is about to happen.

We next get a lesson on the proper use of a weapon, the need to practice using the weapon, and the finesse needed to use the weapon properly. All of this comes up when Hermione tries to explain to Ron how to do a proper Silencing Spell, telling him that instead of waving the wand he needs to jab it (375).

Some spies train with all sorts of weapons, not just guns. Spies need to be proficient in using guns, knives, swords, and even ropes and whips. A spy needs to be more than proficient in the use of these weapons—he or she must become an *expert*. But while this is true, for the most part spies do not carry guns; it's more important that they use their heads!

163

ALONE IN SIBERIA WITHOUT A GUN

At one point while I was in Siberia, I left my translator in the small town of Chara and, on my own, exited the town and walked along the railroad tracks until I came upon some very extensive overhead electrical wires heading away from town. I found a trail—covered with a couple of inches of recent snow—that generally followed in the same direction as the power lines and headed that direction, knowing that it went to an undisclosed military site. About two miles along the trail and into a forested area, I noticed two people around five hundred yards behind me. As the trail turned, I went ahead about forty yards, then walked backwards in my own steps; then I left the trail, covering up my tracks leading into the forest as I went, the whole time wishing that I had a gun with me. Hiding in the trees, I crouched down low as the two persons passed by. By this time it was getting dark, and after the coast was clear I returned to Chara, camera in hand, but with no pictures!

—Lynn Boughey

Just as one should always select the right tool for the job, a spy is obligated to pick the best weapon for what needs to be done. In close-quarters combat, a small gun or knife will do, but it can also involve otherwise innocuous objects that can become deadly: a pen and pencil, for example. A person alone can become a weapon, simply by using karate or some other form of hand-to-hand combat.

Spies also have to understand what type of force is best in a particular situation—everything from deadly force to use of a well-positioned pressure point. Although very few humans are capable of doing a neck pinch that makes somebody pass out (like Spock in *Star Trek*), all spies can disarm or temporarily disable an adversary. Killing is rarely necessary and should be avoided at all costs; often, you need only force your opponent into a room and lock them in, or simply prop a chair underneath the handle so that person is out of your way long enough to do what needs to be done and escape.

NOTE TO SELF: *Don't forget to use your brain so you don't have to resort to force!*

Now, another word about politics: **POLITICS**! (A four-letter word for some, no doubt!)

ANALYSIS: *How is it that the Gryffindor Quidditch team is allowed to reform?* Our heroes correctly analyze the situation and assume that either Professor McGonagall or Professor Dumbledore overruled Umbridge's misuse of power (376). We find out later this is exactly what occurred (416).

The children next reevaluate their plan (a risk analysis) to have Harry teach the other students Defense Against the Dark Arts. Once again, we see the importance of reexamining any plan in light of any new facts or added risks (377).

Hermione, it turns out, is now questioning the plan because *Sirius thought it was a good idea.* Here we have another excellent intelligence analysis: Hermione perceives Sirius as someone who is too willing to take risks—and since he thinks it's a good idea, she now questions whether it might in fact be a *bad* idea (377–78).

In analyzing information, it's always important to look at the source of that information. Does that person have a bias? Does that person have a perspective that would put his or her judgment in doubt? Does that person make rash decisions? Hermione also performs a psychological assessment on Sirius: is Sirius living vicariously through Harry, Hermione, and Ron and enjoying watching *them* take risks while he is stuck at number twelve, Grimmauld Place? Luckily, Hermione concludes that the risk is worth it—even if Sirius thinks it is a good idea—and that it is important to continue training themselves and the other students. There is still the problem of *where* they can secretly train, however.

Harry next receives another of his occasional disconcerting communications with Voldemort through the searing pain of his scar and his ability to perceive Voldemort's emotions. Harry senses that Voldemort is angry, that he wants something done and it's not happening fast enough. Harry reflects back on the pain he felt when he was in detention in Professor Umbridge's office and thinks that Voldemort was happy, perhaps because the Dark Lord realized what was happening to Harry (381–82).

Harry and the others analyze why it is that Harry is able to perceive Voldemort's emotions. Harry wonders what type of weapon Voldemort is trying to obtain and once again dreams about walking down the long corridor (383–84).

Now, a word about a very special friend: **DOBBY!**

Dobby wants to help Harry Potter, since Harry freed him from being a house-elf of the Malfoys (386). This is yet another example of how doing a good deed and befriending somebody can bring great good fortune.

NOTE TO SELF: *Always be willing to make new friends—they may come in handy!*

GOOD DEEDS AND THE THORN IN THE LION'S PAW

Although we personally choose to do good deeds because we think they *should* be done (without any thought of reward), doing good deeds often delivers its own rewards. The person who benefits from that good deed may become a very good friend indeed!

If you're in the position to help another, consider the tradition of asking those you help to repay you by assisting another person who needs it in the future. Instead of asking the recipient for a favor to do something for *you* in return, ask that person instead to do something *for somebody else*. This is an old tradition, but today many simply say, "Pay it forward."

But perhaps we digress.

Wait a minute! **Telling you to pay it forward is a good thing!** Harry pays it forward and reaps the benefits. How? Well, let's get back to the story and see!

~~~~~~

Dobby knows the perfect place for them to meet! It is called the Come and Go Room, or the Room of Requirement. Dobby explains that it's known by very few people and is very secure (386). More importantly from a security standpoint, when one person (or a group of people) is using it, no one else can get in!

Although Harry would love to go see the room immediately, he realizes that getting caught out of his dormitory late at night—on the seventh floor, opposite the tapestry of Barnabas the Barmy—would *not* be a good idea. In other words, Harry performs a risk analysis and determines that it would be best *not* to seek out the Room of Requirement tonight. Rather, he must wait for a more appropriate time (387). Harry is indeed maturing as a spy—and as a person.

~~~~~~

MATURITY DEFINED

Maturity, according to the definition of a federal judge with whom I used to work, is the ability to perceive the results of one's actions *before* taking those actions. A good definition indeed!

—Lynn Boughey

~~~~~~

In her analysis of the Room of Requirement, Hermione seems very concerned—at least until she hears that Dumbledore is familiar with the room (388). Specifically, Professor Dumbledore mentioned

PART 1

the room in book 4, *Harry Potter and the Goblet of Fire*, relating how he found a magnificent room filled with chamber pots while he was in search of the bathroom—but was unable to find it again (*GF* 417–18)!

Here, Hermione is doing good analysis by considering the source as well as the information: she distrusted Sirius's idea because of his history of risk taking, but she trusts Professor Dumbledore. The fact that Dumbledore knows about the Room of Requirement gives Hermione confidence that it is safe to use, and therefore she agrees to the plan (388). A good spy analyzes the source of the information *and* the trustworthiness or credibility of the agent providing the information when evaluating the information gleaned.

So, off we go to the Room of Requirement! Harry wisely brings the Marauder's Map, the wonderful map that shows the location of everybody inside the grounds of Hogwarts. As we all know, the map looks like a blank piece of parchment paper until Harry uses his wand and promises that he is "up to no good," thereby activating the map (389). When Harry is done using the map, he again uses his wand and says, "Mischief managed," and the map returns to what *appears* to be a blank piece of parchment. And as we all know from book 3, *Harry Potter and the Prisoner of Azkaban*, this wonderful map was created by Harry's father, James Potter, and his three best friends: Sirius, Peter Pettigrew, and Lupin (*PA* 347, 355).

The Marauder's Map uses a magical version of invisible ink. While Muggles obviously don't have access to magic, invisible ink is still employed by spies throughout the world.

Once the trio knows the coast is clear, they enter the Room of Requirement, which is exactly as Dobby tells them: a room that provides the user with exactly what he or she needs. In their case, it is already stocked with everything they need for their training. Ron points out that the cushions will be great for stunning practice. To Hermione's great pleasure, the shelves are stocked with numerous books about the Dark Arts and defense against them. Harry even finds a coach's whistle! There are Dark Detectors—instruments that determine whether there's any Dark Magic around. These are

CHAPTER 18

of course used for counterintelligence (to see if there is another spy in the area), but it is also noted that these instruments can be fooled (390).

Now that they have found the room, it is important that they develop an **organizational plan** or scheme and formally select a leader. Since Harry will be providing the instruction, it makes perfect sense that he should be the leader (391).

Now to organization. It is important to select a name for the group. Identification with a group and a name creates camaraderie, that sense of belonging that builds loyalty to your fellow members. The students realize that they need a name that can be spoken without revealing what they are talking about or relaying any secret information to eavesdroppers (392). They need a word or phrase that will sound innocuous on the surface but that conveys meaning to those in the know.

Cho first suggests *Defense Association,* or DA for short. Ginny then suggests Dumbledore's *Army* because that is the Ministry's worst fear—or, should we say, *Fudge's* worst fear: that Dumbledore is going to use the students to create his own army. The group immediately agrees to the name, making Dumbledore's Army official (392)!

When it comes to training, as always we should start at the beginning. (If you're now humming "Do Re Mi" from *The Sound of Music,* then you already know this simple rule! Now *that's* what we call a real digression!) A witch or wizard cannot do sophisticated spells or sophisticated acts until she or he has learned the basics. In learning karate, we begin with katas, which are very formal steps in a progression from position to position, used to perfect specific movements one at a time. The same is true in the first position, second position, third position, fourth position, and fifth position of the feet in ballet.

The basics are essential and should never be ignored. Thus, when the members of the newly named Dumbledore's Army begin their training, Harry begins with a very basic defense: *Expelliarmus* (the Disarming Charm). One student objects to learning such a simple spell, until Harry mentions that he used it himself against Voldemort.

PART 1

Suddenly the spell does not seem so basic, and the training begins (392). Harry provides encouragement to Neville and instruction to everyone.

It is important to note that Harry, by becoming the teacher and leader of Dumbledore's Army, has assumed a leadership role. He grows in this role by developing class plans ahead of time and then, during class, working with the students one-on-one to help them develop their skills (393–96).

Harry also has an *organizational plan*—he directs the students to work in teams so that he can circulate through the room and assist them in perfecting the spells or jinxes as they practice. Harry finds it strange that the students are doing exactly what he asks of them, following his instructions. He has never been a teacher or leader before, but he is one now (392–93)!

NOTE TO SELF: *Being a leader is much more than just issuing orders: being a teacher and a leader involves understanding the people you are leading and their abilities, and helping them become better at whatever they need to learn.*

FURTHER NOTE TO SELF: *A leader also needs to have and convey empathy, and to treat people with respect.*

In the film version of *Harry Potter and the Order of the Phoenix,* Harry wisely points out that every great wizard had to begin at the beginning: no wizard or witch knew these spells or jinxes until they were first taught to use them.

Harry does quite well as a teacher, somewhat to his surprise. He does well teaching not only because he has prior experience in dealing with Voldemort and Dementors (experience that gives him credibility), but also because he has *humility*. Remember when Harry told his soon-to-be followers at The Hog's Head that when in danger, he often did not know what to do, that he survived as much by luck as by skill? Humility (but never false humility) will assist you every day of your life. No one likes a braggart or an egomaniac, as we all know, and beyond that, few people find those self-aggrandizers credible.

And as most of us know, the more you learn, the more you realize how little you know!

During practice, a comment from Cho makes Harry wonder whether Marietta could be a **security risk** because her parents told her not to do anything that would make Umbridge mad. Thus, security remains a concern, and a careful watch for anyone who might betray them continues throughout their training (395)—as it should be, as long as secrecy is required!

The students also appreciate the need not to get caught, and Harry soon realizes that the time has gone quickly and the students need to get back to their common rooms before they are caught in the corridors after 9 p.m. Thus, Harry checks the Marauder's Map to make sure the coast is clear and then sends everybody out in small groups so they will not be observed. The first Dumbledore's Army meeting has been a great success, and Harry and the others all feel quite proud of this accomplishment (396)!

And now a word about *esprit de corps*: **IT'S IN FRENCH!**

Okay, fine, that was *three* words.

Esprit de corps simply means "the spirit of the group." Developing camaraderie among friends—and among fellow spies—is essential. The members of Dumbledore's Army are taking a risk by meeting secretly against Umbridge's express orders. Mutual risk and mutual danger create mutual respect, cohesion, and—dare we say it?—esprit de corps!

Soldiers put themselves in harm's way to save other soldiers or to remove an injured comrade from the battlefield—not because they want to be heroes or put themselves at risk, but rather because all soldiers realize that they must be willing to save the others, just as the others must be willing to save them.

Dumbledore's Army is indeed becoming a real army of soldiers willing to protect each other, take risks for each other, and when the day comes, fight together against Voldemort and his minions and Death Eaters and spiders and giants and whatever else the Dark Lord may use!

PART 1

Tomorrow's warriors are being trained in the Room of Requirement—in secret, among friends, and very much *against* Educational Decree No. 24!

19

STICKS AND STONES MAY BREAK MY BONES . . . BUT YOUR TEMPER MAY GET YOU BANNED FROM QUIDDITCH

This chapter, "The Lion and the Serpent," teaches us lessons also about *equanimity* (not losing one's temper), *application of power* and authority, *bias* in that application, and a blatant grab by Professor Umbridge for even *more* power.

The chapter begins with the realization that holding DA meetings along a regular schedule is impossible—which actually turns out to be a plus. The meeting times have to be moved regularly to make room for Quidditch practice and other important events. As a result, there really is no pattern (or routine) to the meetings, which makes them even more secure (397).

As we discussed in our very first chapter, routine can be your enemy, unless you set a pattern intentionally to allow the routine to *assist* you in spying.

Hermione once again proves her intelligence and magical talent by developing the fake or **counterfeit** Galleons that can send messages to alert DA members to the time and date of the next secure meeting. Harry holds the master Galleon, on which he sets the date and time, and then the edges of the other Galleons change to show the same date and time (398). Harry's primary Galleon **signals** the other Dumbledore's Army members by getting hot to the touch when the new date is set. This is obviously a very secure method of relaying information—all the more so because it uses a common and innocuous object. For most students, having a Galleon in a pocket would not be an extraordinary thing—except for Ron, who has very rarely seen—nonetheless owned—a real Galleon (398). What a wonderful invention!

HERMIONE'S WONDERFUL COIN—AND ONES JUST LIKE IT IN THE REAL WORLD

Hermione's coins are a wonder of clever thinking and inventiveness. We believe that the CIA's Directorate of Science and Technology would be proud to have invented them—assuming it hadn't been done years ago! People have used coins for covert means before: the International Spy Museum has on display an American nickel with a hollow core in which to hide a message. And the Polish spy Colonel Kuklinski communicated by a Discus, a small electronic device that sent out a burst of encrypted information to the Warsaw station.

Harry and Hermione discuss the fact that, at least in part, her idea stems from the method used by Voldemort to signal his Death Eaters—that is, by the Dark Mark they bear on their arms. As we all know, the Mark is activated when touched with the owner's wand (or perhaps the wand of another?) and immediately relays a communication to Voldemort. The Death Eaters are therefore able to signal Voldemort by pressing the sign on their arm. By the same token, when Voldemort touches his mark, the result is a signal for all the Death Eaters to immediately Apparate to his location (399).

This is a fine example of how technology is *neutral* in *its use*—that is, both you *and the enemy* may use the same or similar technology, or the same and similar ideas! It is said that all's fair in love and war, and that is certainly true of spying as well.

NOTE TO SELF: *Stealing a good idea from the enemy is not just a good tactic, it's a commendable one!*

Chapter 19 also delves into the use and misuse of power. A relatively minor misuse of power occurs when Professor Snape refuses to believe the truth about a Slytherin hexing one of the Gryffindor's Quidditch players. Snape, because of his bias and as the head of the Slytherin house, refuses to believe (or at least acknowledge) the *fourteen* eyewitnesses who saw his student cast the hex (400).

We next see an example of PSYOPS, or psychological gamesmanship. The song written by Draco Malfoy, "Weasley Is Our King," is a clear and blatant psychological operation. The Slytherins are well aware that Ron, the new Gryffindor Keeper, does not play well under pressure, and that they are in a position to make him very nervous—therefore making it harder for him to be an effective Keeper. Their mean-spirited badges and song work, as is evident during the Quidditch match (402, 407).

Indeed, it gets to the point that Harry quits looking for the Snitch because he's so worried about Ron. Finally, Angelina reminds Harry to pay attention to his job, and luckily he is able to find and catch the Snitch—pulling a win out of what otherwise could have been a clear defeat. However, as we soon find out, Gryffindor's win is a **Pyrrhic victory** (407–11).

Even though Gryffindor had just won, Draco Malfoy's **provocation** of Fred, George, and Harry by insulting Harry's mother ("fat and ugly"), Harry's father (*"useless loser"*), and Harry's willingness to stay at the Weasleys' home ("Can't see how you stand the stink, but I suppose when you've been dragged up by Muggles even the Weasleys' hovel smells okay") results in the Weasley twins and Harry losing their tempers—with George and Harry using their fists to beat up Draco Malfoy like Muggle duelers (412).

PART 1

Once again, spies need to remember that it is essential to keep your cool and be in control of your emotions at all times. Draco Malfoy's taunting works, and both twins and Harry end up in a great bit of trouble indeed (412–13)!

NOTE TO SELF: *If you know your opponent well enough, a well-placed insult or taunt can goad your opponent into making a mistake or losing his or her focus.*

~~~~~~

PYRRHIC VICTORY—TURNING A WIN INTO A LOSS

The term *Pyrrhic victory* relates to two battles waged against the Romans by King Pyrrhus of Epirus in 280 and 279 BC. Although King Pyrrhus won both battles, he did so at great cost, losing many, many soldiers and his best leaders. The Romans were able to replace the men they lost, but King Pyrrhus was unable to recruit more soldiers from what would, centuries later, become part of Italy. According to the great historian Plutarch, King Pyrrhus said, after winning the battle, "One more such victory will utterly undo me!" You will find it in Plutarch, IX Parallel Lives, *Life of Pyrrhus*, 21:8, page 418 (translated by the poet John Dryden, by the way!).

Thus, even though Harry won the Quidditch match, his and George Weasley's attack on Malfoy resulted in a significant loss: Professor Umbridge declares them banned forever from playing Quidditch. (Fred had tried to attack as well, but he was forcibly restrained and unable to partake in the "fun" [413].)

~~~~~~

As we all know, discipline is normally handled by the head of house, which in this case would have been Professor McGonagall.

CHAPTER 19

She is understandably upset and about to pronounce discipline on Harry and George when she is interrupted by you-know-who (414).

No, not You-Know-Who, the *other* you-know-who. Perhaps we might give you a clue: "*Hem, hem.*"

Yes, Professor Umbridge comes to step in and "help" Professor McGonagall in properly disciplining the boys. We find out that the Gryffindor team was able to reform because Professor McGonagall had gone over Professor Umbridge's head and had Dumbledore intercede. Obviously, Professor Umbridge would have none of that, and she shows up with Educational Decree No. 25, which allows the Hogwarts High Inquisitor to have final decision-making power over punishment of students (415–16).

Obviously Professor Umbridge has the power, through the influence of the Ministry of Magic, to get what she wants, and she has planned ahead this time. As a result, Harry and the twins receive a *lifetime* ban on playing Quidditch. (Fred is banned—if his teammates had not restrained him, he would have attacked Malfoy as well [416].)

NOTE TO SELF: *You can be punished not only for the act, but also the attempt!*

Professor Umbridge is now clearly in control—and we wonder what is left of Professor Dumbledore's power as Headmaster.

Hermione and Harry, back in the common room, wait late into the night for Ron to return. When he does, he claims that he will be resigning from the team the next day. Harry notes that his departure would leave very few players, and Hermione explains about the lifetime ban (418). Things are looking very dire indeed.

And then, Hermione, looking out the window, suddenly smiles and tells her two friends something that she knows will cheer them both up: Hagrid's back (419)!

20

HAGRID AS SPY AND DIPLOMAT—RECRUITMENT AND THE CONSEQUENCES OF A CHANGE IN LEADERSHIP

Chapter 20, "Hagrid's Tale," deals primarily with analysis and perspective. We learn about recruiting people who are different from ourselves, the psychology of recruitment, and how a situation can change abruptly due to changes among those in power. We are, in fact, dealing with the area of diplomacy!

When they see that Hagrid's lights are on, the trio uses the Invisibility Cloak to run as quickly as possible to Hagrid's hut. They find a Hagrid who has been obviously beaten up—repeatedly. Hagrid, one of the worst secret keepers *ever*, immediately states that he can't tell the kids where he was, that "it's top secret." However, once Hermione asks, "Did the giants beat you up?" Hagrid tells all (422).

Hagrid notes that the Ministry has Dumbledore and "anyone they reckon's in league with him" under surveillance, so his trip had to be kept secret. He undertook this secret mission with Beauxbatons Headmistress Olympe Maxime (424–25)—another half-giant, though she refuses to admit it, who we met in book 4, *Harry Potter and the Goblet of Fire* (243–44). The pair took careful steps to conceal themselves and to lose anyone who was trying to tail them.

Imagine Hagrid and Olympe trying to lose a tail! One wonders how anybody could ever lose track of such two large individuals—but apparently they shook off their trackers before they located the giants (425–26).

We learn a lot about recruitment in this chapter, including the fact that you must do a careful analysis of the person you're trying to recruit. In this situation, Hagrid is aware that the giants' leader, known as the Gurg, is the one who has to be convinced to ally with Dumbledore's forces. In giant society, the others will follow whatever the leader decides (427).

Hagrid brings a gift for the Gurg, presents it to him, and then promises to come back the next day with another gift. The purpose of coming back a second time, as Hagrid states, is to allow the Gurg to realize that the gift is indeed a good one and not a fake or a trick—that will get him excited about receiving yet another gift. This also creates a level of *trust* when Hagrid keeps his promise by showing up the next day with a second gift. As we all find out, this goes terribly wrong when the first Gurg is killed by a rival leader that night; it soon becomes clear that the Death Eaters are there as well to recruit the giants to Voldemort's side (428–31).

ANALYSIS: *Isn't it interesting that the Gurg is killed the same evening that Hagrid and Olympe make contact with him and immediately following his acceptance of Hagrid's gift?* Based on everything that happens, it seems quite likely that the new Gurg was probably given the idea to make his move by the Death Eaters—who might also have offered some convenient *assistance*! Certainly the giants don't seem to mind their magic, though they hate Hagrid and Madam Maxime for using theirs!

NOTE TO SELF: *Always analyze any significant events and ask yourself whether they are coincidence or possibly something planned by one of your enemies.*

PART 1

~~~

CUI BONO—WHO BENEFITS?

The Latin phrase *Cui bono,* which means "To whose benefit?" is still used today when someone suspects a hidden motive.

~~~

In any event, things went quite badly for Hagrid and Madam Maxime. Although he was not successful in getting the giants to join the fight against Voldemort, Hagrid notes that "we did wha' we meant to do" and that some of the giants might remember that Dumbledore was friendly and lend support when they are needed (433). Of course, they do come to the final battle, but on the side of Voldemort (*DH* 626, 647–50, 702–3, 727, 733)!

This mission illustrates the essence of diplomacy: communicating facts to a potential friend, or even an adversary, in an attempt to persuade while at the same time laying the groundwork for a potential alliance.

NOTE TO SELF: *Diplomacy is a patient art requiring many attempts, occasional failures, and the careful application of subtlety while being as honest as the situation allows.*

Then there's a knock at the door, and the kids hide under the Invisibility Cloak. The guest is of course Professor Umbridge, who attempts to interrogate Hagrid about where he has been. Hagrid does very poorly in answering her questions, claiming that he wanted to get a bit of fresh air for his health. His health obviously had not improved while he was gone, and, as Umbridge points out, gamekeepers don't need to travel to get fresh air because they *work* outside. During her interrogation, Umbridge makes a reference to mountain scenery, which Harry and Hermione immediately perceive as a hint that *she knows* where Hagrid was and what he was doing (437).

CHAPTER 20

ANALYSIS: *How does Umbridge know so much about where Hagrid had been?* Because the Ministry of Magic has its *own* sources—and certain people (such as Lucius Malfoy) are able to obtain inside information from Voldemort and his Death Eaters and relay that information to the Ministry.

In other words, *Voldemort is playing one side against the other.* He is using the Ministry to inform the Wizarding world that he has *not* returned, while at the same time using his own agents to sow discord. More importantly, he can use the unknowing Cornelius Fudge and his sycophants at the Ministry to do his bidding—like taking over Hogwarts, discrediting Harry and Dumbledore, and preventing the students from learning the truth or practicing Defense Against the Dark Arts. Voldemort is *very* good at sowing disinformation and confusion—all to his own ends.

NOTE TO SELF: *At repeated denials of the existence of something, people tend to quit looking for any evidence of its existence— and when evidence of its possible existence comes to light, they tend to disbelieve it.*

Chapter 48 will cover some of the mistakes and weaknesses of intelligence analysis, such as groupthink, mirror imaging, stereotyping, blindness, overload, and politicization. But we have a ways to go first!

21

HAGRID'S UNSEEN LESSON—HARRY'S "WET" KISS—A SNAKE'S·EYE VIEW TO A KILL

Chapter 21, "The Eye of the Snake," also deals with analysis and perspective, the psychology of those you are teaching, the complexities of human emotion, and the importance of perspective, including that of a snake.

Hagrid is back as a teacher, with Professor Umbridge evaluating him (446–49). Hagrid's lesson, as Hermione notes, is actually a very good one (450). Hagrid brings Thestrals to class, but of course, as we all know, Thestrals can only be seen by those who have witnessed death. Thus, Harry, Neville, and one other student are able to see the Thestrals, while the other children only see meat being devoured by some invisible animal (443–46).

Once again, *perspective* comes into play as Professor Umbridge evaluates Hagrid—though, here, the right word might be *bias* or *prejudice* instead. (Or possibly *ridiculous* is the most appropriate term!) It is obviously unfair to be evaluated by somebody who is *biased* against you.

CHAPTER 21

ANALYSIS: *Is Professor Umbridge likely to be fair to Hagrid when she evaluates him?* In a word, no. Let's analyze what we know: 1) As Sirius mentioned earlier, Professor Umbridge loathes part-humans (302). 2) We also know that Professor Umbridge is *against* Professor Dumbledore (308) *and* that Hagrid is employed at Hogwarts *because* of Dumbledore (*PA* 93). 3) We also know that Hagrid is completely loyal to Dumbledore. 4) Hagrid has just returned from a secret mission *for* Dumbledore (424–25)! So, no surprise—the evaluation doesn't go well (446–49).

We next observe a discussion between Ron and Harry about Sirius and the upcoming Christmas break. Harry will be at the Burrow with Ron and his family. Harry is understandably concerned about Sirius and unhappy that Sirius has to spend Christmas by himself at number twelve, Grimmauld Place. This is yet another example of Sirius having to "tough it out" and stay put so he is not captured—and at the same time demonstrates that sometimes the secret agent's primary duty is to lie low, despite the loneliness and isolation (452).

Harry continues to teach the members of Dumbledore's Army (452–55). It is clear that they have progressed quite nicely. After reviewing and practicing what they have learned so far, the members leave in twos and threes so they will not be observed in a large group leaving the Room of Requirement (455). This is obviously good trade craft.

Harry sees that Cho is waiting around and has sent her friend Marietta away, so he—absorbing this fact—hangs around pretending to straighten pillows (a pretext!). This gives Harry an opportunity to talk to Cho one-on-one (455). Good observation, Harry!

Part of their discussion includes why it was that Cedric died and whether he might have survived, had he known the defensive magic they are practicing now. Harry explains, with a great deal of compassion, that Cedric *did* know these spells and that he was really good at magic—but if Voldemort wants you dead, you're going to end up dead (455).

ANALYSIS: *Why didn't Voldemort kill Harry at the same time he killed Cedric?* Because Voldemort *needed* Harry so he could return to a more normal form. And, as you'll remember, the only reason Harry was not killed the previous June was that Voldemort needed Harry's blood to get his body back (*GF* 642).

Cho tells Harry that he is a good teacher, and Harry finally gets to kiss Cho (457).

Back at the common room, Hermione and Ron ask him about that kiss, and Harry mentions that it was "wet" because Cho was crying at the time (459). Ron, in his normal state of girl-related oblivion, suggests that Harry's kissing ability might have produced this result. Hermione corrects him and describes in short—even abrupt—fashion all of the emotions that were most probably going through Cho's mind: grief over Cedric's death, confusion about her feelings for Harry, and concern about betraying Cedric by dating Harry are just a few (459). Hermione has just demonstrated her ability to apply psychological analysis.

Ron points out that nobody can have that much inside them at one time—they'd explode! Hermione quite correctly rebukes Ron, suggesting that the fact that he doesn't (yet) have the ability to read emotions or another person's psychological make-up doesn't mean everybody is like him—though not in so many words: "Just because you've got the emotional range of a teaspoon doesn't mean we all have" (459). Ouch!

Harry, reviewing the day's events as he tries to fall asleep, decides that he needs a class explaining how to understand the opposite sex. This, he feels, would be much more worthwhile than Divination (462). How right he is!

The chapter ends—as we all know—with Harry falling asleep and dreaming about slithering down a familiar hallway, seeing what the snake sees and even feeling that he *is* the snake—as he is attacking Mr. Weasley (462–63)! Professor McGonagall—who had been summoned because Ron, Dean, and Seamus thought Harry was ill—immediately believes Harry's story and takes him to see the Headmaster (465).

ANALYSIS: *Why did Professor McGonagall believe Harry?* Because she had knowledge of several essential facts: 1) Mr. Weasley was at the Ministry of Magic, guarding something; 2) Voldemort owns a gigantic snake; and 3) Harry is somehow able to read Voldemort's mind or perceive his emotions.

So—on to the next chapter!

22

SEEING THROUGH THE EYES OF THE ENEMY— SLITHERING TOWARD BETHLEHEM—A PORTRAIT IS WORTH A THOUSAND WORDS

Chapter 22, "Saint Mungo's Hospital for Magical Maladies and Injuries," teaches us the value of observing what is going on in real time, seeing things through the eyes of the enemy (*perspective*, or more accurately *point of view*), and the importance of rapid communication in an emergency.

Harry—who had just seen Voldemort's snake, Nagini, attack Mr. Weasley—has been rushed to Dumbledore's office by Professor McGonagall, thanks to her quick analysis of the situation. Once again, we see that you have to use a password to enter the Headmaster's office—this time "Fizzing Whizzbee" (466).

ANALYSIS: *Who gets access to the password to be able to get into Professor Dumbledore's office?* Let us note that it is the *professors* who know the password; it is not bandied about and given to the students so that they could all go rushing up to ask the Headmaster unimportant questions or bother him about matters more appropriate for the Heads of Houses!

CHAPTER 22

NOTE TO SELF: *Professors always have inside information!*

Dumbledore, it turns out, is still awake (467). Does the man ever sleep?

Upon learning that Mr. Weasley may be injured and that Harry saw it happen, Dumbledore immediately—well, not quite immediately—acts. Instead of issuing quick and decisive orders, Dumbledore asks Harry for the details of what he saw and how he saw it. Only then does he instruct the portrait of a former Headmaster, someone named Everard, to "raise the alarm, make sure he is found by the right people" (468–69).

Obviously Mr. Weasley is in enemy territory (what spies call a denied area) and could be found by the wrong people. Dumbledore can use the headmasters' portraits for immediate communication—a powerful tool indeed! As Dumbledore discloses, certain headmasters are so famous that their portraits hang in more than one place—and Everard's portrait in particular hangs not only in Dumbledore's office, but also at the Ministry of Magic (469).

Dumbledore's next step is to keep the reality of the event out of the public eye—or at least from Ministry officials.

ANALYSIS: *Why does Dumbledore want to keep the attack on Mr. Weasley secret from the Ministry?* Because the Order of the Phoenix is sending its members into the Ministry—without permission from the Ministry—to protect something (as we later learn, the prophecy). This is a covert mission, and Dumbledore wants to keep it that way. He does not want the Ministry officials to know the importance of the prophecy or the fact that the Order is secretly guarding it. If the attack on Mr. Weasley is discovered, or, more accurately, if the *location* of the attack on Mr. Weasley becomes known by the Ministry, the operation will no longer be covert.

Moreover, if the Ministry finds out that Dumbledore was

able to discover the attack *before* the Ministry knew about it, then the Ministry would realize that Dumbledore has agents or sources *inside* the Ministry, thus putting those **sources and methods**—the people who provide information and the tools they use to get it—at risk. Thus, Dumbledore is taking the necessary steps to prevent the Ministry of Magic from learning about his covert operation!

Dumbledore tells Fawkes, that wonderful phoenix, "We, will need . . . a warning" (470). Although Dumbledore doesn't say why he needs a warning, it is easy to guess that a certain toadlike woman who has powers of inspection and seems to be nosing into everything might suddenly appear. As such, Fawkes is assigned to be a lookout, prepared to inform Dumbledore when Professor Umbridge (or anyone else) shows up (470).

ANALYSIS: *Why does Dumbledore care whether Dolores Umbridge shows up? What is being said or discussed that needs to remain secret?*

Although we don't find out until book 7, *Harry Potter and the Deathly Hallows*, it is clear that Dumbledore already suspects that Harry has a connection with Voldemort, that Harry is able to perceive Voldemort's feelings or emotions when they are extremely high or low, and that, in this particular instance, Harry was actually able to *see* through the eyes of Voldemort's snake. This incident convinces Dumbledore of Harry's special connection to Voldemort. He has determined, through intelligence analysis, that there is in fact some concrete and important connection between Harry and Voldemort.

Thus, the second reason Dumbledore wants to keep this incident secret is because he does not want anyone to know about that connection. Of course, we could argue that Dumbledore is just protecting Harry from further accusations or ridicule. But there is a bigger issue at hand: the ability to see what Voldemort is doing has both value and danger!

The *value* of these visions is clear. Knowing what Voldemort is up to would give an advantage to the Order of the Phoenix. However, the connection comes to Harry on a very irregular basis and could not be used often. The *danger* is that the *converse* might happen—that is, Voldemort being able to see *through* Harry's eyes and determine what *Harry* is doing. In addition, if Voldemort became aware of the connection between his own mind and Harry's mind, he might be able to read Harry's *thoughts* as well.

ANALYSIS: *Why would Voldemort want to see into Harry's mind?*
We all know that Voldemort wants to kill Harry. Were he in a position to see where Harry is and what he is doing at all times, and to know (more importantly) when he is *not* protected by Dumbledore or other members of the Order of the Phoenix, Harry would be an easy target indeed!

Dumbledore understands all this and realizes that the connection, like most communication devices and technologies, can be used by both sides!

NOTE TO SELF: *Communication devices and technologies can become double-edged swords, with your opponent using the same device or technology to find out what you are doing!*

While they wait to see whether Mr. Weasley has survived the attack, Professor Dumbledore uses several magical instruments and technologies. When a wisp of smoke in the shape of a snake comes out from one of his instruments, Dumbledore says "naturally, naturally" (470).
Perhaps this is the moment when Professor Dumbledore realizes that Harry is himself a Horcrux and that the snake is a Horcrux as well! *If this is true, should he have taken Harry aside and told him what he suspected?*

ANALYSIS: *Why doesn't Dumbledore tell Harry he is a Horcrux?*
The answer is obvious: telling Harry at this point that he has a piece of Voldemort inside him would be psychologically

harmful. Dumbledore, still looking at his instrument, says, "But in essence divided?"

Dumbledore is most probably referring to the splitting of souls and creation of Horcruxes by Voldemort (470). Perhaps he knows by now (from the prophecy and his analysis) that the only way to kill Voldemort is to destroy *each* of the Horcruxes, which by definition means that Harry, our hero, must die!

Wow! What a twist! But surely J. K. Rowling won't let Harry die! No way! There must be a way out of it, don't you think? Time (and book 7) will tell!

There is another reason for Dumbledore to hide what he has just surmised: Dumbledore doesn't want Voldemort to know how much *he* knows on the subject of the Dark Lord's soul, and disclosing this fact to Harry or anyone else might result in Voldemort learning the truth or at least learning what Dumbledore knows.

Former Headmaster Everard reappears, reports that he shouted until someone came running to assist Mr. Weasley, and informs Professor Dumbledore that they had indeed found Mr. Weasley, badly injured. Everard then adds information obtained by another portrait, one of Dilys Derwent, that Mr. Weasley has been sent to St. Mungo's Hospital for Magical Maladies and Injuries (471).

Dumbledore plans to send Fawkes to alert Mrs. Weasley to the emergency when the phoenix is done serving as lookout, pointing out that "that excellent clock of hers" might already have alerted her to her husband's state of "mortal peril" (471).

After the Weasley children have joined them, Dumbledore decides to send everyone first to Sirius's home (headquarters)—once again employing number twelve, Grimmauld Place, as a safe house—and he asks the portrait of Phineas Black to advise Sirius that they will be coming shortly (473).

Dumbledore makes a Portkey to transport everyone to the safe house (472), informing them that it is a much more secure method of transportation than Floo powder because "the Network is being watched" (474). Once again, we see spy craft at its best: analysis used to determine modes of transportation to a safe house that is not being observed by the Ministry of Magic.

Fawkes gives the warning that someone is coming, and everybody uses the Portkey to make a hasty exit (474).

ANALYSIS: *Why didn't everybody go directly to the hospital, as would normally be the case?* The answer is that Dumbledore does not want anyone to know that he is running a covert operation inside the Ministry or that Harry was able to observe Nagini attacking Mr. Weasley. If they showed up *before* the message had gotten to Mrs. Weasley ("his children knowing about it seconds after it had happened"), those loyal to the Ministry of Magic (and especially to Voldemort) would wonder how they came to know *before* the Ministry learned that Mr. Weasley was injured (476). In other words, rushing to the hospital at that moment would have indicated their prior knowledge of the event and resulted in disclosure of their sources and methods.

PROTECTING SOURCES AND METHODS

In the spy world, some of the most closely guarded secrets are sources and methods. *Sources* are the individuals providing the information or, in some situations, the technology used to obtain information. *Methods* include both the manner in which information is gathered and technology used to gather it.

If the enemy knows *how* you are receiving information, it can take **countermeasures** to *defeat* that method or *remove your source*. Thus, in the spy world, the person ultimately receiving the intelligence usually receives *only* the information, and no data on the sources or methods, in order to protect the source's identity.

PART 1

The difference between intelligence itself (the end product) and the person or device *providing* the intelligence is an important aspect of spying, for obvious reasons. By restricting the number of people who actually know the sources or methods, you reduce the chances of that information getting out to the other side.

∿∿∿∿∿∿∿∿∿∿∿∿∿∿∿∿

As hard as the decision might have been to make, Dumbledore was right to make the Weasley children and Harry wait at head-quarters while no one else knew what happened (476–77). While the children wait for information, Ginny—becoming a spy in her own right—uses analysis to figure out a cover story and other basis of information so that they will not disclose the way in which they found out about Mr. Weasley's injury (476).

Although the development of a cover story might be beneficial, in reality there's not much difference between waiting at headquar-ters and waiting in a room at the hospital. In addition, Sirius rightly points out that Mr. Weasley would not want his role with the Order discovered: "Your father knew what he was getting into, and he won't thank you for messing things up for the Order! . . . This is how it is—that is why you are not in the Order—you don't understand—there are things worth dying for!" (477).

There is a higher duty and a higher cause at issue here. But, to Sirius's credit, he *does* understand the children's viewpoint and, even when Fred unknowingly hits a sore spot, shows compassion for their worries: "I know it's hard, but we've all got to act as though we don't know anything yet." Begrudgingly, the children accept the decision to stay put.

While waiting for news on Mr. Weasley, Harry analyzes how he was able to witness the snake attacking Mr. Weasley. He realizes that *he* wasn't the snake, but he is confused about the intense hatred that he felt when he saw Dumbledore (477–78).

Fawkes arrives with a message from Molly that defuses some of the tension: Mr. Weasley is still alive (478). Everybody is relieved, and there is time for them to relax or sleep—and time for Harry to tell Sirius it was as if he had a snake inside him and describe his confusion about his connection with Voldemort (480–81).

When it's finally time to go to the hospital, they disguise themselves as Muggles so as to arrive unnoticed. Tonks and Mad-Eye escort them to the hospital. When Tonks realizes that Harry is seeing not the future, but the present, she says, "It's odd, isn't it? Useful, though . . ." (481–82). Indeed, seeing what your enemies are doing or who they are attacking is especially useful, though, as discussed above, also can create a risk that the enemy can see back through to you as well.

NOTE TO SELF: *When using a device to spy on an enemy, consider whether the enemy can use the same device to see what you are doing!*

It is clear on the way to the hospital that Harry is under protection: Mad-Eye seizes his shoulder to prevent the two of them from being separated (483). Harry is indeed a valuable asset who is being protected not only because Voldemort is trying to kill him, but also because Dumbledore knows the prophecy about Harry and Voldemort and how it relates to their mutual destiny.

As at the train station at platform nine and three-quarters, the Muggles do not see Harry and the others entering a department store that is closed for refurbishment (483–484). The store, of course, is St. Mungo's itself!

As everyone enters the hospital, they see the portrait of Dilys Derwent, who was a healer and then Headmistress at Hogwarts. That explains why Derwent's portrait hangs both in the Headmaster's office and at St. Mungo's (485).

After the children are reunited with Mr. Weasley, Fred asks his father, who is reading the *Daily Prophet*, whether the attack is in the paper. Mr. Weasley answers, "No, of course not," for the Ministry wouldn't want everyone to know that "a dirty great serpent" had gotten into the Ministry of Magic (489). Nor would the Ministry

PART 1

want everyone to know that Mr. Weasley was attacked, assuming
that the Ministry is even aware where Mr. Weasley was when he was
injured or what he was doing (489). Odds are, Mr. Weasley and his
rescuers lied about where he had actually been attacked, don't you
think? Otherwise, there would be some explaining to the authorities
about why Mr. Weasley was in a corridor leading to the Department
of Mysteries!

In the discussion of what happened, Mr. Weasley starts to make
a statement about where he was when he was injured, but is quickly
interrupted by Mrs. Weasley. George understandably jumps in,
stating, "You were guarding it, weren't you? The weapon? The thing
You-Know-Who is after?" (489–90).

Fred then confirms with Harry the fact that Voldemort has a
snake—thereby demonstrating his own conclusion that the attack is
tied to Voldemort himself (490). Fred and George are clearly using
proper analysis of what has happened and why, and have reached a
proper conclusion about what Mr. Weasley was doing at the Department of Mysteries.

Handily, the twins have their Extendable Ears at the hospital.
Thus, the young spies all overhear Mad-Eye's statement that Voldemort might be *possessing* Harry (491). If Harry wasn't concerned
enough before, he certainly has every reason to be concerned now!

BEING BUGGED IN THE MUGGLE AND WIZARDING WORLDS

We already know about Fred and George's Extendable
Ears, but the best bugging device is described in book
4, *Harry Potter and the Goblet of Fire*. When puzzling
over how muckraking journalist Rita Skeeter seems able
to overhear very private conversations, Harry explains
to Hermione the Muggle world's methods of bugging
someone:

194

"Maybe she had you bugged," said
Harry. . . . "Bugged?" said Ron blankly.

"What . . . put fleas on her or something?" . . . Harry
started explaining about hidden microphones and
recording equipment. Ron was fascinated, but
Hermione interrupted them. "Aren't you two ever
going to read *Hogwarts: A History*? . . . All those
substitutes for magic Muggles use—electricity,
computers, and radar, and all those things—they all
go haywire around Hogwarts, there's too much magic
in the air. No, Rita's using magic to eavesdrop, she
must be" (*GF* 574–75).

Later on, Harry reminds Hermione that she is supposed
to be trying to figure out Rita's "magical methods of
bugging!" (*GF* 613). Harry's second reference to "bugging"
gives Hermione an epiphany, and she heads to the library
(of course) "just to make sure" (*GF* 613–14).

By the end of the fourth book, Hermione has captured
Rita and explains to Harry and Ron how they were
"bugged":

"How was she doing it?" said Harry at once.

"How did you find out?" said Ron, staring at her.

"Well, it was you, really, who gave me the idea,
Harry," she said.

"Did I?" said Harry, perplexed. "How?"

"Bugging," said Hermione happily.

"But you said they didn't work—"

"Oh, not electronic bugs," said Hermione. "No, you
see . . . Rita Skeeter"—Hermione's voice trembled
with quiet triumph—"is an unregistered Animagus.
She can turn—"

PART 1

Hermione pulled a small sealed glass jar out of her bag.

"—into a beetle."

"You're kidding," said Ron. "You haven't . . . she's not . . ."

"Oh yes she is," said Hermione happily, brandishing the jar at them (*GF* 727–28).

So once again, Hermione applies wonderful intelligence analysis, capturing the eavesdropper, blackmailing her, and making her promise not to write for a full year (*GF* 728). And, of course, it is Hermione who brings Rita out of retirement the next year to write the truth about Harry in *The Quibbler* (564–69).

But we aren't there yet!

23

TO BE OR NOT TO BE (A SNAKE)—BRAVERY, RISK, AND THE CONSEQUENCES TO THOSE WHO SERVE—KEEPING, REVEALING, AND ACKNOWLEDGING FAMILY SECRETS

Chapter 23, "Christmas on the Closed Ward," provides a superb description of analysis, bravery and risk, and the importance of family history and family secrets. Much of the analysis in this chapter is directly related to Mad-Eye's statement Voldemort might be *possessing* Harry (491).

Harry's subsequent analysis in this chapter—though incorrect in its conclusions—is an important example of *reviewing each of the possible explanations* for an event. In this case, Harry is analyzing all possible reasons for his own ability to see through Nagini's eyes as she attacked Mr. Weasley (492–93). This is the essence of intelligence analysis.

It should also be noted that Harry, who is understandably exhausted, is not at his level best when he performs this analysis.

NOTE TO SELF: *Try not to think things out when overly tired.*

PART 1

Let's review Harry's analysis in detail, looking specifically at each *conclusion*, the *basis* of that conclusion, and the information that results in the *rejection* of that conclusion. We will also observe that Harry does not reach the *correct conclusion* until he has the assistance of his two best friends and, significantly, Ginny Weasley—the only person who has *actually been possessed by Voldemort* and lived to describe what it was like (500).

We will review each of Harry's concerns and assumptions one by one until, at the end of the chapter, Harry finds the answers (or at least the realization that he is not being possessed by Voldemort, or putting his friends at risk) by using the basic tools of intelligence analysis.

CONCERN NUMBER 1: *Professor Dumbledore is unwilling to look Harry in the eye because he believes Harry is being possessed by Voldemort.* Harry wonders how it would feel if Voldemort came bursting out of his head as he did out of Professor Quirrell's head in book 1, *Harry Potter and the Sorcerer's Stone* (*SS* 293). He wonders if his green eyes would turn into snakelike slits when looking at Dumbledore. He feels dirty and tainted, fearful that there is something inside him, perhaps a piece of Voldemort (a Horcrux perhaps?) (492).

CONCERN NUMBER 2: *Harry did not just see through the snake's eyes, but actually became the snake* (491).

And therefore,

CONCERN NUMBER 3: *Harry is the weapon that Voldemort is after.* Harry concludes that he himself is the weapon that Voldemort wants and that the guards surrounding Harry are not for his protection, but rather for the protection of *other* people (492).

CONCERN NUMBER 4: *Harry was the snake that attacked Mr. Weasley at Voldemort's behest.* Harry concludes that Voldemort could be inside him right now, listening to his thoughts (492).

Once arriving at Grimmauld Place, Harry is allowed to go upstairs to go to sleep, but instead he paces about, trying to figure out how he became a snake (493–94).

CONCERN NUMBER 5: *Harry could be an Animagus.* He quickly rejects this proposition because he would know if he were an

Animagus (493).

CONCERN NUMBER 6: *Voldemort could be an Animagus who takes the form of a snake.* When he does so, both of them might transform into the snake, due to their mysterious connection. Harry concludes that this is unlikely because it would not explain how he got to and from London in the space of about five minutes (493).

CONCERN NUMBER 7: *Voldemort is able to transport himself and Harry because he is one of the most powerful wizards in the Wizarding world.* Harry concludes that Voldemort would have no problem transporting people, including Harry, to the places where he wanted them to go (494).

CONCERN NUMBER 8: *Voldemort might be able to see through Harry's eyes and read his thoughts.* This would give him knowledge of headquarters, members of the Order, Sirius's location, and the information Harry has heard that he should not have heard (494).

CONCERN NUMBER 9: *If Harry is actually an unwitting spy for Voldemort, he must leave Grimmauld Place immediately.* Harry concludes that he would have to spend Christmas at Hogwarts so as to not allow Voldemort to see what he is seeing (494).

CONCERN NUMBER 10: *Harry cannot go to Hogwarts because Voldemort might turn him into a snake again, and there are plenty of people to harm and maim at Hogwarts.* Based on this conclusion, Harry determines that he will have to return to number four, Privet Drive, six months earlier than planned and certainly to the great disappointment and consternation of his Uncle Vernon, Aunt Petunia, and Cousin Dudley (494).

CONCERN NUMBER 11: *Once at Privet Drive, Harry would have cut himself off from any contact in the Wizarding world.* Harry therefore begins to pack (494).

But he is being watched, by a painting no less!

The portrait of Phineas Nigellus concludes that Harry is running away and informs Harry that such lack of bravery suggests that he perhaps should not be a Gryffindor. Harry exclaims, "It's not my own neck I'm saving!" Harry says that he is not running away, and Phineas concludes that Harry is not running away *to save himself,* as any good Slytherin would do, but is instead *being noble* and running away to protect the others *from* himself (494–95).

Don't forget that these paintings are lovely communication devices! Phineas Nigellus relays a message to Harry from Professor Dumbledore—to stay where he is—and Harry rejects his noble plan to escape and finally lies down, exhausted, and heads off to sleep (495–96).

We would like to make a note at this point about Phineas Nigellus's critique that children think they are the only ones who know what's going on. He tells Harry quite bluntly that those in charge do not need to tell him *why* they have told him to do something—that is, he needs to accept that he does not have the *need to know*. Phineas Nigellus also sternly reminds Harry that following Professor Dumbledore's orders has never caused him any harm (496).

CONCERN NUMBER 12: *If he is under Voldemort's control, Harry might attack someone else once he falls asleep.* Harry, after hearing Dumbledore's orders, concludes that it is okay not only to stay, but also to sleep. However, he is still worried that he will become the snake again and attack somebody (496).

When Harry does fall asleep, he returns to the recurring dream of walking down the corridor and going up to a black door. He understands that on the other side of the black door is something he desperately wants; or perhaps it is something that *Voldemort* desperately wants (496–97)?

Harry wakes up at Ron's announcement that dinner is ready. Ron tells Harry that he can come down for dinner, or stay there and continue to sleep if he wants (497).

CONCERN NUMBER 13: *Ron, by leaving immediately, implies that he does not want to be in the same room alone with Harry.* Surely none of Harry's companions would want him at Grimmauld Place anymore now that they know what is inside him. Harry turns back over and finally gets a restful sleep, waking up very early in the morning with Ron asleep in the next bed. Harry notes that Phineas Nigellus is observing him again from his portrait (497).

CONCERN NUMBER 14: *Professor Dumbledore has assigned*

Phineas Nigellus to watch over Harry—to ensure that he does not attack anyone else. Harry cannot help but wonder whether it would be better for him to just leave and go live at Privet Drive. He again feels unclean, tainted (497).

Harry continues to hide from everybody, not going down for dinner, and actually going up another level to Buckbeak's room (498).

Around 6 p.m. the doorbell rings, and we subsequently find out that the new arrival is none other than Hermione herself, who has decided to spend the holidays at Grimmauld Place instead of with her parents. At Hermione's insistence, Harry returns to his room, where there is a warm fire, sandwiches, Ron, and to Harry's great surprise, Ginny (498)!

Hermione explains that she had to stay at Hogwarts until the term ended. Dumbledore told her what had happened, and she tells Harry that Umbridge was livid that Harry and the Weasley clan had left Hogwarts without her knowing about it, "right under her nose" (498).

ANALYSIS: *Why was Professor Umbridge so mad about the Weasleys' secret departure?* Umbridge and the Ministry are watching the movements of anyone who is in league with Dumbledore, particularly Harry and the Weasleys. The fact that they could get out of Hogwarts without Umbridge or the Ministry of Magic knowing about it shows that there is a weakness in their surveillance of Harry Potter, Professor Dumbledore, the Weasleys, and indeed all of Hogwarts.

Dumbledore, once again, has pulled a fast one on the Ministry and on Umbridge—and those in the Ministry are very unhappy to think that Dumbledore can still do things without their knowledge.

One of the best things about having friends is that they will speak the truth to you, even inconvenient truths. Hermione asks how Harry is feeling, and when he says he is feeling fine, she immediately scolds him for lying to her. She confronts him with the fact that he has been hiding from everybody. Ginny, quite unabashedly adds that his friends wanted to talk to him, but "you've been hiding" since they got back from the hospital (499).

CONCERN NUMBER 15: *Harry's friends have not been able to look him in the eye.* Hermione puts that issue to rest by asserting that they are all taking turns and happen not to be looking at each other at the exact same time (499). She tells Harry that he should quit feeling sorry for himself and informs him that she is aware of what they overheard last night by the Extendable Ears (499).

Ginny tells Harry quite bluntly that it was stupid of him to hide from the others, and that he actually knows someone who has been possessed by Lord Voldemort: herself! She informs Harry that she can tell him exactly how it feels to be possessed by Voldemort (499–500)!

Suddenly, Harry realizes that Ginny is indeed the only person who has the knowledge necessary to determine if his propositions are correct!

In short order, Ginny presents evidence that convinces Harry that he has *not* been possessed by Voldemort. He does not know of large sections of time where he does not remember things, and he does not suddenly wake up at a place without recalling how he got there (500).

Harry counters with a reference to the dream he had about Mr. Weasley and the snake, and Hermione quickly explains (*correctly*) that he has had dreams before in which he was able to observe things that were happening to Voldemort. Harry asserts that this was different, that he was *inside* the snake, and that perhaps Voldemort had transported him to London so that he could attack Mr. Weasley (500).

Hermione scolds Harry again, wishing that one day he might actually read *Hogwarts: A History* and find out that wizards and witches cannot Apparate or Disapparate into or out of Hogwarts, and as such Voldemort could not have transported him anywhere. Ron confirms this conclusion when he tells Harry that he was watching him for at least a minute *while* he was having the nightmare (500).

Thanks to his two best friends and Ginny, Harry quickly concludes that his analysis (all fourteen parts!) is incorrect. What his friends told him makes sense, and Harry *finally* concludes that he is not the weapon after all (500)!

Harry is thinking much more clearly now due to three important differences: *first*, he has had a good night's sleep; *second*, he is among friends who help him to analyze the situation (four heads are better than one!); and *third*, he is finally eating, receiving the sustenance so necessary to keeping a clear head (500).

NOTE TO SELF: *It's very hard to think logically or correctly when you are tired or hungry.*

Whew! Who would have ever thought that doing analysis was so tough?

ANALYSIS: *What is the real reason why Harry was able to see the attack on Mr. Weasley?* We find out in the next chapter that Voldemort had actually possessed the *snake* when it attacked Mr. Weasley. Harry was able to see through Voldemort's eyes, which were also the snake's eyes at that moment (532–33).

Christmas comes, and Harry is finally able to enjoy himself now that he has worked through the correct analysis. One of Harry's Christmas gifts is a gift from Sirius and Lupin, a Defense Against the Dark Arts book, which Harry realizes will be quite useful in teaching his fellow students (501–2).

Hermione, always thinking of the house-elves, has prepared a present for Kreacher, a quilt. This gives the children an opportunity to look for Kreacher's "bedroom." He is not there, but they find numerous items that he has collected, the most prominent of which is a broken picture of Bellatrix Lestrange (503–4).

ANALYSIS: *No one seems to have seen Kreacher lately: is it possible that he has left?* Sirius and the children discuss when they had last seen Kreacher—and it appears that he was last

PART 1

observed on the night when they arrived at Grimmauld Place, when Sirius told Kreacher to get out of the kitchen. Or rather, looking back a bit to the previous chapter, when Sirius said, "OUT!" (475).

Hermione (correctly, we might add) wonders if it is possible that Kreacher has left. Sirius asserts that Kreacher could not leave the home without his permission—but what if he had, by shouting "OUT," inadvertently given him permission to leave? Harry also notes that permission may not be needed, referring to the fact that Dobby had left his master's house two years ago to warn Harry about returning to Hogwarts, though he had to punish himself afterward. Sirius looks disconcerted for a moment, but then moves on to other issues (504–5).

ANALYSIS: *Where in the world could Kreacher go? Or want to go?*
Let the framed picture displayed prominently in Kreacher's hovel in the boiler room be your guide (504)!

Obviously, if Kreacher is allowed to leave Grimmauld Place, it would make sense for him to go to a prominent member of the Black family whom he adores, Bellatrix Lestrange, or *perhaps* to the home of Lucius Malfoy, where the entire clan might be found (including Lucius's wife, Bellatrix's sister, Narcissa).

Meanwhile, the Weasleys head for St. Mungo's Hospital for Magical Maladies and Injuries. Because the Underground is closed for Christmas Day, everybody is transported to the Wizarding hospital by none other than Mundungus Fletcher, who, we find out, "borrowed" a car (505). Harry surmises that, knowing Mundungus, the car was most likely *stolen*, or is at least being used without the owner's consent (505)!

Once again, a security team assembles to take Harry and the others to the hospital, made up of Moody and Lupin, with Mundungus driving (505).

The streets are fairly empty, given that it is Christmas Day.

When they arrive at the entrance of the hospital, the group enters by stepping through the glass. Mundungus drives away and parks nearby (505). We wonder, will he disappear this time? Could be a good opportunity around the corner!

When an argument starts between Mrs. Weasley and Mr. Weasley about the use of a Muggle medical technique (we call them "stitches"), the kids decide to go have some tea in the tearoom (507). Note that Harry knows what floor the tearoom is on due to his observation of the sign over the Welcome Witch's desk (508). Sounds like open-source material to us!

NOTE TO SELF: *Always try to observe and remember small details—you never know when they may be useful!*

While on the way to the fifth floor, the children see their old professor, Gilderoy Lockhart, at the landing of the fourth floor (509). As we recall from book 2, *Harry Potter and the Chamber of Secrets*, Professor Lockhart tried to erase Harry and Ron's memories using Ron's broken wand (*CS* 303). The powerful memory charm that was supposed to affect Harry and Ron backfired onto Professor Lockhart, who now can barely recall anything, but is still more than happy to provide signed autographs. A kindly nurse ropes the children into spending a few minutes visiting with Professor Lockhart as he is signing autographs in the locked ward (510).

Two very important things occur in the locked ward, one relating to a plant that was delivered to one of the patients, and the other relating to their good friend Neville Longbottom.

We can just hear Mad-Eye Moody challenging the children to *use your powers of observation*! Remember details! And constantly shouting, CONSTANT VIGILANCE! (*GF* 213, 217, 571).

But we digress, so back to the story!

The children make several observations about the locked ward. First, it appears that the individuals living there are there permanently; they have rooms or personal areas that include their personal possessions (511).

They see that someone named Broderick has been given a plant, delivered by a nurse (512). It is unfortunate no one who is adept at Herbology (Neville Longbottom, perhaps?) takes the time to look carefully at the plant. Broderick, we will soon find out, has not long to live, thanks to this nefarious Christmas gift!

The other significant observation is the presence of Neville Longbottom and his grandmother. As Neville and his grandmother are leaving, they run into Ginny, Ron, Hermione, and Harry (512).

Neville is immediately embarrassed—realizing that his *family secret* about his parents will now be known by his fellow students (513).

Harry, thanks to Professor Dumbledore, is already aware of the secret, but Ron, Hermione, and Ginny are not. Neville's grand-mother, upon seeing Neville's embarrassment, chastises Neville about that embarrassment: "You should be proud, Neville, proud! They didn't give their health and their sanity so their only son would be ashamed of them, you know!" (514).

Now all four children know that Neville's mother and father were well-respected Aurors who were driven to insanity by torture at the hands of Voldemort's followers. Harry, of course, knows that it was Belletrix Lestrange who used the Cruciatus Curse on them (514).

We get a glimpse of Neville Longbottom's fortitude when he receives, with great seriousness, an empty wrapper from his mother and looks at his classmates with defiance, seemingly daring them to laugh. Of course, that would be *the last thing* Harry, Ron, Hermione, or Ginny would think of doing. Each of them now has a much better understanding of Neville Longbottom and what he has dealt with for most of his life (515).

NOTE TO SELF: *A person's true character is often shown by the little things that that they do, particularly through a defiant act unconcerned about what others may think.*

Ron, Hermione, and Ginny all state that they had no knowl-edge of any of this, but Harry acknowledges that he *did* know about

Neville's parents and what had happened to them, stating quite honestly that he *had* known but he had promised that he would not mention it (515). His friends, significantly, fully accept Harry's decision not to tell them about the potentially embarrassing fact, even though he has shared other discoveries with them. A promise is a promise, after all.

NOTE TO SELF: *There are many types of loyalty, and one of the most significant is keeping a secret that might embarrass someone.*

Hermione considers the fact that Bellatrix Lestrange, who tortured Neville's parents, appears in a portrait in a place of honor in Kreacher's nest (515). Nothing gets by Hermione! However, despite her newfound knowledge of what Kreacher's heroine Bellatrix has done, Hermione continues to treat the house-elf with kindness and encourages Ron and Harry to do the same. As we all know, this will pay off in book 7!

NOTE TO SELF: *Kindness, like mercy, is twice blessed: it blesses the giver and the one who receives the kindness.*

~~~~~~~~~~

"THE QUALITY OF MERCY . . . IS TWICE BLESSED."

We really wish we'd come up with this phrase on our own, but we must confess that it is from a little-known writer named William Shakespeare—perhaps we've mentioned him before?

The famous quotation is derived from the famous trial scene in *The Merchant of Venice,* when Portia asks Shylock to show mercy to Antonio:

The quality of mercy is not strained;

It droppeth as the gentle rain from heaven

Upon the place beneath. It is twice blest;

PART 1

It blesseth him that gives and him that takes.

'Tis mightiest in the mightiest . . .

(Act IV, scene i, lines 182–86)

~~~~~~

Let's now take a few moments to talk about the importance of *family*, *family history*, and *family connections*. Spies must be aware how family factors into their own lives and into the lives of their friends *and* enemies: family connections in particular can help a spy gain access to information or predict another person's choices. Also a person's perception of his or her family history and values often yields insights into that person and assists in evaluating that person's actions, motives, and beliefs.

Analysis of Family History and Connections

Harry and His Mother, Lily: As we all know, Harry's mother stepped in to protect him, and the bond that choice created protects him still (*SS* 299). Even Voldemort realizes the power of Lily's act and the protection it gave Harry: "Your mother died to save you. Yes, that's a powerful counter-charm. I can see now . . ." (*SS* 317).

Harry and the Dursleys: Despite their mutual dislike, it is the connection between Harry and his relatives that makes number four, Privet Drive, a safe haven for Harry by fostering and maintaining Lily's protective charm (836).

The Weasley Family: The Weasley family is highly interconnected. Each member is very aware of how the others are doing at any moment—and likely to nose into each other's business to make sure everyone is safe. The aftermath of Percy's departure makes it clear that the bonds of the Weasley family are powerful and deeply felt—and anyone working with or against the family should take those bonds into consideration! And of course, half of them end up in the Order of the Phoenix, and by the end all are on the same side, fighting against Voldemort!

The Longbottom Family: We all know of the complicated and interconnected family history that surrounds Neville Longbottom. With that knowledge in mind, we can see how family history and connections affect Neville's choices: when Bellatrix Lestrange escapes from Azkaban, Neville redoubles his efforts in Harry's Defense Against the Dark Arts classes (553). He wants to be prepared for the upcoming fight and his own personal revenge against Bellatrix Lestrange.

Note the not-so-subtle similarities between Neville's family background and Harry's: Neville's parents paid the ultimate price in the previous war against Voldemort, driven to insanity (though not killed, as Harry's parents were). Both boys were instead raised by relatives: Neville by his grandmother, and Harry by his aunt and uncle. Of course, Neville was raised in a *loving* home, something Harry did not have.

We note that, by the end of this book, Harry will have his own family connection to Neville—even beyond the link that the prophecy created. Bellatrix Lestrange will kill Sirius, Harry's godfather, closest living family member, and father figure (805). Harry and Neville are now connected by a mutual loss, and a mutual enemy!

Family history matters. Things that happened years ago, while Harry and Neville were children, or even before they were born, shape those two young men as they grow up. The actions of our family members have consequences for us for years afterward, and even today. Many of the morals examined in the Harry Potter series help us *all* to realize this vital point.

NOTE TO SELF: *What you do and say today has profound implications for the future. Think about what you do today, realizing that there could be consequences—to you and your children not yet born.*

24

READING MINDS—THE ART OF SUBTLETY— MEMORIES AS WEAPONS

Chapter 24, "Occlumency," understandably focuses on what Muggles call the *reading* of *minds*. Believe it or not, it *is* possible to read minds and tell what people are thinking—even if you do not have Wizarding powers!

We Muggles are not dealing with magic here, or with the use of Legilimency, but rather with *the ability to comprehend what people are thinking and what their motivations are.* A good spy must be able to perceive subtleties, such as the proper interpretation of a grimace or a smile. A spy must also understand not only what a person has said, but also what that person is *really* saying—or *not* saying.

NOTE TO SELF: *You can, through careful observation, often understand what people are thinking and their motivations!*

CHAPTER 24

THE USE AND STUDY OF BODY LANGUAGE

Spies are trained in interpreting body language, for obvious reasons. Much can be "said" without talking at all! People communicate in many forms, including body language, and most people don't stop to think about what their bodies are saying, even when they think they're keeping mum!

The chapter begins as Sirius finally finds Kreacher—who has *supposedly* been hiding in the attic the whole time (516). (But we know better, don't we?) Harry, using his rapidly developing analytical skills, doubts whether Kreacher had indeed remained in the home the whole time he was missing.

ANALYSIS: *Why does Harry suspect Kreacher has been away?* Harry shrewdly notes various subtle differences in Kreacher's mood and actions, such as the house-elf being in a better mood, muttering less, and obeying more (516). Harry cannot help but wonder if Kreacher has left the house, perhaps on some secret mission, and whether he is now back at headquarters with a mission of his own! This would of course make Kreacher a mole.

Mrs. Weasley interrupts Harry and Ron's game of wizard chess to say that Professor Snape is at headquarters to see Harry (517). Harry is understandably *thrilled* to see his good friend Professor Snape. . . .

ANALYSIS: *Were we being serious about Harry being thrilled about seeing Snape?* See, *you can read our minds,* even when we really mean the *opposite* of what we said!

PART 1

Harry enters the kitchen and sees not only Professor Snape but also his godfather, Sirius, each looking away from the other—silent and clearly in a bad mood. By observation of their expressions and positions, Harry can easily surmise that the two continue to loathe each other, despite being in the Order together (518) and *supposedly* on the same side.

We soon find out that, although Snape had hoped to meet Harry alone, Sirius, as Harry's godfather, has demanded to stay; it is, of course, *his* house, so Snape has no choice. The Potions Professor has come to tell Harry that, on Dumbledore's orders, Snape will be giving Harry private lessons in Occlumency, the magical defense against mind reading, upon his return to Hogwarts.

The tension and hatred between Sirius and Snape are obvious from every word they speak to each other, and Snape is more than happy to bait Sirius about his trip to the train station and being spotted by Lucius Malfoy. Snape goes so far as to taunt Sirius about this incident (using PSYOPS, perhaps?) asserting that Sirius did it on purpose so that he'd have an excuse to "hide" at headquarters afterward (520).

Sirius's reaction is predictably bad, and by the end of the meeting the two Wizards have come very close to blows, each pointing his wand at the face of the other. Harry has stepped between them, both arms outstretched, trying to prevent either from harming the other—just as the others enter the room (521).

NOTE TO SELF: *An affront or sense of loathing between two people or groups of people—even when derived from some long-ago incident—rarely dissipates.*

We will soon find out—through Harry's observation of Snape's worst memory (645–47)—why Snape hates Sirius (and his best friends, James Potter and Remus Lupin), but we are not there yet! What we do know is when Snape asserts that Sirius is a coward, Harry becomes concerned that Sirius might respond by acting rashly and doing something risky. Here, Harry is applying psychological analysis or assessment. And his assessment is correct: at the end of this book, Sirius does exactly that when he goes to the Ministry of Magic to protect his godson and ends up being killed by Bellatrix Lestrange (805).

But we're getting ahead of ourselves! At this moment, the entire Weasley family enters the kitchen, stumbling in upon quite a scene indeed! Mr. Weasley, they report, is okay, for the Healers have found the proper antidote to the snake's magical venom (522).

This should have been a happy ending to Harry's holiday break. But Harry does not want to leave Sirius, and for the first time he is not thrilled about returning to Hogwarts for the new term, particularly with the prospect of *special lessons* from Professor Snape at least once a week. In order to prevent others from learning that he is learning Occlumency, Harry has been instructed to say that he is seeing Professor Snape for Remedial Potions (519). This is a very good cover story: anyone who has seen Harry in Potions knows that he does have trouble with that subject, and given the obvious hatred between Snape and Harry, *no one* would suspect that Professor Snape is *helping* Harry to defend himself against Voldemort! Still, Harry can't be looking forward to actually *using* this cover story! On top of that, there is also the unsavory prospect of returning to Professor Umbridge's classes (517, 522).

NOTE TO SELF: *A good cover story must be credible and based on facts readily accessible to those who might be analyzing the story.*

As Harry gets ready to leave Grimmauld Place, he tries to visit with Sirius privately, hoping to tell Sirius not to do anything too risky (523). But there isn't much time. Sirius gives Harry something to use to communicate "if Snape is giving you a hard time," but warns him not to open the package immediately because Mrs. Weasley wouldn't approve. Harry takes the package but decides that he will never use whatever the device is. He does not want Sirius to risk coming to Hogwarts to help him, perhaps resulting in his arrest and return to

Azkaban (523).

 This decision is a mistake on Harry's part—the device is a mirror that provides secure communications direct to Sirius (857-58)—but we won't know that until it's too late!

ANALYSIS: *Why didn't Sirius tell Harry to open the package and use the mirror instead of trying to communicate through cryptic messages or the fire?* Our best guess, honestly, is that it would have ruined the exciting roller-coaster plot planned for readers! Or, if you like, perhaps Sirius forgot about it? Or just lost his head in the fire?

OK, bad joke. Perhaps we should just go back to digressions!

 Once again, Harry heads back to Hogwarts with a security detail (524). This time he is escorted by Nymphadora Tonks and Remus Lupin. Tonks is disguised as a very tall woman with gray hair. As they leave headquarters, Harry watches as headquarters is "squished" out of existence (524).

~~~~~~~~

NUMBER TWELVE GRIMMAULD PLACE, STEALTH TECHNOLOGY, AND STEGANOGRAPHY

The magic that keeps people from being able to see number twelve, Grimmauld Place, is a use of what the Muggles call *stealth technology* to prevent anyone, Muggle or Wizard, from seeing headquarters. In the Muggle world, certain composites and designs allow stealth planes to come very close to invisible (to radar, at least). These include the B-2 Stealth Bomber and the F-117 Stealth Fighter. Most missions flown by such planes take place at night so the planes cannot be easily seen by the naked eye. The same is true in the spy world. Meetings are often scheduled at night so as to lessen the chance of being seen, and, if seen, being recognized.

Another interesting aspect of "invisibility" is the concept or use of *steganography*, the art and science of writing messages hidden in plain view. The term comes from the Greek word for "concealed writing." Steganography can be writing or even a set of pictures with a meaning obvious to the recipient, but innocuous to anyone else, a **microdot** found at a pre-planned location, or even invisible-ink writing on the page itself.

~~~~~~

Once headquarters has disappeared, Tonks seems quite nervous. A moment or two later, a three-decker purple bus—known as the Knight Bus—arrives. Tonks, protecting her asset (Harry) at all times, rushes Harry into the bus and only then assists in getting the others in. The conductor, Stan Shunpike, immediately recognizes Harry and begins to say his name out loud—but Tonks tells him to shut up or she will curse him to oblivion (524)!

Tonks is using forceful language—indeed, a direct threat—to keep her asset safe. Stan understandably shuts up!

Tonks is well aware that the enemies of the Order can use a trace on specific words. (We see this in action in book 7, when Death Eaters or snatchers show up whenever someone speaks the name *Voldemort* [*DH* 164, 444].)

~~~~~~

EDWARD SNOWDEN'S DISCLOSURE OF SURVEILLANCE PROGRAMS

It is now public knowledge that the National Security Agency's computers intercepted hundreds of thousands of telephone discussions and had a computer "listen" for certain combinations of specific words and phrases. Where the Death Eaters zoomed in on anyone using the word *Voldemort*, the NSA scanned individual phone conversation for words (we suspect) such as *bomb, jihad, kill,* and *president.* While many may have suspected as much for years, the use of this technique was publicized by Edward Snowden's disclosure in June 2013 of the NSA's collection of telephone metadata and the PRISM and Tempora Internet surveillance programs.

~~~~~~

Although Tonks and Lupin want to keep everyone together, there is not enough room on the bus for everyone to sit in one area. As such, the group has to split up—with Fred, George, and Ginny taking seats below, protected by Lupin, and Harry, Ron, and Hermione on the top deck with Tonks (525).

The bus—a form of Wizarding public transportation—is already full of Wizarding people, all of whom are staring at Harry. This is no surprise, given that the *Daily Prophet* has been trashing him for many months. Harry, it seems, is even *more* of a celebrity than he used to be—although, just now, they might be thinking he is a "nutter" (525).

In any event, Tonks wants to get Harry to safety as soon as possible, and so she tips the driver extra money to move their destination to the head of the line—after dropping off somebody who is ill (526).

NOTE TO SELF: *A good tip to a waiter, hotel bellhop, or cab driver can go a long way!*

The Knight Bus goes through Hogsmeade and then drops Harry and the others off in front of Hogwarts. Tonks still seems quite nervous and tells Harry that he will be safe as soon as he steps onto the grounds of Hogwarts (526), a secure area where Harry is safe from Voldemort. When Harry looks back at the Knight Bus, it has already left. He is once again safe at Hogwarts—or at least that *seems* to be the case.

CHAPTER 24

NOTE TO SELF: *Generally, it is not what you know that should frighten you—it is what you do not know that should give you the greatest concern.*

Now, we know that each of you is perfectly capable of reading another's mind, and that you all have the prescient ability to know *exactly* what your friends, boyfriend or girlfriend, and husband or wife are thinking. Thus, a course in how to "read people's minds" might be unnecessary for any of you reading this.

But, on the off chance that *some of you* may not have this ability, we will discuss *how to discern what someone is thinking* by the careful observation of facial movements, eye contact, style and tone of speech, and other nuances essential to perceiving—as best we can—what others are thinking.

For those of us not yet skilled in the art of Legilimency, J. K. Rowling provides us an excellent example of an all-too-common failure of precise communication that can occur even among friends and with the best of intentions. We speak, of course, of Cho and Harry's discussion about the upcoming Valentine's Day excursion to the village of Hogsmeade (528–29).

Let's first discuss Hermione's situational awareness when Cho arrives. While Harry, Ron, and Hermione are visiting in the corridor, Harry's putative girlfriend Cho arrives and stops by to say hello to Harry. Hermione—realizing immediately that the two might want to be alone—grabs Ron by the elbow and drags him away (528). Hermione understands the situation and the probable wishes of Cho and Harry, while Ron, as usual, is basically clueless. Off he goes, escorted away by Hermione, proving herself a keen observer as well as a powerful witch!

The discussion between Cho and Harry is one that many of us have had before—and hopefully do not have very often after that first awkward event!

Cho mentions the excursion to Hogsmeade, and Harry initially misunderstands why she is even *talking* about Hogsmeade because he is focused on setting up the next Defense Against the Dark Arts meeting. Cho then mentions that the date for the excursion is on Valentine's Day. Harry *still* doesn't get what she's driving at—and again thinks she's just asking when the next DA meeting will be (528).

Cho leaves, obviously disappointed, and Harry, his mind working furiously, *finally* realizes with a literal "clunk" what Cho was really asking about! Harry chases after Cho and invites her to go to Hogsmeade on Valentine's Day. Remember Harry's suggestion that instead of having a class on Divination, it would be much better to have a class on how to understand girls (462)? He's dead right on that one!

Too soon, it is time for Harry to attend his special class with Snape: Occlumency (529).

Snape explains to Harry that *Legilimency* is the ability to extract feelings and memories from another person's mind. Chillingly, he notes that Dark Lord is highly skilled at it (530). Occlumency is the *defense* against Legilimency, a method by which you defend yourself by sealing your mind against magical intrusion and influence (531).

There is a Muggle spy version of Legilimency based on careful surveillance. Is there also a Muggle version of Occlumency? Yes! In the spy world, it's known as *countermeasures*.

Harry inquires whether or not Voldemort can read minds, and Snape chastises him, saying, "You have no subtlety, Potter—you do not understand fine distinctions" (530). This could be said about a lot of people, we would imagine!

Snape goes on to tell Harry that "the mind is a complex and many layered thing" (530). Voldemort, through Legilimency, is able to tell when someone is lying. Snape explains that eye contact is normally necessary for effective Legilimency, but Harry seems to be an exception to this general rule. Thanks to Harry's mysterious connection with Voldemort, Snape says, "you are sharing the Dark Lord's thoughts and emotions" (531).

Snape tells Harry that only through the proper use of Occlumency is someone able to tell a lie in Voldemort's presence without being caught. Occlumency shuts down the feelings and memories that contradict the lie (530–31). Harry asks if Voldemort could know what they are talking about right now. Snape informs Harry that they are too far away from Voldemort for this to occur; plus, Hogwarts has special magical protections. "Time and space matter in magic," Snape tells Harry (531).

Importantly, Snape answers Harry's concern about seeing through the snake's eyes: Voldemort, it turns out, had actually possessed the snake at the time it attacked Mr. Weasley, so Harry was able to observe the snake through the snake's eyes. In other words, Harry was able to see what Voldemort and the snake were *both* seeing (532–33). Just as importantly, Voldemort perceived Harry's intrusion! When Voldemort attacked Mr. Weasley and Harry saw it, the Dark Lord realized that Harry was "there" and able to see the attack through the snake's (or Voldemort's) eyes.

Professor Dumbledore and Snape are therefore concerned that Voldemort may be able to read Harry's mind, observe what Harry is seeing, or plant false images in Harry's mind. Dumbledore wants Harry to close his mind to the Dark Lord via Occlumency so that he does not inadvertently become a spy on Voldemort's behalf.

In the world of spy craft, what we are dealing with here is basic counter intelligence or countermeasures. Dumbledore is aware that Voldemort is going to try to obtain information through Harry and has instructed Snape to teach Harry Occlumency as a countermeasure to such intrusion or surveillance by Voldemort (531).

UNDERSTANDING HOW IT WORKS IN ORDER TO DEFEAT IT

Just as I needed to consult an expert in order to understand the use of a laser mic on our cabin—and how to counter it—Harry's Occlumency lessons deal *first* with understanding the method used to obtain information and how it works. Once we know what our opponent is using to spy on us, *then* we get to the issue of how to defeat it.

—Lynn Boughey

PART 1

When Harry asks how Snape knows all this, Snape merely states, "It is enough that we know" (533). Once again, we are dealing with the need-to-know rule, and Harry does *not* need to know that Snape knows this because he meets with Voldemort regularly! As the Order's spy on Voldemort, Snape's job is to observe and relay to Dumbledore what Voldemort is saying, doing, and thinking. Note that Dumbledore, the case officer, relays the information to the Order of the Phoenix *without disclosing his source*!

Note also that Snape, before doing the Occlumency lessons, uses his wand to take out three silver strands of his memories and puts them in the Pensieve. These memories, which Snape does not want Harry to see, will be important later! For now, this interesting session reveals bits and pieces of Harry's memories as he attempts to prevent Snape from seeing things that he considers personal. But it doesn't go too well: at one point, Harry is apparently shouting instead of closing his mind (535).

Snape tells Harry to use his brain and not to expend unnecessary energy shouting or using his wand. Harry must empty his mind, shut down his feelings and memories, so that the person trying to extract them is unable to do so (535).

On one of his attempts to see into Harry's mind, Snape is able to see numerous things that have caused Harry fear, such as being chased by Aunt Marge's dog, being surrounded by a hundred Dementors, seeing Cedric's dead body. Snape informs Harry, "You are allowing me access to memories you fear, handing me weapons!" (534–36).

NOTE TO SELF: *Memories can indeed be used as weapons.*

Just as a person's wants or desires can be used to entice or coerce them into doing something, a person's memories, personal information, or greatest fears can be used against them.

Being a spy—and particularly being an agent **handler**—involves using basic concepts of psychology to your advantage. Knowing what makes a person tick, what a person desires or fears, is essential in order to manipulate or use that person. Although it sounds some-what unsavory, *the ability to use or manipulate people is an essential tool in being a spy.* It is impossible to recruit, direct, or sustain an agent without understanding that person well enough to influence his or her actions. Thus, we need to employ psychological assessment.

Lynn has often said that the two rules of child rearing are fear and bribery. Although this is a simple rewording of the concept of a carrot or a stick, this simplistic use of positive or negative enforce-ment is essential to the useful application of basic psychology.

But, as Professor Snape mentions, one cannot simply read on the inside of somebody's skull what they are thinking, or elicit their memories or desires or fears by a simple wave of the wand. A person's motives and thought processes are also exceedingly complex and must be analyzed carefully.

At the end of the Occlumency lesson, Harry visualizes what he thinks is his repeated dream of walking down a corridor up to a door that he cannot open. However, this time Harry goes much farther and follows Mr. Weasley to the left and goes down the stairs. Harry recognizes the hall immediately as the corridor leading to the Department of Mysteries—which he had passed when going to his trial earlier in this book (536–37).

Thanks to his vision, Harry now knows that the hallway in his dreams is a real place, *and* he knows where it is in the Ministry of Magic. He surmises that he now knows *where* the weapon is that Voldemort is seeking. Note that all this occurs while Snape is attempting to "read" Harry's mind (537).

Although Harry may now know *where* the weapon is, he does not yet understand that there are nonphysical as well as physical weapons, and that *information itself can be a weapon.* At the very least, information can be of great value to the person who desires it—as Voldemort needs the information contained in the Department of Mysteries.

The chapter ends on a humorous note, thanks to Fred and George Weasley. If the Wizarding world has a science and tech-nology division, we strongly suggest that they hire Fred and George immediately! Their latest amazing invention is what they call Head-less Hats. You simply put on the hat, and the hat *and* your head disappear. Take off the hat and your head reappears (540)!

We cannot help but wonder how soon it will be before they develop their own Invisibility Cloak—and what entertaining twist they might employ! Hermione might be the smartest witch of her age, but it's pretty clear Fred and George—despite their mediocre grades—are smart wizards as well (540)! The CIA's Directorate of Science and Technology would certainly want to recruit these two bright young lads!

The chapter ends with Harry perceiving that Voldemort is very, very happy about something that has just happened (542). Harry wonders what it might be, but he does not have long to wait. One look at the next day's *Daily Prophet* will reveal the answer and prove that, on occasion, the *Daily Prophet* actually publishes the truth (543–44). Or parts of it, anyway!

25

YOUNG LOVE IN SHAMBLES—THE GREEN MONSTER OF JEALOUSY—BRIBING SOMEONE WHO BUGS YOU—USING THE PRESS

Chapter 25, "The Beetle at Bay," focuses on the escape of ten Death Eaters from Azkaban and continues with the theme of miscommunication between our would-be young lovers, Cho and Harry—with disastrous results. We also observe Hermione—once a young first-year who would never violate a rule—blackmailing Rita Skeeter into writing a truthful account of Harry's previous year!

We begin with the revelation that ten Death Eaters have escaped from Azkaban. Hermione is the first to find out, since the news features on the front page of the *Daily Prophet*. However, very few of the students get the daily paper, and hardly anyone seems to appreciate what has happened. This is *not* the case with the faculty, who are clearly in serious discussions about the escape (543–44).

ANALYSIS: *How could ten Death Eaters escape Azkaban? Why not any other prisoners? Why only Death Eaters? Is the Ministry still in control of the Dementors and, if so, why would it authorize such an escape? Who gives orders to the Dementors? Is that*

person in league with Voldemort or under an Imperius Curse?
Or, worse yet, has the Ministry lost control of the Dementors?
Are they working on their own, or with someone else (Volde-
mort, perhaps)?

Important questions indeed!

As we found out at Harry's trial, the Dementors are *supposed* to be under the control of the Ministry of Magic. By the same token, the Ministry is *supposed* to be responsible for the issuance of orders to the Dementors. But as Dumbledore suggested to Fudge when a pair of Dementors wound up in Little Whinging without an order to be there, perhaps they are taking orders from someone *besides* the Ministry of Magic (145–46).

It is also possible that the Dementors *aren't* answering to Voldemort directly, but instead are answering properly to an employee of the Ministry of Magic—perhaps someone who is under the Imperius Curse?

Interestingly, Harry discovers who is now in control of the Dementors as he talks to Cho during the first part of their Valentine's Day date. On their stroll through Hogsmeade, the pair looks at a poster in a shop window that announces a large reward for any information about the ten escaped convicts. Our two friends note the bold portion of the notice: "By Order of the Ministry of Magic" (558).

Cho then makes an excellent observation: "Remember when that Sirius Black escaped, and there were Dementors all over Hogsmeade looking for him? And now ten Death Eaters are on the loose and there aren't Dementors anywhere. . . ." (558). Harry, who hadn't put a lot of thought into the matter until this point, realizes that the Dementors not only let the Death Eaters escape, but also aren't even bothering to look for them! Harry concludes that "it looked as though they really were outside Ministry control now" (558).

Let us return to the breakfast table and Hermione's edition of the *Daily Prophet*. She mentions the article about Broderick Bode's death at St. Mungo's Hospital for Magical Maladies and Injuries (546–47). It turns out that Bode was killed by a cutting of Devil's

Snare that was placed in a pot and brought to him on Christmas Day.

Harry realizes that they had actually seen the plant being delivered to Bode (512) and goes on to assert that one of them should have been able to stop it from happening by using observation and proper analysis: "How come we didn't recognize Devil's Snare? We've seen it before . . . we could've stopped this from happening" (547). Once again, Harry's strong ethical sense and duty to protect others shines through.

ANALYSIS: *Was the delivery of the Devil's Snare a stupid mistake or something more malevolent?* Hermione immediately realizes that nobody would make that mistake: "I don't think anyone could put Devil's Snare in a pot and not realize it tries to kill whoever touches it! This—this was murder."

She correctly states that it was not their fault: whoever sent the plant is to blame. But one additional point is not lost on Harry or the others: CONSTANT VIGILANCE!

But for now, back to Harry's Valentine's date. Harry and Cho's discussion goes well as they talk about Quidditch (always best to find a common interest and go from there!), and they soon find themselves at a coffee shop—surrounded, Harry uncomfortably notes, by other couples, all of whom seem to be holding hands, and one couple is kissing (559)! Then Harry mentions his prearranged appointment with Hermione, and things begin to go badly, very badly. Harry completely fails to apply **situational awareness**!

Though he had mentioned to Hermione that Cho might want to spend the entire day with him (555), Hermione convinced Harry that the meeting was important and that, if he had to, he should bring Cho along (556). If Hermione thinks it is important, it is important! However, the Valentine's date becomes, if you will allow us, Harry's own St. Valentine's Day Massacre.

THE ST. VALENTINE'S DAY MASSACRE OF 1929

The famous St. Valentine's Day Massacre of 1929 took place when seven members of Bugs Moran's gang were killed by four unknown assassins, probably at the direction of mobster Al Capone. The assassins arrived in a police car, serving as their cover. Two of the assassins wore police uniforms as a disguise. Two more assassins, wearing civilian clothes, opened fire and killed their targets; they were then "escorted" away from the murder scene by the two "police officers," their hands up. The four assassins drove away in the police car and were never caught.

NOTE TO SELF: *Situational awareness must be applied not only to physical danger, but also to otherwise mundane discussion with friends, potential lovers, and especially potential enemies.*

It is clear that Cho perceives Hermione as a threat—or, at the very least, dislikes that she is *not* Harry's only focus on this special day—and scheduling an appointment with Hermione during their date does not sit well with her. Indeed, Cho asks if he will be meeting with *other* girls after seeing Hermione (562)!

The green-eyed monster of jealousy has shown itself, but Harry fails to discern how to calm the savage beast!

THE GREEN·EYED MONSTER OF JEALOUSY

The color green was associated with jealousy even before William Shakespeare used the phrase in *Othello*, act III, scene iii, line 166:

> Iago: Oh beware, my lord, of jealousy!
>
> It is the green-eyed monster, which doth mock

CHAPTER 25

The meat it feeds on.

Of Shakespeare's amazing body of work, we particularly recommend this scene, in which Othello begins as a loving husband but is, by the end, ready to murder his wife. This drastic change is due to Iago's treacherous manipulations, which convince Othello that his wife has been unfaithful to him. You'll note, above, that it is *Iago* who warns Othello of jealousy, even while doing everything he can to make him jealous! Did we also note that this tragedy does not end well—particularly for Othello's wife, Desdemona? It is a fascinating portrait of expert manipulation, and also a warning of the ease with which anyone, even a successful general can be manipulated!

~~~~~~

Harry perceives the oncoming train wreck but is thoroughly unable to prevent it. Following a strained discussion about Cedric and his death—including an inquiry about whether or not Cedric said anything about Cho before he died—and Cho pointing out that Harry has already discussed what happened with Ron and *Hermione* (but *not* her), Harry *finally* understands why Cho is upset. Unfortunately, he cannot stop himself about *laughing* about the prospect of him and Hermione (562). Whoops!

NOTE TO SELF: *When you are having a serious and perhaps heated discussion with your significant other (boyfriend, girlfriend, husband, or wife), do not laugh!*

Cho's reaction is swift, and she leaves the establishment—making a scene in the process (562).

Harry tries to catch up with Cho but cannot see her in the driving rain, so instead goes to The Three Broomsticks earlier than planned to meet Hermione (563). On the way to her table he runs into Hagrid, who mentions the importance of family but refuses to disclose why he has even more fresh cuts and injuries (563–64).

PART 1

ANALYSIS: *Why is Hagrid focused on the importance of family, and is there a connection with this oblique reference and his fresh wounds?* Of course there is—but Harry does not make the connection or have time to analyze what he has just heard.

After Hagrid leaves, Harry sees Hermione and goes to join her at a table across the crowded room (564). To Harry's great surprise, Hermione is not alone. She is there with former news reporter and current least-wanted person, Rita Skeeter! Luna Lovegood is also there.

Harry knows full well that Hermione dislikes Rita Skeeter and is very confused by her presence and that of Luna Lovegood. We soon learn that Hermione wants Rita Skeeter to write Harry's true story and threatens to turn her in as an unregistered Animagus if she does not agree to do the story. Hermione has already arranged to have Luna's father publish the interview in *The Quibbler*, which explains her presence (566–68).

Don't you love J. K. Rowling's implicit slam on the press, implying that the only way to get the papers to print the truth is to force them to do so—if necessary by the nefarious means of bribery?

Time for a little review. What are the three primary methods of getting someone to do what you want? Said most succinctly: gold, fear, and duty. Said another way: Carrot, stick, principle.

Bribery uses the promise of gain—the gold, or the carrot—to get a person to do something you want done, creating a positive consequence if the action is taken; in other words, using a *payment* or *incentive* that the person *desires*. Extortion, on the other hand, uses the threat of punishment or damage—using fear, or the stick—to reach the same goal; in other words, providing a *negative* consequence (a disclosure or attack) if the action is not taken.

We assert that the third method, principle, would not apply here, because Rita Skeeter has no principles!

In this situation, Hermione uses the threat of disclosing personal and private information to *force* Rita into writing the truth about what Harry saw (569). Since Rita will not be receiving any money, it's technically not bribery (bribery involves paying somebody to do something) and is instead an act of extortion. Be that as it may, it works, and Rita agrees to interview Harry—not that she has much choice!

26

THREE EASY TASKS: USING THE MEDIA, FINDING DOUBLE AGENTS, AND UNDERSTANDING WOMEN (YEAH, RIGHT!)

The next chapter, "Seen and Unforeseen," delves into predictions, visions of the future, analysis, and proper use of the media. The chapter is filled with numerous significant tidbits, including the disclosure that the Order has penetrated Voldemort's organization—though neither we nor our heroes initially understand the significance of Snape's revelation, "Yes, Potter, that is my job."

The chapter begins with Harry and the others' great anticipation of the release of Harry's interview in *The Quibbler*. Although Harry understands that this is his one opportunity to tell everyone the truth, he is concerned about the poor reputation of *The Quibbler*, which is known for its strange articles. Many people may not believe the truth simply because of *where* it is being printed (570). Will everyone disregard the interview because of *The Quibbler*'s reputation? This relates to importance of credibility: Harry's *as well as* that of the magazine in which his interview appears.

Credibility of a *person* is necessary for that person to be believed, and credibility of a *publication* is important for the same reason.

CHAPTER 26

However, Harry really has no choice in this situation because the *Daily Prophet* is controlled by the Ministry of Magic and has spent the last eight or nine months doing nothing by impugning Harry's character (567)!

Significantly, Harry's story is believed by many, regardless of where it was printed, and provides an understandable **alternative explanation** of what is happening in the Wizarding world. Of course, now that ten Death Eaters have escaped from Azkaban, the Wizarding population will certainly start to have doubts about what is *really* going on. Indeed, the Ministry's own cover story—that Sirius Black assisted with the breakout—is now seen by many as questionable at least (579).

The changing attitude of the Wizarding world soon becomes clear from the letters Harry receives after *The Quibbler* interview— and more personally by the changing minds of some of Harry's schoolmates, particularly his fellow Gryffindor Seamus Finnigan (583).

Before *The Quibbler* arrives that morning, however, the children discuss the need for the public to know what Voldemort is capable of. Neville adds an important expansion of this thought: the people also need to know what the *Death Eaters* are capable of (571).

ANALYSIS: *Why does Neville add this point about the danger of the Death Eaters?* As we now know, it was Bellatrix Lestrange, one of the escaped Death Eaters, who tortured Neville's two parents into insanity!

On a happier note (or maybe not!), Hermione asks Harry how his date with Cho went, allowing Harry to tell the complete, sordid story (571–72) and analyze what went wrong. Hermione explains to Harry—almost as a parent would to a child—how he could have relayed the same information "differently" (572). She suggests that he should have explained that Hermione had *made* him promise to come, that he really *didn't want to* but he had no choice, and if she came along with him it would go much faster. Hermione also suggests—to

Harry's great shock—that he should have also mentioned something about how Harry thinks Hermione is ugly (572).

Hermione is trying to teach Harry the art of *subtlety*, as well as the need to understand and perceive what another person is thinking and what motivates that person (that is, situational awareness and psychological assessment). She explains to Harry—with Ron and a few others listening in at dinner—that Cho was simply trying to find out whether Harry liked her by seeing how he would react—with jealousy or anger?—when she asked about Cedric or mentioned that Roger Davies had asked her out (572–73).

Hermione is correct on all accounts, as usual. Harry asks why Cho wouldn't just ask him outright whether or not he likes her. When Ron tries to support his mate, Hermione reminds him that he has even less tact than Harry. Ron states quite matter-of-factly that Hermione should write a book about how to figure out girls (573). (Lucky for Ron, he will get that wished-for book from his two older brothers and use it to great effect—with Hermione!—in *Harry Potter and the Deathly Hallows*. But we are not there yet!)

Fred and George show up, looking forward to the Quidditch game and unconcerned about the upcoming tests. They hint that Quidditch was the only thing keeping them there, while at the same time mentioning that some of their products are being perfected (574). Hermione suggests that Quidditch is not as important as the boys think it is, and that the competition between the houses is not a good thing at all. Fred, George, and Harry are incredulous (574–75). But try as they might, Gryffindor—without Fred, George, or Harry—loses the match.

The discussion about Quidditch also shows Ginny's abilities in analysis when she corrects Harry and tells him that he is *not* banned for life, but only for as long as Umbridge is at Hogwarts: "There's a difference" (575). Ginny is astutely noting that the ban actually depends on who is actually in power—and those in authority can change or be replaced.

CHAPTER 26

NOTE TO SELF: *What can be done, can be undone. Not only do the people in power have the ability to change their minds, it is also possible for people in power to be replaced with others having different views and positions.*

~~~~~~~~~~~~~~~~~~~~~~~~~~~~~~~~

LEADERSHIP CHANGES AT THE CIA

American leadership changes with the presidential election every four years, and also depending on who has control of the House or the Senate. The head of the CIA often changes with the inauguration of a new president, though this is not necessarily the case, as shown when George Tenet (initially appointed by President Bill Clinton) stayed on after the election of the new president, George W. Bush.

~~~~~~~~~~~~~~~~~~~~~~~~~~~~~~~~

The Quibbler finally arrives during breakfast, along with many letters from people who had read the article the previous day, when it first came out. Luna Lovegood's father, the editor of the paper, also sends Harry a courtesy copy (578–79).

The article has had its intended effect (582): the truth is out for all the Wizarding world to read, and the battle waged by the Ministry against Harry has turned into a war of *information* and *influence* between the Ministry of Magic and Harry Potter (and those who believe him). It is said that having numerous independent newspapers creates a "marketplace of ideas" in which all ideas are presented and discussed, to be decided by the people based on cross-referenced facts and an appropriate and thorough search for the truth by an independent press.

~~~~~~~~~~~~~~~~~~~~~~~~~~~~~~~

PETER'S TIME IN ATHENS—AND THE VALUE OF HAVING MORE THAN ONE NEWSPAPER

When Peter was stationed in Athens, there were more than twenty different newspapers, each with its own point of view. All of these papers, along with other media outlets, such as radio and television, had to be monitored by the case officer. Only through a thorough reading, listening, and viewing of all the country's media is an intelligence officer able to fully grasp the mood of the people, the countervailing forces (political and social), and the political situation, which otherwise would be indiscernible.

~~~~~~~~~~~~~~~~~~~~~~~~~~~~~~~

Harry's first salvo in this new battle is a complete rendition of what happened that fateful night when Cedric Diggory was murdered by Voldemort and Voldemort returned. Harry is trying to "win the hearts and minds" of the Wizarding world, or at the very least trying to educate them to another version of the facts!

~~~~~~~~~~~~~~~~~~~~~~~~~~~~~~~

THE MARKETPLACE OF IDEAS—AND WINNING THE HEARTS AND MINDS OF THE ENEMY

The concept of a "marketplace of ideas" found its earliest champion in Justice Oliver Wendell Holmes, Jr., who used the phrases "free trade in ideas" and "the competition of the market" in a 1919 dissent asserting that the defendants' distribution of leaflets (against sending troops to Russia to undo the Russian Revolution) should have been protected under the First Amendment. Justice William Brennan, in a 1965 concurring opinion, merged the two phrases into one, the "marketplace of ideas."

The phrase "winning the hearts and minds" of the enemy (or even of friends) originates from the British military and political campaign in Malaysia from 1948 to 1960. The term was subsequently co-opted by President Lyndon Johnson in the early 1960s and used extensively in his speeches in support of the Vietnam War.

〜〜〜〜〜〜〜〜〜〜〜〜

The letters Harry received from the readers of *The Quibbler* provide a glimpse into what the Wizarding world thinks about Harry's version of the truth. Some call Harry a nutter, while others inform Harry that they believe him (579–80).

Perhaps the most interesting letter is from a reader who *does not take a position*, but instead states that what the Ministry of Magic is saying does not make sense, but he does not want to believe that Voldemort is back. Fred's reaction to this lack of ability to form a conclusion is insightful: "Blimey, what a waste of parchment!" (579).

When providing a report or an intelligence analysis, it is important to *make a decision* and not waste words—or parchment!

NOTE TO SELF: *If asked a specific question, answer it, or at least explain why you cannot answer it.*

FURTHER NOTE TO SELF: *When providing a conclusion, you should include the basis of that conclusion, in the form of both facts and your analysis.*

In reporting, just as it is important to provide an opinion when asked or to make a decision when a decision needs to be made, it is equally important to *tell your reader what you do not know* and to include in your report any *assumptions* that you had to make in reaching your *conclusions*. These opinions and decisions are often based on the information you have and what you *think* is true. We therefore remind you of the title of this chapter, "Seen and Unseen." You must tell your reader (or decision-maker) *what you can see*, as well as *what you cannot see*.

PART 1

~~~~~~

DONALD RUMSFELD'S "SEEN AND UNSEEN"

Former Secretary of Defense Donald Rumsfeld described in his memoir his thoughts about what we know and don't know:

"Reports that say that something hasn't happened are always interesting to me because as we know, there are known knowns: there are things we know we know. We also know that there are known unknowns: that is to say that there are some things [we know] we do not know. But there are also unknown unknowns—the ones we don't know we don't know. And if one looks throughout the history of our country and other free countries, it is the latter category that tends to be the difficult one."

—Donald Rumsfeld, Author's Note, *Known and Unknowns: A Memoir* (2010)

~~~~~~

How do you think Umbridge will react to Harry "telling more lies" in a national newspaper?

No surprise here!

Umbridge observes the sudden increase in owl deliveries to Harry; she is aware that Harry normally receives very few owls (as Harry, himself, mentions). After making this observation, she takes an active step toward investigation (580).

~~~~~~

A PECK OF OWLS—AND TRAFFIC ANALYSIS

One of the things studied by the intelligence community is *traffic analysis*, the observation of the amount (both number and size) of electronic or other communications. For example, if a known **cell** group suddenly starts calling each other much more than normal, or if the email messages exchanged by a group under surveillance suddenly increase substantially, the intelligence community will take a close look to determine whether the individuals are initiating a plan or operation.

~~~~~~~~~~~~~~~~~~~~~~~~~~~~~~~~~~~~~~

Umbridge asks Harry, "Why have you got all these letters?" Fred, at a little bit of risk to himself, asks Umbridge, "Is that a crime now?" (580).

ANALYSIS: *Should Harry tell Umbridge the truth—that he did an interview for* The Quibbler? Harry does this very analysis and quickly concludes that Umbridge will find out about *The Quibbler* interview eventually—and indeed probably quite quickly. Harry correctly concludes that it's just a matter of time before Umbridge knows anyway, so he decides to tell her the truth (580).

Harry tells Professor Umbridge that the owls are due to people reading the interview with him published in *The Quibbler*. He then boldly throws his copy of *The Quibbler* to Umbridge, whose reaction is certainly *not* "unforeseen." She is furious, takes fifty points from Gryffindor, and gives Harry even *more* detentions (581)! She immediately bans *The Quibbler* and places notices throughout the school that anyone caught with it will be expelled (581).

Hermione, to Harry's great surprise, seems to smile every time she sees one of the declarations outlawing *The Quibbler*. Hermione explains that the best way to make sure everybody reads *The Quibbler* is to ban it (581–82)!

The article is now understandably the talk of the school—among students and professors alike—though no one can admit that they have read it or own a copy. The students are forced to use spy craft or trade craft to disguise their copies as pages from textbooks so Umbridge won't catch them (582).

Although the professors are forbidden from discussing anything outside their specific areas of expertise with the students (thanks to Educational Decree Number 26), it is clear that many of the professors are *quite* pleased with Harry's actions and give him rewards or additional points for other reasons—clearly to make up for the fifty points deducted by Professor Umbridge (582). Indeed, Professor Trelawney, in Divination Class *and* in Umbridge's presence, retracts her previous prediction of Harry's certain death and replaces it with her new prediction that Harry will "live to a ripe old age, become the Minister of Magic, and have twelve children" (582–83). One can only wonder what Umbridge thought of that new prediction—and Umbridge's "predictable" retribution against Professor Trelawney comes soon enough.

CENSORSHIP AND TYRANNICAL REGIMES

One of the tools used by governments or regimes that want to control their citizens is censorship. Severely limiting the flow of information, while at the same time promoting only the party line, is a tactic used successfully and all too often by despotic regimes and dictatorial governments.

The change in **public opinion** about Harry is palpable—shown most directly by Cho telling Harry that he is brave and giving him a peck on his cheek. Another indication of the article's effects is Seamus Finnigan's retraction of what he said at the beginning of the year and statement that he now believes Harry—and has gone so far as to send a copy of *The Quibbler* to his mother (583)!

Although public opinion is mixed, it is clear that at Hogwarts, at least, the majority of students are on Harry's side. That is, of course, except for Malfoy, Crabbe, and Goyle—whose parents were *specifically named* as Death Eaters by Harry in the article. However, any reactions on their part are severely hampered by the decree itself; they cannot even admit that they had read the paper for fear of expulsion (583)!

CHAPTER 26

We find out from Luna that Harry's edition of *The Quibbler* has sold out and that her father is going to reprint the issue (583). Obviously lots of people are reading the article, which is significant. Harry was already a celebrity in the Wizarding world, due to defeating He Who Must Not Be Named the first time, when he was just a baby; now he is a celebrity again. Indeed, one of the letters he receives includes a photo of the woman who believes Harry (580).

Blimey! As Ron would put it.

It's now time to say a word about dreams: DREAMS!

Harry's dreams and his connections with Voldemort through those dreams allow Harry to be his own inside source because Harry is "inside" Voldemort's head! Thus, Harry is able to find out what Voldemort is doing and thinking regularly. Perhaps the only thing close to this level of effectiveness is Rita Skeeter's ability to become a bug and listen and observe mostly unseen—though this is an extremely risky action, because someone could step on her or swat her like a fly . . . er, beetle!

In any event, in this chapter Harry has one *dream* and one very enlightening *vision* while doing his lesson with Professor Snape.

In the dream, Harry is once again in the same hallway approaching the same door—but this time the door is ajar, and he can see a crack of light through it. Just as he is ready to open the door, Ron snores loudly and Harry wakes up (577).

In the next dream, which turns quickly into a *vision*, Harry is again seeing things through Voldemort's eyes (584–86)! Through this literary device of letting a character see what another character is doing (naysayers would call it a contrivance—sacrilege, we say!), J. K. Rowling provides very important information about what is going on in Voldemort's life at that moment.

The vision begins with Voldemort stating that he has received bad advice from Avery. Rookwood is at Voldemort's feet, fearing retribution; he tells Voldemort that he used to work at the Department of Mysteries and that he knew that Bode would not be able to retrieve the item (584–85). As a former employee of the Department of Mysteries, Rookwood has inside information that would be helpful to Voldemort. As he gives his report, Rookwood reveals that Lucius Malfoy used the Imperius Curse to make Bode go and get the item that Voldemort is seeking, and also why he failed. "Bode could never have taken it, Master," Rookwood says, "Bode would have known he could not . . . undoubtedly that is why he fought so hard against Malfoy's Imperius Curse . . ." (585). Voldemort tells Rookwood that he will need his help and all the information Rookwood can give him (585).

Voldemort then concludes that he has wasted months on fruitless schemes, and dismisses Rookwood, telling him to send Avery to him. Avery, who passed the bad advice to Voldemort, is obviously in for punishment. Harry then catches a glance of himself in a mirror— *as Voldemort.* Harry is indeed seeing what Voldemort sees at that moment! Harry understandably wakes up screaming (585–86).

Although Harry does not yet know what the Death Eaters are seeking at the Department of Mysteries, he does know precisely *where* the weapon is located. Harry and his friends are also able to determine—from this information and through analysis—Voldemort's previous plan to get the weapon and who he was using. Good information indeed (588)!

ANALYSIS: *Who was Voldemort using, in what way did he use him, and why was Bode murdered?* We know directly from Voldemort's interview of Rookwood that Bode was forced to go into the Department of Mysteries by Lucius Malfoy's Imperius Curse. We also now know that Bode's mind must have been rattled by being forced to do something that was impossible, or that he was the recipient of a powerful spell or curse protecting the item he attempted to retrieve. Hermione recalls that the nurse had said that Bode was getting better (588). That is why Bode was killed: once he recovered, he would be in a position to describe why he did what he did and perhaps be able to inform the Healers and others that it was Lucius Malfoy who placed him under the Imperius Curse.

CHAPTER 26

Significantly, Hermione is also able to figure out through intelligence analysis how Sturgis Podmore was arrested. She had assumed that Order of the Phoenix member Sturgis Podmore—who had been there the night Harry was being moved but didn't show up to help escort Harry to the train station at the start of term—was most probably on guard duty at the Department of Mysteries to protect the item being sought by Voldemort.

Hermione takes the information available to her and concludes that Sturgis Podmore was using Mad-Eye Moody's Invisibility Cloak while on guard duty, and surmises that Lucius Malfoy must have sensed he was there and had placed Podmore under the Imperius Curse to have him get the weapon, leading to his arrest by the Ministry for "attempting to force his way through a top-security door at one o'clock in the morning" (287). Thus, through the inside information Harry has obtained and careful analysis, our three good friends now know *where* the item is that Voldemort is seeking *and* the fact that the adult members of the Order are attempting to prevent Voldemort from obtaining the item by protecting it (588–89).

Now a word about using a pretext: **PRETEXT**!

When Harry is still in his room, telling Ron about his dreams, two other students enter. In order to not be overheard Ron has to use some of his own spy craft abilities. He moves closer to Harry so he can hear him, without the others being able to hear Harry, on the pretext of getting a glass of water (587). Our two friends are becoming good spies indeed!

There are just two scenes left in this important chapter, one involving Harry's Occlumency lesson (and the vision he sees during it) and the unfortunate firing of Professor Trelawney by Professor Umbridge.

During the next Occlumency session, Harry sees glimpses of Snape as a young boy—including observing Snape's parents arguing when he was a very young age (592). As Snape uses Legilimency on Harry's mind, he sees Harry's recurrent dream. But then an amazing thing happens: during the sparring bout with Snape, Harry actually gets *through* the door and *into* the Department of Mysteries (593).

Let's observe what Harry sees and then analyze *why* he is able to see it while being connected with Snape's mind.

Harry is once again in the corridor at the Department of Mysteries. He gets to the door, and in the previous dream, the door was ajar. But this time, when he is connected with Snape's mind, the door bursts open and Harry goes through it! Harry is then able to see inside the Department of Mysteries, a black-walled, black-floored, circular room lit with blue-flamed candles—with more doors all around (593).

As a result of this vision (as you surely understand, in his dreams he is sleeping, and in his visions he is awake!), Harry now knows exactly where the weapon is! The vision ends—perhaps because Snape himself stops it so Harry does not learn more. Snape demands that Harry explain himself, and Harry confesses that he doesn't know why he was able to open the door this time (593).

ANALYSIS: *Why was Harry able to get through the door this time?* In our view, it is possible that when Snape's and Harry's minds were connected, Harry was able to "see" Snape's memories of the Department of Mysteries.

This gets us to an important point: when retrieving information from a contact or agent you are running, you must take care not to *give* information to that contact or agent (accidentally or intentionally) while you are receiving the information from them.

NOTE TO SELF: *When debriefing an agent it is important to collect the information without disclosing what you already know or tainting that information by sharing outside details with the person being debriefed.*

It is important to *first* get the information—every detail—without any response, reaction, or confirmation. Once you have the information, then and only then is it appropriate to discuss anything else with or relay anything to your agent. FBI agents, when they interview a suspect, are very careful to take detailed notes of every-thing said; they subsequently type that up in a Form 403—the standard form used to document interviews. If any outside infor-mation is provided to the suspect (perhaps a lie or deception, like "we have your fingerprints at the scene and on the weapon that was used"), it is carefully documented.

If, as we believe, Harry was able to get through the door because there was *bleed-through* of Snape's mind and memories into Harry's vision, it must not have been something that Snape expected—it certainly was not information the Professor wanted Harry to have. Tricky thing, this mind reading!

The most significant discussion between Harry and Snape, however, occurs when Professor Snape asks Harry how many dreams he has had about the Dark Lord. Snape tells Harry, "It's not up to you to find out what the Dark Lord is saying to his Death Eaters." Harry retorts, "No, that's your job isn't it?" Harry thinks he has stepped over the line and awaits retribution—but instead Snape gives him a satis-fied expression and says, quite significantly, "Yes, Potter, that is my job" (591).

Wow! A clear revelation—that Harry instantly ignores. And brilliantly, Rowling too immediately moves on, knowing full well that she has just told us *exactly* the truth about Snape's work as a double agent!

You should also take the time to note that Harry asks Professor Snape why he always refers to Voldemort as "the Dark Lord." Harry, being a bit cheeky, explicitly notes that the Death Eaters also refer to Voldemort by that title and never by name. But before Snape has an opportunity to answer, they hear a scream from above—and then a second scream (593–94).

On to the next scene—the firing of Professor Trelawney.

As we know, and could have certainly *foreseen* after Trelawney's revised predictions about Harry, Umbridge was clearly planning to fire Professor Trelawney. While Umbridge certainly has the *power* to fire Professor Trelawney, we find through a very good piece of *legal* analysis that Dumbledore still has authority over the grounds—and who *lives* at Hogwarts (596).

As Harry observes the firing of Professor Trelawney, he proves his increased skills by noticing something else taking place away from the center of attention. Professor Dumbledore enters *not* from the direction of his office but rather *from the grounds*. Harry has the cognizance to wonder why Professor Dumbledore would be coming in from outside.

So what occurs? Umbridge fires Trelawney and tries to kick her off school grounds; Dumbledore states that she can stay in her quarters. Umbridge asserts that the new Divinations teacher will need her quarters. Dumbledore just smiles knowingly (596–97).

ANALYSIS: *Why was Professor Dumbledore coming from the grounds?* The answer becomes clear when Professor Umbridge asserts that Professor Trelawney cannot stay because the new Divinations teacher will need her lodgings. Dumbledore has a quick answer: he has already hired the new Divinations teacher who, he says, would prefer lodgings on the ground floor (597)!

Of course, Professor Umbridge thinks that Educational Decree Number 22 allows only *herself* to make hiring decisions . . . but a careful reading of the *exact language* of the complete decree, as you will recall, reveals that she can choose the replacement *only if the Headmaster isn't able to find a suitable teacher* first (307). As we soon find out, Dumbledore was outside talking with Firenze (a centaur) and convincing him to take over the Divinations Class (597–98). Thus, Umbridge is once again outwitted by Professor Dumbledore— to her great consternation!

27

A CENTAUR'S LOYALTY— A SNEAK'S DISLOYALTY—SECRETS DISCLOSED— CAPTURE AND ESCAPE

This chapter, "The Centaur and the Sneak," begins with the students asking Parvati Patil and Lavender Brown about their favorite teacher, Sybill Trelawney. The two girls had gone to Trelawney's office to visit her, and Lavender provides inside information on how she is doing— which is not very well (599).

NOTE TO SELF: *Much information can be obtained, often with little trouble, by merely asking or listening to what many people would term "gossip."*

When Hermione mentions that she thinks that Umbridge is just *starting* to be evil, Ron retorts, "Impossible," asserting that she can't get any worse (600). Hermione claims that Umbridge will want to retaliate against Professor Dumbledore for overruling her decision to make Trelawney leave the castle (600). Sounds like excellent analysis and proper use of a psychological assessment to us!

There are many surprises in store for the students of Divination, and they take all of them in stride. First of all, they have a new class-room on the main floor, Classroom 11, which to their amazement has been transformed into a forest by Professor Dumbledore's magic (600).

Their new teacher, Firenze, informs his new students that he has been banished from his herd because he has agreed to work for Dumbledore (601–2). A couple of students are foolish enough to make assumptions and misstatements (or thoughtless enough to ask profoundly tactless questions) about Firenze, such as whether Hagrid bred Firenze "like the Thestrals" (601). An enemy can be quickly made by failing to take into account differences in others' views or culture.

NOTE TO SELF: *When dealing with a person from another land or a different culture, frame any questions or statements carefully so as not to offend.*

When Harry arrives, Firenze recognizes and greets him directly, at which point Harry observes a hoofprint on Firenze's chest (601).

ANALYSIS: *Why was Firenze injured, and who most likely did that injury to him?* Harry analyzes this one on his own and real-izes that Bane, in the process of banishing Firenze from the herd, most likely injured Firenze. Harry bases this conclusion on his own prior observation of the strained relationship between Firenze and Bane (602). As we recall from book 1, it was Firenze who rescued Harry and allowed him to ride on his back—to Bane's great disgust, if not anger. Bane insulted Firenze that day, denouncing his choice to serve like a common mule (*SS* 256–57).

Firenze's first lesson to his new students becomes—to the well-trained intelligence analyst—a further indication (or prediction) of the coming war against Voldemort.

The class begins in earnest as the lights go dim and the children lay back on the soft forest floor to see the heavens (602). Significantly, some of the discussion includes the position of the planet Mars (603), the planet named for the Roman god of war. Mars has been mentioned before, most specifically when Harry first met Firenze nearly four years ago (history!), when the centaur interceded between Harry and Voldemort in the Forbidden Forest (*SS* 253, 253, 254).

Through these discussions of Mars the centaur is—as best he can within the bounds of his cultural customs—telling the humans that another war (against Voldemort) is quickly approaching. Even Professor Trelawney gets into the act, telling her class in book 4, *Harry Potter and the Goblet of Fire*, that the position of Mars "meant that people born in July were in great danger of sudden, violent deaths" (*GF* 345–46).

Did we mention that both Harry *and* Neville were born in July, and that they both come very close to violent death before, not to mention during, the final battle?

But we digress (only slightly) from Firenze's first lesson!

Firenze discusses the difference between fortune telling and predictions based on centuries of observation of the heavens by the centaurs (602). Firenze asserts that tides of evil can be divined from the sky, but that human fortune telling is "human nonsense" (603).

According to Firenze, the position of Mars shows that there is presently "a brief calm between two wars" but that "the fight must break out again soon" (603). Firenze provides a caveat, telling the class that even the centaurs are sometimes wrong. Harry properly understands that no one's knowledge is foolproof, not even the knowledge of centaurs. Ron, of course, wishes for more details about the war and thinks additional discussion of this topic would be more helpful to him and his friends, given that Voldemort is now back (603–4).

PREDICTIONS IN THE MUGGLE WORLD

Two of the main goals of the intelligence community are predicting war between other countries and assessing threats against our own country. Firenze is using the tools of his community—the centaurs—to warn the human community of an impending war. The intelligence community—through the President's Daily Brief and other intelligence final products—attempts to do the very same thing. But prediction, in either world, is not an exact science.

So how do we reach a definitive conclusion about anything? We must step back and analyze whether our perceptions are true, our assumptions sufficiently correct, and our conclusions properly supported. Although there is rarely certitude, we are obligated to make decisions based on a robust attempt to be accurate and a thorough questioning of that which we do *not* know.

This is as far as we dare go in a discussion about *epistemology*, though we gladly refer you to any liberal arts college (such as Grinnell College in Grinnell, Iowa) for support in delving that subject. Philosophy classes are a good starting point, but classes in science, history, religion, literature, art, and almost any other subject taught at such a fine institution of learning will give you the basics.

Whoops, bit of a personal recommendation there! Back to the story!

NOTE TO SELF: *Almost all knowledge is based, at least in part, on uncertain facts and unverified assumptions. You must take into account the fact that you can only see the world through a glass darkly.*

As the class ends, Firenze asks Harry to stay for a moment—and allows Ron to stay as well. The doors close (creating a secure meeting place), and Firenze gives them a warning to be relayed to Hagrid: Hagrid's attempt is not working, and it would be better to cease his attempt. When Harry inquires about what it is Hagrid is attempting, Firenze states that he will not betray his friend's secret—showing his loyalty to and respect for Hagrid. Firenze then mentions, as an aside, that he also refuses to answer the question because Hagrid has recently done Firenze a favor (604–5).

When Harry later relays Firenze's warning to Hagrid and confronts him about what it means, mentioning that he is concerned that Hagrid could lose his job, Hagrid says simply, "There's things more importan' than keepin' a job" (605). Hmmm, something as important as *family*, perhaps, as we discussed earlier?

We are also reminded at this point in the chapter that the O.W.L.s (Ordinary Wizarding Levels) are coming up, and the fifth-years are becoming quite nervous about tests. Some even need the assistance of the school nurse, Madam Pomfrey, to quell their nerves (605–6).

NOTE TO SELF: *The best way to calm yourself at testing time is to spend enough time studying that you needn't worry so much about it!*

The members of Dumbledore's Army are still doing well, and Harry takes solace—if not pleasure—in thinking about what Umbridge's reaction will be when all of the members of the DA not only pass their O.W.L.s but also receive top marks in the Defense Against the Dark Arts—despite her lousy Ministry-approved teaching (606).

The DA students are practicing their Patronuses, and some of them are doing quite well. However, Harry reminds the class that there is a huge difference between doing it in a brightly lit room where there is no danger, and performing such magic when surrounded by Dementors (606). This reminder is a wonderful analysis of the difference between a classroom setting and the "real world," and of being able to do things under pressure.

OPERATION SPY AT THE INTERNATIONAL SPY MUSEUM

One of the wonderful activities at the International Spy Museum (for those who are at least twelve years of age) is Operation Spy, a live-action spy adventure. Operation Spy is an opportunity to spend an hour working as a spy in a real-world setting with five to fifteen other "intelligence operatives," conducting surveillance, figuring out a spy mystery, and generally using your wits to conduct a mission in a foreign country. It is quite fun!

But this will end up being the last DA meeting. As we know, house-elves are obligated to keep the secrets of their masters and if they are disloyal in any way, they have to punish themselves. Dobby arrives and keeps trying to punish himself while trying to relay something important to Harry (607–8). Dobby finally blurts out the word "she" several times, and Harry surmises correctly that Umbridge is on her way! The group disbands, with Harry hoping that they can find closer places to hide instead of going directly to their dorms, because they're still allowed to be out for ten more minutes (608).

LEAVING IN TWOS OR THREES—GOOD SPY CRAFT

Not arriving and departing at the same time—or leaving in twos or threes—is good spy craft. If all members of Dumbledore's Army left at the same time and arrived at their houses in a group, anyone waiting at the house entrance would know that they were all fleeing the same meeting!

In hindsight, we wonder whether Harry or the others had developed an explicit *escape plan*—it sounds like they had not. In the spy business, you should always have an escape plan in mind, both a way to extricate yourself from the location you are at, and a way to get back to your home base, a safe house, or headquarters.

~~~~~~

Unfortunately, as Harry runs from the Room of Requirement, he is tripped up by a Trip Jinx, performed by none other than Draco Malfoy (609). Umbridge grabs Harry and leads him to Dumbledore's office, using the password "Fizzing Whizzbee" to enter the Headmaster's office. Umbridge does not use the knocker on the entry door upstairs—as Harry notes—but barges unannounced into Dumbledore's office, where we find Dumbledore, McGonagall, Minster of Magic Cornelius Fudge, Auror Kingsley Shacklebolt, a tough-looking wizard (Dawlish), and our least favorite sycophant, Percy Weasley (610).

Fudge begins his interrogation of Harry immediately, stating, "I expect you know why you are here?" Harry is ready to say yes, but at a subtle signal from Dumbledore, Harry quickly changes it to a no (610–11). It is now Spymaster Dumbledore's turn to teach the young spy a thing or two about keeping your mouth shut and refusing to answer an enemy's questions!

NOTE TO SELF: *If you have been captured, never admit to anything. Make them prove it!*

Fudge presses on, asking Harry if he is aware of having broken any school rules or Ministry decrees; Fudge also asks if it's news to Harry that an illegal student organization has been discovered. Harry, following Dumbledore's lead, says it certainly *is* news to him (611).

Having failed to extract a confession, Umbridge suggests they "fetch our informant" (611), who turns out to be Marietta, Cho's friend. We find out from the adults' discussion that Marietta's mother works at the Ministry of Magic, in the Department of Magical Transportation, and has been monitoring the Hogwarts Floo Network to make sure no one (such as Sirius!) is using it without the Ministry's knowledge and consent (611–12).

Harry is proud to see that Hermione's jinx (a form of coun-terespionage) works quite well indeed: Marietta's face has the word *SNEAK* spelled out in purple pustules (612). Marietta understand-ably refuses to speak (612–13).

~~~~~~

HERMIONE'S SNEAK JINX AND USE OF THE POLYGRAPH ON ROBERT HANSSEN

Hermione's jinx reminds us of an interesting tidbit about the use of **polygraphs** on FBI Special Agents. Beginning in 1982, there was a discussion about whether or not polygraphs should be used for those who had extremely high-level clearance (SCI or COMSEC clearance and access to counterintelligence information). In 1985 there were several high-profile spy cases in which the United States had discovered several Americans who were acting as spies for foreign governments. In addition, some US spies had been caught in the Soviet Union, which made many counterintelligence officers concerned that there was a mole somewhere within the US intelligence community.

After the arrest of John Walker, senior FBI counterintelligence agent David Major gave a briefing on August 7, 1985, at a National Security Council staff meeting and to President Ronald Reagan in the Oval Office. The issue was whether or not to require persons with high counterintelligence clearances to present themselves for polygraph tests. President Reagan approved the change in policy by signing National Security Decision Directive Number 196 on November 1, 1985, directing that this policy be implemented. However, Secretary of State George Schultz threatened to resign over the issue. The policy was therefore not implemented for *all* persons who had access to such information.

CHAPTER 27

The liaison for the intelligence group deciding whether polygraphs should be used on our own counterintelligence people argued that the polygraph was not sufficiently reliable and should not be used. Curiously, that same liaison, when considering applying for a different position that would give him even more access to confidential information, decided against applying for it when he learned that the job required a polygraph.

You have probably already guessed the great irony of these facts. The liaison was none other than Robert Hanssen, who had already received money from 1979 to 1981 to provide secret information to the Soviets, and in October 1985 he restarted his spying operations. He was eventually discovered in 2001—after the unfortunate loss of a number of clandestine US sources in the field. Had the policy changed, perhaps Robert Hanssen would have been caught sooner!

~~~~~~~~~~~~~~~~~~~~~~~~~~~~~~~~~~~~~~~

Since the informant won't talk, Umbridge tells Fudge and the others what Marietta had previously told her—that "Potter had met a number of fellow students in the Hog's Head in Hogsmeade" (613). When asked for proof, Umbridge discloses that at the meeting at Hogsmeade someone named Willy Widdershins, who was heavily bandaged at the time, heard everything that Harry had said and immediately went to the school and told Umbridge (613–14).

Professor McGonagall notes sardonically, "Oh, so *that's* why he wasn't prosecuted for all those regurgitating toilets! What an interesting insight into our justice system!" (613–14). Professor McGonagall considers cutting such a deal an abomination. While her comment borders dangerously on accusing Fudge of misusing the prosecutorial system, the Minister and Umbridge are more interested in discrediting Harry. After all, the students have been caught organizing a group!

PART 1

<hr/>

THE POWER OF PROSECUTION—HELPFUL TOOL OR ABUSE OF THE SYSTEM?

Those in power can use the justice system—particularly the prosecutorial system—to their own advantage. Dropping the charges and letting someone go free in return for information or an agreement to spy for you is in reality *legalized* bribery or extortion—and an unfortunately common way of doing business in many judicial systems. In the United States, it is a common tactic in many drug cases.

Of course, in the spy world, when an adverse agent is caught, one of the first things attempted is to "turn" that agent and use him or her to spy for the other side—that is, to become a double agent.

One well-known example of "striking a deal" with a captured spy is the treatment of Robert Hanssen. Once caught, Hanssen was subject to the federal death penalty. The prosecutor took the death penalty off the table in exchange for Hanssen's cooperation; in addition, Hanssen's wife was allowed to retain some of his pension. The government was willing to accept this plea bargain in return for the option to interview Hanssen at any time and conduct a thorough damage assessment to determine what secrets had been given to the other side.

<hr/>

A good spy can think on his or her feet and use logic to his or her advantage, and Dumbledore is a *really* good spy. Unperturbed, the Headmaster calmly disagrees with Professor Umbridge's assertion that Harry was attempting to recruit students to join an illegal group. Dumbledore—always the able analyst—explains that his disagreement isn't with any of the facts, but rather notes that *at the time* the organizing meeting took place, student organizations were *not yet illegal* because Educational Decree Number 24 wasn't enacted until two days *after* the students returned from Hogsmeade (614–15).

Under almost all systems of modern law, a person cannot be charged with a crime for doing something that was not at that time illegal. If a government could prosecute its citizens retroactively for acts that it later made illegal, it could place everyone in jeopardy (if not in jail) because no one could have known what was or would be against the law. The United States Constitution explicitly prohibits the government from passing such laws, which are called *ex post facto* laws.

Dumbledore, it seems, understands this basic legal tenet. Umbridge then counters, what about all the meetings that took place *after* the decree was issued (615)? Dumbledore quite shrewdly asks whether there is any evidence that these meetings *continued*. Umbridge once again inquires of her informant—but before Marietta can speak, Harry hears Kingsley Shacklebolt whispering something and then feels "a gentle something" go by him (615).

ANALYSIS: *What was it that Kingsley Shacklebolt did?* It seems clear to us that Kingsley used a memory charm, which Dumbledore later confirms (621). In any event, Marietta, when asked about what she observed, now shakes her head no repeatedly (616).

This is where we see the true nature of Dolores Umbridge, a person who is glad to use any means—even illegal ones—to reach the end she desires. Umbridge physically assaults Marietta, shaking her—at which point Dumbledore quickly steps in and uses magic to force Umbridge to stop, resulting in Umbridge waving her hands in the air as though they had been burned (616).

Kingsley Shacklebolt, who to all outward appearances is a Ministry man and aide to Fudge, mentions it would not be a good idea for Professor Umbridge to get into trouble—and Umbridge dolefully agrees. At this point Harry realizes that Shacklebolt had modified Marietta's memory to get her to say the opposite of what was true, as confirmed by his observation of Marietta's blank eyes and general confusion (616–17).

Umbridge still has no proof, and Dumbledore is, once again, about to pull the proverbial wool over her eyes. Unfortunately for Harry and Dumbledore, Slytherin student Pansy Parkinson had run into the Room of Requirement when the door was open and grabbed the list of the members of Dumbledore's Army, which each person had signed (617). Umbridge discloses that she does indeed have proof that a meeting had occurred (617).

Dumbledore—realizing that this is the evidence needed to convict Harry and his friends—immediately steps in, admitting that the game is up and asserting that he himself had recruited the children. Indeed, their first meeting was to be tonight! In one move, Dumbledore has prevented Harry and the other students from being expelled and proved that he, their Headmaster, is the only one to blame (618).

Harry bravely *tries* to tell the truth, but Dumbledore tells him he will have to leave if he continues to try to say another word—and of course Fudge abruptly tells Harry to shut up (619). Percy has been documenting Dumbledore's "confession" and is sent out to make an additional copy and get it to the *Daily Prophet* so that it will arrive in time for tomorrow's paper (619). Once again, we note Fudge's use (or misuse) of the press to discredit Dumbledore and manipulate public opinion.

Dumbledore has admitted to violating several decrees and laws; he is trapped—surrounded and ostensibly in custody. It is at this point where Fudge tells Dumbledore that he will be escorted to the Ministry, formally charged, and sent to Azkaban to await trial (619). Once again, the justice system will be used to punish and silence an opponent of those in power.

Dumbledore, always calm, thinks otherwise: "Ah, yes. Yes. I thought we might hit that little snag" (619). Fudge—not the brightest bulb on the tree—has a difficult time understanding what Dumbledore means, so Dumbledore spells it out for him: Dumbledore advises Fudge that he is laboring under the delusion that Dumbledore would be willing to go "quietly" (620).

Fudge—finally understanding Dumbledore's intentions—signals Shacklebolt and Dawlish to attack. Within moments Harry finds himself on the floor, being protected by Professor McGonagall (who also got Marietta out of the way). As the dust settles, Harry observes that all the Ministry people had been knocked out, including Shacklebolt (621).

Dumbledore instructs Harry and Professor McGonagall to give the cover story that they were knocked out as well, so that no one will realize that they had time to talk. Dumbledore once again explains to Harry the importance of closing his mind and continuing the Occlumency lessons with Professor Snape, telling him to do whatever Professor Snape asks. Some of the Ministry minions start to wake up, and Dumbledore nonchalantly reaches up to touch Fawkes's tail, and both Wizard and phoenix disappear (622).

When the others wake up, Dawlish, Shacklebolt, and Umbridge go chasing out of the office, looking for Dumbledore—assuming that he (like everybody else) cannot Apparate out of Hogwarts (622–623). Obviously Dumbledore has many tricks up his sleeve, including using Fawkes as a method of transportation.

Fudge, who seems to think he was victorious, tells Professor McGonagall, "I'm afraid this is the end of your friend Dumbledore" (623). McGonagall, however, thinks otherwise. As do we all!

As the chapter ends, Phineas Nigellus speaks from his portrait, stating that even though he sometimes disagrees with Dumbledore, the Headmaster certainly has style (623)!

28

HOGWARTS WITHOUT DUMBLEDORE—
EFFECTS OF CHANGES IN LEADERSHIP—
THE POWER AND POIGNANCY OF
HISTORY AND MEMORIES

Chapter 28, "Snape's Worst Memory," finds Hogwarts in turmoil, some seen and some unforeseen. Anticipating what Hogwarts would be like with Umbridge in charge is not difficult, and perhaps we would have just as easily surmised the subtle rebellion of the professors. But George and Fred's outright and anonymous rebellion is indeed a sight to behold!

Let us discuss for a moment the change of leadership and *who* selected the new Head of Hogwarts. Please forgive our use of a four-letter word here: POLITICS!

OK, OK, it's still eight letters—perhaps the equivalent of *two* four-letter words!

As we all know, Professor McGonagall is the Deputy Head-mistress and should be next in line to replace Dumbledore upon his absence. However, that transition did not occur as expected.

CHAPTER 28

ANALYSIS: *Why didn't Professor McGonagall, as the Deputy Headmaster, step in to take Dumbledore's place?* Because Professor McGonagall sided with Dumbledore at the time of the Minister of Magic's attempted arrest of Dumbledore. McGonagall clearly indicated that Dumbledore would *not* be alone and that she would assist him in preventing his arrest (620). Dumbledore did not need her assistance and told her precisely that—and also subtly indicated that her job, when the time came, was to protect the two students in the room (620).

Thus, it was clear with even the slightest application of analysis that Professor McGonagall would *not* be selected to take over as Headmaster. The Ministry would clearly want one of its own in charge—and the obvious candidate is our least favorite toadlike woman, Professor Umbridge (624).

It is understandable that the people in power would appoint people who agree with them to hold important positions—and we can think of very few positions more important than those related to the education of our youth.

NOTE TO SELF: *Just as rank has its privileges, power has it sycophants and minions.*

Let us now compare Dumbledore and Umbridge as leaders, remembering particularly that style and content matter.

Dumbledore—to his great credit—fostered a school that offered intellectual independence and rewards for academic skills or feats of bravery (on and off the Quidditch field). It is an environment in which mistakes can be made and where the students are respected and protected from harm.

Now let us contrast the style and content of Professor Umbridge's rule at Hogwarts. Our prior glimpses of Professor Umbridge torturing Harry by making him write "I will not tell lies" on his hand and her manhandling of Marietta give us a very accurate indication of what we can expect from her as Headmistress. She will attempt to stifle any intellectual independence or honesty, demand that everybody toe the Ministry's party line, and gladly forgo the niceties of social conventions and mores, favoring instead an atmosphere of fear, constant surveillance, and the liberal use of punishment. Strange days indeed.

The chapter began with the presentation of Educational Decree Number 28, by which the Ministry of Magic has replaced Professor Dumbledore with Professor Umbridge as the Head of Hogwarts School of Witchcraft and Wizardry (624). This decree came as no surprise to the students, given that the Hogwarts rumor mill was already buzzing about what had happened (624–25).

By the next morning it was common knowledge that Dumbledore had overcome two Aurors, the High Inquisitor, the Minister of Magic, and his junior assistant—and had then escaped (625). The students are suitably impressed and want to talk about nothing else. We should take a moment to ask ourselves how this information—basically accurate—got out.

ANALYSIS: *Where did the information about what occurred the night that Dumbledore escaped come from?* Certainly Cornelius Fudge and Professor Umbridge would have no desire to tell the students—or anybody else—that Dumbledore escaped even when so completely surrounded by experienced wizards and witches—particularly because they do not know exactly how he did so! The fact that the entire school knew about it the next morning suggests that Harry—who undoubtedly would have had to return immediately to the Gryffindor dormitory—would have told Hermione and Ron and perhaps all the others, who carried the news to the other houses at breakfast.

But how is it that the entire school knew so *quickly*? Marietta, we are told, was taken to the hospital wing, and given her state of confusion (most likely due to the use of the Memory Charm by

Shacklebolt), Marietta probably does not recall what happened. We could surmise that Professor McGonagall told the other teachers, and perhaps they told their students, although the teachers were prohibited from doing so under Educational Decree Number 26 (551).

There is another possibility: the paintings on the wall in Dumbledore's office and throughout the school! We imagine that the former Headmasters and Headmistresses of Hogwarts see and discuss many things with the other portraits throughout Hogwarts.

Notice also the reference to details that had "gone awry in the retelling" (625). That is always a danger with rumors—but inaccurate retelling is dangerous even if in an organized briefing with detailed information. Try as we might, most people cannot remember every single detail of a conversation or an incident. And often, minor changes occur in the retelling.

There have been many studies about the recollection of witnesses of first-hand observation, including witness accounts of important events such as serious crimes. Not only is it hard to remember everything, but most people are also not trained to observe things correctly in the first place, especially in a moment of crisis. Add to this the reality that memories can be altered or at least tainted by suggestion, and it's hard to feel confident about any observation!

The mind is *not* a precise instrument, and memories can fade or, in some cases, be altered. (For example, in book 6, *Harry Potter and the Half-Blood Prince*, Professor Slughorn has *altered* his own memory of his conversation with Tom Riddle about Horcruxes [*HBP* 370–71].) The retelling of Dumbledore's escape ends up fairly accurate—though some details did get a little bit stretched (625).

It is also interesting to note the students' reactions to Dumbledore's departure. Perhaps Ernie McMillan says it best when he asserts that Dumbledore will be back before long and notes that they couldn't keep him away during the second year and they won't be able to do so now (625). Once again, the past is prologue—and history (historical analysis) has significance.

We would also like to point out that the Ministry's change of leadership did not receive unanimous consent, as indicated by the gargoyle's refusal to allow Professor Umbridge into the Headmaster's office (625). We can just imagine the fit that Professor Umbridge had when she discovered that she could not enter that holiest of Hogwarts holy places!

ANALYSIS: *Why wasn't Professor Umbridge able to enter the Head-master's office?* Is it something as simple as Dumbledore changing the password? That is certainly *possible*, but there are other possibilities to consider. Is it possible that Hogwarts—the castle itself—has a mind of its own? Remember in book 7, *Harry Potter and the Deathly Hallows*, when Professor McGonagall uses magic to awaken the statues and suits of armor, telling them "do your duty to our school" (*DH* 602)? Is it also possible that the former Head-masters and Headmistresses sitting around in the portraits have control over *access* to the headmaster's office? Perhaps these former leaders do not consider Umbridge to have been properly appointed, or worthy of the appointment? It seems we'll never know, but we do hope—just a little bit—that the castle *itself* was objecting to Professor Umbridge and preventing her from entering Professor Dumbledore's office!

In any event, Professor Umbridge is relegated to using her own office—where she has now adorned her desk with a very large sign declaring her "HEADMISTRESS," in case anyone has any doubts (629).

The first change implemented by Headmistress Umbridge is the institution of the Inquisitorial Squad, a group of handpicked students (most likely all Slytherins) who have the power to take away points from students (626). Their obvious mission is internal control and enforcement of Professor Umbridge's rules, along with the concomi-tant role of spying on their fellow students (626).

Fred and George have decided to take matters into their own hands, going so far as to shove a member of the Inquisitorial Squad, Montague, headfirst into a Vanishing Cabinet! Hermione tells the

CHAPTER 28

twins that they'll get in trouble, but they don't care (627).

The twins' statements about coming *close* to crossing the line in regards to conduct (and misconduct) are worth a closer look. The twins wisely note that they always knew where the line was, and while they occasionally put a toe over it, they were careful not to cross it. But now that Dumbledore is gone, all bets are off: "we reckon a bit of mayhem," begins George, "is exactly what our dear new Head deserves," completes Fred. Fred goes on to explain to Hermione that they could leave, but they want to "do our bit for Dumbledore first" (627).

The decision to raise mayhem reflects not only the twins' substantial loyalty to Professor Dumbledore, but also an equal disdain for the new Headmistress. It is clear that the twins have a plan for causing disorder and chaos, and they go so far as to mention that "phase one is about to begin," and by the way, it would be best for their friends to be in a location where there are *a lot of witnesses* when the action begins, so that they have a solid **alibi** (627).

Alibis are an interesting thing. They are used in both criminal law and spy craft. An alibi is simply the ability to present proof that you were *not* at the location where a particular incident occurred. An alibi can be created by an eyewitness who saw you at a particular time and a particular place. Alibis can be made by more mundane methods as well: a receipt showing that you purchased gas a hundred miles away from the incident around the time it occurred, or security camera footage with a date and time stamp showing that you were entering a hotel, getting a candy bar, or filling your car up with gas at the time in question. Indeed, as Cornelius Fudge said when bringing in Umbridge's informant Marietta, "There is nothing like a good witness" (612). A good alibi is a close second!

So, back to the story. . . .

Filch advises harry that Umbridge wants to see him. Harry's response is a not-very-spylike "I didn't do it." Filch responds, "Guilty conscience, eh?" (628). It turns out that Umbridge "merely" wants to have a social visit and a spot of tea (629–30).

PART 1

NOTE TO SELF: *Diplomacy is the art of war while having tea!*

~~~~~~~~~~~~~~~~~~~~

PEOPLE LOVE TO TALK—
AND GENERALLY TELL THE TRUTH

In my experience as a lawyer, I have found that most witnesses are quite honest and more than happy to tell you anything you ask—even things that would hurt their case, or the case of a friend. For the most part, people are quite honest, and Veritaserum is not usually necessary!

—Lynn Boughey

~~~~~~~~~~~~~~~~~~~~

When one is being interrogated, one should be very careful about what is said. This does *not* mean you have to lie.

NOTE TO SELF: *When being questioned or interrogated, remember that you always have the option of not answering.*

~~~~~~~~~~~~~~~~~~~~

THE OUTING OF COVERT OFFICER
VALERIE PLAME WILSON

Many a person has gotten into trouble by lying to the FBI. For example, Scooter Libby, Vice President Cheney's Chief of Staff, was convicted *not* of disclosing confidential or secret information about one of our covert officers, but instead of *lying* to the FBI agents who interviewed him! The person who had actually disclosed the information did not lie to the FBI agents (he was with the State Department) and nothing bad happened to him—except, we suppose, the public response to the news that it was he who outed CIA operative Valerie Plame Wilson to the press!

~~~~~~~~~~~~~~~~~~~~

CHAPTER 28

Off goes Harry to "visit" Professor Umbridge—that is, to be interrogated by Professor Umbridge. Filch is naturally gleeful: "Things are changing around here, Potter," he tells Harry. Once again we face the reality of the change of leadership at Hogwarts and the parallel changes in politics at the school. Filch is just about salivating when he mentions his anticipation of Educational Decree Number 29, which he claims will allow him to torture students and hang them up by their ankles in his office! Harry correctly surmises that Umbridge wants Filch on her side; his knowledge of the school's secret passageways and hiding places is probably second only to that of the Weasley twins (628–29).

NOTE TO SELF: *When assigned to an unfamiliar place, take the time to befriend someone who has been there a long time and knows the territory.*

FURTHER NOTE TO SELF: *When making new friends at your new location, remember that it is the unseen folks—such as a janitor or desk clerk—who quite often see and hear the most.*

Harry joins Professor Umbridge in her old pink-colored office, under the gaze of the kitten plates and before her new "HEADMIS-TRESS" sign (629). We don't know about you, but in our experience the people who love titles love power as well, and those who love power are the most apt to abuse it.

GOOD LEADERSHIP AND RESPONSIBLE USE OF POWER

There are many good leaders, though, who are humble and attempt to truly do the public good. One quick example of such a leader: according to the great historian Livy, approximately 2,500 years ago, in 458 BC, a man named Cincinnatus was appointed dictator ("master of the people") when the Roman leader and his soldiers had

265

been trapped by an enemy. Cincinnatus was plowing a field when he was appointed dictator for a term of six months. He ordered all men of military age to report and quickly organized against the enemy, securing victory. Once he had done so, he resigned his position and went back to his farm. In 439 BC, Cincinnatus was brought out of retirement and again given absolute power to quell a conspiracy; once he had done so, he again immediately relinquished his absolute power and returned home. If you would like to read more, go to Livy, *Ab Urbe Condita* 3.26–29.

~~~~~~

So, do you think Harry should drink the tea presented to him by Headmistress Umbridge?

Harry initially declines the tea she offers, but then finally agrees when she persists. It would be rude to decline, don't you think? And one never wants to be rude (630)!

Or maybe not.

Wasn't it *ever so kind* of Professor Umbridge to offer Harry a spot of tea upon arriving at her office? And what do you think of the fact that, when she poured the tea and added milk, her back was to Harry so he could not see her pour? Harry is ready to take a drink when the sight of one of the cats on the plates in Umbridge's office—one with very large eyes—suddenly reminds Harry of Mad-Eye Moody (630)—and what would Mad-Eye Moody say to drinking tea served by an enemy?

CONSTANT VIGILANCE!

Harry *pretends* to drink—and Umbridge begins her "friendly" questioning, more accurately called an interrogation. Where is Albus Dumbledore? she asks. No idea, Harry answers—quite truthfully, by the way. Drink up, drink up, Umbridge insists. Harry pretends to drink again. Where is Sirius Black? Harry pretends to drink again and lies, saying he doesn't know (630–31).

Umbridge discloses to Harry that she almost caught Sirius in the fire—and once again asks where Sirius is. No idea, Harry lies—doesn't have a clue (631).

Umbridge's pretended kindness and her attempt to use Veritaserum have failed. So, perfectly in character, Umbridge tries the only other tactic she knows—she attempts to instill fear, or at least assert her control of Hogwarts: "be warned: The might of the Ministry stands behind me. All channels of communication in and out of the school are being monitored" (631).

MAIL COVER—A LONG HISTORY OF INTERCEPTING "OWLS"

Mail cover is a request by an intelligence agency to obtain information from a country's mail service (public or private) to examine the outside aspects of an envelope or package, normally without opening the item (though some countries will allow the package to be opened and then carefully resealed so it appears to be intact).

From 1917 to 1929, Herbert Yardley headed various code-breaking organizations, including, in 1919, the Black Chamber, a secret group of code-breakers that worked out of a private residence at 22 East 38th Street in New York, reading mail and deciphering diplomatic codes, particularly Japanese cables. Unfortunately for Yardley, in 1929 President Herbert Hoover appointed Henry L. Stimson as secretary of state. When Stimson was shown a transcribed cable and found out what Yardley and his group were doing, he angrily shut down the entire operation, asserting, "Gentlemen do not read each other's mail."

Umbridge mentions that the Floo Network Regulator is observing all the fires at Hogwarts (except her own) and her new

PART 1

Inquisitorial Squad is opening and reading all mail that comes in and out of the castle via owl—and, of course, Filch is observing all the secret passages (631). Umbridge is, though not in so many words, telling Harry that he is trapped, that he will not be able to communicate with anyone outside of Hogwarts, and that any attempt to do so will be discovered. Does the word *incommunicado* come to mind?

In the midst of Umbridge's warning there is a large BOOM (631)! Harry, it turns out, has the best alibi ever: Professor Umbridge *herself*!

The explosion provides a distraction that allows Harry to pour his tea into a vase of dried flowers (631). This is really quite smart of Harry, and very spylike. Equanimity! Opportunity! Spy craft!

ANALYSIS: *Why did Harry want to dump his tea?* Because his cup was still full, Umbridge would realize that he had not drunk any of the truth serum. By pouring it into a vase, he ensures that Umbridge will see the empty cup and *assume* that Harry had indeed drank the truth serum and was telling the truth when he said he did not know the locations of Dumbledore or Sirius. Great spy work indeed, Harry Potter!

When Umbridge and Harry enter the common areas, pandemonium reigns. Fireworks everywhere! Dragons, bats, everything you could imagine (632). Gee, who is well known for making fireworks?

The Weasley twins are engaging in PSYOPS, or psychological operations. They are creating mayhem, chaos, and distraction, and also—by the way—generally having a great time watching Umbridge trying to deal with the fireworks! Umbridge attempts to use a Stunning Spell on the fireworks, which results only in the fireworks exploding and causing *even more* mischief (632). The fireworks themselves are clearly infused with a responsive spell—and Umbridge's countermeasures activate a counterspell instead.

The twins tell Harry—while hiding behind a tapestry—that they hope she tries Vanishing the fireworks next, which will result in the fireworks multiplying by ten (633). Fred and George certainly know their stuff!

For the rest of the afternoon, smaller fireworks rebound throughout the castle, even in classrooms; these smaller explosions are just *somewhat* bothersome (a low-intensity conflict?). The other teachers do not seem to mind—and each time these fireworks cause any type of distraction in the classroom, the teachers send a student to tell Umbridge (633–34). Thus, instead being free to pursue her own tyrannical business, Umbridge is forced to deal with dozens of little problems throughout the school.

The smaller fireworks are quite the diversionary tactic, and Umbridge spends most of the day dealing with issues that would otherwise be dealt with by the professors. Perhaps most telling of the professors' view of Umbridge is Professor Flitwick's apologetic "I could have got rid of the sparklers myself, but I wasn't sure I had the *authority*" (634).

We next find Harry asleep and again (perchance!) experiencing his recurring (and progressive) dream. He is in the corridor, then in front of the door; the door opens, and he enters a circular room lined with doors. He goes across the room and through another door, into a rectangular room full of odd clicking sounds; he goes through this room too, through another door, and finds himself in a large room with rows and rows of towering shelves filled with dusty, spun-glass spheres. Harry is nearly there, but he is awakened by a Weasley firework going off outside his dorm room (635).

~~~~~~~~~~~~~~~~~~~~~~~~~~~~~~~~~~~~

SLEEP, DREAMS, AND J. K. ROWLING'S USE OF SHAKESPEARE

You're probably familiar with that famous quotation about dreams (or is it about death?):

> To sleep—perchance to dream. Ay, there's the rub,
>
> For in that sleep of death what dreams may come,

PART 1

When we have shuffled off this mortal coil,

Must give us pause.

—*Hamlet*, Act III, scene 1, lines 73–76

What about another dreaming quote, when a man named Banquo—who the night before dreamed of the weird sisters—and now cannot sleep for fear of what he shall dream (sound familiar?):

A heavy summons lies like lead upon me,

And yet I would not sleep, Merciful powers,

Restrain in me the cursèd thoughts that nature

Gives way to in repose.

—*Macbeth*, Act II, scene 1, lines 6–9

Banquo cannot sleep because he was with Macbeth when the three witches foretold a prophecy about himself and Macbeth, his fellow general in King Duncan's army. The three witches—referred to in the play repeatedly as *the weird sisters*, gave them both a *prophecy*, in the form of an intellectual riddle, as to each person: To Macbeth, they hail him as the Thane of Glamis (his present title) and then Thane of Cawdor (the title of the man that tried to overthrow the king), and tell Macbeth that he "shalt be king hereafter." To Banquo, the three witches tell Banquo that he will be *lesser* than Macbeth and *greater, not so happy* but *happier*, and, most troubling—that Banquo shall beget kings, "thou though be none."

Witches, prophecies, riddles . . . sound familiar?

Banquo's insomnia is understandable. How can he father kings and yet not be one first? How can the present king be replaced by Macbeth, and yet Macbeth's children not succeed him in royalty? The answer derives from the ambition and evil in Macbeth's heart and the nefarious

270

acts that follow: Macbeth and his wife kill the king as he sleeps in their home; Banquo, next in line for the throne, is murdered that same night, but his son escapes; and upon Macbeth's death, Banquo's son becomes the heir apparent.

Witches, prophecies, evil plots, nefarious people grabbing power through lies, deceit . . . and maybe a few decrees?

In case you have any doubt whatsoever about J. K. Rowling's knowledge and use of Shakespeare's *Macbeth* as a source and foundation of her wonderful series, we ask you only this: What is the name of the popular band mentioned several times in the series and that plays at the Death-Day Party?

The Weird Sisters (*GF* 419, *OP* 286, 867, *HBP* 316)!

Harry realizes—and admits to himself—that he has failed to practice Occlumency, that Snape will be mad, and that he is guilty of not practicing even though Dumbledore had told him to do so (636). But, as we shall soon see, Harry's lessons with Professor Snape are about to end.

Before we reach that point, however, a few words about loyalty and picking your friends—and how to extinguish permanently an otherwise budding relationship with a potential girlfriend.

Harry runs into Cho, who tells him that she never *dreamed* Marietta would tell on them. She continues on, claiming that Marietta is a lovely person who made a mistake. Harry, understandably, thinks that she should have chosen her friends more wisely and reacts with anger. "Made a mistake? She sold us all out, including you!" (637). Cho makes the mistake of trying to defend her friend, stating that Marietta's mother works for the Ministry. Harry retorts that Ron's dad does as well! Cho then makes a fatal mistake: she tells Harry that she considers Hermione's jinx a horrible trick. Harry tells her quite bluntly that *he* thinks it was brilliant. That, as they say, is the end of the matter—or at least of their potential relationship.

PART 1

Harry returns to Snape's office and prepares to practice Occlumency. However, before they can continue, Malfoy interrupts them and informs Professor Snape that Umbridge needs Snape's help: they had finally found the missing Montague—apparently jammed inside a toilet on the fourth floor. Snape dutifully leaves, dismissing Harry and postponing their lesson until the next day. However, Harry lingers, looks around, and sees something *rather interesting* (638–39): the Pensieve, which at that moment contains the memories that Snape *didn't want Harry to see* during their lessons (639).

NOTE TO SELF: *Best not to leave secrets lying around, particularly memories!*

Harry looks over his shoulder, wondering how long it would take for Snape to return (639).

ANALYSIS: *Should Harry take the risk of using the Pensieve to see Snape's memories?* Harry does a risk assessment right then and there. How long will it take Snape to go to the fourth floor and back? Would Snape come directly back, or take Montague to the hospital wing? Does the fact that Montague is the captain of the Slytherin Quidditch team make it more likely that Snape will take him to the hospital wing himself, wanting to make sure he is all right? Harry's risk analysis is superb, and—acknowledging that he is doing so with reckless daring—he heads over to the Pensieve (639–40).

Harry observes young Snape at exam time, age fifteen or sixteen, taking his O.W.L.s. He looks over Snape's shoulder and sees his miniscule and cramped writing (640–41).

ANALYSIS: *Since Harry now knows Snape's writing, why wasn't he able to figure out who the Half-Blood Prince was in book 6?* We guess not all spies are perfect.

CHAPTER 28

Harry looks around the room and sees his father, Sirius, Lupin, and even Peter Pettigrew, aka Wormtail. Harry's father is doodling a Snitch and writing the letters *L.E.* on a piece of parchment. Harry, amazingly, fails to realize who L.E. is (641–42)! (Lily Evans, anyone?)

The exam concludes, and James Potter and his friends head down to the lake to sit under the same tree that Harry and his friends have sat under (644). (Is this a matter of genetics, or is it simply the best tree to sit under? We'll leave that question to someone else.)

Bored, James begins to play with a golden Snitch, which he admits he had stolen (644). (Or shall we say he snitched it? Sorry!)

Harry observes his father and his three best friends and notices that they are egotistical, mean, and cocky. When they see Snape, they taunt him by calling him Snivellus and start bullying him (645–46).

And who comes to Snape's rescue? Someone with the initials of L.E.! Lily Evans, Harry's mother-to-be, is clearly no shy young lady. "Leave him ALONE!" she yells. She goes so far as to call her future husband an "arrogant, bullying toerag." James, who is obviously smitten with Lily, tells her that if she is willing to go out with him, he will never lay a hand on Snape again. Snape, quite foolishly, calls the person who is interceding on his behalf (and probably one of his few friends) a Mudblood (647–48)!

James is understandably incensed (and we assume Lily is as well) and insists on an apology. Instead of an apology, James gets an earful of what Lily Evans thinks of him, concluding with, "You make me SICK!" (648).

Whatever happened next we will not know, because our young spy has just been caught by Professor Snape. "Having fun?" Snape asks. Harry finds himself floating upwards, away from the Pensieve, until he feels his feet connect with the stone floor. Furious, Snape tells Harry never to repeat what he saw, to get out, and that he never wants to see Harry in his office again (649). So much for the continuation of Occlumency lessons!

Harry thinks long and hard about what he observed. His analysis necessarily includes wondering whether Snape's view of his father was right all along. Harry has firsthand experience of being taunted and bullied, humiliated by a circle of onlookers. Harry's conclusion: James was every bit as arrogant as Snape had always told him (649–50)!

Is his conclusion correct? Only partly so, for human behavior is rarely black and white, and all of us at one time or another have done stupid, perhaps even unforgivable, things, in our youth and sometimes well beyond.

NOTE TO SELF: *We cannot judge others, or even ourselves, by the worst of what they have done. You can judge the act, but to judge the person you must consider the whole.*

At the very least, we should try to learn from our mistakes. If possible, we should ask forgiveness of those we have harmed and strive not to make the same mistake again.

FURTHER NOTE TO SELF: *Guilt is intended to be a rudder, not an anchor!*

If you have any question about how to live your life in such a manner, take the time to read *Les Misérables* by Victor Hugo. It really is quite good!

But either way, we will now get back to the story. On to the next chapter!

29

THE PSYCHOLOGY OF RISK—OPERATIONS PLANNING—WHAT WE DECIDE TO DO WITH OUR LIVES—A TWIN EXIT WORTH REMEMBERING

The next chapter, "Career Advice," focuses (unsurprisingly) on careers a wizard or witch might choose, risk (and risky careers!), and the ways in which diversions, explosions, missing students, and other forms of harassment can be used to disrupt a society—and one particular pink lady trying to run it.

The chapter begins with Hermione asking Harry why he is no longer taking Occlumency. Harry keeps his word and does not say anything about Snape's memories—telling Hermione instead that Snape has decided he knows the basics well enough to do it on his own (651).

Harry finds himself unable to focus on his day-to-day activities, thinking instead about what he saw in the Pensieve (652). Most of us have memories of our parents and perceptions built on those memories, and Harry—who had no opportunity to grow up with his parents in his life, but who knows now that they are considered heroes—has understandably placed James and Lily on a pedestal.

Throughout the previous years, Harry has consistently rejected the negative things Snape said about James Potter. Now, having seen a young James acting disgracefully, Harry is confused. He was sure that his parents had been wonderful people—but is now reviewing what others have said about his father and reinterpreting that commentary in a new light.

One of the things spies must do, especially those who run or control other spies, is psychological assessments of those with whom they work. This begins when the spy is recruited and continues as long as the agent–case officer relationship lasts.

BECOMING A SPY—BACKGROUND CHECK

In order to become a spy or to get a security clearance, you are required to fill out a very detailed form describing everywhere you've lived, all of your relatives, and all of the people who have known you at various times throughout your life. A person is assigned to investigate your life thoroughly (a background check), including interviewing the people you have listed and then, often, interviewing people named by the people you listed. No stone is left unturned, for a person's *history* and *background* demonstrate much about the person's *character*, which is what the agency is really trying to evaluate.

The investigators are also looking for anything that can be used *against* the recruit as blackmail. There is a whole division that performs background checks and security clearance checks on those who have applied to enter the spy world, as well as those presently in the spy world. Additional reviews are performed in conjunction with a promotion or new position—or after some negative fact comes to light.

In this reevaluation of James's character, Harry will hear from numerous others that James did these things when he was quite young. This is not a very satisfying excuse, given the fact that Harry is presently the same age! Harry concludes that his father's actions were less then admirable and that his father's age is *not* an excuse (670).

In addition, Harry knows exactly what it's like to be bullied or embarrassed while a circle of fellow students watches. He is rightfully concerned that James justified his actions toward Snape *not* because of anything that Snape had done *to him*, but rather simply because he *exists*. Harry realizes that this is, in reality, a form of prejudice, and the excuse that a person deserves bullying because of what or who he or she is can be used to justify any improper or even evil actions (653). Indeed, one could argue that Voldemort is trying to kill Harry exactly because Harry *exists* (oh, and that thing about the prophecy).

Harry is also confused by the fact that his mother, at the age of fifteen, gave every indication of *loathing* James Potter and considered him a conceited bully. Harry goes so far as to wonder whether his father *forced* his mother to marry him (653). These ruminations are naturally quite disconcerting for Harry, particularly given how proud he was of his father *before* he delved into the Pensieve and saw Snape's memories.

Harry is growing up. There are points in our lives where we begin to see our parents not just as our parents, but as fellow adults. We analyze what they did in their childhood and while raising us with the eyes of maturity instead of youth.

Harry finally settles at the library, trying to study, but he is still worried about these issues. Ginny Weasley comes over to talk, bringing him a package that had clearly been opened and searched by the High Inquisitor before being distributed. Easter is coming, and the package contained nothing but chocolate eggs and other candy sent by Mrs. Weasley (654).

Harry is not his usual self, and Ginny asks him if he is okay, mentioning that he could always talk to Cho. Harry tells her firmly it is not Cho that he wants to talk to. When Ginny presses to know what he is concerned about, Harry says that he wants to talk to Sirius. Ginny—raised in the presence of her twin brothers—states, based on her observations of her brothers' actions, that *"anything is possible if you've got enough nerve"* (655)!

NOTE TO SELF: *If you walk in and look like you know what you're doing, odds are people will assume that you're supposed to be there and think nothing of it.*

This of course brings us to the perennial problem of risk, when to take a risk, and risk analysis. Ginny has indicated that "anything is possible if you've got enough nerve." Is it?

Meanwhile, the teachers seem intent on keeping Hogwarts more or less on schedule, and it is at this point in their education that the teachers discuss with each of the students career options. Numerous pamphlets have been distributed in the common room so that the children can look at their different career options. Each career field has certain minimum requirements that must be met if a student wants to enter that field (656).

When Ron sees the extremely high qualifications required to become a Healer, he says, quite simply, "Blimey" (656). (Anyone who has looked at the requirements for Muggle medical school will sympathize!) Hermione indicates that being a Healer is a very important job, and one cannot help thinking, when hearing this compliment to doctors, that J. K. Rowling's husband just *happens* to be a physician!

Fred and George come to talk to Harry, having been told by Ginny that he wants to speak to Sirius. The Weasley twins inform Harry that they think they have a way around Umbridge's surveillance of all the communications in and out of Hogwarts. The twins state, "It's a simple matter of causing a diversion" (657). Diversion! Yeah!

ANALYSIS: *Where could Harry safely talk to Sirius?* We know that communications via owl are being intercepted and that the Floo network is under surveillance, controlled and monitored by Marietta's mother (631). But the Weasley twins have an idea, one that Harry has already considered and mentions even before the twins have a chance to do so: *Umbridge's office!* You may recall that, in the last chapter, Umbridge told Harry that her fire was the only one not being watched (631).

RULES AND RULE-MAKERS

Isn't it nice that rules often do not apply to those who make them? For example, did you know that some of the laws passed by Congress and applying to all US citizens and all US businesses do *not* apply to Congress itself?

Hermione overhears them talking about getting into Umbridge's office and asks, understandably, "Are—You—Insane?" Harry doesn't think so: he mentions Sirius's knife—the knife that can magically unlock any door. What a wonderful device, and what a wonderful example of a spy's use of technology (658).

As we've mentioned before, the CIA's Directorate of Science and Technology has created many wonderful technological spy tools over the years. Of course, many of their inventions are still classified, so that they can be used secretly. Thus, the best we can do is refer you to the many James Bond movies and to the fictional head of science and technology for the British secret service, Q. (So secret a person that they only give him a LETTER!)

One more word about technology: TECHNOLOGY. (Just had to do that!)

Harry uses many clever devices throughout the series to spy or not be seen. In addition to Sirius's knife, we have the Marauder's Map (which tells you where everybody is at Hogwarts at all times), the Invisibility Cloak, the two-way mirror Sirius gave to Harry (which he has not yet used), Portkeys for transportation, expanding charms so that the trunks and Hermione's purse can hold much more than they normally would, and numerous diversionary devices, such as the Weasley twins' fireworks and, later, their Decoy Detonators. But science and technology are your friends as well as your enemies: just as a jinx usually has a counter-jinx, a device used to spy on someone can be used just as easily *against* you, or can be *countered* by some other device or method.

The next step toward getting into Professor Umbridge's office is of course the planning stage, properly called *operation planning* in the spy world. When dealing with covert operations (and this is one), it is essential that everyone knows what they are to do, when they are going to do it, and how long the diversion will last so they are not discovered. The planning also includes an **intelligence briefing**, in which an intelligence officer will update the **operations team** on what the intelligence entity knows about the location, the individuals who could be there, and other details important to the mission.

Most intelligence agencies have access to a **Sensitive Compart-mented Information Facility (SCIF),** which is often literally kept in a large vault. By means of computer, the intelligence officer can look through all of the classified information relating to a particular location, person, or organization. Obviously this person would have to have the proper clearance, which is normally determined on a need-to-know basis.

Let us pretend for a moment that we are in the intelligence briefing at the planning stage for breaking into Umbridge's office. Here are some of the things that the planners need to know and that the intelligence officer must be able to provide:

1. What is the security used *to prevent access*? Obviously Umbridge's door, which is magically protected—but hopefully that magic will be countered by Sirius's knife.

2. What are the risks associated with *getting in*? The most obvious risk is being observed in the hallway. The solution is use of the Invisibility Cloak and the diversion planned in order to make them unlikely to be seen as they enter the office.

3. What is the **layout** *of the location?* The students know
    the layout of the corridor adjacent to the office and can
    choose a proper location for the diversion, away from those
    corridors. In addition, they need to know the layout of
    the room itself—which Harry knows all too well from his
    detentions in Umbridge's office.

4. Once in the room, what are the risks relating to being
    observed while *in the room?* In other words, are there any
    cameras or other devices (such as a Sneakoscope) that
    could observe Harry when he enters and alert Umbridge?

5. Are there any particular security alerts or magic spells that
    alert anyone when someone is in the office—such as the
    loud screaming that occurs when Harry, Hermione, and
    Ron Disapparate in a street in Hogsmeade in book 7 (*DH*
    554)? (In the film version of *Harry Potter and the Order of
    the Phoenix*, the kittens on the plates in Umbridge's office
    not only move, but also, when Harry sneaks into the office,
    can exit the plates to alert Umbridge, just like the portraits
    throughout Hogwarts.)

6. What technology or method will be needed to *activate* the
    communication device? In other words, if Harry is going
    to use Umbridge's fireplace and the Floo network, what
    will he need to use? He will need Floo powder—which, by
    the way, he does not bring with him; good planning would
    have called for that, but instead he finds some sitting on
    the hearth.

7. What are the time constraints? *How long can the operation
    last?* Harry needs to determine how long it will take to
    communicate with Sirius and needs to have some way of
    keeping track of the time so that he can get out promptly.
    This too should have been considered in planning: Harry
    should have some form of stopwatch to alert him when his
    time is up.

8. What is needed to ensure that the place is *left exactly as you found it*? How can they be sure that Harry *leaves no trace* or any evidence that the operation had occurred? The whole point of a *covert* operation is to go in, do what you need to do, and get out—*without anybody knowing you were there*! Thus, Harry needs to think about leaving NO trace of his presence. He must put the Floo powder container back *exactly* where it was when he arrived. He needs to make sure he doesn't change *anything* in the room. (For proof of that, think of the consequences of his stealing Mad-Eye Moody's eye off Professor Umbridge's door in book 7 [*DH* 251].) This includes, for example, tidying up after using the fireplace, using a broom to put back any ashes that might have come out onto the floor. In our experience, many operations include bringing a digital camera—often with night vision capability if the operation is being run at night—and taking a photo when entering the room. The initial photo is then compared with (or, better yet, superimposed over) a photo taken right before leaving the room, making sure the pictures match.

BLACK BAG JOBS— COVERT OPERATIONS AT THEIR BEST

A **black bag job** is a surreptitious or covert entry into a home, office, or other location without the knowledge of the owner. The term originates from the need to bring a black bag full of tools by which to gain entry to the home or office, such as lock-picking tools. A black bag job is a success when the person gains entry, obtains the information desired or places surveillance devices, and leaves, undetected and without the knowledge of the person who resides, works, or lives there.

9. Once the mission is complete, what needs to be done so the **egress** or escape is executed without being seen? Will Harry leave under the Invisibility Cloak? Will he simply open the door, step out, and walk away? Will there be somebody outside the door watching as a lookout? All of these concerns must be addressed in the planning stage if this covert mission is to be a success.

10. Is there a method to communicate that the *plan is to be aborted*? It is essential in any plan to have a way to communicate that something is going wrong. Harry needs to know right away if Umbridge isn't where she's supposed to be, or if she's on her way back. The ability to abort a plan is a very important aspect of every covert operation and should be taken into account in the planning stage.

NOTE TO SELF: *Planning a mission is almost as fun as conducting it!*

The operations planning done by Harry and the Weasley twins is substantially less detailed, but sufficient for this particular mission. The Weasley twins intend to set off the diversion in the east wing right after classes are over, so that everyone is in the corridors when it happens. The twins tell Harry that they can guarantee him twenty minutes and the diversion will begin around five o'clock. Thus, the planning includes not only the *location* of the mission, but *when* and *where* the diversion will occur (659).

By creating the diversion when classes have just gotten out, the twins are planning for the maximum number of people in the corridors and accounting for whether most will go *toward* the diversion or *away* from it, depending on what *type* of diversion they employ. By definition, the diversion has to be something that Umbridge would learn about and feel compelled to attend to immediately. Of course, the planners should know where Professor Umbridge would normally be at that time—whether in her office or teaching a class.

Throughout the rest of the chapter—at least until the operation is completed—Hermione repeatedly attempts to persuade Harry *not* to go through with it. Hermione is concerned for Harry's welfare and even goes so far as to mention that Dumbledore sacrificed himself so Harry could stay in school, and if Harry is caught, he will surely be expelled (657–67).

Thus, in addition to the general risk analysis, Hermione has attempted to use a pang of guilt to dissuade Harry from completing the operation. She also mentions the risk that Professor Umbridge will "*force* you to drink Veritaserum" (660). (Hermione and Harry had both correctly concluded that Professor Umbridge's tea had included the truth serum, Veritaserum [629–31].) Not surprisingly, Hermione's attempts to stop Harry are to no avail.

We will now discuss the **psychology of risk**, and the motivations for taking risks. We note that Harry is *not* taking this huge risk for the purpose of learning about Voldemort, or to develop information about the "weapon" hidden in the Department of Mysteries. Harry's sole purpose is one of *personal privilege*: he wants to ask Sirius about his parents. In other words, Harry is taking this risk *not* in furtherance of the greater good, but rather in furtherance of his own personal desires and emotional needs.

In deciding whether to take the risk and proceed with the plan, Harry specifically recalls Sirius's dig when Harry was unwilling to take the risk of having Sirius show up in Hogsmeade: "You're less like your father than I thought . . . the risk would have been what made it fun for James" (667).

Now a word about retribution: RETRIBUTION!

While the plan simmers, Harry is dealing with retribution from Professor Snape himself! The Potions Professor now ignores Harry completely—which is just fine by him. He's used to the silent treatment at the Dursleys'. But when Harry does a fairly decent job on his potion and turns it in on Professor Snape's desk, amazingly it *somehow* falls to the floor and breaks. "Whoops," says Snape, "another zero, then, Potter" (660–61).

CHAPTER 29

NOTE TO SELF: *It is always dangerous to alienate or offend somebody who has power or control over you.*

Harry is furious—but what can he do?

Before "Operation Fireplace," Harry has an appointment with Professor McGonagall, the Head of the Gryffindor house, to get career advice. But Professor McGonagall is not alone! Headmistress Umbridge is there, quietly—and then *not* so quietly—taking notes (661).

Professor McGonagall asks Harry if he has any thoughts on a future career, and he tells her that he has thought about being an Auror. Professor McGonagall notes that he will need top grades for that and goes on to list the classes that he would be required to take in the sixth and seventh years, including Transfiguration (Aurors frequently Transfigure and Untransfigure in their work). Harry finds out, to his great disappointment, that to be an Auror he would need not only to take Potions, but also achieve an "Outstanding" on his Potions O.W.L. Professor McGonagall sees his disappointment, but explains to Harry that "poisons and antidotes are essential study for Aurors" (662–63).

Let us discuss for a moment what an Auror does. An Auror is a highly trained spy or security agent who focuses on the application of the Defense Against the Dark Arts, finding those who are using the Dark Arts, and stopping them—in essence, combating Voldemort, Death Eaters, and others who use Dark Magic. Aurors also serve as protectors of *high-security assets*—as we saw when the Ministry of Magic attempted to arrest Dumbledore with Shacklebolt and Dawlish in attendance. (Shacklebolt is later assigned to protect the Muggle Prime Minister in book 6, *Harry Potter and the Half-Blood Prince* [*HBP* 17].) Thus, in the Muggle world, Aurors are the equivalent of US Marshals in Texas in the late 1800s, FBI and Secret Service agents today, and the Royal Mounted Police of Canada. Where necessary, CIA officers protect their assets and defectors—though often, in the United States, with the assistance of the FBI.

In addition to doing well in all these classes, Harry would be required to go through a stringent series of character and aptitude tests. Sound familiar? When Harry asks, "What sort of character and aptitude tests?" Professor McGonagall states that he will "need to demonstrate the ability to react well to pressure and so forth! Perseverance and dedication . . . Very high skills in practical defense" (664–65).

The abilities and character of anyone wanting to be a spy are thoroughly investigated, as well as their ability to think well under pressure. One of our favorite scenes in the *Men in Black* movie series is in the first movie, when they are recruiting soon-to-be Agent Kay (played by Will Smith). He and a few highly trained military officers are given a test in which they have to determine which person or caricature to shoot at. While the others shoot at the monsters, Kay shoots at the little girl holding books that were clearly not suitable for her age. The film example is exaggerated for the humor of it, but the CIA and other agencies do look for the ability to think outside the box and analyze things differently—but also correctly.

One ability not covered in Professor McGonagall's list, or indeed at Hogwarts (perhaps because there are magical solutions?), is learning a different language. Speaking two or more languages will open many, many doors in all branches of government and business. Anyone who speaks native English and also one or more other languages, such as German, Mandarin Chinese, French, or Arabic, could literally choose whatever he or she wanted to do for the rest of their career in the spy world.

The next portion of Harry's career advice relates to *Professor Umbridge's* view of his capabilities and the humorous interplay (normally called an argument) between Professor McGonagall and Professor Umbridge (663–66).

Professor Umbridge has already interrupted Professor McGonagall's advice, wondering "whether Mr. Potter has *quite* the temperament for an Auror?" (663). The argument begins over Harry's high marks in Defense Against the Dark Arts. Professor Umbridge takes umbrage (yes, we know!) at his test results, indicating that Harry did quite poorly in *her* class. Professor McGonagall corrects herself, albeit clearly for the purpose of insulting Professor Umbridge: "He has achieved high marks in all Defense Against the Dark Arts tests set by a competent teacher" (663–64). Whoa. That had to hurt!

Umbridge mentions that Aurors must have no criminal record, and Professor McGonagall retorts that Harry has been cleared of all charges (665). Professor Umbridge then declares that "this boy has as much chance of becoming an Auror as Dumbledore has of ever returning to this school," to which Professor McGonagall replies, "a very good chance, then" (665). The argument really gets going, with Professor McGonagall stating that she will tutor Harry nightly if necessary to assist him in getting the marks necessary to become an Auror (665)!

The issue of politics raises its ugly head when Umbridge says, "The Ministry of Magic will never employ Harry Potter," and Professor McGonagall states, "There may be a new Minister of Magic by the time Potter is ready to join" (665). Harry's session of career advice is clearly over.

It is important to note that a part of Defense Against the Dark Arts at Hogwarts seems to involve what Muggles call *conflict resolution*. Although young boys are often interested in action, fights, and daring adventures (such as spy craft, of course!), one of the chapters in Harry's Defense Against the Dark Arts books is entitled "Non-Retaliation and Negotiation" (666).

Yes, in order to be a spy one needs skill in both offensive and defensive fighting, including close order fighting (the proverbial knife fight in a phone booth). But it's just as important to be able to accomplish your aims *without* a fight! Non-retaliation is one method—as is negotiation.

MAHATMA GANDHI AND THE CONCEPT OF NONVIOLENT PROTEST

Mahatma Gandhi brought the greatest international power of his time, Great Britain, to its knees by his method of **nonviolent non-cooperation**. Martin Luther King and others used similar methods, including sit-ins, work holidays, and boycotts of the public bus transportation system, as ways to create change in the southern United States in the 1960s.

~~~~~~

Negotiation is almost always the best way to find a *common path to a common solution*. Every negotiation must begin with analysis of what one side wants or needs, what the other side wants or needs, and in what ways the two sides can come together to a mutually desirable solution. In book 7, you will note, Voldemort repeatedly negotiates with his opponents in Hogwarts Castle to turn Harry over, telling them that none of them will be harmed if they do so, but also explaining the risk of what will happen if they don't (*DH* 610, 660).

Following his career advice with Professor McGonagall, Harry reanalyzes the risk of his *mission*, receives Hermione's admonition that Dumbledore had sacrificed himself to keep him in school, and thinks about the consequences of being caught right after Professor McGonagall has vouched for him and his character (666–67). What type of *loyalty* would he be showing Professor McGonagall by doing something so stupid right after she had informed him of the steps she was willing to take to ensure that he became an Auror?

As we soon find out, when the time comes Harry does indeed continue the mission, in part because Sirius's hurtful words are still at the front of his mind: "You're less like your father than I thought. . . . The risk would have been what made it fun for James" (667–68). The diversion begins, and Harry is off!

The corridor outside Umbridge's office is deserted, and Harry is able to run up to Umbridge's door unseen and use Sirius's knife to open the door. The room is empty but for the kittens on the plates. Harry pulls off his Invisibility Cloak, finds the Floo powder on the hearth, gives the address—number twelve, Grimmauld Place—and then gets down on his knees and puts his head toward the fire (668).

CHAPTER 29

ANALYSIS: *How smart was it for Harry to go into an enemy's office and say* out loud *the address of the secret headquarters, the place where the infamous Sirius Black is presently located?* Not very. If there was anybody else hidden in the room, or if the room was under surveillance, or if there was a recording device in the room, Harry would have just provided the Ministry of Magic (and specifically Professor Umbridge) with the address of the Order's secret headquarters *as well as* the location of Sirius Black, who is of course being sought as the supposed mastermind behind the Death Eaters' breakout! A bad idea indeed!

And why is Harry taking such a huge risk? Because he wants to find out whether his father was a good man or a pompous jerk!

Looking out of the fireplace at number twelve, Grimmauld Place, Harry sees Lupin. He asks Lupin to get Sirius (669). Lupin and Sirius think there must be something dreadfully wrong for Harry to take such a risk and are somewhat surprised that the questions Harry poses relate to his father (669).

Harry guesses that some five minutes has already passed, though it is important to realize that in moments of crisis or great risk there is such a thing as a situational time shift (669). That is, as many of you probably already know, the feeling, when you are in an emergency situation—such as an automobile accident—that *time changes* dramatically; it changes *differently* for each person.

While you might perceive the accident almost in slow motion—one car hitting your car and then your car heading in a different direction, and all the little details about it—another person may hardly observe any details and instead claim that everything happened "in an instant." Thus, as we noted earlier, Harry should have brought a stopwatch or some device to tell him when his twenty minutes was close to being up.

PART 1

Sirius tells Harry that he should not judge his father on what he saw in the Pensieve, that James Potter was only fifteen at the time. Of course, Harry's reaction is, "I'm fifteen!" Harry and his father's two best friends discuss James Potter and the hatred that he and Snape had for each other (670). Sirius says that he's "not proud of" what happened, but that they were all idiots at the time. Lupin was perhaps not so much of an idiot, Sirius points out (670).

Lupin, to his credit, objects to the compliment—rightfully stating that he had observed everything that was going on but never "had the guts" to tell them to lay off Snape (671). Lupin probably refused to partake in the bullying because he, as a hidden were-wolf, knew very well what it's like to be an outcast, shunned by the Wizarding world.

One other fact deserves mention at this time: when Lupin claims he didn't have the guts to tell them to lay off Snape, does that remind you of how Gryffindor won the House Cup at the end of Harry's first year at Hogwarts, thanks to Neville Longbottom? He tried to prevent Harry, Ron, and Hermione from breaking the rules (*SS* 272). And do you remember what Dumbledore said to all the students and staff of Hogwarts when Neville received the final points that resulted in Gryffindor's win?

"It takes a great deal of bravery to stand up to our enemies, but just as much to stand up to our friends" (*SS* 306).

Now, as Harry is perhaps misapplying his bravery, Sirius tells him that yes, James Potter did show off at that point in his life, but his head was deflated by his seventh year and he stopped hexing people for the fun of it. Sirius explains that Harry's father was a good person and that he grew out of the character flaws that Harry saw in Snape's memories (671). When Sirius and Lupin find out that Harry is no longer taking Occlumency lessons, they react very badly, telling Harry that it is the most important thing for him now (672).

CHAPTER 29

Harry should have been long gone by this point. He hears footsteps and leaves the fire to hide under the Invisibility Cloak. Lucky for Harry, the person who enters Umbridge's office is Filch, who comes in to get a form for whipping a student. After Filch leaves, Harry is able to leave as well, undetected, and follows the noise to the entrance hall, where he finds that Fred and George have been caught—and are cornered (673)!

The diversion, it turns out, was Fred and George turning a school corridor into a swamp! Fred shows absolutely no fear of Professor Umbridge or of being caught. Filch hands Umbridge the form for whipping, and she tells the Weasley twins that they are about to learn what happens to wrongdoers "in my school" (674).

Fred replies, "I don't think we are." He then comments to George, "I think we've outgrown full-time education." George agrees. They summon their brooms from Professor Umbridge's office and declare to everyone there that it's time to take their talents into the real world—announcing their new premises, Weasleys' Wizard Wheezes at Number 93, Diagon Alley. And with that, away they go, instructing Peeves to "Give her hell from us." The poltergeist not only accepts the order, but respectfully salutes the twins as they escape the confines of Hogwarts and the toadlike grip of Professor Umbridge (674–75)!

30

SECRETS REVEALED: LARGE (GIANT) FAMILY SECRETS, SMALL TWIN SECRETS, SECRETS OF THE HERD AND HAGRID'S INTERVENTION

Chapter 30 is entitled "Grawp." As might be expected, Fred and George's exit becomes legend at Hogwarts. However, everyone wants to tell a good story, and sometimes a good story can get better in the retelling, particularly by the addition of colorful facts that are not entirely accurate, but not entirely wrong, either.

Other students at Hogwarts, inspired by the twins' example, plan similar mayhem, making Fred and George Weasley part of the Hogwarts lexicon (676). A mass movement often begins with such brave acts, which can be used as an example for others. (The Arab Spring started this way!) And, of course, mimicry is often the highest compliment and a form of flattery.

Thanks to the new Headmistress, the types of punishments allowed have changed drastically, and a happy Filch has been empowered with authority to punish—with a horsewhip no less (677)! Members of the Inquisitorial Squad, however, keep having things happen to them—one of them actually sprouting antlers (677). The little war has spread to all of Hogwarts! No staff members other than Filch are helping Umbridge, which must make her life very busy indeed (676–78)!

Ron and Hermione wonder how Fred and George got the money to set up their shop and whether or not Mundungus might have been somehow involved. Harry, unwilling to see Fred and George's reputation besmirched, tells them the truth: Harry gave the Triwizard winnings to the Weasley twins. Harry also gives Ron permission to tell his mother so she doesn't think her twins somehow got the money improperly (680).

NOTE TO SELF: *Everyone cares what his or her mum thinks about them! Even David Letterman!*

Harry continues to have his recurring dream, getting all the way into the Hall of Prophecies and running to the correct row—row ninety-seven—then turning left. However, he still wakes up before finding his target (682).

Preparations are in full swing for the Quidditch match between Ravenclaw and Gryffindor. Ron is understandably nervous, though Hermione notes that since his brothers left Hogwarts he has been handling the pressure much better (683). Everybody handles pressure differently: some with calm stoicism, others with mild concern, and still others with great trepidation. Often the best way to deal with pressure is to put it in perspective: how important is this really, in the larger scheme of things?

NOTE TO SELF: *When feeling pressured, try to think about everything in the big picture: will it be important a week from now, a month from now, or a year from now?*

The Quidditch match begins poorly, as Ron misses a block. Harry and Hermione miss the rest of the match, however, because Hagrid asks them to go with him *right away*. Hagrid won't tell them why, but says, "it's gotta be now . . . while ev'ryone's lookin' the other way" (684–85).

They head toward Hagrid's cabin, thinking that they will stop there. Instead, Hagrid grabs his crossbow and tells them that they're heading into the Forbidden Forest. Harry asks, "Hagrid, why are you armed?" and Hagrid says, "Jus' a precaution." It seems that the centaurs are riled at Hagrid—and, actually, the word *angry* doesn't cover it. "If I hadn' stepped in, I reckon they'd've kicked Firenze ter death" (686). Hagrid explains that he had prevented the herd from killing Firenze.

ANALYSIS: *Why did Hagrid insist on telling his secret in the middle of a Quidditch game?* Though his actions don't always make sense, Hagrid has enough sense to realize that with all the school at a Quidditch match, he would be able to take Harry and Hermione into the Forbidden Forest without being seen. The Quidditch match, in other words, is a diversion!

NOTE TO SELF: *If a diversion already exists, why not use it?*

On their way into the depths of the Forbidden Forest, Hagrid states that it would not be the end of the world if he got fired, because he would then be able to help Dumbledore. Without disclosing exactly what he wanted from Harry and Hermione, Hagrid informs them that he needs their help, and they promise to give it. And then they meet Hagrid's half-brother, Grawp. The promise they made, it turns out, is to look after him when Hagrid's gone and teach him English (688–93). Nothing to it, right?

As Hagrid, Hermione, and Harry are leaving the forest, the centaurs show up, telling Hagrid that he should not have meddled and that "our ways are not yours, nor are our laws." In their view, Firenze has betrayed and dishonored the centaurs and entered into servitude to humans. Hagrid objects, saying that it's not servitude and he is just "doing Dumbledore a favor." The centaurs are not convinced, stating "he is peddling our knowledge and secrets among humans. There can be no return from such disgrace" (698).

CHAPTER 30

These few paragraphs of discussion between Hagrid and the centaur raise issues usually dealt with in full-semester courses at major universities! First we have the issue of social differences between cultures and nations; Hagrid has "meddled" into the affairs of a cultural group accustomed to sovereignty, a separate nation in the Forbidden Forest. The centaurs are an entity independent from the Wizarding world, with their own laws, customs, and mores. Hagrid, by intervening, has violated those laws, mores, and customs. The question becomes, at what point is one group allowed to intercede in the actions of a second group when technically they have no authority?

DIFFERENT CULTURES AND THE IMPORTANCE OF AREA STUDIES

One of the most important aspects of CIA training is area studies, which is used not only by case officers who are sent out to foreign countries, but also by all intelligence officers, including and especially analysts. Beyond just learning the local language, intelligence officers are immersed in the history, morals, customs, and mores of a country in order to understand the place to which they have been assigned. In order to assist intelligence analysts in reaching this understanding, analysts are frequently assigned to live undercover in a country for an extended time, thus learning as much as possible about that country and its people.

The centaurs are mad at Firenze not only because he has supposedly entered into the servitude of humans, but also because he is "peddling our knowledge and secrets among humans" (698). In other words, Firenze is divulging confidential information or secrets to someone who is not allowed that information, and thus has been branded a traitor. According to the centaur, "There can be no return from such disgrace" (698).

~~~~~~~~~~~~~~~~~~~~~~~~~~~~~~~~~~~~~~

SHOULD SECRETS BE SECRET?

Every country has its secrets—and every country wants to keep them. When a person discloses one country's secrets to another country, he or she is properly deemed a traitor, regardless of whether that secret is *important*. When a person agrees to join an intelligence agency or another group dealing with secrets, he or she must agree to keep any classified material secret. Any violation of that promise is both immoral and illegal.

You might ask, why do we need secrets? And what if the secrets you know are those you do not feel should be secret? The first part of the answer is simple: the person learning the secret does not decide whether or not it should be secret; the entity or government providing the information makes that decision. Regardless of their beliefs, the person gaining that knowledge still has a profound moral and legal obligation to keep it secret. A system of secrecy will not work if every person involved has the option of deciding whether or not to abide by it! Thus, a person agreeing to receive secrets is obligated to keep them.

The next question is whether our society should have *so many* secrets. It is true that secrets should generally *not* be allowed and that there must be a valid basis for creating and continuing to hold secrets. Certainly, we can all agree that there are some things that absolutely should be secret, such as the codes used to launch nuclear missiles. And most certainly the names of agents or sources spying for us in the field should not be disclosed.

By the same token, the methods by which we receive information about other nations need to remain secret so that we continue receiving that information. In other words, it would not be appropriate for anyone to disclose how our spy satellites work, how our computers retrieve information without the other side's knowledge, or how we could use cyber warfare to, say, shut down centrifuges in another country (assuming we had anything to do with that!).

We need secrets, but we should also *presume* that everything should be open and known to all *unless* there is a very good reason to keep it secret.

~~~~~~~~~~~~~~~~~~~~~~~~~~~~~~~~~~~~

It seems to us that the centaurs put just a bit too much stock (sorry about that) in the value of their knowledge. Firenze himself said that centaur knowledge is not very specific—and, indeed, the centaurs may not know for a decade whether their interpretation of the stars is correct (604)! As far as we can tell, the only thing they've said of any import is that Mars indicates that a war will be coming soon and that we are presently between two wars. Given what we know from the series so far, it doesn't seem very profound to learn that the Wizarding world might be in between two wars!

Though still angry, the centaurs allow Hagrid to pass because he is accompanied by children, and centaurs do not slaughter foals: harming "the innocent" is a terrible crime. However, the centaurs tell Hagrid to "stay away from this place" and warn, "we know what you are keeping in the forest." Hagrid, always tactful, tells them, "You'll tolerate him as long as he is here; it's as much his forest as yours" (699).

Thus, with more questions than answers, Harry and Hermione return to the school just as the Quidditch game is ending. Hagrid, once again employing great spy craft, instructs the pair to hurry up and blend in with the crowd so no one will realize that they weren't at the game. As Harry and Hermione approach the school, they

PART 1

once again hear the strains of "Weasley Is Our King." However, it is being sung with *new* words (702). Harry is first to realize that it now affirms that Weasley is "our king"—Gryffindor's king!—for *Ron has won the match*. Ron, the hero of the day, raising the Quidditch cup overhead and being carried on the shoulders of his fellow Gryffindors! Harry and Hermione are thrilled for their friend (702).

ANALYSIS: *Did the mirror of Erised actually predict the future in book 1?* Remember back in *Harry Potter and the Sorcerer's Stone*, when Harry brought Ron to see Harry's mother and father standing with him (*SS* 209)? What did Ron see? "I'm alone—but I'm different—I look older—and I'm Head Boy! . . . and I'm holding the house cup and the Quidditch cup—I'm Quidditch captain, too!" (*SS* 211). And here, four years later, is Ron, the prefect (although not Head Boy) of Gryffindor, holding the Quidditch cup!

Let's look again at what Harry saw in the Mirror of Erised: a crowd of people standing behind him, including his mother and father. In book 4, *Harry Potter and the Goblet of Fire*, after Cedric was murdered and Harry was making his escape, his parents stand again behind and beside him (*GF* 667)! And in book 7, Harry's parents and closest friends, though dead, stand behind and beside him as he walks into the Forbidden Forest to meet Voldemort—where he will allow Voldemort to kill him (*DH* 699).

So, did the Mirror of Erised foretell the future or merely reflect what Harry and Ron each desired most? The inscription on the mirror gives us a good clue—more on that in a moment. For now, think about whether it might have been the boys' strong desire for something that made those desires reality, and not some mirror's prediction!

Will you become what others predict for you or what *you* want to become because of your greatest desires? We leave this question to you!

But before we leave our reflection on the Mirror of Erised, let's have one more word about **code breaking**. All right, *two* words.

Do you recall the engraving on the top of the Mirror of Erised? Let us remind you.

Erised stra ehru oyt ube cafru oyt on wohsi (*SS* 207).

Just out of curiosity, have you by chance written those letters in reverse order, *as they would appear in a mirror?* If you've done so, this is what the engraving says:

ishownotyourfacebutyourheartsdesirE.

Now let's add spaces where appropriate and make it into a sentence:

I show not your face but your heart's desire.

We have just broken the code!

In book 1, Dumbledore explains the mirror without breaking the code or telling Harry how to read the inscription, saying simply, "The happiest man on earth would see himself exactly as he is." Harry figures out on his own (sound familiar?) that the mirror "shows us what we want," and only then does Dumbledore confirm that, "It shows us nothing more or less than the deepest, most desperate desire of our hearts" (*SS* 213). But Dumbledore never tells young Harry how to break the code contained in the inscription.

This motif of Dumbledore explaining part, but not all, appears throughout the seven books, leaving Harry to figure things out on his own. Only in the last book do we understand why Dumbledore wanted it that way . . . but we aren't there yet!

31

LET THE TEST BE WITH YOU—THEORY MEETS PRACTICE—TOAD·FACE MEETS OLD WIZARDING FACES—A "STUNNING" OBSERVATION FROM THE ASTRONOMY TOWER

Chapter 31, "O.W.L.s," begins serenely—and ends in screams and terror. Many strands of the story coil us ever closer to an exciting end to an exciting book.

The chapter opens with Harry, Ron, and Hermione sitting under the same beech tree beneath which James Potter and his friends had sat so many years ago (703). Harry and Hermione had suggested going outside so they would have an opportunity to tell Ron—without being overheard—what Hagrid has in the Forbidden Forest. Selecting a *proper place to disclose confidential information* is yet another example of good spy craft.

～～～～～～～～～～～～～～～～～～

AGENT MAXWELL SMART AND THE CONE OF SILENCE

We are probably—definitely!—dating ourselves, but the meeting under the beech tree reminds us of the 1960s television series *Get Smart* (1965–1970), in which Maxwell Smart (Agent 86) and other operatives would use "The Cone of Silence."

Whenever Maxwell Smart needed to talk to the Chief or someone else without being overheard, the speakers would enter a very secure area and a secure room, where a transparent glass or plastic cone was lowered over their heads. The cone supposedly prevented eavesdropping.

The actual spy equivalent is the modern SCIF (Sensitive Compartmented Information Facility), a room where case operatives can talk without being overheard. But without access to the secure facilities of headquarters, a remote outdoor spot with clear lines of sight will do!

Ron is still reliving his win at the Quidditch match the day before, but eventually Harry and Hermione have to admit that they did not see the entire match—indeed, they saw only his first miss before answering Hagrid's summons (704–5). After hearing what Hagrid has done, Ron concludes that their friend is crazy and that Harry and Hermione should *not* keep their promise. After all, he points out, all of Hagrid's creatures have caused great turmoil—think of Norbert the Norwegian Ridgeback Dragon and Aragog the spider (705). However, Harry and Hermione intend to keep their word—as Hermione simply states, "we promised" (705). (Though they all hope that Hagrid doesn't get sacked, so they will not have to attempt to teach Grawp English!)

Now, a few words about keeping your promise: **KEEP YOUR PROMISE!**

The importance of keeping promises is a factor throughout the Harry Potter series. In book 2, *Harry Potter and the Chamber of Secrets*, Harry makes a "rash" promise to attend a Deathday Party at the request of Nearly Headless Nick instead of the Halloween feast (*CS* 129–31). Hermione says it best: "A promise is a promise," and they all go to the party instead of the feast. And when Harry promises Fudge in book 3, *Harry Potter and the Prisoner of Azkaban*, to stay at the Leaky Caldron and not leave Diagon Alley, he keeps his word (*PA* 49). Also in book 3, Hermione doesn't tell Harry or Ron about the Time-Turner (*PA* 430). And, as we discussed earlier, Harry does not tell his friends about Neville Longbottom's family secrets (*GF* 602–4; *OP* 515).

We note as an aside that there are times in life where we make promises we wish we had not made, perhaps in the heat of the moment, or after a mug or two of Firewhisky. Nonetheless, it is very important to keep your promises, no matter how hard it is to do so. Keeping of a promise you'd like to forget is especially important, if only to teach you to imbibe less Firewhisky next time!

While sitting under the beech tree, we also find out an interesting tidbit about the previous day's game. The win was a result not only of Ron's superb goalkeeping, but also of Ginny Weasley getting the Snitch "right under Cho's nose" (704). (And as we will see by the final book—and indeed, the final chapter of the final book—Ginny will win much more than the coveted Snitch!)

June is now upon the students, and with it their O.W.L.s (706). While the students are studying, Draco is overheard stating that it is "not what you know, but who you know" (707). Draco is asserting *special influence* based on his family connections.

Hermione wonders if Draco's family really can influence the witches and wizards who will be conducting the tests. Ron states stoically that there is nothing they can do about it anyway. Neville, however, is of the opinion that it is most likely not true—and he has interesting inside information to back that up. It turns out that Neville's grandmother knows Professor Marchbanks, the head of the Wizarding Examinations Authority. Neville tells the others that she's very strict (and therefore very honest, perhaps?). Neville implies that Draco's family has no known connection to Professor Marchbanks, based on the fact that Professor Marchbanks has never even mentioned the Malfoys while visiting Neville's grandmother (707).

CHAPTER 31

ANALYSIS: *Will the testing depend on who you know, or what you know?* We have no doubt that Draco would say so to make the others nervous, but it is just as possible that he believes it because his father has indicated—throughout his pathetic life—that using *connections,* not merit, is the way to get ahead.

The Malfoys are an established and well-known Wizarding family, and one that has money. So it appears that Draco *believes exactly what he is saying.* But is it true? Let's analyze it a bit, discerning who has *influence* and who is well-enough connected (through power, access to those in power, or even family connections) to have influence over the testing process at Hogwarts.

First, even the students know that outside influence during testing would be blatantly unfair and inappropriate. We already know that influence is used throughout the Wizarding world by the likes of Lucius Malfoy: remember him talking to Fudge at the Ministry after Harry's trial (154–55)? And Mr. Weasley's subsequent condemnation of Lucius Malfoy and his use of wealth and influence (155)? But when it comes to testing, it is clear that cheating is condemned and testing is taken very seriously.

As the children prepare for the tests, Professor McGonagall informs them that there will be many anti-cheating charms in force. She also sets her own expectation that none of the students in Gryffindor, her house, will cheat. Finally, Professor McGonagall notes that Professor Umbridge has indicated quite clearly that the results will reflect on the new regime. Professor McGonagall's view of the "new regime" is clear when she advises the students to do their very best because they have their futures to think about (708–9). In other words, although bad results would harm Umbridge's regime, it's not a good reason to intentionally flunk! Thus, the mores of the Wizarding community seem to indicate that improper influence during testing would never be allowed.

Second, we have Neville's assertion that the head of the Wizarding Examinations Authority has never mentioned the

Malfoys, at least not socially (707). Given the Malfoys' connection to Voldemort's Death Eaters, what do you think the odds are that Neville's grandmother would invite a friend of Lucius Malfoy over to her house for dinner?

Thus, taking all the facts we know into account, we can conclude the following: first, Draco, based on what his family has always said, believes that his family's influence will help him in testing; and, secondly, what he says is not true.

NOTE TO SELF: *Influence through power, money, and family connections is a fact of life, but that does not make it right. However, such influence can and should be used for the greater good if necessary.*

Meanwhile, many of the students are discussing and buying brain-stimulating potions in order to become smarter or do better on the tests. Of course, Hermione rejects all of these as fakes, some of them potentially harmful (708).

NOTE TO SELF: *There are many charlatans willing to prey on the fears and weaknesses of the masses, and it's important to perceive them for the fakes they are.*

The examiners, most of them quite elderly, arrive, to everyone's interest. Professor Marchbanks is the head of the examination team and apparently also somewhat hard of hearing, making it easy for Harry and his friends to overhear what she is saying. They nonetheless employ *basic spy craft techniques* and find a pretext to get closer and hear everything she says. They take their sweet time in walking by as Professor Marchbanks and Professor Umbridge talk, with Ron at one point finding it "necessary" to retie his shoe so that the trio can listen to what is being said. And what is being said is interesting indeed (710–11)!

Professor Marchbanks asks Professor Umbridge if she's heard from Dumbledore. Of course she hasn't. Professor Marchbanks then asks whether she has any idea where he is. Umbridge, to her great disappointment, has to answer, "None at all." Umbridge, always presenting the Ministry party line, tells Professor Marchbanks that "the Ministry will track him down soon enough"; Professor Marchbanks immediately pops Umbridge's bubble, saying, "I doubt it! Not if Dumbledore doesn't want to be found." She informs the new Headmistress that she herself had tested Dumbledore in his seventh year N.E.W.T.s and exclaims for all to hear that Dumbledore "did things with a wand that I've never seen before!" (711).

We'd like to make three points about this fascinating discussion:

The first point is that eavesdropping—particularly in public—is quite often easy to do. By definition, you're in a public place and you're allowed to go where you want. You are also able to make pretextural excuses to be in the area and to delay the time you are in that area, such as when Ron tied his shoe.

The second point is that it *appears* that not everybody in the Wizarding world is in favor of what the Ministry of Magic is doing, or, at the very least, not everyone is falling hook, line, and sinker for the party line.

Third, Professor Marchbanks's statement that Dumbledore will not be found unless he *wants* to be found can be interpreted two ways: first, as a mere statement of fact that the Ministry of Magic fails to comprehend; or second, as a subtle indication that Professor Marchbanks is secretly rooting for Dumbledore and thinks the Ministry of Magic is incorrect in its views—and perhaps in more than that!

Testing begins the next day, and it turns out that the vision Harry saw in Snape's memory is an accurate one (640). The tables are distributed exactly as they were when James Potter and his friends took the test so many years ago (712).

The tests proceed, with written tests (theory) in the morning and practice (practical application) in the afternoons—with the exception of Astronomy, of course, which must be done at night (708). As expected, Harry does quite well in his Defense Against the Dark Arts tests. Even better, Harry performs these various feats of magic while Umbridge is looking, and even receives extra credit when he—at the request of the tester—produces a corporeal Patronus Charm (714–15).

NOTE TO SELF: *When Harry and Ron have a day off from their O.W.L.s, they relax over a game of wizard chess. Playing chess is a great way to develop strategic skills—and it's a lot of fun!*

When the students find out that another Niffler has gotten into Umbridge's office, Ron and Harry both exclaim, "Good!" Hermione, however, counters that it's *not* good, because Professor Umbridge thinks that Hagrid is doing it, and she will use this as a reason to chuck him out. Harry looks outside and sees that Hagrid is at that moment teaching on the grounds. She can't blame Hagrid, Harry opines, because he was teaching and has an alibi! Frustrated, Hermione says, "Oh, you're so naïve sometimes, Harry. Do you really think Umbridge will wait for proof?" (715–16).

ANALYSIS: *Is Hermione's statement about Harry being naïve justified?* Hermione's criticism is both justified *and* unjustified. It is *unjustified* because Harry has often figured out whether or not things would occur, and because Harry has two reasons why Umbridge will wait to sack Hagrid: first, she should want Hagrid to finish out the school year; and second, Hagrid has an obvious alibi, and normal, reasonable people would wait for proof.

However, Hermione's comment is *justified* by the fact of her spot-on psychological assessment of Professor Umbridge. Hermione understands that Umbridge is not the type of person who cares about *proof*, but is rather concerned only whether her target agrees with her and her position—and Hagrid is a Dumbledore man "through and through."

Although there will always be some facts that are unknown and some conclusions based on assumptions or pure analysis, *your starting point must always be the facts—carefully gathered and carefully considered.* In the intelligence world it is very important that all decisions have a basis in fact and all *conclusions* and *assumptions* be based on some *demonstrative* fact.

This reminds us of a famous statement made by Senator Daniel Patrick Moynihan: "Everyone is entitled to his own opinion, but not his own facts." The fact that Umbridge makes decisions based on *biases or prejudices* instead of real evidence says a lot about whether she is the type of person you would want as a headmistress, or in any other leadership position.

ANALYSIS: *Why does the testing include theory AND practice?* The O.W.L.s show us a useful point about theory and practice, and the importance of having both. Harry—unlike many of the other students at Hogwarts—has had more opportunity than most to put his book learning into practice, especially (and unfortunately) in Defense Against the Dark Arts. The only bright spot in his Potions test, in fact, is that he can answer a question about the effects of Polyjuice Potion because he and his two friends had used the potion themselves (716). We can easily see how book learning supports practice, but remember that experience can help with book learning (and exams) as well!

When Harry shows up for his nighttime Astronomy exam, though, certain things draw his attention—and soon everybody else's attention—away from the test and instead to the grounds of Hogwarts (718–22).

We will now analyze what occurs while Harry is in the Astronomy Tower and differentiate between *observations* and *conclusions* on the way to evaluating whether or not the conclusion reached has sufficient basis in fact to be considered *reliable.* The task of making observations and reaching conclusions based on those observations plus prior knowledge is the very essence of intelligence analysis—which is, in essence, critical thinking. Based on his observations, Harry makes assumptions and reaches conclusions derived

PART 1

from both his observations and his use of logic. In other words, Harry uses his five senses and reaches rational conclusions based on common sense and what he observes.

Let us now chart these out, with the observation on the left column and the conclusion on the right:

OBSERVATION	CONCLUSION REACHED
Harry observes front doors of castle opening.	
Harry sees five to six shadows crossing the grass.	
In the moonlight, Harry recognizes a squat person as the leader.	Umbridge is taking a stroll with five others.
Harry sees that Hagrid's light is on; the six people are silhouetted in the light.	
The door opens, and the five to six people enter Hagrid's cabin.	
Harry hears a roar from the cabin.	It is Hagrid.
Harry hears a loud bang.	
Harry sees Hagrid's door burst open.	
Harry sees Hagrid fighting six at one time.	A fight has begun.
Harry sees Dawlish try to Stun Hagrid.	

OBSERVATION	CONCLUSION REACHED
Harry hears a dog bark and sees the dog Stunned.	Fang has been hit.
Harry hears Hagrid's howl of fury.	Hagrid is furious.
Harry sees a single long, black shadow crossing the lawn toward the hut.	A seventh person is entering the fray.
Harry hears McGonagall's voice: "How *dare* you!"	McGonagall is interceding.
Harry sees four Stunning Spells hit McGonagall, and she falls to the ground.	McGonagall has been injured.
Harry sees Hagrid knock out two attackers and bend down.	Hagrid *may* be hit or hurt?
Hagrid gets up and puts something that looks like a bag over his shoulders.	Hagrid is retrieving Fang.
Harry sees Hagrid turn and run through the gates.	Hagrid has escaped and *might* be joining Dumbledore?

As you can see here, Harry is able to reach certain conclusions because he knows who the squat lady is, he knows Hagrid's voice, he knows the sound of Fang's barking, he knows McGonagall's voice, and he can guess what Hagrid had picked up and put across his shoulders before he left the grounds. Harry has used logic, prior knowledge, and his observations to reach first *assumptions* and then valid *conclusions*.

Another interesting aspect is the reactions of the adults. We first observe McGonagall's reaction as she intercedes, yelling, "On what grounds are you attacking him?" (721). But even more interesting is the statement by Professor Tofty, the Astronomy examiner, when McGonagall is hit by four Stunners at once: "Not so much as a warning! Outrageous behavior!" (722). Once again, it appears that most witches and wizards, and certainly the more experienced adults, think that Headmistress Umbridge's conduct is inappropriate!

ANALYSIS: *Why did Professor Umbridge decide to sack Hagrid at night?* Ernie McMillian provides one analysis: Umbridge wanted to avoid another scene like her dismissal of Professor Trelawney, with the entire school watching (723). Whether she wanted to prevent another scene or just take care of Hagrid when he was least suspecting it and had no one who could help him, we leave to you.

FURTHER ANALYSIS: *Why did Professor Umbridge decide to sack Hagrid while school is still in session?* Hermione made the point that Umbridge hates part-humans, and also that Umbridge thought Hagrid was putting Nifflers in her office. Lee Jordan confessed that *he* was the one putting the Nifflers in the office, but the students conclude that Umbridge would have sacked Hagrid anyway because he was too close to Dumbledore.

EVEN FURTHER ANALYSIS: *Where did Hagrid go?* The students are relieved that he's not in Azkaban and suspect—perhaps correctly—that he went to join Dumbledore. We later find out that he hid in a cave in the mountains (854).

MORE ANALYSIS: *Why didn't Hagrid go to Dumbledore?* Most probably because he needed to stay nearby and take care of Grawp.

Despite all of the excitement, Harry still has to take his last exam, History of Magic. He falls asleep and into his usual dream, but with a new addition.

Harry finds himself in the Department of Mysteries in the room with the spheres—and he sees a human shape on the floor. Voldemort is telling the person on the floor, "I cannot touch it, but you can" (727). Harry approaches and, to his horror, "sees" that Voldemort is torturing Sirius! Voldemort wants Sirius to pick up something that he cannot touch himself. Sirius responds, "You'll have to kill me," to which Voldemort replies, "Undoubtedly I shall in the end . . . We have hours ahead of us and nobody to hear you scream" (727–28). Harry hears screaming and realizes, when he falls off his desk, that *he* was the one doing it (728).

Time for a rescue mission, don't you think?

32

APPLYING INTELLIGENCE ANALYSIS TO A "MISSING" SIRIUS—HERMIONE'S PLAN TO REENTER THE FIRE—CAPTURED!—TORTURE AND THE ART OF LYING CONVINCINGLY

Chapter 32, "Out of the Fire," begins with Harry getting out of a trip to the hospital wing by claiming that he screamed because he fell asleep and had a nightmare during the test. He is focused on figuring out how to rescue Sirius (729).

Harry realizes, for once, that he needs to tell an adult about what he has just seen, and in particular a member of the Order of the Phoenix. He therefore goes looking for Professor McGonagall. Unfortunately, Professor McGonagall is no longer at Hogwarts; after receiving four direct Stunning Spells to the chest the night before, she has been sent to St. Mungo's Hospital (730).

Once Harry learns that Professor McGonagall is gone, he immediately concludes that there is nobody left to tell. Dumbledore is gone, Hagrid is gone, and the always constant McGonagall is also gone. (He realizes too late that there *is* another member of the Order of the Phoenix at Hogwarts: Professor Snape!)

CHAPTER 32

NOTE TO SELF: *In an emergency, it is even more important to think clearly and analyze all options, quickly and objectively.*

Harry looks for Ron and Hermione, and they soon find each other. Harry finds a secure location—an empty classroom—and shuts the door before telling his friends what he saw in his dream (731).

We would like you all to note that the next ten or so pages are an exceedingly good example of intelligence analysis at its best.

ANALYSIS: *Is Sirius being tortured by Voldemort at the Department of Mysteries?*

Harry begins by informing his friends that Voldemort has Sirius. Hermione's first question is, *How do you know?* Harry says that he *saw* it. Hermione asks, but *where, how?* Harry doesn't know the how, but he knows the where: Sirius is being tortured at the Department of Mysteries, at the end of row ninety-seven. Voldemort will torture Sirius until he gives the Dark Lord what he wants—something that Voldemort can't get himself—and then murder him. Instead of analyzing the *situation*, Harry goes directly to analyzing *how to get there* to rescue Sirius (731).

Hermione, quite properly, analyzes the situation first. Her questions are those of an excellent intelligence officer and intelligence analyst:

1. How did Voldemort get into the Ministry of Magic without anyone realizing he was there?

2. How would Voldemort and Sirius get in without being seen, in the middle of the afternoon?

3. How would the two most-wanted wizards in the world get into a building full of Aurors undetected?

Harry mentions the possibility of an Invisibility Cloak and notes that the Department of Mysteries has always been empty whenever he's been there (732). Hermione properly reminds Harry that he has never *been* there, "You've only dreamed about the place, that's all" (732).

Harry next asserts that these are *not* normal dreams—after all, he saved Mr. Weasley's life using information from a vision (in a dream, but still a vision). In Harry's mind—and Ron's too—this prior incident provides credibility for what Harry just saw and proves that his dreams are more than dreams—that they have a basis in fact. Hermione, however, continues to question whether *this particular dream has a basis in fact* by pointing out that the situation is "so unlikely" (732).

4.   How could Voldemort get hold of Sirius when he's at Grimmauld Place the whole time?

5.   Why would Voldemort use Sirius to get the weapon "or whatever it is"?

Harry and Ron have immediate answers: Sirius has been wanting to get out of headquarters for some time (a psychological assessment). Perhaps Voldemort had learned that Sirius's brother, Regulus, who had been a Death Eater, had told Sirius how to get the weapon (732–33).

Hermione correctly says that there is "no proof for any of this. No proof that Voldemort or Sirius are even there." She is analyzing the situation *objectively*, demanding actual proof (733). Harry does not appreciate her insistence on careful analysis, nor at times does Ron. However, she is simply trying to force Harry to reevaluate what he knows—or *thinks* he knows. This is another example of Hermione's intelligence, and also of her willingness to stand up to her friends when she thinks she is right, just as Neville did in book 1 (*SS* 272).

NOTE TO SELF: *Never get upset if someone is asking you tough questions about what the real facts are or whether your conclusions are sound.*

Hermione, after stating that there's no proof, mentions that Harry has a "saving people thing" and that Voldemort knows Harry— knows that Harry would go to rescue Sirius if he was in danger (733). Hermione is using **character analysis** and **psychological profiling**, not only to convince Harry, but also to extrapolate how an enemy of Harry's might apply that *same* analysis to Harry himself!

Hermione goes on with two more questions:

6. What if Voldemort is just trying to get Harry to go to the Department of Mysteries?

7. What if the dream was just a dream?

Instead of answering these questions, Harry reverts to his personal and emotional concerns that "if we don't go, Sirius is dead" (734). He is convinced that the dream is real.

By posing these questions, Hermione properly questions the validity or credibility of the information being analyzed—the accuracy and validity of the dream—and examines the assumptions employed and conclusions reached. She analyzes the probability of Sirius being at the Department of Mysteries from all angles. How would Voldemort be able to capture Sirius? How would they get into the Department of Mysteries or the Ministry of Magic without being seen or detected? Why would Voldemort need Sirius to get what he is after? This is what intelligence analysis is all about: asking yourself the same questions a good reporter asks: How? Where? When? What? Why?

Ginny and Luna then arrive, having heard Harry's shouting. Harry is initially dismissive of them, but Ginny is no longer the shy girl who cannot talk to Harry; she tells Harry, forcefully, that she just was trying to find out if he needed any help.

Hermione realizes that they need to have proof whether or not any of the assumed facts (most importantly the "fact" that Sirius is being tortured by Voldemort in the Department of Mysteries) can be discounted or proven untrue. Hermione determines that Harry should once again use Umbridge's office fireplace to communicate with Sirius and determine if he is still at headquarters. Thus, having done her work as an intelligence analyst, Hermione turns herself into an operations officer and operations planner and comes up with a splendid plan (735).

She tells Harry that they need to establish whether Sirius has really left headquarters. She notes again that this could be a trick of Voldemort's. She literally begs Harry to listen and to check first whether Sirius is not at home before they "go charging off to London." If Sirius is not there, she tells Harry, "I swear I won't try and stop you" and will even join the rescue mission (735).

Intelligence planner Hermione Granger quickly evaluates the resources at her disposal. While Ron creates the diversion (hopefully using Peeves to draw Umbridge into a different area of the castle), Ginny and Luna will stand lookout outside Umbridge's office and use the excuse of Garrotting Gas (something Ginny's twin brothers had planned to use) to keep people away from that corridor. Harry and Hermione will don the Invisibility Cloak, wait for the coast to clear, and then enter Umbridge's office, now a secure location for Harry to communicate with Sirius (736–37).

Harry does calm down when Hermione plans to go into Umbridge's office with him. He realizes that this is a sign of solidarity and loyalty, and the fact that Hermione is putting herself at risk as well brings her back to his good graces. Perhaps this also helps him start thinking more rationally about finding proof before rushing off to the Department of Mysteries (737).

The students also discuss how much time Harry will have in Umbridge's office before getting caught. They conclude that he has no longer than five minutes, due to the fact that Filch and the Inquisitorial Squad are roaming the halls, checking everything. Harry runs to get his Invisibility Cloak and Sirius's knife, and the operations plan is put into action (737–38). They decide that the warning signal, to be used if Umbridge approaches, is a loud chorus of "Weasley Is Our King" (739).

CHAPTER 32

THE USE OF IMPERSONAL SIGNALS DURING AN OPERATION

Most, if not all, covert operations include the use of a "wave-off" or danger signal that results in the operation or contact with the other agent being aborted. By the same token, there is often an "all-clear" or safe signal indicating that the operation should proceed as planned.

Ron reports to Umbridge that Peeves is smashing up something a long ways from her office; Ginny and Luna warn students about the gas; the crowd thins, and Harry and Hermione use the Invisibility Cloak to approach the office door. Upon reaching the office door, Harry inserts his knife into the lock and opens the door. The office is empty. Hermione seems shocked by this (738–39).

Hermione was certain that Umbridge would have added extra security after the second Niffler appeared in her office. (She is correct, as we soon see.) Hermione stands guard at the window, her wand out. Harry uses the Floo powder and places his head into the fire after requesting number twelve, Grimmauld Place (739–40). (Once again, Harry has just told any eavesdroppers the address of headquarters *and* Sirius's location!)

When Harry's head enters the fire at headquarters, he is in the deserted kitchen. Harry hears a noise and yells out for Sirius. Instead, Kreacher comes over to the fire, looking delighted. Kreacher states that master has gone out, that nobody is here but Kreacher, and Harry asks whether Sirius has gone to the Department of Mysteries. Kreacher responds, "Master will not come back from the Department of Mysteries" (740–41).

By mentioning the Department of Mysteries, Harry has inadvertently given information to the enemy; this allows Kreacher to use that information *against* Harry. As discussed previously, when questioning or interrogating somebody, it is essential not to accidently give them the information you are looking for—or any *additional* information. When you are attempting to determine what some-body knows, you should never give them information that can be used against you. When you give your source information and your source relays that same information back to you, you have the risk of giving *credibility* to the source based on the information you yourself provided! This is exactly what happens here to Harry.

At this point Harry is captured by Professor Umbridge, who informs him and the others that she had indeed protected her office with special security, Stealth Sensoring Spells, placed all around her doorway. Harry finds himself detained, along with all of his friends, and his wand (that is, his weapon) seized (741–42).

Let's take stock of just *who* has been captured. Obviously Harry and Hermione were in the office and have been captured by Umbridge and the Inquisitorial Squad. In addition, their two lookouts, Ginny and Luna, have also been captured. Ron has been captured as well, in part because Professor Umbridge immediately rejected the diversion because she knew that Peeves was actually doing some other mischief at a different location. Lastly, Neville Longbottom attempted to come to Ginny's aid when the Inquisitorial Squad was capturing her, and so he was captured as well (742).

Professor Umbridge is delighted and is already planning on expelling the entire group and making Hogwarts, as she puts it, a "Weasley-free zone" (742).

Umbridge's Stealth Sensoring Spells are a form of countermea-sures. Such stealth devices alert the user to any unauthorized entry while the person or persons entering the room have no knowledge that the device has been activated; thus, Professor Umbridge had time to get back to her office and determine who had entered illegally.

Umbridge is naturally very interested to know why Harry was using the fire—and, more specifically, with *whom* he was trying to communicate. She therefore begins her interrogation by asking Harry why he was there. Harry lies, stating he was there to get his Firebolt. Umbridge knows it's a lie because she previously told Harry that his Firebolt is in the dungeon (742).

Umbridge then asks with whom Harry was communicating, and

he says it's none of her business. Umbridge then applies her own intelligence analysis, wondering whether he was talking to Dumbledore, Hagrid, or Professor McGonagall. (Though she doubts it would be Professor McGonagall, who is still recovering from the four Stunning Spells she received!) Harry refuses to answer, and so Umbridge concludes that she will need to use other methods to obtain the information. She then tells Draco to fetch Professor Snape (743). As Draco leaves to get Professor Snape, Harry suddenly realizes that there is indeed another member of the Order at Hogwarts!

Snape arrives, and Professor Umbridge requests another bottle of Veritaserum. Snape tells Professor Umbridge that she used his last bottle on Harry, and that it will take a month to make more. Displeased, Umbridge places Snape on probation and sends him away (744–45).

Before Snape leaves, Harry at first tries to "think" the information to Snape, though this obviously doesn't work (perhaps because you have to be using Legilimency in order to read the other person's mind, which would be rather obvious indeed). As Snape begins to leave, Harry yells out to him, "He's got Padfoot at the place where it is hidden!" (745). Once again, Harry has used his head and figured out a way to relay essential information in open code—without disclosing the information itself.

ANALYSIS: *Who is "Padfoot" and where is "the place where it is hidden"?* Obviously Padfoot is the nickname of Sirius Black, who is able to turn into a dog. (You may recall that the Marauder's Map lists its makers as Padfoot, Prongs, Moony, and Wormtail.) As to "the place where it is hidden," everybody in the Order has been guarding something at the Department of Mysteries, and Snape would of course understand Harry's reference.

Umbridge asks Snape what Harry was talking about. Snape, always able to control his reactions, tells Professor Umbridge that he has "no idea." Before he leaves, Professor Snape continues to add credibility to the view that he hates Harry Potter by mentioning that he would be more than happy to bring Umbridge a poison to use on Harry (745).

Professor Umbridge is now desperate to get her information. What has she tried so far? She first tried coercion, and Harry refused. She then attempted to drug Harry to get the truth, but there is no Veritaserum left. Umbridge, thinking out loud and actually trying to convince herself, then decides that the issue involves Ministry security more than school discipline, and so convinces herself to torture Harry to get the information, using the Cruciatus Curse (746).

As we all know, many a wrong can be committed in the name of patriotism using the shibboleth "national security." Certainly, the security of our nation is important, but so are the values and principles that form the basis of our nation. Most Western governments grant individuals certain fundamental, inalienable rights, including the rights of liberty and to be left alone. The US federal government is intended to be one of *enumerated* or *limited* powers, and indeed the Bill of Rights were passed for the specific purpose of *limiting* the federal government so that it does not become abusive or tyrannical. In addition to the Bill of Rights, the US government has various internal checks and balances, with each of the three branches of government limiting the reach of the other three branches (executive, legislative, judicial). Umbridge, it seems, has decided that there will be no checks and balances on her!

As Umbridge is arguing with herself, she indicates that it would be appropriate to use the Cruciatus Curse on Harry (although illegal, as Hermione points out), but that it would be best for the Minister of Magic not to be informed of this illegal use of the Cruciatus Curse. In the process, Professor Umbridge discloses to Harry and the others that it was she who sent the Dementors to attack Harry last summer, asserting that she was the only one who had the fortitude to actually do something to shut Harry up instead of just complaining about him (746–47).

Just as Professor Umbridge begins to use the Cruciatus Curse against Harry, Hermione pretends to break down—stating that she will tell her everything. Pretending to cry, Hermione "admits" that they were indeed trying to speak to Professor Dumbledore and they were trying all the various pubs to see if he was there. Professor Umbridge reacts disdainfully, stating the obvious—that Professor Dumbledore would not be in a public place when he is being sought for his arrest (747–48).

Hermione's "disclosure" is yet another excellent use of psychology; by asserting something that would clearly not work, she appears to be an inferior thinker and allows Umbridge to consider herself superior (which isn't too hard for Umbridge!). Hermione continues to "confess" that she needed to tell Dumbledore something that is important, that "it's ready." She tells Professor Umbridge that the kids were building a weapon. Umbridge accepts this "revelation" completely, even adding a couple of details of her own: that the children were building it at the instructions of Dumbledore and that it was to be used against the Ministry (748).

Umbridge demands that Hermione lead her to the weapon. Hermione realizes she will increase her odds of escape by decreasing the number of people guarding her. She therefore objects to the Inquisitorial Squad members coming along (749).

Using reverse psychology, Hermione asserts that, on second thought, she would be *glad* if all the other students found out about the weapon, so that if Professor Umbridge does anything that they don't like, they can use it against *her*. Umbridge buys into this argument as well, always fearing any chance that her power could be taken away or reduced, and decides that she will look at the weapon herself. She even goes as far as to reject help from Malfoy, stating, "Do you really think I cannot manage two wandless teenagers alone?" She decides that just Hermione, Harry, and herself should investigate (749–50).

"Lead on," Professor Umbridge orders, and away they go!

33

INTO THE FORBIDDEN FOREST—HOW TO TURN FRIENDS (OR NEUTRALS) INTO ENEMIES—A LITTLE HELP FROM A REALLY BIG FRIEND

Chapter 33, "Fight and Flight," begins as Professor Umbridge escorts the captured Harry and Hermione out of Hogwarts. Harry, of course, has no idea what Hermione is planning—or even if she *has* an escape plan (751).

Harry does realize, however, that he needs to *appear* as if he knows where they were going! Like a good spy, Harry must hide his emotions and thoughts and use equanimity. He stays about half a length behind Hermione so that he can follow her—wherever it is that she's going! Harry is acting as a good spy here, too, *going with the flow* and following Hermione's lead. The two of them can't even communicate with each other because Professor Umbridge is exceedingly close to them, with her wand out (751).

Hermione leads the way downstairs, through the entrance hall, out the front doors, and across the grass. Professor Umbridge asks if the secret weapon is in Hagrid's hut, and Hermione answers forcibly, "Of course not, Hagrid might have set it off accidentally." Umbridge immediately agrees (751–52). Hermione is using psychology and psychological assessment to manipulate Umbridge. By asserting that Hagrid is a blundering buffoon, Hermione is giving credence to her cover story by playing into Professor Umbridge's biases and prejudices.

Hermione leads the group into the Forbidden Forest (752). Harry attempts to analyze what Hermione is doing and performs his own risk analysis, concluding that entering the Forbidden Forest without wands is perhaps the most foolhardy thing they've done all day! Worse yet, Harry realizes that they are *not* heading to where Grawp is hidden, but instead toward the *center* of the Forbidden Forest—where Aragog the giant spider and his many descendants reside (752–53)!

Armed with this knowledge of Aragog—which Harry realizes Hermione does not have—he finally asks Hermione if she's sure this is the right way. She responds, "Oh, yes" (753).

Harry also notes, to his consternation, that Hermione is making a lot of noise as they travel through the forest. Harry has a heightened awareness of the dangers that lurk in the Forbidden Forest. He assumes that it would be best to be walking as quietly or covertly as possible, but Hermione obviously has other ideas (753)!

When Umbridge asks her a question, Hermione answers quite loudly—increasing Harry's nervousness. He finally tells Hermione to keep her voice down, but she responds, "I want us heard. You'll see" (753).

ANALYSIS: *Who does Hermione want to be heard (or perhaps herd) by?* (Sorry about that.)

Kind of gave it away, didn't we!

Sure enough, an arrow hits right above Hermione's head, and there is a sound of hooves. Fifty centaurs arrive, bows nocked, arrows aimed at Harry, Hermione, and Professor Umbridge (753)!

ANALYSIS: *What in the world was Hermione thinking when she went straight to the centaurs' territory?* She had analyzed the fact that she and Harry had been disarmed; that Umbridge had captured them and *did* have a weapon; that she needed a way to disarm Umbridge—*or have someone else disarm her.* In addition, Hermione knows that Umbridge dislikes half-breeds and considers the centaurs to be inferior sentient beings (as officially defined by the Ministry of Magic's laws). Umbridge perceives herself to be superior in power and authority (both legal and moral) over the "beasts." So, when Hermione puts Umbridge in the middle of a herd of centaurs, what could possibly go wrong?

A centaur asks Umbridge, "Who are you?" The Headmistress answers by stating her name and all of her many titles (754).

NOTE TO SELF: *Inferior people attempt to create a sense of superiority by the overuse of titles, awards, or accomplishments.*

The centaurs are not impressed that she is a Ministry official. Umbridge is then foolish enough to threaten them, telling the centaurs to "be very careful" because any attack on a human by a *half-breed* is against *the law* (754)!

Well now, what do you think? You're surrounded by fifty armed persons—oh yeah, right, "inferior sentient beings"—just one wand against fifty centaurs armed with bows and arrows. Clearly, you should quote the law and insult them . . . We're *sure* that will work out *just* fine!

Obviously Headmistress Umbridge has never taken a class in diplomacy or, for that matter, in strategic studies! Maybe she should be required to take a *cultural sensitivity* class as well, if by some slim chance she survives! Hermione analyzed Umbridge's character exactly and made the most of her psychological assessment.

The centaur Bane yells back, "What did you call us?" (754). Things are not looking very good now!

Hermione yells furiously at Umbridge *not* to call them that, a clear attempt to put Harry and Hermione on the centaurs' good side

CHAPTER 33

(754). Good thinking, Hermione!

NOTE TO SELF: *When at all possible, indicate to potential opponents that you are really one of them, or at least understand or have empathy for them!*

Does Umbridge properly analyze the situation, regroup, and apologize, given the fact that she is outnumbered and surrounded? Oh no, dear me, hem, hem—that would not be right as defined by the Ministry of Magic's view of her and its own superiority! Umbridge presses on, of course, continuing to assert the party line without any situational awareness or further analysis. She quotes another Ministry of Magic law that makes it a crime for a creature with "near human intelligence" to attack a wizard (754). *Near* human intelligence? Big surprise . . . this offends the centaurs even further!

NOTE TO SELF: *Calling another culture, society, or person stupid is usually a big mistake.*

A different centaur asks what Umbridge is doing in "our forest." "*Your* forest?" Umbridge retorts with indignation. She informs the centaurs that they live there *only* because the Ministry of Magic "*permits*" them certain areas of land (755). This is understandably the last straw for at least one centaur. An arrow whizzes by Umbridge's head, and she quite unwisely yells at the centaurs, calling them "filthy half-breeds" and "beasts" (755)!

Hermione, again attempting to get on the right side of the situation, yells at Professor Umbridge to be quiet. Umbridge will have nothing of it and attacks using magic, conjuring ropes to bind one of the centaurs. The centaurs return the attack, capturing Umbridge and carrying her away (755).

We think that perhaps now would be a good time to discuss how to make friends and get along with people—even centaurs.

Instead of trying to communicate calmly with the centaurs, Umbridge did everything possible to turn them against her. She asserted her higher legal authority and her moral authority; she threatened them; she patronized them by saying they are "allowed" the land they consider home; she denigrated their intelligence and called them racially charged names; she disregarded their claim not only to their own land, but even to exist under their own laws and customs; *and* she was the first to attack.

The art of diplomacy involves learning to project your most important principles while taking into account the other group's cultures, norms, and laws.

NOTE TO SELF: *When you have no authority (or are in a position of lesser power), persuasion must be the first tool you use.*

Remember also how Hagrid—considered a buffoon by Umbridge—attempted to get the giants on his side, acting with respect and caution, providing gifts as their culture expected, and working to earn the giants' trust (427, 429). Now consider what Umbridge said and did to the centaurs.

FURTHER NOTE TO SELF: *Understanding and appreciating a different culture is the first step in working with people who are different from you. If you do not offer well-mannered honesty and respect, you will receive none in return.*

So, back to the story!

What are the centaurs going to do with Harry and Hermione? This is where Hermione makes the same unfortunate mistake as Professor Umbridge—but at least not at the same level!

When asked why she and Harry had come into the forest, she discloses that she was hoping that the centaurs would drive Umbridge away (756). In other words, she admitted to wanting to *use* the centaurs for her own ends! And she says this *despite* her prior knowledge (through Firenze's situation) that the centaurs object—strongly—to doing the bidding of humans. Whoops!

The centaurs react negatively, stating, "We do not help

humans! . . . We do not recognize your laws. We do not acknowledge your superiority" (757). As things go from bad to worse, it appears that Harry and Hermione will suffer the same fate as Professor Umbridge—that is, until there is a loud crash and a *big* friend appears (756–57).

It is Grawp, who is looking for Hagrid. Grawp looks around and does not see Hagrid, but he *does* see people he knows and recognizes as friends of Hagrid: Harry and "Hermy" (758).

Grawp reaches down to pick up Harry (or perhaps Hermione) and in the process knocks a centaur aside. The centaurs perceive this as an attack and immediately shoot fifty or so arrows at Grawp, splattering his blood on Harry and Hermione. A huge fight ensues, ending with the centaurs' retreat into the forest, Grawp in pursuit (758–59).

Well, things did not go exactly according to plan, but you have to admit: Harry and Hermione are now free.

NOTE TO SELF: *When a plan does not go exactly as intended, quickly reanalyze, apply flexibility, and improvise.*

Despite the fact that the plan worked, Harry is extremely upset with Hermione, believing that they're now in an even *worse* place than before, and farther than ever from being able to rescue Sirius. "Smart plan," says Harry derisively, "Where do we go from here?" (759). Hermione says they need to get back to the castle and asks Harry, "How do you plan to get all the way to London?" (759–60).

"Yeah," Ron says, "we were wondering about that." Harry looks up to see Ron, Ginny, Neville, and Luna! The other members of Dumbledore's Army have escaped the Inquisitorial Squad and come to return Harry and Hermione's wands to them (760). Blimey, we say!

When Ron asks whether Harry had confirmed that Voldemort has Sirius, Harry says yes, *and* that he is sure that Sirius is still alive (760–61).

PART 1

ANALYSIS: *What is the factual basis for Harry's conclusion that Sirius has been captured and is being tortured by Voldemort at the Department of Mysteries?* Harry, like all intelligence officers, should—before executing a plan—take every opportunity to evaluate and reevaluate the situation, review what is known and unknown, and ask himself whether the *facts* add up to the *conclusion* reached. But Harry is too close to the situation and cannot be *objective*. Based mostly on his dream, Harry once again leaps several steps of logic and takes the fact (or supposed fact) that Sirius is *not* at head-quarters as proof that Sirius is being tortured by Voldemort in the Department of Mysteries.

Once again, someone asks, "How are we going to get there?" The issue of transportation is essential when planning a rescue mission (761).

All are silent *except* for Luna, who states matter-of-factly, "we'll have to fly." None of the others have yet figured out that Luna has good ideas—and she has one now. They can fly to London on the backs of Thestrals (761)!

NOTE TO SELF: *Do not reject a person's ideas merely because he or she appears different or even odd. Odd people often have odd ideas—which are often exactly what you need!*

Two Thestrals have already shown up because (as we learned in Hagrid's Care of Magical Creatures Class) they are drawn by the scent of blood—in this case, Grawp's blood. Transportation problem solved! Thank you, Luna (762)!

As the Thestrals slowly approach Harry and the others, the rescuers discuss who should go and who should stay (763).

There are Thestrals enough to bring everyone to London, and the group decides (against Harry's better judgment) that *everyone* will come to assist. Dumbledore's Army has just accepted its first real-life mission.

They mount the Thestrals, and off they go to London!

34

THE FLIGHT OF THE THESTRALS—THE MAGIC OF CODE BREAKING—MY KINGDOM FOR A MAP!—LEAVING MAGIC BREADCRUMBS (ON DOORS!)—A PROPHECY (AND CURIOSITY) KILLS THE DOG, AND MAYBE HARRY'S FRIENDS, TOO!

In chapter 34, "Department of Mysteries," Harry finally travels the path of his dream, but not with the expected results. This chapter has both high adventure and profound tragedy. Harry has taken the bait and led his friends into grave danger.

Once everybody has mounted the Thestrals (a challenge for those who can't see them, of course), Harry tells his Thestral where he wants to go, and they take off into the sunset. It is soon twilight, then night (764–66).

Traveling at night is a good idea when you don't wish to be seen, and therefore good spy craft. If you're familiar with Muggle military tactics, you'll know that for the last twenty years or so, US air forces have begun almost every battle at night, when the planes could not been seen. The first planes to go in are almost always the F-117 stealth fighters (which should really be called stealth bombers), as well as the newest stealth bomber, the B-2.

PART 1

~~~~~~

STEALTH TECHNOLOGY AND NIGHT MISSIONS

Stealth technology allows a large aircraft (as well as some ships) not to be seen, or, more accurately, to seem *much smaller* than they are. Planes and surface ships are "seen" by radar, an electronic signal emitted from the viewer's position (land, sea, air, and even space!) outward; when the electronic signal hits the object, the signal reflects back toward the viewer's position and is visible to watchers, just as you can see your reflection coming back at you from a mirror.

Stealth technology works by using design and certain types of materials to send radar reflection away at a different angle, so that it does not return to the sender. The signal may also actually be absorbed by special *radar-absorbent materials* on the exterior of the plane. Thus, a plane that is over fifty feet long and weighs tons will "send" back a signal so small that it appears to be the size of a sparrow!

Because these planes can be seen easily by the eye, the initial missions by stealth fighters and bombers take place at night. As you would expect, when initiating an action with airpower, the first goal is to take out all radar sites so the enemy cannot see any of your assets. The F-117 stealth fighter and B-2 bomber are very good at this, working with other specialty airplanes to hone in on radar sources and target the radar antennas for destruction.

What's that you say? We digress? Then back to the story once again.

~~~~~~

The thestrals land at the visitor's entrance to the Ministry of Magic (767). All six rescuers squeeze into the telephone box and enter the code Harry remembers (62442), and state their names and their purpose—to save someone (768). A friendly sounding female voice

CHAPTER 34

responds, and badges arrive stating their names and the purpose of their visit: a rescue mission (768).

Finally, it's time for code breaking!

ANALYSIS: *Why 62442?* Time to use logic! Let's first try assigning letters of the alphabet to the numbers: 1 being *A*, 2 being *B*, and so on. Do we get anything?

A	B	C	D	E	F
1	2	3	4	5	6

6 F

2 B

4 D

4 D

2 B

Applying 62442, we get F B D D B. Not much there.

Let's think some more. Any ideas?

Let's apply *situational analysis*. Where are they?

At the visitor's entrance. Yes, yes. But *what are they physically in?*

A phone booth! Very good!

So what do you think?

Any thoughts on *how to break the code?*

Phone numbers, you say? But phone numbers usually have seven numbers, like 555–5555.

What's that? Oh! You want to apply the letters that are on each number key on the phone itself! Sure, that makes sense!

Any readers out there who have texted someone by using the numeric keys?

Let's add to our list the letters assigned to each number:

6 M N O

2 A B C

4 G H I

4 G H I

2 A B C

See anything?

6 **M** N O

2 **A** B C

4 **G** H I

4 G H **I**

2 A B **C**

MAGIC!

Isn't this great? J. K. Rowling *never tells us* how to break the code, but by using logic we can decode the password for the Ministry of Magic visitor's entrance!

Code breaking, you see, is very much like magic!

Now, back to the story!

The children have been told to check in at the security station, but inside they find the atrium empty, the lights dim. No one is at the security station. Harry thinks this is odd and an ominous sign. His analysis is certainly right! This *alone* should have indicated that something is seriously wrong, something far more worrisome than Sirius's capture!

CHAPTER 34

ANALYSIS: *Why would the entire atrium be left unguarded?* To allow Harry and his friends to continue on their mission unopposed! If a security guard stopped them, Harry would never get to the Department of Mysteries, would he? And who, pray tell, is capable of killing or otherwise removing the security guards? Why, the Death Eaters who await Harry's arrival, of course!

Harry leads his friends across the atrium to the lift, noting as they walk the fountain with the five prominent statues of a witch, a wizard, a centaur, a goblin, and a house-elf (769), designed to suggest that these groups work together for a common cause.

The six students descend to level 9, the location of the Department of Mysteries (769). Anybody think a *map* would be handy about now? Perhaps the map that Bill Weasley so quickly Vanished when Harry and his friends entered the kitchen at headquarters as an Order meeting was concluding (80)?

They continue down the so-familiar corridor to the plain black door. But then Harry stops to suggest leaving a lookout there (769–70).

ANALYSIS: *Does it really make sense to leave a lookout here?* No. We suggest that Harry is actually trying to lessen the number of people continuing on with him, most likely so fewer of his friends will be in danger. A noble thought, but one rejected by the others. No one wants to stay behind as a lookout, and logic prevails when Ginny rightfully states that there is no way to communicate a warning anyway. Thus, they continue on together and enter the Department of Mysteries (770).

The door swings open as in the dream, and the six find themselves in a large circular room with approximately twelve black doors. But then the door shuts behind them and the room goes absolutely dark! Worse yet, the room spins or rotates, which Ginny correctly surmises is a way of preventing them from knowing what door they first entered (770–71).

The spinning stops, and the children light their wands. Which door to enter? Harry analyzes that he should simply continue with his dream and goes to the door directly in front of him. Beyond it is a room with a large tank containing free-floating brains (771). Not the right room at all!

Before they try the next door, Hermione marks the first so they know which ones they have already entered (772). This is a good idea that demonstrates good intelligence analysis and spy craft.

ANALYSIS: *Would there be an easier way to figure out which door to use?* There is, but they don't learn it until the end. All you have to do is *ask* which door is the exit, and it will open up! In other words, sometimes the simplest action is the best one: *ask* for the proper door to be opened, please.

NOTE TO SELF: *Sometimes the simplest solution is the best! Shades of "ask and you shall receive" in Matthew 7:7 and Luke 11:9, and "when a door closes, a window opens" in Acts 16:6!*

The next room has a large, old stone amphitheater (773). On a dais at its center is an old stone arch hung with a tattered veil (773). Harry and Luna can hear voices through it, and Harry focuses on them, forgetting his mission. Hermione tells Harry to be careful and suggests that they leave, but Harry comes back to reality only when Hermione mentions Sirius and the fact that he needs to be rescued (774).

The students continue onward. When they reach a locked door, they try to use Sirius's knife—and the blade melts! They then try another door, and Harry realizes that "*This is it!*" They enter first the room with the clocks—a space dedicated somehow to the issue of time—and see a hummingbird in a bell jar being born, growing, and then going back into its egg in much the same way that a phoenix is reborn (776–77).

CHAPTER 34

The children get their wands out and enter the room of glass spheres. Harry carefully goes to row ninety-seven, but no one is there! He goes down the row, looking for Sirius—but again, there is no one else there (777–78)!

Confused and upset, Harry starts searching feverishly up and down the rows for Sirius. While he's doing so, Ron happens to look up at the row where Harry thought Sirius was being tortured and sees a sign with Harry's name on it right below a round sphere. Ron asks Harry, "Have you seen this? . . . It's—it's got your name on it." And it lists a date of about sixteen years ago (779).

Harry comes over and reviews the card (780), which states

S.P.T. to A.P.W.B.D.
Dark Lord
and (?) Harry Potter

Before we proceed with our story, perhaps now would be a good time to discuss again abbreviations and codes. Ready for another exercise in code breaking?

Remember the Mirror of Erised, where the letters carved into the mirror needed only to be read backwards to reveal its message? Here we have a code based on *abbreviations*, though Harry does not know it yet.

Does anybody remember what *SPT* stands for, or *ABWBD*?

Let's think about it for a bit. We are dealing with a prophecy, a prophecy about Harry. First of all, *who* delivered (that is, spoke out loud) the prophecy?

And who *heard* the prophecy being given?

Perhaps a certain Divinations teacher and a certain Headmaster?

Quite correct you are!

SPT stands for Sibyl P. Trelawney!

And APWBD stands for Albus Percival Wulfric Brian Dumbledore!

Thus, the abbreviations stand for "Sibyl P. Trelawney to Albus Percival Wulfric Brian Dumbledore"!

But there is more to figure out.

Why is there a question mark? Because the prophecy could apply to Harry Potter, but it could *also* apply to some other boy born at the end of July whose parents thrice defied Lord Voldemort. And we all know who that boy is, don't we?

We will get to that in a bit, but now, back to the story!

Hermione tells Harry she doesn't think Harry should touch it, and Neville (who four years ago bravely tried to stop his friends from leaving Gryffindor tower) also says, "Don't, Harry!" (780).

But Harry feels reckless. It's got his name on it, after all, and feeling rather risky—he picks it up (780).

And, to his great surprise, nothing happens . . . yet.

Then, from behind Harry, the drawling voice of Lucius Malfoy says, "Very good, Potter. Now turn around, nice and slowly, and give that to me" (780).

35

THE ORDER OF THE PHOENIX AND THE DEATH EATERS DO BATTLE—THE CONSEQUENCES OF MISTAKEN INTELLIGENCE ANALYSIS AND HUBRIS—A PROPHECY LOST (BUT PERHAPS REGAINED)

Chapter 35, "Beyond the Veil," sets six members of Dumbledore's Army against Lucius Malfoy and the other Death Eaters. The members of the Order of the Phoenix arrive to intercede on their behalf. And then, finally, the moment we've all been waiting for, Dumbledore versus Voldemort, mano a mano (or perhaps "professor to snake"!).

By the way, *mano a mano* is Spanish for "hand to hand," as in hand-to-hand combat. In modern terms, it means dealing with an adversary face-to-face or one-on-one.

This chapter does not deal very much with spy craft, except perhaps as an example of how incorrect or faulty intelligence analysis can make things go very badly. The chapter is really a fight scene, with the members of Dumbledore's Army not doing very well. Ginny ends up with a broken ankle, and Neville a broken nose (792, 795). Although the children do succeed in injuring or incapacitating some of the Death Eaters, it seems clear that, without the arrival of the Order of the Phoenix (799–801), all would have been lost.

We do, however, have an opportunity to obtain some information from the discussion between Lucius Malfoy and Harry. Lucius explains to Harry that Sirius was never there, and that Voldemort had set this trap by interjecting the dream of Sirius being tortured into Harry's mind (782).

ANALYSIS: *Why don't the Death Eaters kill Harry and his friends immediately?* They are there to get the glass sphere, and although they would have no problem killing any of the others, they have been ordered by Voldemort not to harm the prophecy—and therefore cannot harm Harry while he is holding it. Harry refuses to hand over the prophecy, realizing that it is the only thing keeping them all alive.

In order to "convince" Harry to hand over the prophecy, Bellatrix Lestrange proposes torturing Ginny (783). Harry goads her into an attack, and the six students scatter, going from room to room as the battle begins. Eventually those still on their feet end up in the room with the veiled gateway (787–800).

Observe the way that, throughout these scenes, Harry uses the prophecy as leverage, almost to the point of taunting his opponents, reminding them that their master will not be very happy if the sphere is destroyed or broken (783, 799, 804). Harry also learns, through Lucius Malfoy, that the only people who can retrieve a prophecy "are those about whom it was made." Since the prophecy is about "Voldemort and (?) Harry Potter," only Voldemort and Harry can pick up the prophecy. Voldemort can't come to get it without letting the Ministry of Magic know that he has come back. Indeed, Voldemort wants the Ministry of Magic to continue ignoring his return as he develops and organizes his forces (786–87).

At the last possible moment, the members of the Order of the Phoenix, including Sirius, Lupin, Moody, Tonks, and Kingsley, arrive to assist Harry and his friends (801). Unfortunately

CHAPTER 35

for Voldemort—and Harry, who has been using the prophecy as leverage—the sphere falls out of Neville's pocket, gets kicked across the room, and shatters against the bottom of a stone step—its contents unheard by anyone in the room (804–5).

The battle rages, but it appears that, thanks to the members of the Order of the Phoenix, the tide has been turned.

Now a word about hubris: **HUBRIS**.

Hubris is when a person is egotistical to the point of arrogance: the person often holds an unshakeable belief in his or her personal superiority that results in a fatal mistake and grave consequences. Most Greek tragedies use this underlying weakness as the foundation of the play's plot.

While battling with his cousin Bellatrix, Sirius deflects a spell and *laughs*, telling her, "You can do better than that" (805). While taunting his cousin, his focus and concentration are momentarily diverted from the fight, and Bellatrix aims a killing curse that hits Sirius directly on the chest (805). Sirius falls backwards, surprised and shocked, passes through the veil, and disappears (806).

Sirius is dead. Harry is first shocked—and then furious.

36

HARRY'S RISKY THIRST FOR VENGEANCE— VOLDEMORT ARRIVES—DUMBLEDORE VICTORIOUS—AN ENEMY NOW SEEN FLEES (YET AGAIN)

Chapter 36 is entitled "The Only One He Ever Feared." Although Voldemort's intention was primarily to obtain the prophecy, he still hungers to kill Harry. Harry fails to take this simple fact into account and, in his anger, chases Bellatrix Lestrange with every intention of killing her (809). Harry would have been better served by staying where he was, with the members of the Order of the Phoenix. But in his anger, he dismisses the risk and runs after the fleeing Death Eater.

Bellatrix asks Harry for the prophecy, and Harry tells her that it's gone—*and* that Voldemort knows! Harry laughs at Bellatrix, knowing that it will incense her still more (812). Harry is using psychological operations (PSYOPS) against Bellatrix Lestrange— taunting her—but with enough presence of mind to avoid his godfather's mistake.

Voldemort arrives and aims a killing curse at Harry (812). Fortunately, Dumbledore arrives and knocks the golden statue of the wizard into the curse's path (813). The battle between Voldemort and Dumbledore begins. Just as Harry thinks that Dumbledore has triumphed, Voldemort possesses Harry's body, causing him unspeakable pain (815–16). We later learn that Voldemort possessed Harry in the hopes that Dumbledore would kill him (sacrifice him, for the greater good?) in order to kill Voldemort (828). Dumbledore refuses, and Harry's remembrance of Sirius and the rush of emotion it sparks once again defeats Voldemort, who flees Harry's body (816).

Fudge and many others arrive—and see Voldemort just as the Dark Lord Disapparates with Bellatrix Lestrange (816–17). Dumbledore chastises the Minister of Magic, telling Fudge and the others that they have seen with their own eyes proof that what he has been telling them the entire year is true (817).

Instead of explaining everything at that point, Dumbledore informs the Minister of Magic that he will not do so until he gets Harry back to Hogwarts. Dumbledore has clearly taken charge of the situation: he is the one making decisions, not the Minister of Magic (818).

ANALYSIS: *Why is it so important to get Harry back to school?*

First Possibility: We could argue that once he's at school he will be better protected—it is the equivalent of a safe house. Dumbledore realizes that it is *possible* that Voldemort and his followers could begin a counterattack.

Second Possibility: Perhaps Dumbledore doesn't want Harry to hear the explanation he provides to the Minister of Magic, or perhaps he realizes that Harry needs to digest what has happened *before* Dumbledore tries to explain what happened and why. Or, perhaps, Dumbledore was trying to protect Harry from being questioned, not only by the Minister and the Aurors, but by the newspapers as well.

Third Possibility: Dumbledore intends to tell Harry some things that he's *not* going to tell Fudge—such as what the prophecy actually said. We will never find out what Dumbledore told Cornelius Fudge, of course, although it would have been a very enjoyable session to overhear!

PART 1

In order to get back to the school, Dumbledore creates a Portkey—right in front of Fudge and the others. Fudge objects, apparently because Dumbledore's actions are illegal or perhaps can only be done with permission of the Ministry of Magic. Perhaps they have a Portkey Department or a Department of Magical Transportation! In any event, Dumbledore ignores Fudge's objections and instructs Fudge to take three actions: first, remove Umbridge from Hogwarts; second, tell the Aurors to stop looking for Hagrid; and third, reappoint Dumbledore as Headmaster (818–19). (Well, technically, Dumbledore doesn't actually *demand* to be reappointed as Headmaster; he merely *informs* Fudge that if there is any need to contact him, he can be reached at Hogwarts by letters to the Headmaster.)

Dumbledore knows full well that he is addressing Fudge as one would address a servant, something noticed, no doubt, not only by Fudge, but by all the others who have just witnessed Voldemort's return.

Dumbledore, it is clear to all, is back!

37

PROFESSOR DUMBLEDORE DISCLOSING TRUTHS (BUT MAYBE NOT ALL OF THEM!)

Chapter 37, "The Lost Prophecy," is quite cleverly mistitled. The prophecy *was never lost* because the person who had heard it still has the memory and can repeat *exactly* what the prophecy said. That person is Professor Dumbledore, and he heard it from Professor Trelawney. Harry learns as well that the first portion of the prophecy was also overheard by an eavesdropper (indeed, a Death Eater!) who shared that information with his master, Voldemort (843). Who was the Death Eater? We find out much later that it was Professor Snape (*DH* 677).

The chapter begins with Harry locked into Dumbledore's office for his own safety while Dumbledore finishes his explanations at the Ministry of Magic. Harry is very upset, thinking obsessively that it's his fault that Sirius is dead. Harry has gained insight into his own character and concludes that Voldemort was banking on Harry to play the hero—just as Hermione had said! (820–21).

Dumbledore returns via the Floo network and informs Harry that his friends will be fine and no one will suffer lasting damage (822). Harry is still upset with himself and angry that Sirius is dead. Dumbledore explains to Harry that the fact that he can feel pain like this is his greatest strength: because Harry feels empathy and love, he hopefully will be able to defeat Voldemort. Harry, however, is dejected and pretty much tired of the whole thing. "I've had enough. I've seen enough. I want out. I want it to end" (823–24).

Dumbledore claims that it is in fact *his* fault that Sirius is dead, but then retracts his assignment of blame slightly, saying "almost entirely my fault" (825). Dumbledore admits that he should have been more open with Harry and that he should have explained to him that Voldemort might try to lure Harry to the Department of Mysteries (825–26).

Dumbledore explains that he guessed fifteen years ago—when he saw the lightning-bolt-shaped scar on Harry's forehead—"that it might be the sign of a connection forged between you and Voldemort" (826–27). When Harry saw through the snake's eyes during the attack on Mr. Weasley, Voldemort became aware of the connection. Because of that fact, Dumbledore expected that Voldemort would attempt "to force his way into your mind, to manipulate and misdirect your thoughts" (827).

In other words, Dumbledore was concerned that Voldemort would use Harry *to spy on* Dumbledore—and therefore the Headmaster stayed clear of Harry throughout the year. Dumbledore even anticipated that Voldemort might try to possess Harry, hoping that Dumbledore would kill Harry while Voldemort possessed him. Dumbledore arranged the Occlumency lessons as a countermeasure to prevent Voldemort from using Harry as an unwilling spy (828).

Professor Dumbledore next discusses with Harry the security at the Department of Mysteries and confirms that Voldemort would have had to pick up the prophecy himself or use Harry to do so (829).

Dumbledore also reveals that Kreacher "has been serving more than one master for months" (829). In other words, the house-elf was a mole. As we all suspected in previous chapters, Kreacher took Sirius's order to get out as an explicit order to leave, going to the only place which still had a connection to the Black family—that is, the home of Narcissa Malfoy (830). Although Kreacher was unable to disclose the location of the headquarters or the fact that Sirius was there, he was able to provide intelligence that was helpful to Voldemort (831).

CHAPTER 37

Once Harry warned Snape that Voldemort has "Padfoot at the place where it is hidden," Snape was able to use "more reliable forms of communication than the fire in Dolores Umbridge's office" to determine that Sirius was indeed at Grimmauld Place. When Harry and his friends did not return from the Forbidden Forest, however, Professor Snape properly analyzed that Harry still believed that Sirius had been captured by Voldemort and was most likely on his way to the Department of Mysteries (830).

Meanwhile, Voldemort had learned, from Kreacher's disclosures, that the person Harry cared about most was Sirius, his father and brother figure—and that Harry would go to any lengths to rescue Sirius. Voldemort used this psychological assessment of Harry to his advantage (831).

Dumbledore notes that he had warned Sirius to treat Kreacher kindly, perhaps, in a sense, to recruit him to their cause, but Sirius refused to do it (832).

The issue of whether Snape is friend or foe comes up yet again, with Harry noting that Snape didn't take him seriously when he gave him the warning (832). However, Dumbledore rightly informs Harry that Snape *pretended* not to take Harry seriously in order to maintain his cover (832–33). Snape had actually given Professor Umbridge *fake* Veritaserum to use on Harry (833). As always, Professor Dumbledore reminds Harry of his complete trust in Severus Snape (833).

Dumbledore also makes the point, with Kreacher as his example, that "indifference and neglect often do much more damage than outright dislike" (834). Dumbledore describes the night he left baby Harry at the Dursleys' in order to keep him protected through his mother's love and blood bond (835–39).

Dumbledore next tells Harry that Voldemort first tried to kill him because of a prophecy made shortly before Harry's birth (839). Voldemort wanted the prophecy—the *complete* prophecy—so he could obtain "the knowledge of how to destroy you" (839–41). It is at this point that we finally find out the complete prophecy:

"THE ONE WITH THE POWER TO VANQUISH THE DARK LORD

PART 1

APPROACHES.... BORN TO THOSE WHO HAVE THRICE DEFIED HIM, BORN AS THE SEVENTH MONTH DIES... AND THE DARK LORD WILL MARK HIM AS HIS EQUAL, BUT HE WILL HAVE POWER THE DARK LORD KNOWS NOT... AND EITHER MUST DIE AT THE HANDS OF THE OTHER FOR NEITHER CAN LIVE WHILE THE OTHER SURVIVES... THE ONE WITH THE POWER TO VANQUISH THE DARK LORD WILL BE BORN AS THE SEVENTH MONTH DIES..." (841).

Dumbledore takes several minutes to analyze the prophecy, and we should do the same.

ANALYSIS: *What does the prophecy mean?* The prophecy first refers to a boy born to parents who have already defied Voldemort three times. Professor Dumbledore notes that the prophecy could apply to *two* wizard boys, Harry and Neville Longbottom. However, Voldemort himself played a role in selecting the subject of the prophecy: he chose to hunt down Harry, a half-blood, and *not* Neville Longbottom, who is a pureblood. While trying to kill Harry, Voldemort marks him with the famous lightning scar (841–42).

Professor Dumbledore also points out to Harry the significance of Voldemort being more afraid of the half-blood, Harry, than of the full-blood, Neville (842).

Voldemort did not have the complete prophecy because his eavesdropper was detected a short way into Professor Trelawney's recitation of the prophecy and thrown from the building (843). Thus, Voldemort learned only that the person who could defeat him was a boy born in July to parents who had thrice defied him (843).

At long last, Harry realizes that he must kill Voldemort or be killed by him: "One of us has got to kill the other . . . in the end?" "Yes," replies Dumbledore (844).

Having read all seven books, we must ask ourselves whether Dumbledore was completely honest with Harry, or instead provided *incomplete* information. Did Dumbledore know at this point that

CHAPTER 37

Harry was himself a Horcrux?

ANALYSIS: *Does Professor Dumbledore know about Horcruxes yet—and that Harry is one?* Dumbledore realizes, at the very least, that there is a connection between Voldemort and Harry signified by the scar—but it appears he does not yet know the details surrounding that connection. Perhaps Dumbledore suspects, but we guess at this point that he is providing to Harry what *he believes* to be complete and truthful information. But perhaps not . . .

In the next two books, we learn that Dumbledore did not share *all* of the information he had available to him. For example, in book 6, *Harry Potter and the Half-Blood Prince*, Dumbledore tells Harry (after securing Slughorn's unedited memory), "Four years ago I received what I considered certain proof that Voldemort had split his soul" (*HBP* 500). Then, in book 7, *Harry Potter and the Deathly Hallows*, after Harry lets Voldemort kill him and he talks with Dumbledore in King's Cross, Harry asks, "And you knew this? You knew—all along?" Dumbledore answers, "I guessed, but my guesses have generally been good" (*DH* 708–10). And at the end of book 7, in Snape's released memory, Dumbledore explains, "We have protected him because it has been essential to teach him, to raise him, to let him try his strength" (*DH* 686–87).

I leave you to judge Dumbledore, as did Snape (who is, we note, somewhat aghast when he finds out that Dumbledore has "been raising him like a pig for slaughter" [*DH* 687]).

In the world of spying, we almost always have to make decisions based on incomplete information, or *assume* that the information we have is as complete as possible (yet still likely incomplete). In other words, we must make decisions based on what we know, but also realize that there is a significant chance that there are things we do not know—things that are both "seen and unseen."

NOTE TO SELF: *It is essential to keep an open mind, as long as it doesn't fall out!*

38

THE PRESS FINALLY PRINTS THE TRUTH—DUMBLEDORE RETURNS— DEATH BE NOT PROUD

The final chapter of *Harry Potter and the Order of the Phoenix*, "The Second War Begins," opens with the students reading the *Daily Prophet's* many articles about the return of Voldemort.

They obtain a great deal of information—this time *truthful* information—through this open source. Cornelius Fudge confirms that Voldemort has indeed returned. Fudge also acknowledges the mass revolt of the Dementors, who are no longer under the control of the Ministry. The article further states that Dumbledore has been reinstated to all of his previous honors, including his position as Headmaster of Hogwarts (845–46).

The *Daily Prophet* also mentions that Dumbledore had for over a year been telling everyone that Voldemort was back and gathering followers (846). Instead of ridiculing Harry, the *Daily Prophet* now refers to him as the "lone voice of truth . . . perceived as unbalanced . . . forced to bear ridicule and slander" (847).

Hermione notes that this ridicule and slander was emanating from the *Daily Prophet* itself—something the *Daily Prophet* doesn't mention (847)!

The paper includes an article—a piece of historic analysis, in fact—describing Voldemort's attempt sixteen years ago to take over, a blame-placing article entitled "What the Ministry Should Have Told Us," and one dispensing credit and blame entitled "Why Nobody Listened to Albus Dumbledore" (847).

In addition, the paper includes an "exclusive" interview with Harry Potter—even though Harry hasn't given any new interviews. It turns out that the *Daily Prophet* purchased the exclusive interview published by *The Quibbler*. This, of course, gives Luna and her father great delight—and no doubt a significant financial advantage (847–48).

While tying up loose ends, we find out that Professor Umbridge is recovering in the hospital wing after Professor Dumbledore retrieved her from the Forbidden Forest—without a scratch on him. Professor Umbridge lies silently on her bed, nearly catatonic, although Ron has some fun making the noise of hooves, which scares her nearly out of her bed (848–49)!

When the subject of Divinations comes up, Ron questions whether it should even be a course, and Hermione notes that there are indeed real prophecies—as they had just found out (849). We wonder whether any of them feel at least a little bit guilty about destroying hundreds if not thousands of prophecies and the information contained therein.

Harry, it should be noted, has decided for the time being to keep secret the fact that he knows the contents of the complete prophecy. When his friends start discussing the prophecy, now supposedly forever lost, Harry is glad to change the subject (849–50).

On his way to see Hagrid, Harry runs into Malfoy, Crabbe, and Goyle, and Malfoy threatens, "You're dead, Potter" and "You're going to pay. *I'm* going to make you pay for what you've done to my father" (851). It turns out that Lucius Malfoy—now exposed as a Death Eater—presently resides in Azkaban. However, since the Dementors are no longer guarding the Wizarding prison, Draco (and the others) assume that Lucius and his fellow Death Eaters will escape soon enough (850–51).

Just as Harry and Draco begin drawing their wands to attack each other (Harry is the fastest!), Professor Snape intercedes. Harry, it seems, will always have enemies at Hogwarts, even though he is again the hero, lauded as "the lone voice of truth" (851–53).

Harry finally gets to see Hagrid, who reassures him that "everyone knows you've been telling the truth now," though it doesn't make Harry feel any better about the death of Sirius (854). Hagrid points out that Sirius died in battle, and surely he would have preferred to go that way. However, Harry still wishes that he had not had to go that way—or any way—and was still here (854–55).

Harry leaves Hagrid and spends some time alone, contemplating what Dumbledore had told him. He feels isolated and now truly understands that he is a marked man. He knows what he will have to do: either murder Voldemort or be murdered by him (856).

The end of the term is upon them, and Harry begins to dread going back to Privet Drive. However, thanks to Dumbledore's explanation, Harry now understands the necessity of going back each summer (856). At least there is the humorous departure of no-longer-Professor Umbridge, who tries to sneak out unseen. However, Peeves will have none of that, and he chases her out of the castle and through the grounds to everyone's great delight—except for Filch (856–57)!

Harry still doesn't feel like talking about Sirius or being seen by others or even his friends. He chooses not to go to the end-of-term feast and instead stays upstairs, packing his trunk to go back to the Dursleys' (857).

While packing he sees the package that Sirius had given him and finally opens it, discovering a two-way mirror that he could have used to talk to Sirius any time he wanted (857–58). It was, according to Sirius's note on the back, a mirror that he and James had used to talk to each other while they were in separate detentions (858).

We must wonder how long it will be before Harry realizes that, had he taken the time to open Sirius's gift, he would have been able to talk to his godfather anytime, without owls, fireplaces, or any of the other complicated methods he used all year. And, of course, he could have quickly and easily determined that Sirius was at Grimmauld Place and *not* being tortured at the Ministry of Magic.

Harry wonders if he can still use the mirror to see Sirius. When it doesn't work, he decides that Sirius must not have had the mirror on him when he fell through the archway. Frustrated, he throws the mirror into his trunk, and it shatters (858). As we know, that isn't the last that we'll hear of the mirror . . . but that's another book (or two)! Still hopeful, Harry thinks that Sirius might come back as a ghost and asks Sir Nicholas if this is possible. But it's most likely that Sirius has chosen to have "gone on" (859–61).

Still wishing to hide from everyone, Harry accidentally runs into Luna in the hallway. Luna is putting up posters asking for her things to be returned to her (862). As with most everything, Luna takes her missing things in stride, believing that they will all turn up eventually (863). Harry pities Luna and offers to help her find her things, but she declines, and they have a genuinely good discussion about Sirius, and about Luna's mother, who died when she was nine years old. Luna is steadfastly convinced that there is an afterlife and that she will eventually see her mother, noting that both she and Harry were able to hear the voices on the other side of the veil (863). Suddenly Harry feels much better about his situation (864).

NOTE TO SELF: *After something bad happens, talking with a trusted friend is always a good idea.*

Several minor things happen on the way home on the Hogwarts Express. Cho walks by, and Harry realizes that he feels nothing about her, even when he finds out she is dating Michael Corner (865–66). Ron is thrilled to hear this for a different reason: Michael Corner had previously been dating his sister Ginny. Though Ginny quickly destroys his good mood by saying that she is now dating Dean Thomas (866).

Finally, the members of the Order of the Phoenix—Mad-Eye Moody, Tonks (wearing a Weird Sisters T-shirt!), Lupin, and Mr. and Mrs. Weasley—meet Harry at the train station between platforms 9 and 10 for the sole purpose of ensuring that the Dursleys understand what will happen to them if Harry is not able to communicate with the members of the Order of the Phoenix or his friends during the upcoming summer months (867–70).

And so ends book 5, *Harry Potter and the Order of the Phoenix*. We have learned all about spying, friendship, truth in politics, humor, and sadness.

We have seen the tools of trade craft used frequently and well, and we have observed Harry and all of his friends becoming quite good at intelligence operations and analysis, defense, and teamwork. We have watched our friends become adept at critical thinking, perhaps the most essential trait of intelligence work. The usual gang of three—Ron, Hermione, and Harry—has expanded to include Neville Longbottom, Luna Lovegood, and Ginny Weasley. We now have a gang of six (which, by the way, will eventually consist of *three pairs of couples*). We have watched these young children become young adults, and it has been very fun indeed!

In Part 2, we will review what we have learned and apply it to specific areas of the art of spying, drawing on examples from all seven books.

PART 2

THE ART OF SPYING IN THE WIZARDING AND MUGGLE WORLDS

39

TYPES OF SPIES

- For Hire (or Money)—Mundungus Fletcher

- For Cause, Patriotic—Death Eaters, Professor Quirrell, and Kreacher

- For Cause, Personal Feelings—Severus Snape

- For Cause, Personal Revenge and Glory—Draco Malfoy

- For Adventure—The Weasley Twins

- The Fearful—Peter Pettigrew

- The Cursed—Bode

- The Possessed—Ginny Weasley

- A Desire for Mayhem—Barty Crouch Jr. as Mad-Eye Moody

- A Spy in the Light of Day—Dolores Umbridge

- The Duped, on a Fool's Errand—Katie Bell and Bode's Nurse

- With a Little Help from My Friends

CHAPTER 39

It is now time to discuss the topics introduced in part 1 in an organized manner based on the real-world art of spying. We will still use examples from the Harry Potter series when appropriate, but this section covers the various aspects of spying topic by topic, as applicable in the real world.

First we will discuss spies themselves. What are the types of spies? Why do they do it? What are their motives? How do they become spies? How are they recruited? Who runs them? How do they receive their orders or instructions? And how do the people in charge of spies, called handlers, keep track of them safely and without giving them away? All of these issues are very important to spy craft and will be discussed one by one.

There are many types of spies, and the proper classification often depends on the individual spy's motive. It is essential to understand motive when recruiting, running, and using a spy. And it is equally important to reevaluate the spy's motive on a regular basis. Let's look at some of the different types of motives and perforce the different types of spies, both in Harry Potter's Wizarding world and the real world.

THE SPY FOR HIRE (OR MONEY): MUNDUNGUS FLETCHER

In a system where you get what you want through material gain, money can be a significant incentive. We are not just talking about the incentive of holding a job and getting a paycheck here. We are talking about individuals who spy for financial compensation, usually a fairly large amount of money. (Aldrich Ames was promised over $2 million; yet, amazingly, some of the spies caught in the United States have spied for a ridiculously low amount of money.)

In the Harry Potter series, at least, most of those who spy are not doing it for money alone. The one possible exception is our less-than-ethical friend Mundungus Fletcher. Interestingly, Mundungus is first mentioned by Mr. Weasley in book 2, *Harry Potter and the Chamber of Secrets*, when he mentions having had a tough night and the fact that Mundungus Fletcher tried to put a hex on him (*CS* 38). In book 4, *Harry Potter and the Goblet of Fire*, Mundungus is described as putting in a false claim for an expensive tent supposedly ruined at the World Cup (*GF* 151). And yet, by the end of the same book, Dumbledore is referring to Mundungus (and Mrs. Figg and Remis Lupin) as part of the old crowd that needs to be brought back due to Fudge's unwillingness to believe Harry or that Voldemort is back (*GF* 713). We cannot help but wonder, since Mundungus is always trying to make a buck, whether there is some way that his connection with the Order allows him to sell—or, as we find out after Sirius's death, *steal*—more items and panhandle them on the street (*HBP* 247).

MUNDUNGUS FLETCHER ANALYSIS

Recruitment by: Most probably Dumbledore

Incentive Used: A strong sense of what is right combined with a touch of personal gain or an opportunity for larceny—and perhaps a slight fear of Dumbledore. He is referred to as part of the "old crowd" by Dumbledore.

Handler: Order of the Phoenix leadership, but ultimately Dumbledore

Method of Communication: Group meetings at number twelve, Grimmauld Place

Memorable Quote:

"It . . . it was a very good business opportunity, see . . ." (*OP* 23).

CHAPTER 39

THE SPY FOR CAUSE—PATRIOTIC: DEATH EATERS, PROFESSOR QUIRRELL, AND KREACHER

Many spies work for cause, usually the cause of their nation. The spy's cause might be patriotic, as one hopes is true of most of our spies, but it may also be related to views or the adoption of an ideal espoused by a particular country (or group). The ideal does not need to be tied to a particular country to be "patriotic."

NOTE TO SELF: *A true ideal has no borders.*

Patriotism does not necessarily mean that the cause the spy holds dear is related to a nation or the security of a specific nation, as is clearly evident by Voldemort's Death Eaters. They are *against* a nation, and indeed, the whole Wizarding world *and* the world of Muggles. Their cause *is* Voldemort, or perhaps the desire to obtain power *through* Voldemort.

DEATH EATERS ANALYSIS

Recruitment by: Presumably Voldemort himself

Incentive Used: Assertion of Wizarding superiority, the opportunity to wreak havoc and assert extraordinary power over Wizards and Muggles alike

Handler: Voldemort or a Death Eater who has a close connection to Voldemort

Method of Communication: Direct assignments from Voldemort, messages sent through another Death Eater, or use of the Dark Mark on the Death Eater's arm

Memorable Quote:

Sirius: "Well, you don't just hand in your resignation to Voldemort. It's a lifetime of service or death" (112).

A good example of someone assisting Voldemort, and gladly so, is Professor Quirrell. Quirrell knows that Voldemort has gotten, you might say, *inside* his head. At the end of book 1, *Harry Potter and the Sorcerer's Stone*, Quirrell seems more than happy to have assisted Lord Voldemort in his endeavors: he says so quite clearly—*without any stuttering or nervousness*! And, as we see when he touches Harry and is overwhelmed with pain, his fingers, then palms, and then his face blistering (*SS* 294–95), Voldemort abandons Quirrell without hesitation, once again on the run as an ephemeral spirit looking for the next minion to help him return to physical existence.

PROFESSOR QUIRRELL ANALYSIS

Recruitment by: Voldemort in a forest in Albania

Incentive Used: The promise of receiving great power

Handler: Voldemort himself—under Quirrell's turban

Method of Communication: Direct—he's, like, right behind you, man!

Memorable Quotes:

"A foolish young man I was then, full of ridiculous ideas about good and evil. Lord Voldemort showed me how wrong I was. There is no good and evil, there is only power, and those too weak to seek it. . . . Since then, I have served him faithfully, although I have let him down many times" (*SS* 290).

"Sometimes," he said, "I find it hard to follow my master's instructions—he is a great wizard and I am weak—" (*SS* 290).

CHAPTER 39

Note also how Quirrell seems to be a bumbling, frightened idiot. But his stupidity is in reality a superb act.

~~~~~~~~~~~~~~~~

RECRUIT SMART SPIES WHO APPEAR STUPID

General Sun-Tzu at Part XIII 11 discusses the need for a spy to look "stupid":

"As living spies we must recruit men who are intelligent but appear to be stupid; who seem to be dull but are strong in heart; men who are agile, vigorous, hardy, and brave; well-versed in lowly matters and able to endure hunger, cold, filth, and humiliation."

~~~~~~~~~~~~~~~~

A spy who could be deemed patriotic without connection to a particular nation is Kreacher. As a member of and servant to the House of Black, he has absorbed all of the biases and prejudices of that family. Kreacher's patriotism lies with his understanding of the history and values of the Black family. Importantly, in the last book, Kreacher is able to *unlearn* these biases and prejudices (as we all are able to do) and actually assists Harry, Hermione, and Ron when they are hiding out at number twelve, Grimmauld Place, and in the final battle.

KREACHER ANALYSIS

Recruitment by: Presumably Voldemort himself

Incentive Used: At first simply an obligation to the House of Black, but then specifically to R.A.B. (Regulus Black) and subsequently to his perception of what R.A.B. believed or desired. This changed once he discovered that Regulus betrayed Voldemort (with Kreacher's help), thus allowing Kreacher's recruitment by Harry through friendship and acceptance of the parallel ideals of Harry and his friends.

Handler: Initially Regulus Black; later Harry, after Kreacher was turned

Method of Communication: Face-to-face

Memorable Quotes:

Hermione: "What do wizard wars mean to an elf like Kreacher? He's loyal to people who are kind to him, and Mrs. Black must have been, and Regulus certainly was, so he served them willingly and parroted their beliefs" (*DH* 198).

Kreacher: "Fight! Fight! Fight for my Master, defender of house-elves! Fight the Dark Lord, in the name of brave Regulus! Fight!" (*DH* 734).

The patriotic spy normally owes allegiance to his or her own country. In most countries, when people assume a public office, they take an oath. In the United States the oath includes the obligation to support and defend the Constitution from any enemies, foreign or domestic. In other words, it is possible that we might need to defend our country and Constitution not only from those outside its borders, but also from those *within* it.

Although there are some who argue convincingly that the nation-state is disintegrating or becoming less important, and that we are entering instead a clash of civilizations (discussed at pages 572-73 in the Appendix), spies are presently and primarily organized by nations and thus are sent out to do a *nation's* bidding.

CHAPTER 39

THE SPY FOR CAUSE—PERSONAL FEELINGS: SEVERUS SNAPE

Another type of spy that works for a particular cause is those who become spies for a *personal* reason or cause. The foremost of this type of spy in the Harry Potter series is Professor Snape, who has been, like Harry, "Dumbledore's man through-and-through" (a disparaging statement, you might remember, by the ineffectual Minister of Magic Scrimgeour describing Harry's allegiance to Dumbledore [*HBP* 348]). Snape became a spy for Dumbledore the day Voldemort began hunting down Lily Potter. Snape's motive is his love for Lily—or, more accurately, his *unrequited* love of Lily.

But let's not forget that Snape was a Death Eater before making his bargain with Dumbledore, and his prior loyalty was to Lord Voldemort. Why would Snape initially go over to the dark side? (No, this is *not* intended to be a reference to the Star Wars trilogy. So quit giggling!)

Let us now do an introductory psychological assessment of Professor Snape. (We will thoroughly discuss Snape's background and history in chapter 53 of this book.) As we all know, Snape was belittled and bullied, probably by many students at Hogwarts, but particularly by none other than James Potter (*OP* 640–48; *DH* 674). He was understandably not popular. He looked disheveled, had greasy hair, and probably only had one set of clothes (*OP* 591, 641; *DH* 663). He grew up in an abusive family. J. K. Rowling does not explicitly explain or show us Snape being recruited as a Death Eater, but she provides hints as to his motivation and we are told through Lily Evans that Snape "couldn't wait" to join Voldemort while still attending Hogwarts. This desire to become a Death Eater is based most likely on Snape's views relating to the superiority of purebloods, a desire for a sense of belonging to a group, and an adolescent thirst for power (mixed of course with a desire for revenge against his tormentors).

So how do we analyze Snape's motives and steadfast loyalty to Dumbledore? Snape did not know love except through his feelings for Lily Potter, which, due to many factors, was unreturned; once his chance of winning Lily Evans was gone, Snape continued to love her, or at least perceived the ideal of love based on how he felt about her. Snape's love of Lily was the linchpin for his actions, and yet understanding how and why that love continued even after her marriage to James Potter and then her death is perhaps the most complicated aspect of the Harry Potter story. Can such a love be that powerful an incentive?

By the time he left Hogwarts Snape was, in many ways, a broken (but powerful) man.

NOTE TO SELF: *It is often the outcasts of society who are willing to do things that others cannot fathom.*

Personal injustices are easily transferred into generic and nationalistic affronts. It is also a trait of human psychology to blame others for your own situation: "I am poor because of the government," or "I am treated unfairly because of the government," or "The government and the people in power do not understand me," or "The people in power as well as the people themselves insult me by not understanding or accepting my viewpoints." A battered tree has a hard time standing tall on its own—and will often, too easily, bend to the winds of some nefarious ideal or opportunity, no matter where those winds may be heading.

SNAPE ANALYSIS

Recruitment by: Initially Voldemort; then Dumbledore, when Severus is turned and they make the bargain

Incentive Used: Initially Voldemort's promise of power and revenge; later love of Lily Potter, then being true to her after her death

CHAPTER 39

Handler: Voldemort; then Dumbledore, while Voldemort still thinks himself the handler

Method of Communication: Face-to-face, and the Dark Mark; Voldemort may be able to communicate with Snape through other means

Memorable Quotes:

Harry: "Yes, Dumbledore's dead," said Harry calmly, "but you didn't have him killed. He chose his own manner of dying, chose it months before he died, arranged the whole thing with the man you thought was your servant. . . . Snape was Dumbledore's [man], Dumbledore's from the moment you started hunting down my mother" (*DH* 740).

Snape: "You can carry my words back to the others who whisper behind my back, and carry false tales of my treachery to the Dark Lord! Before I answer you, I say, let me ask a question in turn. Do you really think that the Dark Lord has not asked me each and every one of those questions? And do you really think that, had I not been able to give satisfactory answers, I would be sitting here talking to you?" (*HBP* 26).

Dumbledore: "Do not think that I underestimate the constant danger in which you place yourself, Severus. To give Voldemort what appears to be valuable information while withholding the essentials is a job I would entrust to nobody but you" (*DH* 684).

Snape: "I have spied for you and lied for you, put myself in mortal danger for you. Everything was supposed to be to keep Lily Potter's son safe. Now you tell me you have been raising him like a pig for slaughter—" (*DH* 687).

PART 2

THE SPY FOR CAUSE—PERSONAL REVENGE AND GLORY: DRACO MALFOY

There is one other personal reason to spy or to do Voldemort's bidding. Revenge!

ANALYSIS: *Why would Draco Malfoy agree to try to kill Dumbledore in book 6,* Harry Potter and the Half-Blood Prince?

Because by that point in the series, Draco's father is imprisoned and derided as a known Death Eater, servant to Lord Voldemort. Draco is given the assignment by Voldemort himself, which makes him feel powerful and important. But one must wonder, just as Professor Dumbledore wonders when he is visiting with Snape about Draco, whether Draco's heart is really in it.

Draco is not evil at this point, but simply terribly misdirected. His motive is revenge, not hatred, and the difference between the two is significant. Draco seems somewhat apathetic to Lord Voldemort's cause. In book 7, *Harry Potter and the Deathly Hallows*, Draco observes Lord Voldemort torturing and killing people—including Hogwarts's Muggle Studies teacher, Professor Charity Burbage, the woman twisting above the drawing room table (*DH* 3, 11). When he sees his father forced to give his wand to Lord Voldemort, we imagine that he begins to understand Voldemort quite well and perhaps has terrible misgivings about the Dark Lord's presence in his family's home (a point raised by Voldemort at the time—perhaps by use of Legilimency!).

We assert that Lucius and Narcissi Malfoy come to the same conclusion by the end of the series, as shown in the final installation of the film series: during the last battle, they grab Draco and quietly leave the scene, no doubt to go into hiding—away from Lord Voldemort, in case he is successful, and in a position to claim they did not fight for him if the tide is turned. A shrewd move indeed, Mr. and Mrs. Malfoy!

You will also note that, in the movie version, Draco has a hard time leaving his friends when asked to do so. He is clearly conflicted; after all, he had been saved just a little while ago by Harry Potter (to Ron's great chagrin!) when the Room of Requirements went up in magical flames (*DH* 633–34).

DRACO MALFOY ANALYSIS

Recruitment by: Voldemort himself, no doubt

Incentive Used: Revenge for father's downfall

Handler: Voldemort, perhaps through Lucius Malfoy or other Death Eaters when necessary (as when Lucius is in prison)

Method of Communication: Face-to-face

Memorable Quote:

"I haven't got any options! I've got to do it! He'll kill me! He'll kill my whole family!" (*HBP* 591).

Dumbledore: "A frightened teenage boy is a danger to others as well as to himself. Offer him help and guidance, he ought to accept, he likes you—"

Snape: "—much less since his father has lost favor. Draco blames me, he thinks I have usurped Lucius's position" (*DH* 682).

~~~~~~~~~~

THE CIA LEARNS TO TAKE CARE WHEN DISMISSING CASE OFFICERS

Revenge is a significant motive for some, and under the "lessons-learned" category, the CIA decided to make some changes after it botched the firing of Edward Lee Howard. Howard was dismissed rather abruptly for using illegal drugs. Partly as revenge, and partly due to his ego (he wanted to bask in the appreciation of the KGB for using his connections to provide important information), Howard sold secrets to the Soviets to get back at the agency. Based on this experience with Howard, the CIA "changed gears" and set up an office to deal with employees who have problems.

—Peter Earnest, *Business Confidential* 12, 172

THE SPY FOR ADVENTURE: THE WEASLEY TWINS

Another type of spy is one who does so for adventure. Although adventure is a great incentive indeed, it should never be the *primary* incentive. A spy's primary incentive should be a value or principle on which you can always rely. Adventure knows no country, nor any morals. Adventure is a rush of excitement that satisfies a specific purpose; such a flimsy or ephemeral rationale is not in and of itself a purpose worthy of action.

NOTE TO SELF: *Without an underlying and worthy purpose, actions are just that: action without meaning or principle.*

In the Harry Potter series, we identify two individuals who are in a sense spies (or at least operatives) and do so for adventure: Fred and George Weasley. Fred and George clearly enjoy the adventure of spying on people and have even designed the Extendable Ears to do so. But they are also principled and have a moral belief about what is right.

CHAPTER 39

THE WEASLEY TWINS ANALYSIS

Recruitment by: None needed

Incentive Used: The desire to always be up to no good!

Handler: Themselves

Method of Communication: Face-to-face (via quick-witted banter)

Memorable Quote:

A thin piece of flesh-colored string descended in front of Harry's eyes. Looking up he saw Fred and George on the landing above, cautiously lowering the Extendable Ear toward the dark knot of people below (76–77).

"George," said Fred, "I think we've outgrown full-time education." "Yeah, I've been feeling that way myself," said George lightly (674).

THE FEARFUL SPY: PETER PETTIGREW

The next type of spy is motivated by fear. Our example is Peter Pettigrew. As we all know, Peter Pettigrew was brought into James Potter's circle despite the fact that the other three (James, Sirius, and Lupin) would not automatically or normally have included him in their group. James and Sirius were good-looking and popular, as well as egotistical. Lupin, as a werewolf, was an outsider; that at least indicates that James and Sirius were not so full of themselves that they would be unwilling to befriend and assist somebody strange or different. Peter Pettigrew was the one in need of friends, but we wonder why the other three allowed him into their midst. It's hard to say how they became friends, and we're never really told.

Thus, it's possible that they brought in Peter Pettigrew not necessarily because they felt sorry for him, but rather because they observed that he was different and allowed him into their fold. Whatever the reason, Peter Pettigrew became one of the foursome, but unfortunately not one who could be trusted in the end. For, as we all know, Peter Pettigrew was the Secret Keeper who told Voldemort where James and Lily Potter, and their toddler son, Harry, lived.

When we meet Peter Pettigrew as an adult, he seems like a weak and spineless rat (and, of course, he can turn into a rat!). He seems to fear Voldemort, but is thrilled by the prospect of receiving power *through* Voldemort. He is willing to give Voldemort not merely the shirt off his back, but, literally, his right hand. Now that's really a right-hand man! (Sorry about that!)

Let us also remember that, thanks to Harry's refusal to allow Sirius and Lupin to kill Peter at the Shrieking Shack (after the rat returned to human form and confessed to his betrayal of James and Lily Potter), Peter Pettigrew is indebted to Harry (*PA* 375). As Dumbledore explains to Harry, "The consequences of our actions are always so complicated, so diverse, that predicting the future is a very difficult business indeed. . . . Pettigrew owes his life to you. You have sent Voldemort a deputy who is in your debt. When one wizard saves another wizard's life, it creates a certain bond between them . . ." (*PA* 426–27).

Harry understandably wants no connection to Peter Pettigrew, but Dumbledore wisely opines, "the time may come when you will be very glad you saved Pettigrew's life" (*PA* 427). And, to Peter Pettigrew's great surprise, he does falter for a moment when coming to check on Harry and the others imprisoned in the dungeon of Malfoy Manor—and the new hand that Voldemort gave Pettigrew immediately turns on him and kills him (*DH* 470)!

PETER PETTIGREW ANALYSIS

Recruitment by: A Death Eater or Voldemort as they searched for James, Lily, and toddler Harry Potter

Incentive Used: Desire for power and fear of Voldemort

Handler: Probably Voldemort himself

Method of Communication: Face-to-face

Memorable Quotes:

Sirius: "But you, Peter—I'll never understand why I didn't see you were the spy from the start. You always liked big friends who'd look after you, didn't you? It used to be us . . . me and Remus . . . and James. . . ." (*PA* 369).

Voldemort: "You returned to me, not out of loyalty, but out of fear of your old friends" (*GF* 649).

Narrative: "The silver tool that Voldemort had given his most cowardly servant had turned upon its disarmed and useless owner; Pettigrew was reaping his reward for his hesitation, his moment of pity; he was being strangled before their eyes" (*DH* 470).

THE CURSED SPY: BRODERICK BODE

Another type of spy specific to the Harry Potter series is one who has been cursed. The example closest to hand would be Broderick Bode, who was subjected to an Imperius Curse by Lucius Malfoy in an attempt to get the prophecy from the Department of Mysteries. When under the Imperius Curse, a person is spying not of their own free will, but rather is being forced to do so by someone

PART 2

else and as such should *not* be held responsible for those misdeeds.

BODE ANALYSIS

Recruitment by: Under Imperius Curse, so no real recruitment

Incentive Used: None—subjected to the Imperius Curse

Handler: Lucius Malfoy

Method of Communication: Imperius Curse

Memorable Quote:

Rookwood: "Bode could never have taken it, Master. . . . Bode would have known he could not. . . . Undoubtedly that is why he fought so hard against Malfoy's Imperius Curse . . ." (*OP* 585).

THE POSSESSED SPY: GINNY WEASLEY

Another type of spy unique to the Harry Potter series is one who is possessed, such as Ginny Weasley in book 2, *Harry Potter and the Chamber of Secrets*. Ginny Weasley is possessed by Lord Voldemort—or, more precisely, by Tom Riddle through the diary—but she does not remember what she did at Tom Riddle's behest. As such, Ginny should not be held accountable for painting warnings on the walls or her other actions while being possessed.

GINNY WEASLEY ANALYSIS

Recruitment by: Tom Riddle's diary, via the part of Voldemort's soul contained therein

CHAPTER 39

Incentive Used: Initially curiosity; then possession, with no choice given

Handler: Tom Riddle

Method of Communication: The diary

Memorable Quotes:

Tom Riddle: "Yes, of course, she didn't know what she was doing at first. It was very amusing. I wish you could have seen her new diary entries . . . far more interesting, they became. . . . Dear Tom, I think I'm losing my memory. There are rooster feathers all over my robes and I don't know how they got there. Dear Tom, I can't remember what I did on the night of Halloween, but a cat was attacked and I've got paint all down my front. Dear Tom, Percy keeps telling me I'm pale and I'm not myself. I think he suspects me. . . . There was another attack today and I don't know where I was. Tom, what am I going to do? I think I'm going mad. . . . I think I'm the one attacking everyone, Tom!" (*CS* 310–11).

Ginny: "Well, that was a bit stupid of you," said Ginny angrily, "seeing as you don't know anyone but me who's been possessed by You-Know-Who, and I can tell you how it feels. . . . Well, can you remember everything you've been doing?" Ginny asked. "Are there big blank periods where you don't know what you've been up to? . . . When he did it to me, I couldn't remember what I'd been doing for hours at a time. I'd find myself somewhere and not know how I got there" (499–500).

PART 2

SPYING OUT OF A DESIRE FOR MAYHEM—BARTY CROUCH JR. AS MAD·EYE MOODY

Another spy who does not fit exactly into the categories listed above comes from book 4: Mad-Eye Moody, who was in reality Barty Crouch Jr. using Polyjuice to impersonate the irascible professor. Moody, as we find out at the end, had been imprisoned inside his own highly secure trunk in his office. Barty Crouch Jr., disguised as Moody, was spying for the purpose of getting Harry into the Triwizard Tournament and succeeding in it, so that, at the final moment, he would touch the trophy—in reality a Portkey that would take him directly to Lord Voldemort, who needed Harry's blood to return to physical prowess.

BARTY CROUCH JR. ANALYSIS

Recruitment by: A Death Eater or Voldemort

Incentive Used: Antisocial and anti-authority tendencies

Handler: Voldemort at the Riddle house, and also probably a Death Eater, given Voldemort's weakened state

Method of Communication: Face-to-face

Memorable Quotes:

Sirius: "When Voldemort disappeared, it looked like only a matter of time until Crouch got the top job. But then something rather unfortunate happened. . . ." Sirius smiled grimly. "Crouch's own son was caught with a group of Death Eaters who'd managed to talk their way out of Azkaban. Apparently they were trying to find Voldemort and return him to power" (*GF* 527).

Barty Crouch Jr.: "He told me he needed to place a faithful servant at Hogwarts. A servant who would guide Harry Potter through the Triwizard Tournament without appearing to do so. A servant who would watch over Harry Potter. Ensure he reached the Triwizard Cup. Turn the Cup into a Portkey, which would take the first person to touch it to my master" (*GF* 688).

Barty Crouch Jr.: "My master's plan worked. He is returned to power and I will be honored by him beyond the dreams of wizards" (*GF* 691).

A SPY IN THE LIGHT OF DAY: DOLORES UMBRIDGE

Another spy who does not fit exactly in the categories listed above is Professor Umbridge, who certainly spied for a cause (the Ministry can do no wrong, hem hem, giggle), but was spying *openly*. In other words, everybody at the school knew that Professor Umbridge was there to spy on Hogwarts, its students, its staff, and its headmaster. We note this simple fact because normally a spy works *covertly* and *secretly*. However, there are situations in which somebody spies openly, particularly when they have been given authority to do so by those in power! The role of such open spying is to assert the authority's control with constant reminders that resistance will be observed, reported, and certainly not left unanswered!

DOLORES UMBRIDGE ANALYSIS

Recruitment by: Cornelius Fudge

Incentive Used: Pure loyalty to the Ministry and the Minister of Magic, Cornelius Fudge

Handler: Cornelius Fudge

Method of Communication: Owl, Floo Network, Educational Decrees

Memorable Quotes:

Umbridge: "Let us move forward, then, into a new era of openness, effectiveness, and accountability, intent on preserving what ought to be preserved, perfecting what needs to be perfected, and pruning wherever we find practices that ought to be prohibited" (*OP* 213–14).

"What Cornelius doesn't know won't hurt him" (*OP* 746).

As an aside, we note two other "open" spies in the series, both appearing in book 3, *Harry Potter and the Prisoner of Azkaban*.

The first is none other than Petunia Dursley, who, it turns out, is quite the nosy neighbor! According to Harry, Aunt Petunia would *love* to be the one to call in and report the spotting of Sirius Black: "She was the nosiest woman in the world and spent most of her life spying on the boring, law-abiding neighbors" (*PA* 17).

Another "open" spy is Tom, the toothless landlord of the Leaky Cauldron, who at the request of Cornelius Fudge keeps an eye on Harry while he stays at the Leaky Caldron for a few weeks after escaping from the Dursleys' (*PA* 46).

THE DUPED SPY, ON A FOOL'S ERRAND: KATIE BELL AND BODE'S NURSE

The last type of spy we would like to discuss is the person who is being used or has been duped. Two examples in the Harry Potter series are Katie Bell, who agrees to deliver the cursed necklace to Professor Dumbledore, and Bode's nurse, who delivers the lethal plant to Bode's bedside.

We are constantly amazed that people can be so friendly and compliant that they will do whatever is asked of them, with little thought or concern as to *why* they are being asked to do it!

It also amazes us on a regular basis how easy it is to get somebody to do something based on a pretext or a lie. For example, it is possible to have a bellhop place something in someone else's hotel room simply by stating that you're traveling with that person and he or she forgot this particular piece of luggage in the car. If you are unsure of what room somebody is in at a hotel, you can have the person paged, or leave a note with the bellhop and then quietly follow the bellhop to the room. (You must first convince the bellhop or the front desk that it is essential that the envelope be placed under the door as soon as possible, but that, because the person is probably taking a nap, it would be best not to call.)

What's that you say?

That we digress?

So, back to the story! Or at least the point we were making about having very nice people do your bidding.

There are numerous ways to get information by trickery and deceit, but good ol' unabashed friendliness works too. For example, go up to somebody and ask, "Didn't I go to high school with you? Well, aren't you from such and such town?" Most of the time you will end up in a conversation in which you will be able to determine that person's name, where he or she grew up, what that person is doing in town, his or her profession, and even a listing of family members!

NOTE TO SELF: *People love to talk about themselves, so let them!*

When we say that these individuals have been duped, we say so *in the nicest way possible.* The best spies do not look upon others with condescension or arrogance, but instead generally *enjoy* people, listening to them, and learning about their lives. Listening closely to people and showing a genuine interest will open more doors than Sirius's famous knife!

PART 2

NOTE TO SELF: *One of the most important traits of a spy is the ability to listen carefully and to appear to show genuine interest in the person to whom you are speaking.*

KATIE BELL ANALYSIS

Recruitment by: Draco Malfoy's use of the Imperius Curse on Rosmerta, who then asked Katie to deliver the package to Dumbledore

Incentive Used: Doing someone a favor

Handler: Rosmerta, at the request of Draco Malfoy

Method of Communication: Through Rosmerta in the Three Broomsticks

Memorable Quotes:

Leanne: "She came back from the bathroom in the Three Broomsticks holding it, said it was a surprise for somebody at Hogwarts and she had to deliver it. She looked all funny when she said it. . . . Oh no, oh no, I bet she'd been Imperiused and I didn't realize!" (*HBP* 251).

Dumbledore: "So poor Rosmerta was forced to lurk in her own bathroom and pass that necklace to any Hogwarts student who entered the room unaccompanied?" (*HBP* 589).

BODE'S NURSE ANALYSIS

Recruitment by: Probably just a person leaving a "gift," and the nurse was just "doing her job"

Incentive Used: Doing someone a favor

Handler: Voldemort, through a Death Eater

Method of Communication: Something simple and ordinary, like a note attached to the "delivery"

Memorable Quote:

Hermione: "I don't think anyone could put Devil's Snare in a pot and not realize it tries to kill whoever touches it" (547).

SUN-TZU'S FIVE TYPES OF SPIES

A famous Chinese general Sun-Tzu lived in the fourth century B.C. and is the author of the earliest known writings on war and spying, including his most famous, *The Art of War*. Sun-Tzu described five types of spies at XIII 5-11: 1) local inhabitants; 2) government officials who could be persuaded to switch their loyalties; 3) enemy spies that could be persuaded to become a double agent; 4) spies who conduct acts of espionage to deceive the enemy (often captured and executed); and 5) spies sent behind enemy lines and return with information.

WITH A LITTLE HELP FROM MY FRIENDS

When you need access to a location or a particular person, it never hurts to have friends in high places or in the right spot!

PART 2

GETTING INTO THE KURCHATOV INSTITUTE IN MOSCOW

When I wanted to gain access to the Kurchatov Institute in Moscow, the place where the Soviets first created a nuclear reactor capable of creating weapons-grade plutonium, a friend with whom I often stayed with in Moscow had a cousin who worked there. Through that connection, I was able to get into the Kurchatov Institute, see the reactor itself, and walk around the grounds—all without having to go through any security! Because of my friend's connections, I and an American engineer entered the Kurchatov Institute in a private car that was not searched and could have been loaded with weapons.

At the time, the Kurchatov Institute had very little security and supposedly housed hundreds of pounds of weapons-grade material that could have easily been stolen. Upon my return to the United States I relayed this story to General Gary Curtain, then head of intelligence for STRATCOM, the US military command in charge of nuclear weapons and analyzing the nuclear weapons capabilities of other countries.

About six months later, money from the Nunn-Lugar Act was made available to Russia so that it could secure the nation's nuclear facilities and weapons-grade material. According to *Newsweek*, reporting around August 1, 1994, one of the first places secured was the Kurchatov Institute and the nuclear materials contained therein!

—Lynn Boughey

Harry receives assistance from his best friends, Ron and Hermione, throughout the book. From the moment Ron and Harry rescue a crying Hermione from a troll in the girls bathroom and she lies to protect them afterward, they are friends who help each other—*even* when they are arguing!

After rescuing Dobby, Harry has a friend for life who assists him numerous times, despite Harry's request, at the end of book 2, that Dobby "Just promise never to try and save my life again" (*CS* 339). Thank goodness Dobby ignored that request!

As we have previously discussed, friends can be made in the unlikeliest places, and with those you had initially considered to be enemies, such as Kreacher. Most people have a great capacity to exhibit the most amazing traits and surprising acts of loyalty—even in the midst of great danger.

So we will end this chapter by reiterating the most important point that J. K. Rowling makes throughout the Harry Potter series:

Never underestimate the power of love or friendship.

40

RECRUITING AND RUNNING SPIES

- **Grindelwald Recruits Young Dumbledore—The Strength of Personality and Ideas, Good and Bad**

- **Dumbledore Recruits Young Tom Riddle—Act of Valor (to Save Tom, or Muggles) or Foolish Mistake?**

- **Hermione's (and Harry's) Recruitment of Dumbledore's Army—Friends Finding a Common Purpose**

- **Hagrid's Attempt to Recruit the Giants—Family Connection Versus Desire for Power**

- **The Reticence of the Goblins to Choose Sides—Pure Avarice or Strategic Disinterest?**

- **Dumbledore Recruits Slughorn to Hogwarts—Dumbledore's Use of Pride and Slughorn's Desire for Influence**

- **Spy Handling: Keeping Track of and Control over Your Spies—The Art of Leadership and the Necessity of Making Decisions**

We will now discuss the tactics of recruiting as described in the Harry Potter series—in a somewhat chronological order.

There are many ways to try to recruit individuals, but the primary issue is always motivation. What are the subject's *personal beliefs*? With whom does the subject's *loyalty* lie? What are the subject's *principles* or *beliefs*? What would *motivate* or *entice* this person to spy for you? *What are you offering* that the person does not have or wants? Importantly, is the subject worthy of being recruited? And perhaps more importantly, will the subject turn on you and betray you?

All good questions, indeed.

A PLACE TO BELONG?

Those who are estranged from their own country are often willing to gravitate toward a new place to call home—and a new object of their loyalty. As George Santayana once said, "People who feel themselves to be exiles in this world are mightily inclined to believe themselves citizens of another."

GRINDELWALD RECRUITS YOUNG DUMBLEDORE— THE STRENGTH OF PERSONALITY AND IDEAS, GOOD AND BAD

Let us look back in the Potter series to perhaps its earliest portrayal of the recruitment of a person toward a particular side: Grindelwald's recruitment of young Albus Dumbledore—enticing him to the banal concept of the common good and the prejudicial and arrogant view of Wizarding superiority. We find out about this in book 7 (*DH* 353).

It is clear that Dumbledore is drawn in by Grindelwald's engaging personality and superb intellect (though we highly doubt it was superior to Dumbledore's own intellect). Believe it or not, it is very easy for those who are young, accomplished, and bright to think they know everything. Hard to believe, but it is true.

The psychology of young Dumbledore is actually described by Professor Dumbledore himself when he explains that he learned—through his *desire for power* in his discussions with young Grindelwald—why he should never become the Minister of Magic: he *liked* power. Based on this discovery, Dumbledore decided that he should not accept a position of great power, but instead confine himself and his talents to a position in which he provides positive influence without the temptation of great power (*DH* 717). As Hogwarts Headmaster, Dumbledore is in a position not only to ensure that he does not abuse his own power, but also to *prevent* the abuse of power at Hogwarts by others—as when Umbridge attempts to throw out Professor Trelawney or to inappropriately "manhandle" the DA snitch, Marietta (*OP* 595, 616).

In any event, Grindelwald attempted to recruit Dumbledore to his view of the world—and came very close to success. However, upon the death of his sister Arianna, Dumbledore reevaluated everything that he had initially considered to be true or intellectually viable and rejected Grindelwald's recruitment profoundly (*DH* 718).

Was this epiphany merely because of guilt? Or was Dumbledore's guilt the catalyst that engendered his insight and the application of a more experienced intellect?

Whatever the reason, Dumbledore learned, in a word, *humility*, both the personal kind and its application to wizards, Muggles, house-elves, and students alike!

TRAGEDY, FAILURE, AND THE ADVENT OF KNOWLEDGE AND HUMILITY

Just as ego and hubris follow great deeds and accomplishments, we have found that humility often follows personal failures or tragedies—some of which are our own making, and some of which are pure chance. Those with talent but not enough humility ask themselves, "What could have been?" Those with humility ask instead, "What now? To what positive end?"

In the Muggle world, many people have reached the conclusion—based primarily on Arthur Schlesinger's wonderful biography—that Robert Kennedy did not develop a true understanding of society and real empathy until his brother Jack was assassinated. Afterward, he spent months reading Albert Camus and the Greek poets. This thorough study of great works of literature by the then thirty-eight-year-old attorney general is described best in Schlesinger's *Robert Kennedy and His Times*, chapter 26, part VII (1978).

NOTE TO SELF: *Great literature not only reflects on life and the values worth internalizing, but can also provide personal insight and direction.*

Dumbledore's newfound humility is, in our opinion, a significant development, that of a sense of humanity, and used in the best light possible. It is a view that all beings have value, that might does not make right, and that caring for and protecting others is the aspect of humanity that makes us different and worthy to continue our existence. Dumbledore did, in a word, become human.

DUMBLEDORE RECRUITS YOUNG TOM RIDDLE— ACT OF VALOR (TO SAVE TOM, OR MUGGLES) OR FOOLISH MISTAKE?

Let us look now to the next significant recruitment in the Harry Potter series—the recruitment of young Tom Riddle by a young Professor Dumbledore, as described in book 6, *Harry Potter and the*

PART 2

Half-Blood Prince.

As we are all aware, Tom Riddle lived at an orphanage when Dumbledore first met him. We find out through the person running the orphanage that Tom Riddle is a strange child who seems to have certain powers of persuasion that other children do not have. Indeed, it appears that he has not only stolen items from some of the other children, but even gone so far as to use his powers to torture Muggle children (*HBP* 266–68).

Imagine all the red flags that appeared when Dumbledore first met Tom Riddle: a boy who is already willing to use his powers for self-interest and has no empathy toward others at all. Dumbledore had before him a young sociopath and most probably knew it.

ANALYSIS: *Why allow Tom Riddle to come to Hogwarts, where he would learn how to use his talents and magical powers?* Certainly Professor Dumbledore realized that if he allowed Tom Riddle to come to Hogwarts, Tom would become even more proficient at using magic. And if Riddle's initial perverted uses of magic to instill fear in and wield power over others were not altered, he would become a very dangerous person indeed!

Dumbledore most probably analyzed the situation and identified two options: first, he could leave young Tom Riddle at the orphanage, and at some point the boy would be caught violating Muggle rules and be sent away—probably to prison or a psychiatric ward—for the rest of his life. But at what cost or harm to Muggles? The second was for Professor Dumbledore to bring Riddle to Hogwarts and attempt to teach him that he was heading in the wrong direction. Dumbledore, forever the optimist, went with the second option, no doubt believing that he would be in a position to teach Riddle the error of his ways. In addition, Dumbledore probably believed that by bringing Riddle to Hogwarts he was preventing the boy from doing further damage to the Muggles at the orphanage or whatever boarding school he would have ended up in (*HBP* 276).

CHAPTER 40

We could certainly argue that Dumbledore's decision has an element or aspect of pride—based on his understandable view that he would be an excellent teacher to Tom Riddle and that he would be successful in steering the boy along the right path. And even if this wasn't an error of pride, we certainly cannot blame Dumbledore for having a default positive view of all the young wizards and witches in his charge—for Dumbledore is above all things a wonderful optimist. It is very hard indeed to fault Professor Dumbledore for having a positive view of the nature or potential goodness of humans.

NOTE TO SELF: *A person can be recruited as an act of necessity— necessity in terms of the person being recruited, the person doing the recruitment, or both.*

HERMIONE'S (AND HARRY'S) RECRUITMENT OF DUMBLEDORE'S ARMY—FRIENDS FINDING A COMMON PURPOSE

Now let us look to the recruitment process for the members of Dumbledore's Army. We discussed this quite a bit in chapter 16, so we will not dwell too much on the style of recruitment at this time. A quick review will suffice.

Hermione has the initial idea and convinces Harry to teach Defense Against the Dark Arts to his fellow students (*OP* 325). They meet at the Hog's Head and, after some unrelated discussion, focus on the real issue at hand: Harry's special and advanced knowledge, what he has already been able to accomplish as a young wizard, and his willingness to teach the others these same skills (*OP* 335–44).

Harry indicates to everyone at the Hog's Head that much of what he's accomplished has been by luck—half the time he didn't know what to do—and he often had the help of his friends in getting things done (*OP* 327–28, 343).

Once again, we see the humility of young Harry Potter and his worthiness both as a teacher and as a person. The motivation of the prospective students (those who are being recruited) is clear: they believe Harry's assertion that Voldemort has returned and want to learn how to defend themselves, so they are ready when the battle finally comes.

NOTE TO SELF: *A group of people can be recruited based on a common belief, a common enemy, or the need for mutual protection.*

HAGRID'S ATTEMPT TO RECRUIT THE GIANTS—FAMILY CONNECTION VERSUS DESIRE FOR POWER

The next significant recruitment we learn about is Hagrid's attempt to recruit the giants in book 5, *Harry Potter and the Order of the Phoenix*. Again, this is discussed in some detail in chapter 20, but here we will focus on a few of the more salient points. For this assignment, Hagrid has been informed by Dumbledore not only *where* the giants are located, but also *how* to approach them (*OP* 425, 427).

The giants, it seems, are interested in two things: payment and power. Hagrid begins with a gift, which is well liked, and then plans to return the next day with another gift. He is therefore attempting to recruit the giants with a bribe, in the form of a gift, and will return with another item to show his consistency, trustworthiness, and credibility.

~~~~~~~~~~~~~~~~~

SUN-TZU AND THE VALUE OF BRIBERY

The renowned Chinese general Sun-Tzu notes in his famous book *The Art of War*, VIII 2, that bribery is cheaper than war:

"Hostile armies may face each other for years, striving for the victory which is decided in a single day. This being so, to remain in ignorance of the enemy's condition simply because one grudges the outlay of a hundred ounces of silver in honors and emoluments, is the height of inhumanity."

~~~~~~~~~~~~~~~~~~~~

Although Hagrid's initial bribe seemed to work, it turns out that the bribe will not be effective because the next day Hagrid finds a new leader in charge (*OP* 429–30), one who appears more interested in whatever the Death Eaters have promised, most probably access to *power*.

Through this example, J. K. Rowling indicates that the unsophisticated among us can be persuaded by flattery, obsequiousness, self-congratulation, trinkets of wealth, and promises of power. More sophisticated persons are drawn to ideals or a sense of common good. (At least we hope that this is the case!)

~~~~~~~~~~~~~~~~~~~~

FLATTERY AND THE WORD TOADY

Did you know that there are such words as *toady* and *toadyism*? Guess what they mean? A *toady* is a person who flatters or defers to others for self-serving reasons, a sycophant. Can you think of anyone who is described as toadlike and who acts like this? "Hem hem," we say!

~~~~~~~~~~~~~~~~~~~~

The giants, we see, are in a *Hobbesian state of nature*, where life is short, brutish, and nasty. The giants understand power more than principle; immediate wants as opposed to long-term civility or the concept of the common good (in its proper or best sense). They have not yet entered into a social contract, and as such are much more interested in the Death Eaters' offer: help us win, and we will give you great power; help us win, and we will allow you carte blanche in the destruction of Hogwarts and perhaps much of the Wizarding world. Or perhaps the Death Eaters "merely" offered the giants the opportunity to plunder the entire Muggle world with impunity! That might have worked just as well!

~~~~~~~~~~~~~~~~~~~~~~~~~~~~~~~~~~~~~

HOBBESIAN STATE OF NATURE

So what is this Hobbesian state of nature? And why do the conclusions of long-dead philosophers about social contracts apply to how power and goods are distributed and what each member of society owes to his or her fellow members?

Lots.

Let us take a moment to read the most famous portion of Thomas Hobbes's treatise, *Leviathan,* and apply this description to the giants: "No Arts; no Letters; no Society; and which is worst of all, continuall feare, and danger of violent death; And the life of man, solitary, poore, nasty, brutish, and short" (part I, chapter 13, page 62, [original edition, 1651]).

Other, more recent philosophical treatises have also discussed the state of nature and the development of society, including John Rawls's *A Theory of Justice* (1971). Study of human nature and how society developed is important because it leads us to a personal and perhaps societal determination of the nature and extent of our *personal obligation to society*, and also of *society's obligations to its members.* We leave it to you to investigate and determine for yourself how the Muggle world left the state of nature and developed a society—and what truths, social contracts, and values are properly derived from such analysis.

~~~~~~~~~~~~~~~~~~~~~~~~~~~~~~~~~~~~~

CHAPTER 40

THE GOBLINS' RETICENCE TO CHOOSE SIDES—PURE AVARICE OR STRATEGIC DISINTEREST?

Concerning the recruitment of the goblins, we learn in book 7 that goblins tend to be very literal in any agreements they make (*DH* 516–17). And in book 5, Bill Weasley mentions that which side they choose to support may depend on who will provide them the most financial advantage (*OP* 85). The goblins have not yet chosen sides.

DUMBLEDORE RECRUITS SLUGHORN TO HOGWARTS—DUMBLEDORE'S USE OF PRIDE AND SLUGHORN'S DESIRE FOR INFLUENCE

Lastly, in book 6, we observe Headmaster Dumbledore's attempts to convince Professor Horace Slughorn to return to Hogwarts. Dumbledore understands Slughorn well (having applied a psychological analysis) and attempts to massage his ego by introducing him to Harry. Dumbledore knows that Slughorn loves to recruit students, mentor them, and take credit for their subsequent accomplishments. Slughorn demonstrates this proclivity in his own words when he describes to Harry how important and well-connected he is. Indeed, we find out that Slughorn literally collects students and displays them through the photos of former students on his dresser (*HBP* 71). Dumbledore counts on Slughorn's need to feel important by receiving adulation of impressionable students when he offers Slughorn the Hogwarts position, including the opportunity to meet, teach, and mentor the famous Harry Potter, and perhaps convert the illustrious youth into one of his many protégés (*HBP* 74–75).

Thus, Professor Dumbledore knowingly prods Professor Slughorn's ego and vanity—and then excuses himself to go to the loo, leaving Harry to become Dumbledore's personal recruitment incentive. Professor Slughorn first discusses what he and Harry have in common: his mother Lily—and the fact that Harry has her eyes. It is clear that Professor Slughorn had great fondness for Lily Potter (then

Lily Evans) and is reminded through this recollection how much fun teaching can be, particularly when you have students who are more than happy to listen to your every word and greedily receive the information that you offer them. Dumbledore—at the end—prepares to leave rather briskly, asserting quite shrewdly that he has failed in his mission and it is time to go. This too is brilliant: instead of wasting time begging for Slughorn's return, Dumbledore "gives up" and allows Slughorn to accede to Dumbledore's request to teach at Hogwarts (*HBP* 69–70, 74).

You will note that Dumbledore wants Professor Slughorn there not only to teach Potions (though he could, no doubt, find somebody else with equal qualifications), but also, more importantly, to make it easier to obtain certain information about what Tom Riddle was told one night in Professor Slughorn's office after the other students had left (*HBP* 372)!

Although Dumbledore has previously retrieved this memory from Professor Slughorn, he is also well aware that the memory *has been altered*. Dumbledore believes, or at least *suspects* through proper analysis, that the real memory may contain a very important bit of information, a piece that he needs to complete the puzzle of what young Tom Riddle knew about—dare we say it out loud?—*Horcruxes* (*HBP* 371)!

Thus, Professor Dumbledore is recruiting Professor Slughorn not only to teach, but also in hopes that he will get access to the innermost of inside information. Having Professor Slughorn onsite at Hogwarts will create more opportunities for Professor Dumbledore to gather this information—perhaps through the not-so-subtle use of a certain young student named Harry Potter!

SPY HANDLING: KEEPING TRACK OF AND CONTROL OVER YOUR SPIES—THE ART OF LEADERSHIP AND THE NECESSITY OF MAKING DECISIONS

Keeping track of your spies and what they are doing is very

important. The best way to do this, we think, is to get a wonderful clock like Mrs. Weasley's, which lists where everybody is, what they are doing, and whether they are in mortal danger!

In the event you're unable to find such a clock to keep track of all of your family members and fellow spies, then you will have to figure out some other way to accomplish this important task!

Good communication is essential to knowing what your spy *is doing* and conveying what you *want* your spy to do. When handling spies, you should have as much contact with your spy *as is necessary* to obtain the information and to relay what you want done—and no more. Unless you're able to communicate in an entirely secure manner, each interaction puts your spy at risk of being discovered! It is for this reason that any contact with your spy should be limited to the task at hand and, if possible, face-to-face contact should be kept to a minimum. If other methods can be employed to deliver information or to delegate tasks, then resort to impersonal means.

We'll discuss communication in detail in chapter 46, but right now we want to talk about how a spy master keeps track of his or her spies and gives them assignments—in other words, the basics of spy handling.

Let's first discuss Voldemort. The Dark Lord is able to keep *control* of his spies by one very simple method: fear. All of Voldemort's Death Eaters strongly fear him and worry about being punished, tortured, or even killed. These are great incentives indeed to do whatever Lord Voldemort tells you to do!

Compare this to the Order of the Phoenix. We are able to observe, at least in part, numerous meetings of the Order in which they discuss information received and decide what needs to be done. The founder and head of the Order is clearly Dumbledore, but it appears that he rarely comes to headquarters and the group works as a team, discussing openly what needs to be done and reaching a *consensus* about what steps should be taken and what assignments should be distributed.

Yet, at the same time, we suspect that Dumbledore is directing the action, if not actually making (skillfully, and in a friendly manner)

PART 2

all the important decisions for the members of the Order. Even so, he is not overly or even overtly authoritarian in how he does this.

Lord Voldemort, on the other hand, has a clear hierarchy. He is in charge, with everyone else below him and required to do whatever he tells them to do—or else.

Although in the spy business there must always be someone in charge to make the final decision, ideally that leader fosters a genuine opportunity for everybody to speak his or her piece, present his or her own analysis, discuss the reliability of facts and the soundness of conclusions, and have an open discussion of the issue at hand. Again, you can do all of this while at the same time having one person who eventually makes the final decision.

NOTE TO SELF: *If you can lead a group by consensus and genuine discussion, allowing all sides to be considered, but with a clear decision made in a timely fashion, the final result has a better chance of being correct.*

ANOTHER NOTE TO SELF: *Allowing the members of a group to have a real role in reaching a decision results in those members being more committed to the group and the decisions made.*

Leadership requires listening, but also deciding.

In the Harry Potter series there are many examples of Harry listening to what Ron or Hermione have to say, but then clearly and decisively making important decisions *for the group*—most of them correct.

Two examples come immediately to mind. First, Harry's decision at Shell Cottage to go after the Horcruxes instead of the Deathly Hallows—that is, to go after the Hufflepuff cup and the Slytherin locket instead of trying to beat Voldemort to the Wand of Destiny, also known as the Elder Wand (*DH* 484, 537–538). Harry had "seen" the cup and locket before, in book 6—thanks to Dumbledore's Pensieve—and therefore knew what both objects looked like (*HBP* 433–39). An elderly witch named Hepzibah Smith had showed the young Tom Riddle both objects. Most certainly, it was just "an accident" that Hepzibah Smith died a mere two days later by poison—supposedly administered by her elderly house-elf, who took the blame and was convicted. Dumbledore was able to procure this memory from Smith's house-elf, Hokey (*HBP* 436–38).

Significantly, both items—properly considered to be Smith's greatest treasures—were never found by her family. And Tom Riddle? He very soon thereafter resigned his post at Borgin and Burkes and vanished, not to be seen for a very long time (*HBP* 439).

The second example of Harry making a bold decision is when he decides *not* to keep the all-powerful Elder Wand for himself, but instead put "it back where it came from" so that its power will be broken when Harry dies (*DH* 749). (We note that, in the movie version of the final book, Harry decides to destroy that very wand by breaking it in half!)

Importantly, Harry makes his decisions based primarily on his understanding of the history and background of Lord Voldemort and his own role in defeating the Dark Lord. And what is the basis of this knowledge? Albus Dumbledore's years of study, inquiry, research, and information gathering.

Dumbledore has certainly been busy, running around and collecting all the memories he can relating to young Tom Riddle! And he has learned much over the years, important information that he is able to relay to Harry, the Boy Who Lived, the boy who is destined to attempt to defeat the Dark Lord.

This, we think, leads us quite properly to the next chapter and the next subject: intelligence gathering.

41

INTELLIGENCE GATHERING

- **Observation: The Five Senses at Work**

- **Surveillance Techniques: Invisibility Cloaks and Other Methods**

- **Research: Yes, the Library Is Your First Stop**

- **Books, People, and Tall Tales**

- **Target Selection and Preliminary Research**

- **Maps and Physical Attributes**

- **Organizing a Security or Protective Detail**

- **Open-Source Information: History and Present Analysis**

- **Seeing History and the Future: The Sorting Hat, the Pensieve, and Oracles**

CHAPTER 41

OBSERVATION: THE FIVE SENSES AT WORK

The next area we'd like to delve into is *how* we observe and how to develop our *powers of observation*. We've already discussed previously the need to observe not only all around you (180 degrees, both *left* and *right*) but also *above* and *below* you, as if you are observing from inside a sphere.

What we are dealing with here is heightened awareness (or situational awareness), the ability to perceive what is going on around you. Have you ever been walking around a grocery store when someone literally bumped into you, or totally failed to realize you were trying to get by? These people are not focusing on what is going on around them!

A good spy must always be aware of his or her surroundings and what is going on in the area, and then be able to quickly differentiate that which is important from that which is unimportant. A good spy also has to be able to determine whether something that *looks* unimportant really is important. In addition, a spy needs to remember little details that may not seem important at the time but may later be quite important indeed!

For example, Harry notices—thanks in part to his *observation* of Viktor Krum's reaction to it—Mr. Lovegood's necklace, which bears the symbol of the Deathly Hallows (*DH* 139, 148). Hermione makes this important connection when she notices the same symbol on Ignotus Peverell's gravestone (*DH* 326–327). This symbol and its meaning turn out to be very significant to determining and understanding Mr. Lovegood's explanation of the Deathly Hallows as they wait for Luna to return (*DH* 409, 413).

Another example of noticing details occurs in book 5, when the children are cleaning the house and pick up, observe, and try to open a very old-looking locket—yes, we said *locket* (*OP* 116)! Harry and his friends later learn that this locket is a Horcrux—and by remembering what it looks like and that they have seen it at the former home of Regulus Black, our good friends are able to track it down to a certain toady woman who had confiscated it from one Mundungus Fletcher

(*DH* 222)!

Now let's talk about using all of our five senses. We receive information not only by looking (*sense of sight*), but also by use of the other four traditional senses. And perhaps we should add a sixth sense, the use of intelligence and analysis!

Your *sense of sight* can be enhanced by use of telescopes, binoculars, or even night-vision goggles. We've already mentioned that you should always consider using mirrors and windows in order to see behind you—without being seen looking backwards. Although Mad-Eye Moody can look right through his hat and the back of his head to see what's going on behind him, the rest of us need to use devices to observe without being seen to be observing!

When eavesdropping on somebody, you are using your *sense of hearing*. But ears are good for much more than overhearing conversations. Remembering and identifying auditory information such as tone of voice, others' conversations going on around you, and even background noise can enrich information gathered by your other senses. And if you can't use your other senses—you're on the phone, perhaps, or playing back a recording—your ears can pick up more than just words.

The *sense of touch* is also essential, particularly if you are attempting to gather information in a room where you have to keep the lights dim or even entirely off. Whether you're looking for tripwires or determining how recently a gun has been fired, or even cracking a safe, touch will be your guide.

Never forget your *sense of smell* and the fact that many people consistently use the same cologne or perfume. And as for using your *sense of taste*, we'll merely point out that cyanide tastes like almonds!

SURVEILLANCE TECHNIQUES: INVISIBILITY CLOAKS AND OTHER METHODS

Throughout the Harry Potter series we have instances of observation and surveillance. In book 1, for example, Harry and his friends carefully observe their nemesis Severus Snape, noting who he is talking to and what he is doing (*SS* 225–26). Special mention is always made of Snape's facial features and body language. The development of an understanding of body language is an important tool for all spies. And, thanks to his Christmas gift from an anonymous source, Harry can observe things without being seen! Harry of course puts the cloak to good use, such as checking out the restricted section of the Hogwarts library and sneaking around the halls of Hogwarts to visit the Mirror of Erised (*SS* 201, 205, 207, 210, 212).

Hermione also provides us, in book 3, with another excellent example of observation and the use of logic. When Harry and his friends board the Hogwarts Express and enter the only compartment with enough room for them, there is a man asleep in it. The children observe that he is wearing "an extremely shabby set of wizard's robes." When Ron asks, "Who is he?" Hermione has a ready answer: Professor R. J. Lupin, the new Defense Against the Dark Arts teacher (*PA* 74–75). How does Hermione know this? His name is stamped on his luggage (observation), and there is only one vacancy on the Hogwarts staff (logic). Go, Hermione!

Let's look at a few other surveillance techniques used in the beginning of book 5. Our story began with Harry underneath the Dursleys' window, trying to surreptitiously listen to the news (*OP* 4). We find out that Mundungus Fletcher had Harry under surveillance—but had left his post (*OP* 20). The Ministry of Magic, as we all know, is somehow alerted if an underaged wizard uses magic, as Harry quickly finds out after he uses magic to defend himself and his cousin Dudley from the Dementors (*OP* 27, 32–33). And Moody tells the advance guard not to talk about anything as they are rescuing Harry from Privet Drive because of his concern about being overheard, meaning that they may all be under surveillance (*OP* 50).

Another surveillance device used in book 5 is the Weasley twins' Extendable Ears, which are employed in an attempt to overhear a meeting of the Order of the Phoenix after the children arrive at number twelve, Grimmauld Place. Note that Mrs. Weasley applies a counter-jinx (countermeasure) to prevent the extendable ears from working (*OP* 67–69)!

Harry—through careful observation—finds out much about the inner workings of the Ministry of Magic when he goes there for his trial. Harry watches and listens as Mr. Weasley enters (and says out loud) the phone number to gain access to the Ministry of Magic: 6–2–4–4–2 (*OP* 125). You may want to remember that number in case you need to get in at some later time—like to rescue Sirius!

When attending his hearing at the Ministry of Magic, Harry observes the security protocols, the security guards, the process of getting clearance to get in, the methods of internal communication, and internal transportation (*OP* 128–32). He also learns the layout of the Ministry of Magic by simply listening to the kind voice in the elevator that tells him not only what floor he is on, but also what departments are on each floor (*OP* 130–32). Important information indeed!

It used to be that the old trick of turning up the radio to protect yourself from eavesdroppers worked fine, but technology has probably advanced to a point where loud background noise is no longer sufficient to defeat eavesdroppers.

SPYING IN A DENIED AREA AND MOSCOW RULES

Over the years the CIA developed certain techniques for collecting information in denied areas. These techniques were pulled together into a list of street tips that developed over time in Moscow Station and became known as the Moscow Rules. They were operating techniques learned the hard way by case officers working the Moscow streets in the face of nearly round-the-clock surveillance by local intelligence and law enforcement. Tony Mendez, a former senior CIA officer in technical operations support and the man who succeeded in getting the State Department employees out of Iran in 1979 (as depicted in the movie *Argo*) recorded the tips as follows:

- Assume nothing.

- Never go against your gut.

- Establish a distinctive and dynamic profile and pattern.

- Stay consistent over time.

- Be nonthreatening; keep them relaxed; mesmerize!

- Know the opposition and their terrain intimately.

- Make sure you can anticipate your destination.

- Don't harass the opposition.

- Keep your options open.

- Once is an accident; twice is a coincidence; three times is an enemy action.

- Pick the time and place for action.

- There is no limit to a human being's ability to rationalize the truth.

Peter included these tips in his book *Business Confidential,* pages 113–14.

~~~~~~

RESEARCH: YES, THE LIBRARY IS YOUR FIRST STOP

Books, People, and Tall Tales

Throughout the Harry Potter series, whenever the students try to figure out a particular issue, they almost invariably go to the library. Smart kids!

Well, at least Hermione always went to the library. Why? "Because that's what Hermione does," Ron says with a shrug. "When in doubt, go to the library" (*CS* 255). And what does she find there? The answer! It's a basilisk! Just look at the paper crumpled up in her hand, boys (*CS* 290)!

PART 2

The Hogwarts library is the source of a lot of great information throughout the series, just as your library and other resources can provide you not only great knowledge, but often great pleasure.

Most libraries are broken down into reference areas, nonfiction books, and fiction books, with audiovisual and other materials in their own areas. A reference librarian is a wonderful person; you will be absolutely amazed at how much information you can obtain by just asking a reference librarian to show you how to find what you're looking for.

But please, we beg of you, do not allow computers to be your only source. Libraries should be your first stop and computers used to *supplement* what you have found. The library is still your very best source for general knowledge and background information.

ONLINE LIBRARIES—WIKIPEDIA

Wikipedia is an "encyclopedia" created by the users of the Internet. There is no formal editor, so the information contained in Wikipedia may or *may not* be accurate. It is an *open source*, but the reliability of that source, as often as it is correct, is in question. Nonetheless, Wikipedia is usually a quick way to get basic, generally accurate information about a subject. However, don't bet your life savings on any of the factual details it contains!

Target Selection and Preliminary Research

When using the Internet, you will quickly find that you get too much information. This gets us to another research problem: narrowing your search down to what you actually want—and then narrowing it down to credible sources. Doing these two things is in our view the most difficult aspect of Internet research.

We suggest that, when researching particular topics, your best bet remains the traditional encyclopedias, many of which are available in the library and some of which are now online. Indeed,

CHAPTER 41

Encyclopedia Britannica has gone entirely online and no longer publishes a hardcover version. (We were exceedingly disappointed to hear this and will be rushing out to get the last print edition of *Encyclopedia Britannica* so that our children will have a real encyclopedia in which to look up things!)

STEPHEN COLBERT AND READING IN— GETTING BEYOND A GOOGLE SEARCH

When comedian Stephen Colbert came to the International Spy Museum to tape an interview with me for his TV show, *The Colbert Report*, he had already told viewers that the economic crisis had necessitated looking for a "fallback position." He thought that "spy" might be the career he would adopt, just in case he lost his job. Walking into my office, he knew more about me than some people who see me at work every day. He had *read in*. And his producers had collected no end of useful information about me and the Museum.

—Peter Earnest, *Business Confidential*, 115

Sometimes the research you need to do relates not to a particular person, but rather to a particular *place or location*. Knowing how to get to a place (or getting *away* from a place and safely home) can be absolutely essential for a spy!

GETTING TO A DENIED AREA IN SIBERIA— KNOWING THE TERRITORY

While writing my spy novel *Mission to Chara*, I wanted to make it as accurate as possible. I decided to go to Chara soon after the Soviet Union fell. Thus, toward the end of

PART 2

1993, I flew to Moscow and made arrangements to get to Chara, a small Siberian town approximately three hundred miles north of the northernmost portion of China.

Unfortunately, Chara was at that time in a denied area for foreign travelers. I was aware, from my preliminary research, that Chara was close to a military base that was of sufficient significance to be known in the military community and by B-52 pilots who were trained to fly into the Soviet Union. Not surprisingly, I was informed that any request for a visa to Chara would be denied. Nor did the Chara airport have civilian flights. However, the Baikal–Amur Mainline did pass through Chara.

Thus, I chose to arrive by train, requesting and receiving a visa for a popular Russian tourist city about three hundred miles west of Chara, and another authorized city about four hundred miles East of Chara, planning all along to simply get off the train when it stopped at Chara.

—Lynn Boughey

Location research relates to more than just maps, but we will deal with maps first. A spy must be able to read maps quickly and understand them entirely, even topographical maps. In the Harry Potter series, the most famous map is of course the Marauder's Map, which shows both Hogwarts and its grounds and which appears to be a normal piece of parchment until the reader promises that he or she is up to no good. At that promise, the map activates, showing the location and names of everyone on the grounds—in real time (*PA* 192–93). In other words, Harry and his friends can use the Marauder's Map to observe exactly where everybody is at in Hogwarts, even when they are on the move. This is a great map indeed, because if you know where everybody is, including your enemies, you will be able, perhaps, to make it to the Restricted Section while hiding under the Invisibility Cloak!

CHAPTER 41

And now a few words about Muggle maps: **LEARN TO USE MAPS!**

MAPS AND PHYSICAL ATTRIBUTES

Obviously the most important type of map is a local map of the town or location where you are doing your spying. Such maps can be found in phonebooks or other official publications.

You can also purchase detailed United States Geographical Survey maps in many places throughout the United States. They are fairly detailed and show roads, buildings, and even contours. Contours are lines that follow a specific elevation; in other words, by looking at the lines, you can see the specific geography of the area—where there are hills, lakes, roads, or tunnels, as well as boundaries or borders. These maps use symbols to delineate everything from campgrounds to major highways. With a good map and a working compass, you can get just about anywhere you need to go (though the Marauder's Map would also allow you to make sure the coast is clear!).

MUGGLE SCIFS—YOUR ONE-STOP INFORMATION FACILITY

In the military and spy worlds, all information relating to a particular location can be found in a sensitive compartmented information facility, or SCIF. Individuals with the proper clearance are able to get into the SCIF and determine everything about a particular location. Many of the locations are military targets, such as locations of military weapons or missile sites. When a spy returns from a foreign country and has taken photographs, those photographs are looked at very carefully and compared with the location information that already gathered for that location. This is to confirm the accuracy of the information presently held.

PART 2

The US Air Force—and special operations—use SCIFs to plan out a bombing attack and the entire flight path to and from it. In other words, the mission planners put all aspects of the mission onto a CD, including the topographical maps from point A (the location where the plane takes off), past every point on the way to the location—with a listing of refueling locations available in the air or upon landing at, say, the Azores (an archipelago off the coast of Portugal), Guam, Diego Garcia, or even England (usually Mildenhall)—all the way to point B, the destination.

~~~~~~

~~~~~~

MILITARY TARGET SELECTION AND ACCESS TO TOP-SECRET INFORMATION

All information relating to a bombing *target* can be obtained from the SCIF, including any anti-aircraft missiles or artillery in the target area, residential locations near the target, and other information that influences what type of bomb will be used. For example, if the target is an intelligence headquarters in Baghdad just before the beginning of the hostilities in the first Iraq War, then the military planners would need to know everything about the building, especially what it is made of, in order to determine whether the bomb dropped must pierce the roof and go through several floors before detonating, or go through a window or side wall and detonate immediately. Many modern bombs, particularly cruise missiles, have cameras that send pictures back to headquarters (numerous places, but essentially the conference area at the Pentagon directly outside the office of the J-3, the highest military officer in charge of operations).

Indeed, anyone who recalls the Iraq War will remember the numerous videos of cruise missiles entering the buildings and arriving on target, sometimes hitting the exact window or door assigned to the weapon. Obviously, such technology can work only with the guidance of sophisticated global positioning devices and the global positioning system (GPS).

~~~~~~~~~~~~~~~~~~~~~~~~~~~~~~~~~~~~~~

Notice that Harry, when trying to determine the details about the layout and location of the Department of Mysteries, uses information from his recurring dream (*OP* 771–78). Obviously, a map of the Department of Mysteries would have been very helpful! Which reminds us, do you remember when Harry and the others first arrived at headquarters and the members of the Order quickly Vanished a parchment showing what looked like plans for a building (*OP* 80)?

What do you think that document was?

ANALYSIS: *What was the map or building plan that was quickly put away when Harry and the other children entered the kitchen after the Order of the Phoenix's meeting?* We know that the Order is guarding *something:* their members have been assigned "guard duty" (*OP* 68). We also know that Mr. Weasley is attacked in a dark hallway and that Professor Dumbledore is able to communicate via a portrait of a former Headmaster the location where Mr. Weasley was injured (*OP* 469).

In any event, it seems clear to us that the document they were looking at and quickly putting away is the layout of the Ministry of Magic—and probably the floor hosting the Department of Mysteries!

FURTHER ANALYSIS: *Why would the Order of the Phoenix need a map of the Ministry of Magic when they had already been doing guard duty and know the location very well?* Two reasons come to mind.

First, if they are guarding something in secret, they need to be able to get in and out quickly and secretly—and to do so they would need the plans of the building to determine locations at which they could get in and out without being seen. They also would want to know where to place their guards so as to protect the asset without being discovered. These actions are *offensive,* in the sense of selecting the location to place a guard in order to best protect the asset. The second reason is *defensive* in nature: the Order needs to determine—since Voldemort is clearly attempting to get the prophecy—any weaknesses in the layout of the building or secret passageways that Voldemort or his minions could use to get to the asset they are guarding. Thus, this building plan helps them both to get into a location and to protect the location and prevent the other side from getting what it wants.

ORGANIZING A SECURITY OR PROTECTIVE DETAIL

Another use of maps is determining how to get from point A to point B with a high-value asset. If you are protecting an asset, such as Harry Potter, and taking him from number four, Privet Drive to, say, number twelve, Grimmauld Place (or some other location, such as back to Hogwarts), it is essential to know the route that you are taking and to identify any hazards you may encounter as you move your high-risk asset from one place to another.

ORGANIZING A SECURITY OR PROTECTIVE DETAIL

Back in the 1990s (before 9/11), I taught a university course on terrorism. One of my assignments required students to spend one day protecting the president of the university. The Department of Criminal Justice professors were assigned to be the "assassins" and were tasked with trying to "kill" the president by placing a sticky note anywhere on his body.

Before spending the day protecting the president, a team of students was assigned to interview the president and determine all aspects of his life for that particular day and all his usual routines—information vital for proper protection. The students found out what time he normally got up, what route he normally drove from his home to the university, where he normally parked, what door he used to enter the building where his office is, how he got to his office in that building, what time he normally arrived, what was scheduled for that particular day, what other locations he would be at during the day and what routes he would take to get there, what time he would be leaving that day, from what building he would be leaving and the route from there to his car, what route he would take home, and the time he anticipated arriving at home.

As you can imagine, the students who were part of the protection detail had to remember a substantial amount of information about the president's comings and goings for that day. One of the requests the intelligence officers made on that particular day was that the president of the university take a *different* route from home to school, as well as from school back to home, so there would be less chance that he would be "killed" by someone who was aware of his normal route or routine.

The students had a great time protecting the president, and the local TV station did a segment on the protection detail. The university president survived the day, although two professors did place a sticky note on the window of the president's office (which was on the second floor) by use of a ladder—and to this day they both still claim victory in "killing" the president of the university.

Another assignment in my terrorism class was to read Osama Bin Laden's Fatah of 1996. Again, this was about five years before the attacks on the World Trade Center and Pentagon. After 9/11/2001, many of my students contacted me—some of them already employed by various government agencies or police departments—and thanked me for educating them so many years ago about the Al Qaida threat, terrorism in general, and the intelligence necessary to thwart terrorist activities. It was indeed an interesting class!

One of the more enjoyable assignments for my students was training on a Stinger missile simulator. My students learned how easy it was to shoot down airplanes with a Stinger missile and what it felt like to hold and aim the launcher and "fire" the Missile, all through the simulator. One of the reasons for the Soviet Union's defeat in Afghanistan in the 1980s was that the United States was providing Stinger missiles to the Mujahideen, the Afghani Arab resistance fighters, some of whom later became the Taliban or joined Pashtun tribes (some of whom subsequently fought against the United States).

—Lynn Boughey

~~~~~~

OPEN·SOURCE INFORMATION: HISTORY AND PRESENT ANALYSIS

Open-source information is derived from publications that can be purchased or obtained by any member of the public, including newspapers, journal articles, and books, primarily nonfiction books about a particular country or person. Books about people or countries are especially beneficial sources of information about the culture or history of a particular country. Open-source information is valuable to us not only as an explanation of what is *presently* happening in a particular place, but also in allowing us to determine the *historical aspects* of whatever topic we are researching.

This is especially true now that we have the Internet and computer search techniques. For example, it is now possible to use the Internet to review content from a variety of newspapers over many years and search for a particular person, entity, or even location—finding out everything about that subject quickly while covering years at a time. It is also possible to observe the amount of social networking traffic to determine if "something is up"—such as a call to the streets by protesters.

Open-source analysis can also be used to determine the mood of a country or an area within countries. Open-source articles and information were essential following the 2011 revolt in the Arab countries that resulted in the resignations or departures of numerous heads of state.

Films can be useful, too: from an historical aspect, there is much to be learned about Arab culture by watching Peter O'Toole's unbelievable performance in *Lawrence of Arabia* (Columbia Pictures, 1962), or Ben Kingsley's amazing performance in *Gandhi* (Goldquest, 1982). Both movies should be required viewing for anyone who wants to become a spy because it is essential, especially after the 1900s, to have some basic knowledge about the cultures of lands that were once colonized by other cultures. A good operative understands the reasons former colonies dislike the cultures that used to rule them, the nationalistic pride of such countries based on their history and culture, and their national or cultural desire for self-determination. Take the time to understand why some countries reject assistance from outsiders, even those who are attempting to help.

Many operatives receive special language training. And obviously, knowing a second language is exceedingly helpful in performing one's mission as a spy!

PART 2

SEEING HISTORY AND THE FUTURE: THE SORTING HAT, THE PENSIEVE, AND ORACLES

As Shakespeare wrote in *The Tempest*, "What's past is prologue" *(*Act II, scene i, line 254). And, as William Faulkner wrote in *Requiem for a Nun*, "The past is never dead. It's not even the past!" (Act 1, scene 3). For us, as students of history and culture for many years, both statements are true. We can and must learn from the past, for the more we know about the past, the better we can *guess* about the future. But we are still merely guessing. Educated guesses, true, but still guesses—necessarily fraught with complexity, numerous possibilities, and the potential of misreading the tea leaves, if you will.

~~~~~~

GEORGE F. KENNAN AND THE DEVELOPMENT OF THE CONTAINMENT THEORY

George F. Kennan, a longtime US envoy to Russia, discerned the nature of the Russian people in part from his careful study of classic Russian literature. Kennan—who lived in Russia from 1933 to 1936, 1944 to 1945, and in 1953 for some months before being ejected—was said to speak Russian better than most Russians.

To the chagrin of many, Kennan gave a lecture at Yale in October 1946 and spent the majority of his time describing in detail one of Chekhov's short stories, "The New Villa," instead of talking about Soviet duplicity or his famous theory of containment. Chekhov's story and its description of the heroine—who wanted the peasants to build a school but is informed by the blacksmith that the peasants needed time to absorb the concept and indeed the need for such a thing—was to Kennan a perfect representation of *the nature of the Russian people* and the fact that, at some point, those people would reject Communism and eventually defeat it. By truly understanding the nature and culture of the

Russian people, Kennan proposed the *theory of containment*, by which the West was able to stall the Soviet Union's plans while waiting for the system to collapse on its own.

The insight that led Kennan to his famous theory is just this simple: if the nature of a people is to slowly and carefully consider matters and to generally reject authority, then one might carefully assume that, eventually, any authoritarian regime will be overthrown, slowly and carefully, and perhaps without violence. Kennan also fully understood the nature of Stalin and the draconian steps he would take to impose his will on the masses. Kennan understood Stalin's ability to influence the surrounding countries and the likelihood that the Soviet Union could manipulate (by force or otherwise) those countries into the sphere of its control and (if possible) domination.

In book 2 of the Potter series, history is very important: the students learn about the history of the Chamber of Secrets in Professor Binns's History of Magic class (*CS* 148–52), and in the Pensieve, Harry watches Tom Riddle framing Hagrid all those years ago (*CS* 242). In book 6, Dumbledore takes Harry on a journey through memory to discover the history of Voldemort. Dumbledore understands that to defeat this enemy, Harry must understand Voldemort fully. In the Pensieve, Harry observes many important moments of Tom Riddle's life:

- his family background (*HBP* 199–211)

- where his mother came from and how she tricked a Muggle into loving her (*HBP* 199–211)

- Riddle's grandfather Gaunt's ring (*HBP* 207)

- Riddle's realization that he is a wizard when Dumbledore tells him so at the orphanage (*HBP* 270)

- completing his knowledge of Horcruxes through Professor Slughorn (*HBP* 494–99)

- acquiring the Gaunt's ring (*HBP* 363–66)

- his early years working for Borgin and Burkes, which allowed him to gather two more objects from a lonely, elderly woman (*HBP* 433–38), each of which he would later use as a Horcrux (*HBP* 363–66)

All of this history becomes very relevant to Harry and his best friends in finding the Horcruxes and defeating Voldemort.

It has been reported that J. K. Rowling took years to outline all seven Harry Potter books, supposedly during the writing of her second and third book. When one looks at the complexity of the story, as well as the hints even in the first two books about what we later do not discover until the final book, one can be fairly certain that this thorough planning and outlining did indeed occur.

It is no wonder that the series is so professionally done, intricately tied together, and in many ways profound in both plot and structure.

To spend so much time planning and to figure out every plot and permutation—for J. K. Rowling understood that "the past is indeed prologue"—she understood not only the past, but the future of all her characters while writing and completing the early books.

~~~~~~~~~~~~~~~~~~~~

"THE PAST IS PROLOGUE"—ORIGINS AND IMPORTANCE

Where does "the past is prologue" come from?

From *The Tempest*, Act 2, Scene i, line 247 (1611), by **NONE OTHER THAN WILLIAM SHAKESPEARE!** We highly recommend that you get a copy and read about Prospero stranded on an island with his daughter, Miranda, by the cunning of Antonio, who kidnapped Prospero and his daughter Miranda, set them in a small boat at sea, a boat filled only with Prospero's books, and in Prospero's absence Antonio was able to steal Prospero's Dukedom. . . . And Prospero learns magic while stranded on the island, uses his magic to shipwreck a boat carrying Antonio and the King of Naples onto the island, and . . . is able to reap his revenge and set things right. Oh, and did we mention Miranda meets the King's son Prince Ferdinand and they fall in love?

~~~~~~

So, as demonstrated in the Harry Potter series, the past helps us, educates us, and to a slight degree directs us. But a review of the past alone is not sufficient for a master spy or a superb intelligence analyst. To succeed in either of these professions, you must develop a thorough understanding of people, cultures, history, human nature, and indeed yourself to be able to find the right direction and determine accurately and properly what course should be taken.

Without history, we are a map without a compass. Without an understanding of people and their motives, we are a ship without a rudder. And without a fondness for people, we are without the ability to connect with others or discern what makes them tick.

Spying is, above all things, a people business. We necessarily focus on scientific details, military capabilities, geographic attributes, and economic indicators—but cold numbers and statistical details can only go so far. The spy on the ground and the analyst at a desk must learn to see beyond facts and figures and apply that information to the tapestry of human life, human endeavors, human goals, and even human desires. It is *people* who make decisions and implement policy—*and individual people* who agree to spy for you and provide information—and perhaps intercede when necessary to save your life.

42

THE ART OF DECEPTION

- **Red Herrings, Lies, and Other Misdirection Techniques**
- **Disguises: Be Not What You Seem**

RED HERRINGS, LIES, AND OTHER MISDIRECTION TECHNIQUES

A good story—and a good spy—always uses misdirection. We will now discuss the use of misdirection—and the results of acting on incorrect analysis as shown in the Harry Potter stories. The climax of book 5, Harry's rescue mission at the Department of Mysteries, is motivated by Harry's vision of Sirius being tortured there by Lord Voldemort (*OP* 726–28). Another example of misinformation in the same book is Hermione's "disclosure" of the "secret weapon" hidden in the Forbidden Forest as a way to escape capture by Umbridge and the Inquisitorial Squad (*OP* 748–49).

There are numerous other occasions where our heroes must choose a course of conduct based primarily on logic or analysis, such as in book 7, when Harry has to choose between going after the three Deathly Hallows or the remaining Horcruxes (*DH* 484). If he attempts to do both, there will not be enough time for him to succeed in either. He therefore has to *choose* between one or the other: it is, in a sense, a choice between personal power (the three Deathly Hallows that grant ultimate power) and the greater good (defeating Voldemort by destroying all the Horcruxes).

You could argue that the quest for the Deathly Hallows would not necessarily have been an incorrect choice: had Harry succeeded in getting all three of the Deathly Hallows, perhaps he could have used them to defeat Voldemort. However, we personally disagree. Even if Harry were to unite the Deathly Hallows, he would *not* be able to kill Voldemort—or at least ALL of Voldemort—because Voldemort could not die if any of his Horcruxes were still in existence. We will give you two examples that support this view.

Remember what Slughorn said? "Then, even if one's body is attacked or destroyed, one cannot die, for part of the soul remains earthbound and undamaged" (*HBP* 497). And remember what Voldemort himself said about life before regaining his body? "I was ripped from my body, I was less than spirit, less than the meanest ghost . . . but still, I was alive" (*GF* 653).

The Horcruxes contain *pieces* of Voldemort's soul that keep him "alive" until they are all destroyed, making it possible for him to come back even *after* his corporeal body is killed. Thus, we think that Harry would *not* have succeeded in using the Deathly Hallows, and indeed, at one point—as Harry entered the forest to meet his death—he *did* have all three, as he had captured Draco's wand, which had been captured from Dumbledore.

Having to choose between two methods of doing something is a constant reality of life and a *frequent* reality in the spy world. Harry clearly choose correctly—and did so while at Shell Cottage, when he decided whom to speak with first: Griphook or Ollivander (*DH* 484).

Another use of a misdirection is the belief that Voldemort already has the Elder Wand. Voldemort *believes* that, by opening Dumbledore's casket and grabbing the wand, he has acquired the Death Stick or Elder Wand. There is a fair amount of uncertainty about this because Dumbledore's wand was captured by Draco when Draco disarmed the Headmaster on top of the Astronomy Tower (*HBP* 584)—and Draco's wand was subsequently captured and changed allegiances when Harry seized it at Malfoy Manor (*DH* 474).

The Elder Wand—which Voldemort believes he is wielding during his final duel with Harry—will not kill its master. If Voldemort really *did* have the Elder Wand, he would have defeated Harry. But Harry asserts that it is he who technically has the Elder Wand because Draco's wand changed allegiances to Harry. As Harry says to Voldemort, "Does the wand in your hand know its last master was Disarmed? Because if it does . . . I am the true master of the Elder Wand" (*DH* 743).

Another example of misdirection, though one that seems inadvertent, occurs in book 2, when Hagrid tells Harry and Ron to follow the spiders (*CS* 264). Harry and Ron follow them, all right—right into Aragog's den, where both of them are almost eaten alive by Aragog's children and grandchildren! Although Harry does learn some additional, new information from Aragog—such as the fact that Aragog was *not* the monster from the Chamber of Secrets and that it was not *Hagrid* who had previously opened it—the misadventure was indeed a misdirection (*CS* 272–81), though likely an accidental one.

By the way, did you know that J. K. Rowling also has a fear of spiders, just like Ron?

Another important misdirection occurs in book 3, where everyone—including Harry—believes that Sirius is the one who betrayed James and Lily Potter's location to Voldemort (*PA* 205–6). This misdirection was arranged by Peter Pettigrew, who killed numerous Muggles and then made it look like he had died as a victim of the attack, cutting off one of his fingers and leaving it at the scene as proof of his death. He then transformed himself into a rat and eventually became Scabbers, the Weasley family's pet (*PA* 367–69).

When Regulus Black got into the cave and stole the locket, replacing it with a fake locket and note to the Dark Lord telling him what he did, he managed a wonderful sleight of hand, as well as a superb betrayal of Voldemort (*DH* 196). Of course, the Dark Lord never got that note—instead, Dumbledore and Harry retrieve the locket that had been substituted by Regulus Black all those years ago (*HBP* 609).

Perhaps the most clear and enjoyable example of the use of misdirection in the Harry Potter series is when Ron becomes convinced—right before a Quidditch match—that Harry has provided him Felix Felicis, or "liquid luck," as potion-makers call it, in book 6. Using the potion would be a terrible violation of the rules of the game, but Harry hasn't actually given it to Ron—he just allowed his friend to think so! Ron does wonderfully well in the match nonetheless (*HBP* 293–99). Of course, J. K. Rowling is telling us here that confidence is more important than some secret elixir—and that Ron had it in him the whole time, but just didn't know it. He simply needed confidence to do well.

GETTING A TICKET TO SIBERIA BY ASSUMING SOMEONE ELSE'S IDENTITY

When I landed in Moscow in October 1993, intending to do research for my novel, *Mission to Chara*, the city was under martial law. A few days before, Russian President Boris Yeltsin had ordered tanks to fire on the upper floors of the Russian White House—the nation's legislative building—which was at that point controlled by opposing political and martial forces. The day before, around sixty people had been killed, including an American lawyer, in an assault on the Russian television broadcast center. (My friends thought I had been killed until they did the math and determined that, at the time of the assault, I was still in Amsterdam, waiting for my plane to Moscow.) As I entered Sheremetyevo Airport, young men in uniforms wielded automatic weapons, looking scared and a bit trigger-happy. The person with whom I was supposed to stay could not

make it, so another person picked me up—someone I
did not know but had to trust. He knew my name, spoke
English, and had said he was my other friend's replacement.
We exited the airport road to the sight of many trucks and
vehicles being stopped and searched, particularly anyone
who appeared to be from Chechnya.

A few days later, my translator and I flew to Omsk and
then Bratsk. We went to the Bratsk train station around six
in the morning to purchase tickets to Chara. Unfortunately,
the only person authorized to sell tickets to foreigners was
gone and would not be back for three days. By the time we
bought the ticket and actually got to Chara, we would have
had to immediately turn around and return to Bratsk to
catch our flight back to Moscow! We traveled several miles
farther to Bratsk and stayed at a hotel, eventually deciding
we would go back to the train station the next day and try
somehow to get on board.

The next morning we obtained a ride from a Russian taxi,
which is in reality a private person willing to pick you up
and take you somewhere, for a fee. My translator explained
our situation, and to my amazement the driver agreed to
come into the train station, purchase a ticket to Chara using
his passport, and allow me to use the ticket. (Passports are
needed in Russia to purchase any tickets for travel, and the
price of a ticket was five to ten times more expensive for a
foreigner.) The purchaser's name was written on the ticket
itself, as required. Thus, it was necessary for me to assume
the driver's identity for the thirty-six-hour train ride across
Siberia and the trip back to Bratsk. The driver retained
his passport, and so, for the next thirty minutes (before
the train arrived), I studied his passport and memorized
everything about the man.

We boarded the train and went to our assigned berthing
car, me speaking Russian as best I could. We had my

translator (a petite and very beautiful young woman) hold both tickets, and I carried the two suitcases, one in each hand. The attendant assigned to our car reviewed the tickets and took us to our sleeping berth, which we would share with another couple and their young child. Soon the train began to move, and a large, steely-eyed conductress in uniform entered our cabin and demanded passports and tickets. After reviewing the documentation from the other couple, the conductress looked at us and again demanded passports and tickets. Of course, the only passport I had was my US passport, and the name on the ticket most certainly did not match my name!

My translator handed the conductress our tickets. While reviewing the tickets the conductress again demanded passports. My translator looked at me seated by the window, nonverbally inquiring what to do. The conductress again asked for our passports, and I gave her a look of disdain and turned my head to look out the window, basically indicating I was above her mundane demands. The conductress handed the tickets back to my translator, swore at us as elitist Muscovites, and left.

Thirty-six hours later we arrived at Chara, then a small town of around five thousand people (and decreasing rapidly). We got off the train without permission to be there—not knowing where we would stay, not knowing a soul, and wondering how we would fare there for a week.

You see, research can be quite exciting!

—Lynn Boughey

DISGUISES: BE NOT WHAT YOU SEEM

In the Harry Potter series we see the use of many different

disguises. Indeed, in the very first book, before Professor Dumbledore shows up at the Dursleys' home, there is a cat sitting outside number four, Privet Drive. We find out quite quickly that the cat is Professor McGonagall, who has used Transfiguration to turn herself into a cat and observe the Dursleys (*SS* 2–9). Now that's one heck of a disguise!

There are other, less "transforming" disguises in the series, such as Quirrell concealing the face of Voldemort on the back of his head with a turban (*SS* 293). And there are several people in disguise at the Hog's Head during the first DA meeting, including Mundungus Fletcher (370)!

We have already discussed the disguising powers of Polyjuice Potion, which allows you to assume the physical form of another person. It takes a long time to make Polyjuice, and as Hermione found out when she grabbed the wrong hair and turned into a human cat, it can have some unforeseen results (*CS* 225)!

However, disguises are not just making one human appear like another human. A disguise can also include taking steps to blend into your environment. People who are trained in special operations are able to use disguises made of tree branches and brush to blend in with the surrounding plant life so they cannot be seen. But some of the most common disguises involve nothing more than some careful clothing choices and attention to how you move and behave. Blending in can simply mean matching your appearance to what observers expect to see in a particular place, and doing it so well that they don't realize you aren't just part of the crowd. Whenever wizards go out into the Muggle world, they dress up as Muggles—or at least what they *think* Muggles look like—in order to blend in and not violate the Statute of Secrecy. At the end of book 5, you will note that Mad-Eye Moody is wearing a bowler hat in order to hide his magical eye—though he gladly shows the magical eye to the Dursleys to make a point (*OP* 869–70).

An early example of blending in appears in book 3, when Mr. Weasley and Harry (following Mr. Weasley's lead) demonstrate superb spy craft when preparing to cross the barrier at platform nine and three-quarters:

CHAPTER 42

Mr. Weasley strolled toward the barrier between platforms nine and ten, pushing Harry's trolley and apparently very interested in the InterCity 125 that had just arrived at platform nine. With a meaningful look at Harry, he leaned casually against the barrier. Harry imitated him. In a moment, they had fallen sideways through the solid metal onto platform nine and three-quarters and looked up to see the Hogwarts Express . . . (*PA* 71).

DISGUISE IN *MACBETH*— WHEN A FOREST CAN ACTUALLY MOVE

A good literary reference to the use of disguises occurs in Shakespeare's *Macbeth*, when the soldiers approaching Macbeth's castle hide their numbers by carrying tree branches. Earlier in the play, the three witches (the weird sisters!) gave Macbeth a prophecy that he could never be *vanquished* until the forest of Birnam Wood moved:

> Macbeth shall never vanquished be until
>
> Great Birnam Wood to high Dunsinane Hill
>
> Shall come against him.
>
> —Act IV, scene 1, lines 92–94

(Did you happen to notice that Harry's prophecy refers to someone being "vanquished" too?)

So, how is it that the forest moves and Macbeth is defeated? Because the enemy soldiers are disguised as trees and bushes as they come forth from Birnam Wood to attack Macbeth!

In the play, a messenger brings the news to Macbeth, saying,

> As I did stand my watch upon the hill,
>
> I looked toward Birnam and anon methought

PART 2

The wood began to move.

—Act V, scene 5, lines 31–33

The use of disguises is quite old indeed, going back long before Shakespeare's time. We probably have mentioned him before . . . perhaps as the greatest English writer of all time?!

~~~~~~~~~~~~~~~~~~~~~~~~~~~~~~

43

SPIES AT WORK

- **Case Study 1: Mrs. Figg at Privet Drive**

- **Case Study 2: Shacklebolt at the Ministry**

- **Case Study 3: Lucius Malfoy at the Ministry**

- **Case Study 4: Kreacher at Headquarters**

- **Case Study 5: Hagrid and the Giants**

Now let us discuss five case studies of spies at work.

CASE STUDY 1: MRS. FIGG AT PRIVET DRIVE

As we all know, Harry is attacked by Dementors at the beginning of book 5, *Harry Potter and the Order of the Phoenix* (16–18). After the attack, Arabella Doreen Figg shows herself—and tells Harry *not* to put away his wand ("idiot boy!") in case the Dementors return (*OP* 17–19, 143). Since only wizards and witches can see Dementors, it is clear that Mrs. Figg is *not* a Muggle.

Mrs. Figg was assigned to watch over Harry Potter all those many years ago, no doubt by Dumbledore himself. Mrs. Figg is a sleeper agent. She's also in *deep cover* because even the Ministry of Magic does not know she's there, apparently because she is a Squib (a witch with limited or no magical powers). As we discussed in chapter 8, the Ministry of Magic has reviewed the areas near Harry's home at the Dursleys and was unaware of any witches or wizards living near number four, Privet Drive (*OP* 143). Cornelius Fudge is not very happy to find out about this previously unknown, magic-aware neighbor of Harry's! Fudge suspects—*quite rightly*—that Dumbledore had a hand in it (143)!

Mrs. Figg has been near number four, Privet Drive, for a very long time. Indeed, we initially "meet" Mrs. Figg in the very first book, when we find out that she has broken her leg and therefore cannot babysit Harry on Dudley's birthday, resulting in Harry getting to go to the zoo with the Dursleys and Dudley's friend Piers (*SS* 22, 25, 31–32). Harry is unaware of Mrs. Figg's role as a deep-cover agent serving as his protective detail and surveillance agent when he is at the Dursleys' home each summer—that is, until she intercedes and tells him to keep his wand close at hand (19)!

We eventually discover that Mrs. Figg is no new-comer to the Order. Once Harry returns from the cemetery where Cedric has been killed, one of Dumbledore's first actions is to send Sirius to alert "the old crowd" of the return of Lord Voldemort, specifically including in this list Arabella Figg, along with Remis Lupin and Mundungus Fletcher (*GF* 713). Mrs. Figg, it turns out, is a long-standing member of the Order of the Phoenix!

CASE STUDY 2: SHACKLEBOLT AT THE MINISTRY

As we all know, Kingsley Shacklebolt is an Auror. Harry first meets Shacklebolt when he is being taken by members of the Order from number four, Privet Drive, to headquarters (*OP* 49). Throughout book 5, Shacklebolt is working on a Ministry of Magic assignment to *find Sirius Black* (95)—but, as we all know, Shacklebolt knows *exactly* where Sirius Black is at: number twelve, Grimmauld Place, aka headquarters! While pretending to look for Sirius, *Shacklebolt is spying on behalf of the Order of the Phoenix from inside the Ministry of Magic.*

Shacklebolt is a mole, and he must be very good at his job, because he is one of the Aurors who accompanies Cornelius Fudge when he attempts to arrest Dumbledore. During that scene, Shacklebolt appears to have Fudge's back at all times, and yet he also befuddles Marietta's mind so she doesn't disclose information about Dumbledore's Army, even to the point of having her lie for him (*OP* 615–16). And when Dumbledore knocks out everyone in the room but Harry and Professor McGonagall, Shacklebolt is also rendered unconscious in order to maintain his cover as Dumbledore's opponent (621).

We find out at the beginning of book 6 that Shacklebolt has been assigned to protect the Prime Minister of the United Kingdom (*HBP* 17) because the Wizarding world no longer has control over the Dementors and Voldemort is at large, as are his numerous Death Eaters—all of whom are more than happy to kill, torture, or otherwise disrupt Muggles on a mere whim.

CASE STUDY 3: LUCIUS MALFOY AT THE MINISTRY

When we first enter the Ministry of Magic for Harry's trial, who happens to be there after the trial, talking to the Minister of Magic, but Lucius Malfoy! There are numerous references throughout book 5 to Lucius's constant presence at the Ministry of Magic (*OP* 154–57, 588, 610). Even Draco flaunts it: "I mean, she knows my father really well, he's always popping in and out of the Ministry" (*OP* 360–61).

We subsequently find out that Lucius is at the Ministry of Magic because he is assisting Voldemort in reaching the prophecy. He even places an Imperius Curse on Broderick Bode in order to try to have Bode retrieve the prophecy, which luckily does not work (*OP* 585).

Lucius Malfoy is a secret agent of Voldemort, as well as a Death

Eater. After the trial, when Harry asks Lucius why he is there, Lucius tells Harry, "I don't think private matters between myself and the Minister are any concern of yours, Potter" (*OP* 154). There are also references to Lucius Malfoy *buying* his way into the good graces of Cornelius Fudge and the Ministry of Magic, supposedly with gifts or other items of value to Cornelius Fudge or the Ministry itself (*OP* 155)— "Gold, I expect . . . Gets him in with the right people."

In our Muggle world, politicians can receive donations from individuals as well as money from lobbyists. (People who give large donations are called "fat cats.") This is, in reality, nothing more than sophisticated bribery. Yes, yes, we know, these politicians would *never* change their votes based on who gives them money! And they certainly would *never* take the time to talk to a lobbyist who has brought in several million dollars on their behalf over the chance to talk to you or me or one of the other lowly constituents! But perhaps we digress.

CASE STUDY 4: KREACHER AT HEADQUARTERS

Although Kreacher lives at number twelve, Grimmauld Place, he ends up becoming a spy in his own home because the Order of the Phoenix decides to make that place headquarters. Kreacher is introduced to Harry as "The house-elf who lives here . . . , [a] Nutter," according to Ron, against Hermione's objection (*OP* 76).

When the Order shows up, Kreacher's mutterings clearly indicate that he objects to their presence and activities (*OP* 107–8). Kreacher's loyalties lie with the biased and prejudiced Mrs. Black (109–10), whose portrait yells "Mudblood" and other vile comments whenever awakened (180). Kreacher even goes so far as to call Hermione a Mudblood, albeit only when mumbling under his breath (108, 118). Kreacher also attempts to hide the family heirlooms and anything relating to his mistress and his beloved Regulus (117). Kreacher realizes, however, that he will not be sent away because "Kreacher knows what they are up to" and that Sirius "is plotting against the Dark

Lord, yes, with these Mudbloods and traitors and scum" (118). Sirius is of the same opinion, telling the children, "We can't set him free, he knows too much about the Order" (110).

When Sirius tells Kreacher to get out right before Christmas, the house-elf goes to the only place that he would consider appropriate—that is, to another close member of the Black family, Narcissa Malfoy, Sirius's cousin (475). Although Kreacher is unable to tell them explicitly where headquarters is located or what's going on at number twelve, Grimmauld Place (thanks to the rules that bind house-elves), Dumbledore confirms much later that Kreacher was able to provide important information to Narcissa, including Harry's close connection with Sirius (831). Voldemort uses this inside information against Harry to create a vision of himself torturing Sirius at the Department of Mysteries (786).

In the final book, we note, Kreacher becomes friendly not only to Hermione, but eventually to Harry and Ron as well; indeed, Kreacher eventually becomes loyal to them, making them meals and generally assisting them on his own turf (which is also now Harry's property) (*DH* 225).

NOTE TO SELF: *Loyalties can and often do change based on kindness, persuasion through discussion, or positive actions that convince someone that his or her loyalties should change.*

CASE STUDY 5: HAGRID AND THE GIANTS

Hagrid is sent by Dumbledore to try to convince the giants to join Hogwarts in the fight against Voldemort (GF 719, *OP* 424-27). Hagrid and Madame Olympe Maxime make perfect sense as envoys, because they are both part giant. The giants will certainly be more likely to talk to them than to a human wizard. In chapter 20, we described their attempts to negotiate or recruit the giants—and their failure. The Death Eaters seem to have been more persuasive, no doubt because of their love of violence and their promises of great power to the Gurg.

Here, Hagrid has taken a very high-risk assignment. In a sense, he is more diplomat than spy, attempting to get one group of people to join in an endeavor that another group of people wants to undertake (*OP* 427–33). As with the giants, real-world decisions about which side to join often depend primarily on the deciding group's self-interest. No country wants to be dragged into a war just because they were asked to do so. There must be some appeal to self-interest or national interest before a country will agree to engage, even simply wanting to continue a friendship with the country requesting assistance. It is unfortunate that the giants seem to have chosen Voldemort's side because of a love of doing battle or perhaps the chance to have revenge on the Ministry of Magic. However, this is ironic because—as we all know—as soon as the battle is over and Voldemort is victorious, his likely first move will be to further subordinate or kill the giants, centaurs, and any other half-breeds.

NOTE TO SELF: *Choose your friends wisely—and analyze whether a friend might ultimately betray you.*

DETERMINING IF YOUR SOURCE IS LOYAL ONLY TO YOU—BUGGING A DESK

There are times in the intelligence world where you might suspect that your source—who claims he is providing only you the information—is actually providing the same information to your "competitor." I faced this very problem with one of the agents I had handled early in my career. One of the station's senior assets decided to expand his options and opportunities. He was known for producing voluminous reports. In the course of reviewing his reporting, I noticed similarities between the material he reported and what we were getting from another intelligence service. The similarity triggered the question:

Is he talking to them as well as us? I mounted an operation to find out how many services besides ours he might be collaborating with. All I needed to do was bug his office.

For years he had been inviting my wife and me to dinner. Typically, we tried not to mix business and pleasure, and so I had repeatedly declined. In the course of one of our routine conversations after my suspicions surfaced, I moved the discussion to a friendly tone and, once again, he issued the invitation. This time I accepted.

His residence was a kind of townhouse, with a drab exterior—identical to those around it, but opulent inside. This is typical of the region; people want to flaunt their wealth, but they do so in a way they can completely control. The living/dining area, to which he escorted my wife and me when we arrived, was upstairs, but I knew that his office was downstairs. We used to meet there, and at one meeting just before the dinner party, I'd ascertained that there was space between where the drawer of his desk closed and the end of the desk. When he left the room briefly, I had taken a quick look and figured that space would be a good spot to plant a microphone.

The mic I brought with me to dinner that night was strapped to my leg—a foot-long wood block with batteries and a transmitter wire. Fortunately our host had invited another couple so there was a lot of getting-to-know-you chat. I had forewarned my wife that, when I excused myself from the party to go to the bathroom, she had to keep the conversation going and our host distracted. Knowing there was a bathroom downstairs, I headed down there when I excused myself. I got under his desk, lay on my back, took out the silent drill I'd slipped under my suit, drilled some holes near the back of the drawer, and installed the bug. Sawdust rained down over my chest;

PART 2

I collected it carefully, put it in my pocket, and rejoined the party.

In the next few weeks we monitored his conversations, and sure enough, we found him collaborating with multiple other services. So I terminated him. (Keep in mind that this isn't a James Bond movie; by "terminate" I mean I fired him, not killed him.) I didn't tell him why, though. I just ended the relationship and moved on, recruiting a new agent with similar access to the information we desired.

—Peter Earnest, *Business Confidential*, 169–70

～～～～～～～～～～～～～～～～～～～～～～

44

SECURITY: KEEPING SECRETS SECRET AND PLACES SAFE

- Secret Keepers: Hagrid's Slips and Choosing Who to Tell

- Secure Areas: Headquarters, Hogwarts, and the Ministry

- Case Study 1: Security at the Ministry

- Case Study 2: Security at Order of the Phoenix Headquarters

- Case Study 3: Security at the Room of Requirement

- Case Study 4: Security in the Hall of the Prophecies

- Case Study 5: Security at Number Four, Privet Drive

- Case Study 6: Security at Hogwarts

SECRET KEEPERS: HAGRID'S SLIPS AND CHOOSING WHO TO TELL

In the Harry Potter series we have such a thing as a Secret Keeper: a person who learns a secret and is obligated to keep that secret closely and tell no one. Peter Pettigrew was a Secret Keeper for James and Lily Potter—to their great misfortune (*PA* 365). We hope that most other Secret Keepers do a better job!

As we have discussed previously, when Harry receives the location of number twelve, Grimmauld Place, it had been written out in longhand by Professor Dumbledore; when the piece of paper was shown to him, he became a person *authorized to receive that information by Professor* Dumbledore and was required to keep it secret. Since nobody ever got into headquarters, it's clear that everybody in the Order kept that secret. The only way the Death Eaters eventually found headquarters was when Harry, Ron, and Hermione Disapparated out of the Ministry and Yaxley (a Death Eater) grabbed Hermione's arm and Disapparated with them, thus accidently passing into the protected area of number twelve, Grimmauld Place, and breaking security in their headquarters (*DH* 270).

You will recall our previous discussions about Harry speaking out loud the address of headquarters when he used Umbridge's fire to talk to Sirius. This was, in our opinion, a very foolish thing to do (*OP* 668). Okay, fine, we'll be less politic: it was stupid! Had Umbridge or anyone else been in the room and able to overhear Harry, they would have had the address for headquarters and the location where Sirius was hiding! Amazingly, Harry actually speaks the address into the fire at Umbridge's office twice (*OP* 668, 740)! Why did he take this huge risk the first time? Not to find out important information relating to Voldemort or what he's doing, but instead to find out whether his dad really was a sophomoric, bullying prat!

We have already discussed how the members of the Order of the Phoenix had kept the location of headquarters secret for some time. Obviously, everybody in that group was worthy of Dumbledore's trust. We would now like to talk about another person who Dumbledore trusts completely, but maybe he shouldn't!

Yes, you guessed it! Hagrid!

Would you want Hagrid to be *your* Secret Keeper? Think of all the times that he has let information slip out. In the first few books we find out that Hagrid keeps a lot of secrets—though not very well! Hagrid tells Harry (and others) in the first book that his mission to Gringotts is "Hogwarts business" and "Very secret. Hogwarts business" (*SS* 63, 74). When Hagrid discusses his pet, Fluffy, he lets slip more information:

- "I lent him to Dumbledore to guard the—" (*SS* 192).

- "That's top secret, that is" (*SS* 192).

- "You forget that dog, an' you forget what it's guardin', that's between Professor Dumbledore an' Nicolas Flamel—" (*SS* 193).

Finally, Hagrid learns just to keep his mouth shut in book 1: "I'm not sayin' nothin'" (*SS* 197). But he had already told a stranger at the pub the essential fact that Fluffy is easy to handle because if you play music, he simply falls asleep (*SS* 266)!

When Hagrid returns from his recruitment trip to the giants in book 5, it doesn't take long for him to tell Harry, Hermione, and Ron exactly where he had been and what he had been doing on his "top-secret" mission (*OP* 423–33)! In other words, Hagrid means well, but perhaps he isn't cut out for a role as Secret Keeper!

Stated another way, you must not only choose your friends wisely, but also choose who is worthy of keeping your secrets!

NOTE TO SELF: *Tell secrets only to somebody who you thoroughly trust!*

Of course, secrets often have a way of getting out, especially in confined environments, such as a school or a tight-knit organization. Often rumors serve as a great way to obtain information, as Dumbledore himself notes in the very first book: "What happened down in the dungeons between you and Professor Quirrell is a complete secret, so, naturally, the whole school knows" (*SS* 296).

The CIA has an acronym, a joke of sorts, about this type of intelligence: they refer to it as RUMINT—Rumor intelligence!

SECURE AREAS: HEADQUARTERS, HOGWARTS, AND THE MINISTRY

There are, throughout the Harry Potter series, certain secure areas. We will next discuss six of those secure areas.

CASE STUDY 1: SECURITY AT THE MINISTRY

As we know, you can't just walk into the Ministry! Visitors have to go through the phone booth, enter a code, and state their name and purpose; only after they are authorized does the phone booth descend into the Ministry Atrium (*OP* 125–26). The primary way of getting into the Ministry of Magic appears to be the Floo network, although when there are concerns about security, as in book 7, they monitor the Floo Network and allow only senior members of the Ministry to connect their homes to the building (*DH* 6, 46). However, the Ministry, in its infinite wisdom, incorporated an alternative method of getting in by, yes, flushing yourself down a toilet (*DH* 241)!

As you remember, once inside the Ministry, visitors are required to check in at the security station, where their wands are examined (and, amazingly, returned to them) and registered. All visitors are required to have an escort and given a nametag that clearly indicates that they are a *visitor*. The escort is responsible for that person and is required to stay with visitors while they are on the grounds of the Ministry of Magic (126).

As we find out when Harry, Hermione, and Ron attempt to escape from the Ministry in book 7 (while assisting in the escape of wizards and witches with "questionable" bloodlines), the Ministry of

Magic has ways of sealing itself so that no one can get out during a security breach (*DH* 266).

One would assume that the Ministry of Magic—like Hogwarts—would be watched by Aurors and protected by numerous charms and other means, such as Sneakoscopes—counterintelligence devices that alert you when someone is spying on you or otherwise acting duplicitously (*PA* 10; *GF* 342–43). Interestingly, whatever protections are present, in book 5 they did not stop the Death Eaters from entering the Department of Mysteries, or Voldemort from entering the Atrium with the purpose of killing Harry (*OP* 781, 812)!

CASE STUDY 2: SECURITY AT ORDER OF THE PHOENIX HEADQUARTERS

As discussed at the beginning of this chapter, number twelve, Grimmauld Place is kept secure by limiting the knowledge of the address to only those who have a need to know, that is, the members of the Order of the Phoenix. The address is shown to new inductees on a piece of paper—and then that paper is destroyed (*OP* 59).

The fact that the piece of paper is destroyed after being seen reminds us of the breach of security resulting from Neville Long-bottom's solution to forgetting the password to get into Gryffindor House. He wrote down the password, but then *lost* the paper, thus allowing Sirius Black to enter the Gryffindor common room (*PA* 268). However, once you enter the Order's headquarters, there is yet another security "device" that will alert everyone in the house to any intruders: the portrait of Sirius's mother, who yells and screams whenever she hears any noise (usually created by Tonks)! Thus, without wanting to do so, Mistress Black has become an additional safeguard and warning system in case of an intruder at headquarters (77)—assuming that the intruder is noisy enough (although you'd think that most intruders would want to sneak in *quietly*).

CASE STUDY 3: SECURITY AT THE ROOM OF REQUIREMENT

As we find out when the Room of Requirement is first mentioned to Harry, the room is created based on the needs of the person who is asking that the room come into existence (*OP* 388). Once that person enters the room, in theory the room is accessible only to that person and other people who are given permission to be there by the person activating the room. The persons using the Room of Requirement may also request security, which Harry and the members of Dumbledore's Army employ to keep their lessons secure from Professor Umbridge (*OP* 390).

Beyond the room's own capabilities, when the students *leave* the Room of Requirement, they do so in threes and fours so it's not obvious from whence they came (*OP* 396). The Room of Requirement continues to serve as a secure area in book 7, when Dumbledore's Army and others who are hiding out from the Carrows seek refuge there (*DH* 577). Note, however, that an added security precaution has been added: the students have caused the exit to appear somewhere different each time so it can't be found (*DH* 577–85)!

CASE STUDY 4: SECURITY IN THE HALL OF PROPHECIES

The Department of Mysteries is deep inside the bowels of the Ministry of Magic, so the security measures taken for the Ministry of Magic overall act as an outer layer of security on the Department of Mysteries. In addition, as Harry and his friends find out, there are numerous impediments preventing anyone from just waltzing into the Department of Mysteries and the Hall of Prophecies. Once the kids get into the Department of Mysteries, they initially find a room with approximately a dozen doors; after they enter, and whenever a door shuts, the room goes totally dark and then spins, making it difficult to figure out which door you want to enter and which door is the exit. The kids try several different doors before finally reaching the Hall of Prophecies (*OP* 771–77).

But as we know, the prophecies themselves have security. Bode found this out the hard way while under Lucius Malfoy's Imperius Curse: touching a prophecy that does not relate to you can result in serious magical maladies (*OP* 585, 588). Only the person to whom a prophecy applies is authorized to pick it up. Thus, the prophecy relating to Harry and Voldemort can be picked up *only* by Harry or the Dark Lord himself (786).

ANALYSIS: *Could Neville Longbottom pick up the prophecy?* As we know, the tag on the prophecy itself lists Lord Voldemort and "(?) Harry Potter."

In other words, at the time this particular prophecy was made, the person who labeled it had no way of knowing whether it applied to Harry Potter or some other lad who was born at the end of July to parents who had thrice defied the Dark Lord. And as Dumbledore himself tells Harry, the prophecy could apply *equally* to Neville Longbottom and Harry Potter—that is, until Voldemort left his mark on the boy selected by *him* to fulfill the prophecy (*OP* 842). It was only by Voldemort's own actions—his *choosing* and *attacking* Harry Potter, thus marking him "as his equal"—that the prophecy became applicable *presumably* to Harry (*OP* 842).

However, it seems to us that *since the prophecy related equally to Neville Longbottom when it was made*, there is at least a chance that Neville would be able to pick up the prophecy as well. To this point, notice that in the room with the veil, when Harry has to throw the prophecy to somebody else, *he throws it to Neville*—who, unfortunately, later loses it when it falls out of his pocket (804). But the point of the matter is this: Neville was able to touch it without going insane!

More likely, once the person to whom the prophecy applies picks it up, all the charms and protections are gone. Lucius Malfoy certainly seemed to think so: once Harry has taken the prophecy off the shelf, Lucius wastes no time in demanding that Harry hand it over (*OP* 780). In any event, we assert that at the time the prophecy was *made*, there were *three* people who could pick it up: Voldemort, Harry Potter, and Neville Longbottom. The prophecy applied to all three individuals at the time it was given, so we conclude that Neville Longbottom could have picked it up as well!

CASE STUDY 5: SECURITY AT NUMBER FOUR, PRIVET DRIVE

While Harry is at number four, Privet Drive, he is protected by the powerful charm that his mother created when she gave her life to save her son (*OP* 836). This charm is renewed every summer when Harry returns to his Aunt Petunia and the Dursleys' home to live there and call it home. This protection prevents Lord Voldemort, his Death Eaters, and even Dementors from attacking Harry (or his relatives) at number four, Privet Drive (*OP* 836).

We wonder whether this is sufficient security when you're dealing with somebody like Voldemort, but obviously it is—as shown by the simple fact that Harry is never attacked while at number four, Privet Drive. He is, however, attacked by the Dementors *after leaving home*, but again, this attack did not occur while Harry was in the safe house. In addition, further security is provided at number four, Privet Drive, by Mrs. Figg, who serves as a lookout and protector of Harry when the time comes (*OP* 19).

CASE STUDY 6: SECURITY AT HOGWARTS

Under normal circumstances (when Dementors are not being used to protect the school), security at Hogwarts is maintained by the use of passwords.

Harry is introduced to the use of passwords at Hogwarts after he has been Sorted and is on his way to his dormitory for the first time. Percy, as Prefect, shares the password to the portrait of the Fat Lady that serves as the entrance to the Gryffindor common room

(*SS* 129–30). Each house has its own password, which changes regularly—an excellent security precaution! There is also a password to get to the Headmaster's office and, we imagine, passwords and other protections to get into other areas of the school where unsupervised students could get into a lot of trouble.

When there is a real need for extra security at Hogwarts, the Ministry of Magic sends those lovely Dementors to guard "the entrances to the school grounds" (*PA* 66). As we all know, the Dementors are on our side and under the full control of the Ministry of Magic—right? So nothing to worry about there!

SECRET PASSAGEWAYS AT HOGWARTS

There are many secret passageways that can be used to enter and exit Hogwarts. The first passageway we learn about is the tunnel to the Chamber of Secrets, which is found in the second-floor girls' bathroom (*CS* 300–1). In book 3, the Weasley twins give Harry the Marauder's Map, which discloses seven secret tunnels within Hogwarts or leading off the grounds (*PA* 193, 198).

RESTRICTIONS ON CLASSIFIED INFORMATION: SECRECY IN THE MUGGLE WORLD

As we discussed earlier, information that is withheld in some manner from the public is given a security classification based on the importance of the information being withheld. The three basic classifications are *Confidential, Secret,* and *Top Secret.*

The more secret the information is, the higher the classification will be. When a security clearance is required for access to certain information, that information can be disclosed only to people with an equal or greater level of security clearance. In other words, if the information relating to a certain topic is classified *secret*, then only people who have been qualified for levels classified secret or higher may access that information. In addition, there should be a need-to-know requirement for access to any information—that is, the person requesting access should have a good reason to need that information.

Top Secret, obviously, covers things that are more secret then *Secret,* and often this information is further restricted to a specific group of people authorized to receive the information by categorizing it as *sensitive compartmented information.* SCI clearances almost always include a code word or two—often created by a computer—which puts all the information relating to that particular topic in one "compartment." Only people who are cleared *specifically* for that compartmented information can receive it. For example, any information relating to launching or engaging our nuclear assets would be sensitive compartmented information, along with nuclear codes, communication devices, and weapons design.

Much of the information that is designated as SCI is retrieved through a SCIF (sensitive compartmented information facility). These facilities can be used by the intelligence entity as a central source for planning missions, combining all information relating to specific locations, persons, or government entities, and anything else necessary to retrieve and analyze intelligence.

THE INTELLIGENCE WORLD'S MOST CLOSELY GUARDED SECRETS—METHODS AND SOURCES

The CIA and other intelligence organizations place information obtained from their numerous sources into a secure location to which only they have access, all the while protecting their *methods and sources*. In other words, the methods and sources of obtaining that information should not be able to be retrieved by those who use the information. Methods and sources need to be kept separate, and generally speaking, the person receiving the product (the information itself) is never told the source or method. The intelligence officers who are running the sources are aware of the methods used to obtain the information and keep that information in a separate area, providing only the information itself to those who need it, without divulging the sources or methods.

45

COUNTERINTELLIGENCE

- **The Importance of Knowing Thy Enemy**

- **Spies Not by Choice: Understanding the Imperious Curse and Its Use**

- **Finding Death Eaters: Looking for the Mark and Other Signs**

- **Counterintelligence Case Studies**

- **Case Study 1: Using the Marauder's Map**

- **Case Study 2: Hagrid in Search of the Giants**

- **Case Study 3: Finding the D.A. Traitor**

- **Case Study 4: "Friendly" Spies—Umbridge at Hogwarts**

Counterintelligence is the art of determining whether others are spying on you or your organization and preventing them from doing so. It is the art of developing your own Sneakoscope!

Part of the fun of counterintelligence is when people must attempt to figure out how to defeat their *own* system. During the Cold War era, at Nellis Air Force Base in Nevada, American pilots

442

were trained to fly just as the pilots in the Soviet Union flew and then, during so-called Red Flag exercises, young pilots learned aerial combat by flying dogfights with these highly trained "Soviet" pilots. In other words, to do counterespionage, you have to think like the enemy!

THE IMPORTANCE OF KNOWING THY ENEMY

Throughout the Harry Potter series there are references to the importance of knowing your enemy—Voldemort. Throughout book 6 in particular, Dumbledore educates Harry with a trip down memory lane—that is, the memories he has collected relating to Tom Riddle and his transformation into the Dark Lord (*HBP* 198, 260, 360, 430, 494). Dumbledore understands that if Harry is to defeat Voldemort, he must understand why the Dark Lord does what he does—and where his strengths and weaknesses lie. We understand that Voldemort's greatest weakness is his failure to understand the power of love and of compassion. Furthermore, despite his extolling the purity of the Wizarding world, Voldemort is a half-blood himself. Harry learns that fact and uses it to his advantage against Bellatrix Lestrange at the Department of Mysteries (*OP* 784).

It is also essential for Harry to know Voldemort's background so he can figure out what the Horcruxes are and where they might be located. Perhaps the ultimate irony is Harry's eventual realization—through Snape's final memory—that *Harry himself is a Horcrux* who must sacrifice himself and be killed by Voldemort before Voldemort can be killed (*DH* 658–90).

PART 2

ANCIENT CHINESE WARRIOR·PHILOSOPHER SUN TZU—
AND KNOWING THY ENEMY

One of the world's most revered philosophers is Sun-Tzu, an ancient Chinese general who wrote the seminal book *The Art of War*. In that masterpiece, he states the following:

> Hence the saying: If you know the enemy and know yourself, you need not fear the result of a hundred battles. If you know yourself but not the enemy, for every victory gained you will also suffer a defeat. If you know neither the enemy nor yourself, you will succumb in every battle.

—Sun-Tzu, *The Art of War*, section III, number 18

In addition to the memories and explanations shared by Professor Dumbledore, Harry gets to know his enemy by more personal means. On occasion, Harry is able to see what Voldemort sees and know what he is feeling. By the same token, once Voldemort realized the existence of that connection, he was in a position to share visions with Harry. Thus, Voldemort too was able to know his enemy, Harry Potter. Once Voldemort realized that Harry could see through his eyes, he combined that knowledge with the news of Harry's growing connection to Sirius and Harry's own tendency toward heroics. As we all know now, Voldemort turned that information into a highly effective counterintelligence campaign to get Harry to retrieve the prophecy (*OP* 782).

NOTE TO SELF: *In order to defeat the enemy, you need not only know the enemy, but also be able to think like the enemy!*

Let's examine some other examples of counterintelligence in the series.

CHAPTER 45

SPIES NOT BY CHOICE: UNDERSTANDING THE IMPERIUS CURSE AND ITS USE

Perhaps the most dangerous spy in the field of counterintelligence is the friend or colleague who has been *forced* by an enemy to spy on you. In the Harry Potter series, when someone is under the Imperius Curse, they have lost their free will and must do the bidding of the person who cast the curse. Bode's attempt to steal the prophecy for Voldemort while under Lucius Malfoy's Imperius Curse comes first to mind (*OP 585*).

In the Muggle world, the equivalent of an Imperius Curse can be far more mundane things, such as blackmail, fear, or protection of a third person. As we all know, many people have private information that they would prefer to keep private. If an enemy finds out that secret, then the person could be subjected to blackmail. The fear of being exposed is a powerful fear indeed. And, once someone is foolish enough to accede to the first blackmail request, then the acceptance of the initial blackmail *itself* can be used to blackmail the agent. The obvious recourse to being blackmailed is alerting the proper authorities; of course, that means the secret will come out—but better that than to become a traitor and be spying against your own friends simply to hide something in your private life.

NOTE TO SELF: *If you allow yourself to be blackmailed once, you have allowed yourself to be blackmailed forever!*

Fear is another way of forcing people to do things. They can fear for themselves, or for somebody they care about. For example, if somebody's child is kidnapped and held hostage, there is a very good chance that the parent will be willing to do anything to get that child back. Luckily, this doesn't happen very often, but criminals trying to gain access to a bank vault or other such location have been known to use fear in this way.

There are also more subtle ways to force people to spy. For example, if somebody has been allowed into Country A on a visa, it would be possible for Country A—which has allowed that person in—to withdraw that visa unless the person provides information about or does certain things against their homeland, Country B. Some individuals know that if they're sent back to their own country, their enemies will kill them. In such situations, an immigration officer could nonchalantly mention that the person's visa would be renewed, continued, or not withdrawn if the individual would simply do a couple of minor things that need to be done—or provide certain information that the government wants.

FINDING DEATH EATERS: LOOKING FOR THE DARK MARK AND OTHER SIGNS

Death Eaters, as we all know, have the Dark Mark placed on their arm. It shows that they are loyal to Voldemort—and is also used to communicate with Voldemort. Wouldn't it be nice if our counterintelligence officers had the luxury of just looking for the Dark Lord's Mark on somebody's arm to determine if they are an enemy?

~~~~~~~~~~~~~~~~~~~~~~~~~~~~~~~~~~

SPIES SPYING ON THEMSELVES

In the Muggle world, it is very difficult to determine who is spying on you and to find those individuals. A great example is the case of Robert Hanssen. Hanssen worked at the FBI in the counterespionage section; in other words, he was assigned to look for penetrators—of which he was one!

If someone is suspected of spying within an entity, then the entity itself has access—as the employer—to all computer records and other information held by that person. It is also possible to obtain a search warrant (when there is *probable cause*) and search the person's home or other personal property, or to obtain a *covert* search warrant, which allows the government to enter the location without the person's knowledge, search for the items you're looking for, and leave without the person ever knowing!

Thanks to the use of computers, it is very easy today to organize information into certain cubbyholes and then keep track of everyone who has accessed those cubbyholes. By the same token, it's possible to put a bit of *false* information into a document provided to someone you suspect of spying, or for that matter, to provide many people with *different* bits of false information (such as the number of missiles that we suspect are presently operational in Iran) and wait to see whether that information is received by the enemy and, if so, *which* bits of misinformation they were given—which indicates which person provided the information. We may also need one of our own spies in place to gain access to the information received by the enemy in order to see what misinformation the enemy has received.

COUNTERINTELLIGENCE CASE STUDIES

- Case Study 1: Using the Marauder's Map

- Case Study 2: Hagrid in Search of the Giants

- Case Study 3: Finding the D.A. Traitor

- Case Study 4: "Friendly" Spies—Umbridge at Hogwarts

We will now look at four different case studies of finding traitors in the Harry Potter series. And later on, in chapter 53, we will discuss in full Snape's role as a double agent—and how Snape was able to convince Voldemort and his fellow Death Eaters who questioned his loyalty, that he was really on their side.

PART 2

CASE STUDY 1: USING THE MARAUDER'S MAP

The Marauder's Map is first introduced in Book 3, *Harry Potter and the Prisoner of Azkaban*—in fact, chapter 10 is actually entitled "The Marauder's Map" (*PA* 183). The map, described by Fred and George Weasley as the secret of their success, is the twins' early Christmas present to Harry (*PA* 191). Deciding that Harry's need was far greater than their own (*PA* 191), the twins give Harry the best counterespionage device described in the entire series: a map that tells you where everyone is located at Hogwarts, in real time!

After simply saying, "I solemnly swear that I am up to no good," users watch as the blank parchment "draws" the map of Hogwarts and indicates where everyone is located (*PA* 192–93). It even tells you what spell to use to get secret passageways to open (*PA* 195). A lovely, miraculous map indeed!

CASE STUDY 2: HAGRID IN SEARCH OF THE GIANTS

When Hagrid and Madam Maxime go in search of the giants in *Order of the Phoenix*, the two of them observe that they are being watched (*OP* 425). This observation is itself counterespionage. Hagrid goes on to tell our three friends that the Ministry is keeping Dumbledore, and "anyone they reckon's in league with him," under surveillance (*OP* 425). Hagrid knew that they might be followed and watches for pursuers: he perceives the tail, and they lose the tail. Imagine Hagrid and Madam Maxime losing a tail! But they did somehow—around Dijon, France, we are told (*OP* 425–26).

CASE STUDY 3: FINDING THE D.A. TRAITOR

Thanks to Hermione's wonderful jinx, when Marietta tells Umbridge about the D.A. meetings, pustules spelling out the word *SNEAK* appear on her face (*OP* 612). This is a very obvious way to determine who the traitor is—how could anyone doubt it? If only it was so easy in the Muggle world!

CASE STUDY 4: "FRIENDLY" SPIES—UMBRIDGE AT HOGWARTS

As soon as Umbridge gave her first speech (*OP* 212–14), it was clear that she was there to spy on Hogwarts: its professors and its students, particularly Harry Potter and Albus Dumbledore. Hermione—and all of the professors—astutely realizes Umbridge's intent from the meaning of her speech, which, though packed with seemingly meaningless platitudes, clearly indicates (*to those who are closely listening*) that the Ministry of Magic intends to interfere with Hogwarts. The level of Umbridge's spying and her ability to gather information increases with each Educational Decree—to the point where she becomes Hogwarts's High Inquisitor (the *first* High Inquisitor, we might add). Then—upon Dumbledore's departure—Umbridge becomes *Headmistress* of Hogwarts—even though, thanks to the gargoyles, she is not given access to the Headmaster's office (*OP* 307, 624). Everyone knows that Umbridge is a mole from the Ministry of Magic assigned to observe what is going on at Hogwarts and relay that information back to the Ministry of Magic and Cornelius Fudge, and that, in turn, instills fear of reprisal in many students who would otherwise stand up for Dumbledore—and themselves!

THE USE OF DIPLOMATIC IMMUNITY

Many US embassies overseas have military attachés who are the liaisons between our military and state department officials, as well as between our military and the military of the host country. Most foreign countries consider the military attachés to be "open" spies, in the sense that they are certain to absorb whatever information they can while in the foreign country and relay that information to the officials in their own country.

Certain individuals who work at overseas embassies have diplomatic immunity. Those individuals normally carry a black passport indicating this status. Diplomatic immunity means just that: the country they are visiting has no right to prosecute them for any reason, or arrest them, or in any way hinder that individual. If a person with diplomatic immunity is caught doing something they should not be doing, then the host country has the option of demanding that the wrongdoer leave the country—and that person is thereby expelled (designated as a *persona non grata*) and must leave. Diplomats with diplomatic immunity status try very hard to comply with the laws of the host country so that they can remain there on behalf of their own country.

~~~~~~~~~~~~~~~~~~~~~~~~~~~~~~~

NOTE TO SELF: *If you're in a foreign country and don't have diplomatic immunity, don't do anything stupid.*

46

COMMUNICATION AND CODES

- **Communication Methods: From Owls to Dreams**

- **Code and Code Breaking: Secure Communication in a World of Spies**

- **Languages: The Need to Be Able to Talk to Giants, Centaurs, Etc.**

As a spy, you *must* be able to communicate information to your handler or to the entity with which you are affiliated. Gathering information has little value if it is not received by those who need to know it! As such, in this section we will discuss three different aspects of communication in the Harry Potter series—most of which applies to the Muggle world as well!

COMMUNICATION METHODS: FROM OWLS TO DREAMS

The most basic form of communication—and the first one unique to the Wizarding world that we learn about—is the use of owls. As we all know, in book 1, Harry receives his letter (and then many more letters!) from Hogwarts via the owls, who are clearly very tenacious in accomplishing their mission (*SS* 34–42)! Owls bring letters from one person to another in the Wizarding world. Although these letters can be intercepted—and indeed, we find out about such attempts in book 5—for the most part this communication system works quite well.

It is also possible—as we find out when Harry writes to Sirius aka "Snuffles"—that it is possible to send secure communication via owl by using code words, or words and phrases that seem innocuous but that only the other person would understand. One humorous example is Harry's reference to Professor Umbridge as being almost as nice as Sirius's mum (*OP* 280)! There are also special types of letters; Howlers, for instance, are used to communicate great anger, like the one Mrs. Weasley sent to Ron after the boys used the Ford Anglia to get to Hogwarts when he and Harry were unable to enter platform nine and three-quarters (*CS* 87–88).

Another everyday method of communication used in Wizarding offices and homes is the Floo network. In addition to letting you travel from fireplace to fireplace, Floo powder lets you stick your head into, for example, Professor Umbridge's fireplace and look out at number twelve, Grimmauld Place, as Harry did twice (*OP* 668, 740)—not the most secure form of communication, as we've already discussed!

At the Ministry of Magic, interoffice communications proceed via bespelled paper airplanes. We imagine that other offices use such handy, though potentially insecure, means of communicating. As with the Owl Post, a clever spy could send paper-airplane messages that seem to say one thing, while really conveying something else to a person who knows the codes or can read between the lines, as Sirius could.

Hermione's special Galleons communicate the date and time of the next D.A. meeting after Harry inputs the information into a master coin. All the other coins change to show the updated information and then grow hot so that the recipient will know that a new message has just come in. It is interesting to note that Hermione got this idea from, of all things, the Dark Mark on the arms of the Death Eaters (*OP* 398)!

Another unusual communication method appears in book 7, when Shacklebolt sends his Patronus to Bill and Fleur's wedding to advise everyone there that "The Ministry has fallen. Scrimgeour is dead. They are coming" (*DH* 159).

Another interesting Wizarding communication method is the use of slivers of memories. Using the Pensieve, a third person can observe these memories, which convey huge amounts of information. We have already discussed the many things that Harry learns from viewing memories—which are not unlike archived film footage—including information about Karkaroff's trial (*GF* 584–591), Tom Riddle's life (*HBP* 198, 260, 360, 430, 494), and Snape's work as a double agent (*DH* 662–690).

Other communication devices in the Harry Potter series include Tom Riddle's diary, which as we know is a Horcrux. When you write a question into the diary's pages, Tom Riddle's "ghost" is able to respond back. More importantly, the diary is capable of acting as a Pensieve; it shows Harry the death of Moaning Myrtle and Tom Riddle framing Hagrid for unlocking the Chamber of Secrets (*CS* 240–47). (Though, in the case of the latter, Harry did not yet fully understand what he was seeing; Aragog explained it to Harry in his den [*CS* 277–78].)

Wizards and witches can also communicate via the *portraits* located in homes, businesses, public buildings, and offices. After Harry sees the attack on Mr. Weasley, Professor Dumbledore directs one of the portraits to go to the scene and make sure that Mr. Weasley is found—and found by the "right people" (*OP* 469). The portraits can also observe and share important information. Harry and his friends use the portrait of Sir Cadogan to find the Divinations classroom (*PA* 99–101), and after Sirius Black got into Harry's dorm room, it was Sir Cadogan who was able to identify the person he had let into Gryffindor tower—because he had the password—as Sirius Black (*PA* 266–68).

We've already discussed the use of the Pensieve, but perhaps we should also discuss Harry's dreams—and more specifically, Harry's visions. Harry does receive information through his dreams, but it's questionable whether the information is accurate. When Harry is actually seeing through Voldemort's eyes, as when he possessed the snake, Nagini (*OP* 532), and when torturing people for information (*OP* 584–86), Harry's visions were indeed a form of communication—albeit one in which Voldemort was an unwilling sender of that information. Once Voldemort turned that connection to his own advantage, of course, it remained an effective method of communicating *misinformation* instead.

There are also more mundane ways of communicating in the Wizarding world. For example, RAB—Regulus Arcturus Black— left a note for Voldemort inside the substitute locket that he placed inside the stone basin in the center of the lake inside the cave (*DH* 194). Although Voldemort never got the note (Harry did instead), it was certainly one way to communicate, even after Regulus was long dead (*HBP* 609)!

Wizards and witches also communicate through newspapers and books. Although not as fun as a Pensieve or a good Howler, these open methods of mass communication can convey substantial amounts of information (and misinformation—such as Rita Skeeter's book on Dumbledore). We will discuss the press in detail in chapter 49 and pages 557-66 in the Appendix.

THE ART OF "SUBTLE" COMMUNICATION— BEING TAKEN FOR A RIDE

After a drawn-out effort to cultivate an East European official, I finally got him to agree to meet me for dinner in a remote village in northern Greece. By sheer "coincidence," we would both be there at the same time on official business. As we left the restaurant, two of his colleagues, also by sheer "coincidence," showed up and offered us a ride back into town. Not wishing to let on that I was suspicious, I accepted the offer. As the car made a fast U-turn and sped into the mountains of northern Greece toward Bulgaria, I, not wholly naïve and a Georgetown graduate to boot, realized we were not going back into town. As I was unarmed—case officers usually did not carry weapons during the Cold War—I decided my only hope of not visiting Bulgaria (at least at that time, when it was beginning to get quite chilly there) lay in trying to force my way out of the car as it slowed for a mountain curve. Before I could carry out this brilliant and well-developed scheme, my hosts abruptly turned around and headed back into town. Nary a word was said, other than a pleasant "Good night," but the message was plain: We know what you're up to, so knock it off. No more coincidental dinners with our colleague in remote villages. Hey, I got the message, was grateful to actually get back into town, and decided that the young official and I would just never become friends.

—Peter Earnest

CODE AND CODE BREAKING: SECURE COMMUNICATION IN A WORLD OF SPIES

J. K. Rowling employs the use of codes several times in the Harry Potter series. The first one occurs in the very first book, *Harry Potter and the Sorcerer's Stone*, when Rowling writes out the strange language that is carved into the top of the Mirror of Erised. As discussed in earlier chapters, the inscription on the Mirror of Erised is as follows:

Erised stra ehru oyt ube cafru oyt on wohsi (*SS* 207).

This code is exceedingly simple—all you need to do is *reverse the letters*, and when you do so you get the following:
Ishow no tyo urfac ebu tyo urhe arts desire.

If you take away the spacing you get this:
Ishownotyourfacebutyourheartsdeisre.

And then if you put in new spacing, you get this:
I show not your face but your heart's desire.

Although Professor Dumbledore explains what the mirror does—the Mirror of Erised shows you "nothing more or less than the deepest, most desperate desires of our hearts" (*SS* 213)—Rowling never actually tells the reader how to break the code, nor does she provide a translation. Like every good spy master, she lets us figure it out on our own—much as Dumbledore let Harry figure out so many things on his own!

The next code appears in book 2, when Harry finally meets young Tom Riddle in the Chamber of Secrets and Riddle writes his name in the air as follows:

TOM MARVOLO RIDDLE

Tom Riddle's full name, it turns out, is an *anagram* for the following:
I am Lord Voldemort (*CS* 314)

Rearranging letters into a different order is a simple method of creating a code, though it helps to know the way in which the letters will be mixed up!

The third code used in the series is Harry's letter to Sirius in book 5—a letter he knows could possibly be intercepted. In preparing to write the letter, Harry asks himself an important question: "How was he supposed to tell Sirius everything that had happened over the past week and pose all the questions he was burning to ask without giving potential letter-thieves a lot of information he did not want them to have?" (280). This demonstrates the primary difficulty of sending a coded message when the two parties have not yet developed a code!

In his letter, Harry employs what is called, in the spy world, an open code:

> Dear Snuffles,
>
> Hope you're okay, the first week back here's been terrible, I'm really glad it's the weekend.
>
> We've got a new Defense Against the Dark Arts teacher, Professor Umbridge. She's nearly as nice as your mum. I'm writing because that thing I wrote to you about last summer happened again last night when I was doing a detention with Umbridge.
>
> We're all missing our biggest friend, we hope he'll be back soon.
>
> Please write back quickly.
>
> Best,
>
> Harry (280)

As discussed earlier, the letter conveys lots of useful information in a way that anyone intercepting the letter would not understand.

Harry opens by using Sirius's code name, "Snuffles." In the second paragraph, Harry says Umbridge is "nearly as nice as your mum." We all know how awful the portrait of Sirius's mother is! Then he writes, "that thing I wrote to you about last summer happened again." Only Sirius would know what "it" is, that being Harry's scar hurting. The bit about "our biggest friend" is obviously code for the missing Hagrid and a request for any information on when he will return.

Thus, it is possible to send a coded message without a code, employing instead "inside" information that only the recipient would have. But be careful that this inside information cannot be interpreted by any unwanted eyes—or perhaps any toads lying in the weeds!

LANGUAGES: THE NEED TO BE ABLE TO TALK TO GIANTS, CENTAURS, ETC.

We note with interest that in the Wizarding world it is apparently possible to speak numerous languages at the same time. We assume this based on the Quidditch World Cup announcer, who speaks in one language, and the one hundred thousand attendees from all over the world hear what is being said in their own languages (*GF* 96).

Wouldn't it be wonderful if we had such a device in the Muggle world? However, we do not, so learning languages is an absolute essential for every spy. At the very least, a spy must be able to quickly learn the basics of a language in order to function in a country where a different language is spoken.

Although the use of translators is always an option, it is important for a spy to be able to at least understand what is going on and to communicate certain essential requests or information. Of course, there is always an advantage to being fluent in a particular language when the people around you do not know it—such as the Bulgarian and Ludo Bagman at the Triwizard Tournament (*GF* 100, 114-15) There are many types of eavesdropping, and one of the most ironic is when the people around you assume, incorrectly, that you are unable to understand what they are saying!

Some people can pick up languages very quickly and easily and are able to speak many languages, such as Barty Croach, who speaks over one hundred languages (*GF* 89, 100). The ability to speak a language well, or to learn many languages, is indeed a true gift. If you happen to have that gift, please take the time to advance it and learn as many languages as you can!

SCIENCE AND TECHNOLOGY (AND WIZARDRY):

CURSES, CHARMS, JINXES, AND OTHER WIZARDING WEAPONS

One of the great features of the Harry Potter series is its take on magic. Magic is fun and entertaining, of course, but it also involves skill, particularly when one is performing a charm, a curse, or some defensive spell against a practitioner of the Dark Arts. But there is also *science* to be taken into account, particularly when one is dealing with the potions or clever inventions used throughout the books.

Certainly, the Invisibility Cloak is one of the greatest magical inventions, and the one that Harry has is one that really works, as described by Xenophilius Lovegood when Harry, Ron, and Hermione have dropped by to find out about the Deathly Hallows in book 7 (*DH* 410–11):

> Ah, but the Third Hallow is a true Cloak of Invisibility, Miss Granger! I mean to say, it is not a traveling

cloak imbued with a Disillusionment Charm, or carrying a Bedazzling Hex, or else woven from Demiguise hair, which will hide one initially but fade with the years until it turns opaque. We are talking about a cloak that really and truly renders the wearer completely invisible, and endures eternally, giving constant and impenetrable concealment, no matter what spells are cast at it. How many cloaks have you ever seen like that, Miss Granger?

(Well, one, actually.)
But hold on, can they be real? In the Muggle world?

INVISIBILITY CLOAK—TRUTH OR FICTION?

As we all know, Harry's Invisibility Cloak is a fiction created by J. K. Rowling. But guess what? This type of magic is coming to the Muggle world thanks to science and technology! A group of scientists at Duke University has produced a *working* "invisibility cloak" that deflects microwave beams around an object with little distortion, making the object "disappear."

If you are interested in reading the press releases from 2006 and November 2012 (when graduate student Nathan Landy improved the design to eliminate subtle reflections) you should go to http://www.pratt.duke.edu/news/first-demonstration-working-invisibility-cloak and http://today.duke.edu/2012/11/landycloak.

Fiction can indeed become reality, don't you think?

Let us not forget curses, charms, and jinxes. Going through the series, we located the following thirty-one basic spells and what they do:

Hover Charm (*Wingardium Leviosa*)	causes objects to fly or hover in the air	*SS* 171
Leg-Locker Curse (*Locomotor Mortis*)	sticks victim's legs together—although victim can still move	*SS* 222
Body-Bind Curse (*Petrificus Totalus*)	causes victim's body to become rigid and stiff; does not allow movement or speech	*SS* 273
Freezing Charm	causes objects to stay still	*CS* 103
Engorgement Charm (*Engorgio*)	causes objects to grow	*CS* 118
Disarming Charm (*Expelliarmus*)	causes opponent's wand to fly out of his or her hand	*CS* 190
Tickling Charm (*Rictusempra*)	causes opponent to feel a tickling sensation	*CS* 192
Boggart-repelling charm (*Riddikulus*)	repels boggarts	*PA* 134
Fidelius Charm	conceals a secret inside a single living soul known as the "Secret Keeper"—the information is henceforth impossible to learn unless divulged by the Secret Keeper	*PA* 205
Patronus Charm (*Expecto Patronum*)	creates a guardian that acts as a shield between oneself and a threat—a kind of positive force that can also deliver messages	*PA* 237 *DH* 159
Cheering Charm	makes the recipient happy or cheerful	*PA* 294

PART 2

Confundus Charm (*Confundo*)	makes the recipient feel confused or misinformed	*PA* 386
Summoning Charm (*Accio*)	makes things fly to the person producing the charm	*PA* 68
Severing Charm (*Diffindo*)	used to cut things	*PA* 411
Banishing Charm	makes things fly away from the person producing the charm	*PA* 479
Drought Charm	used to dry up puddles and lakes	*PA* 486
Bubble-Head Charm	forms a bubble around the caster's head, allowing the person to breathe normally when underwater	*PA* 506
Stunning Spell (*Stupefy*)	renders victim temporarily unconscious	*PA* 574
Impediment Jinx (*Impedimenta*)	slows down and obstructs attackers	*PA* 608
Reductor Curse (*Reducto*)	blasts apart solid objects	*PA* 608
Four-Point Spell (*Point me*)	makes one's wand point due north	*PA* 608
Shield Charm (*Protego*)	makes an invisible barrier between the person producing the charm and his or her surroundings to deflect minor curses	*PA* 608

Jelly-Legs Jinx	causes victim's legs to go wobbly and collapse	*PA* 608
Unbreakable Charm	keeps objects from breaking	*PA* 728
Memory Charm (*Obliviate*)	erases memories	*GF* 77
Imperius Curse (*Imperio*)	one of the Unforgiveable Curses; makes victim do the bidding of the person casting the curse	*GF* 212
Cruciatus Curse (*Crucio*)	one of the Unforgiveable Curses; causes extreme pain, used as a form of torture	*GF* 214
Killing Curse (*Avada Kedavra*)	one of the Unforgiveable Curses; kills its victims	*GF* 215
Trip Jinx	causes victim to trip	*OP* 609
Levitating Jinx (*Levicorpus*)	causes victim to be hoisted up in the air by his or her ankle	*HBP* 239
Cutting Curse (*Sectumsempra*)	causes victim to bleed excessively	*HBP* 522

Obviously some of the curses are quite dangerous, as shown in book 6, when Harry uses one of the Half Blood Prince's curses (*Sectumsempra*) against Draco Malfoy in the bathroom (*HBP* 522).

Other curses are useful but can be funny, such as the Trip Jinx Malfoy used to catch Harry when he was trying to escape from the Room of Requirement (*OP* 609), or the Body-Bind Curse Hermione used against Neville Longbottom when they were leaving in their attempt to get past Fluffy and go down the trapdoor (*SS* 273).

Some other curses can be used for pranks, including *Levicorpus*, which was used against Snape when he was a young boy at Hogwarts (*OP* 647). But they are also useful, as when, perhaps, you need to disarm a certain troll that is attacking your soon-to-be-good-friend Hermione (*SS* 176)!

Many different types of Wizarding weapons and tools are used throughout the series, and a spy could find a good use for most of them. The first such tool we see is Professor Dumbledore's Deluminator—used initially by Dumbledore himself in book 1—as it takes all the lights away from the streetlamps before Harry arrives for the first time at the Dursleys' (*SS* 9–14). There is the Sneakoscope, which will tell you if anyone is being two-faced or untrustworthy in your vicinity (*PA* 10). Dumbledore considers one of the most wondrous inventions to be the Weasleys' clock, which tells not the time but where everybody is and their situation, including whether they are in mortal danger (*GF* 151).

Expanding charms allow Hermione's purse to hold everything but the kitchen sink—though perhaps there is one of those in there as well (*DH* 162)! The same charm is also used on the Ford Anglia's trunk, which holds much more luggage than should be possible (*CS* 66).

Most of all, we have to give credit to the Weasley twins for their many wonderful inventions! We should take our hats off to them—or perhaps take our *heads* off for them (*OP* 540)! Their work with the fireworks (*OP* 632) and their class-skipping candies, one of which makes you nauseated and another makes you well (*OP* 104), are every child's dream. They also are able to make heads disappear and reappear (*OP* 540), and create a swamp in the corridor (*OP* 674). Their Extendable Ears (*OP* 68) and many other fine inventions can now be found at Weasleys' Wizard Wheezes at number ninety-three, Diagon Alley (*OP* 675).

SCIENCE, TECHNOLOGY, AND THE ABILITY TO BE A GOOD PLUMBER WHEN YOU NEED TO BE

After determining that a Soviet military intelligence officer would be away from his house for the weekend, I accompanied several tech officers TDY (temporary duty assignment) from headquarters on a forced-entry operation to implant listening devices there. After successfully completing the work in the living quarters on the main floor, we ventured down to the basement to complete the work. After a few minutes, one of the more astute team members pointed out that we were "taking water." Somehow we had broken a water pipe and sprung a leak. Unlike the snoopers at Watergate, we had to weigh in as real plumbers. Fortunately, we had time to spare, as it took the better part of the evening and into the morning hours to repair the damage. Our vacationing Soviet Intelligence Officer would never know that he had been the accidental beneficiary of some high-price plumbing assistance from his US counterparts.

—Peter Earnest

PETER'S DESIRE AT A YOUNG AGE TO PERFORM MAGIC

When I was growing up for many years I was very interested in magic. I was an amateur magician, and somebody told me when I was very young, you're going to go into, I don't know what word he used, it might have been "intelligence"—I didn't know what he was talking about—but in later years when I professionally was involved in deception and dealing in deception it dawned on me that I had in fact realized my young desire to be involved in the world of magic, but it was the world of deception.

—Alohomora Interview of Peter Earnest and Lynn Boughey at 58:35 to 59:17 aired 5-17-14. Listen to the full Alohomora Podcast at http://alohomora.mugglenet.com/ episode-84-ootp-7-the-names-potter-harry-potter/

48

INTELLIGENCE ANALYSIS AND
DIVINING SECRETS

- Historical Analysis—Prelude and Prologue

- Understanding Power—Who Has It and
  What They Can Do with It

- Possibilities, Risks, and Other Statistical Permutations

- Trust, Faith, and Other Gut Feelings

Throughout our rereading of *Harry Potter and the Order of the Phoenix*, we spent a fair amount of time applying critical thinking and discussing the analysis employed within the book itself. The ability to conduct analysis is *absolutely essential* for a spy. A spy must be able to analyze the situation, identify what is true, and determine the motives and character of the people involved. We have also described many times the importance of using solid facts and unembellished pure logic in performing analysis. A good analyst does his or her best to assume nothing, and most certainly refuses to involve his or her own (or anyone else's) prejudices or biases.

When performing analysis, you must do so in a neutral and

detached way, just as we expect judges to analyze cases based only on the evidence before them.

~~~~~~

THE MUGGLE INTELLIGENCE CYCLE

The *intelligence cycle* is a sophisticated and organized plan by which a country obtains and uses intelligence information. The gathering of specific intelligence generally serves some important purpose. We do not just gather every bit of information we can; instead, we organize ourselves so as to obtain important and essential information that can be used to determine policy.

Generally speaking, most intelligence entities employ the following intelligence cycle: Planning and Direction, Collection, Processing, Analysis, Production, and Dissemination. Also, there are six specific weaknesses or mistakes common to the use of intelligence: Mirror Imaging, Stereotyping, Blindness, Overload, Timeliness (actually, lack thereof), and Politicization.

The Appendix at pages 545-56 provides an overview of the intelligence cycle and common mistakes made in the use of intelligence.

~~~~~~

HISTORICAL ANALYSIS—PRELUDE AND PROLOGUE

The Harry Potter series tells us not only what happens to Harry and his friends from year one through what should have been year seven at Hogwarts, but also much about what occurred *before* Harry went to Hogwarts. The events of the past permeate the story as it progresses.

Perhaps the best example of how history shapes the series is what we learn about Tom Riddle and the history of Lord Voldemort,

PART 2

especially in the last two books, *Harry Potter and the Half-Blood Prince* and *Harry Potter and the Deathly Hallows.*

We are able to observe this history in many ways, from memories in the Pensieve to the reading of *Hogwarts: A History*—which, according to Hermione, Harry and Ron never seem to get to! Rowling also shares historical information through the story's narrative.

We know that the war that occurs in book 7 is actually the *second* war against Lord Voldemort—and we know much of the history of the first one.

Tom Riddle was a boy with bad if not evil tendencies; as a teenager he was manipulative and began gathering followers while still a student at Hogwarts (*HBP* 369). We see through the narrative the manner in which he recruited first his friends and then his servants— and how he was able to use people to get what he wanted (*HBP* 277). Tom Riddle also had no problem sacrificing others, as when he framed Hagrid for opening the Chamber of Secrets (*CS* 247).

As a young man, Riddle went on to work at Borgin and Burkes, a place where he could learn as much as he could about the Dark Arts, all the while manipulating and stealing items from his clients and contacts (*HBP* 438). Riddle then disappeared and returned as Lord Voldemort and began his rampage against Muggles and then the Wizarding world, his success almost certain until he attacked a certain toddler right after killing his mother (*SS* 12).

With this type of background, we should not be surprised about anything that Lord Voldemort does, for he has done much of it before! He uses Professor Quirrell, manipulates Peter Pettigrew, kills Cedric Diggory without a thought, kills Charity Burbage in front of his Death Eaters, and takes Lucius Malfoy's wand for himself (*SS* 293; *GF* 7–15, 638; *DH* 12, 8).

Thus, Voldemort's *background and history* provide a clear indication of what we can expect him to do. All of this information is provided to Harry as well, so that the boy who is destined to defeat the Dark Lord will know his enemy.

THE IMPORTANCE OF HISTORY ACCORDING TO MUGGLE PHILOSOPHERS

Why is history so important and illuminating? Famous Muggle scribes and philosophers of the ages have told us exactly why: those who do not understand history are condemned to repeat it. This aphorism has been told by many people in many ways:

> **Edmund Burke:** "Those who don't know history are destined to repeat it."
>
> **George Santayana**: "Those who cannot remember the past are condemned to repeat it."
>
> **Winston Churchill**: "Those that fail to learn from history are doomed to repeat it."
>
> **Niccolò Machiavelli**: "Whoever wishes to foresee the future must consult the past; for human events ever resemble those of preceding times."
>
> **G. W. F. Hegel**: "What experience and history teach is this—that people and governments never have learned anything from history, or acted on principles deduced from it."
>
> **George Bernard Shaw**: "We learn from history that we learn nothing from history."
>
> **William Faulkner:** "The past is never dead. It's not even past."

And, of course, **William Shakespeare** said, "the past is prologue" in *The Tempest*, Act 2, Scene i, line 247.

PART 2

UNDERSTANDING POWER—WHO HAS IT AND WHAT THEY CAN DO WITH IT

There are many types of power, as has been demonstrated throughout our review of *Harry Potter and the Order of the Phoenix*. There is the *power of magic* and a person's ability to use his or her wand. There are *powers of fortitude, loyalty, and perseverance*. But most of the time, when we talk about power we are talking about *political power*—the power assigned by a society to political entities or specific individuals. Those who hold these positions of power may wield their power wisely—or not. Cornelius Fudge is a perfect example of a person in power who shouldn't be. As Dumbledore says, "It is a curious thing, Harry, but perhaps those who are best suited to power are those who have never sought it. Those who, like you, have leadership thrust upon them and take up the mantle because they must, and find to their own surprise they wear it well" (*DH* 718).

There are those who rightly believe that the lower an official's rank, the higher the risk that person will misuse his or her power. In other words, petty officials tend to worry about petty things and act accordingly. In theory, everyone in a bureaucracy is answerable to someone. In reality, most people are allowed to do whatever it is they are doing; even when an error is discovered, superiors often either fail to recognize the error or fail to do anything about it and simply leave the person in place. Although there are a lot of good and well-meaning people in government organizations, the reality is that many organizations have ingrained views of their mission, role, and manner of dealing with their people—and a proclivity to leave things as they are.

NOTE TO SELF: *It is very difficult to change the mindset of a large group of people, even if you are the leader of that group!*

In understanding power, you must understand first and foremost how the individual who has power received it. If the person was elected, then he or she will likely be very concerned about public opinion. If the person was appointed, then he or she will be very concerned about what the person who appointed him or her thinks about his or her actions or conduct. Thus, knowing how the power was obtained by those in power gives you insight into ways of persuading that person to do what you want.

You must also analyze intent. An opponent may have the capability to do something, but will he or she really do it? Here are two real-world scenarios to shed light on the difficulties of determining capabilities and intent.

~~~~~~~~~~~~~~~~~~~~~~~~~~~~~~~~~~~~~~~

CAPABILITIES AND INTENT: THE CUBAN MISSILE CRISIS AND JOHN F. KENNEDY'S INSIDE INFORMATION

We handed President John F. Kennedy a slim blue folder. It contained the latest intelligence from our top source in Moscow, Soviet military intelligence Colonel Oleg Penkovsky, the weapons and military affairs expert who volunteered to provide his country's most carefully guarded secrets to the West. Passing the top-secret material to us covertly, using a **dead drop** under terrible pressure, he revealed the startling limitations of Soviet missile capabilities. Now the young president realized that the Soviets could not launch an effective attack on the United States, thus giving President Kennedy the upper hand in facing down Nikita Khrushchev during the Cuban Missile Crisis of 1962.

—Peter Earnest, *Business Confidential*, 7

~~~~~~~~~~~~~~~~~~~~~~~~~~~~~~~~~~~~~~~

CAPABILITIES AND INTENT—SADDAM HUSSEIN'S INVASION OF KUWAIT

Saddam Hussein amassed his troops at the gates of Kuwait, but the intelligence question remained: Would he invade? Regardless of having the tanks and people ready, and understanding what he had to gain or lose, the decision rested solely with Saddam Hussein, and he could do what he had done many times before—change his mind at the last minute. Even having his right-hand man in your pocket at the moment would not have made a difference if Saddam himself had not yet made his decision.

In short, even with the best information in the world, you may not know what the outcome will be. On the question of **weapons of mass destruction**, Saddam Hussein led his own generals and commanders to believe that he was pursuing the development of such weapons. He was deceiving his own people. So even if we had communications with sources close to him, we would have gotten a false reading.

—Peter Earnest, *Business Confidential*, 103

POSSIBILITIES, RISKS, AND OTHER STATISTICAL PERMUTATIONS

As we have discussed many times in our rereading of *Harry Potter and the Order of the Phoenix*, risk is a part of being a spy—and an analysis of risk must be made before you undertake any action.

NOTE TO SELF: *The more important the task, the greater the risks that may be justifiable in completing that task.*

CHAPTER 48

On several occasions in book 5, Harry thinks about whether he should take a particular risk or not. Some of this thought pattern and analysis is his own doing, and much of it occurs thanks to Hermione's repeated, concerned questions—such as the decision to sneak into Umbridge's office the first time and use her fireplace to talk to Sirius (*OP* 666).

Because there is nothing certain in the world, there is nothing certain with regard to risk. You will never know for sure if the risk is justified or, for that matter, how much risk really exists. You must make the best guess you can, analyze the situation, and make a decision. There is always a risk of being caught—and a risk of being wrong.

There is another type of risk: the risk of doing nothing!

NOTE TO SELF: *A decision to do nothing is still a decision.*

FURTHER NOTE TO SELF: *Indecision almost always leads to failure.*

INDECISION AND ALBERT CAMUS'S THE PLAGUE

Joseph Grand, a character in Albert Camus's *The Plague*, spends most of the novel attempting to write the first sentence of the greatest novel ever written. Grand continues to try to make that first sentence perfect—and it seems he will never succeed because he is too much a perfectionist. (Spoiler alert: The plague forces Grand to become a hard worker taking care of the people. He becomes the secretary of a group of workers and, by the end of the novel, has finally started to write *his* novel.)

PART 2

TRUST, FAITH, AND OTHER GUT FEELINGS

Throughout the Harry Potter series, and particularly in book 7, Harry trusts his gut feelings and is almost always correct. When it comes to analysis, we are obligated to analyze situations as intellectually and rationally as possible. But that is only one half of the equation. It is also important to step back and ask yourself whether the actions you plan on taking are fair, just, and appropriate—whether they "feel right." Odds are, when you first meet somebody you have a gut reaction about whether you like them, whether you think you would like them to be a friend, and generally what you think of that person. It is sometimes impossible to even explain gut feelings, but we all have them, and for the most part we should take them into account when making decisions, particularly when choosing friends or accomplices in a common endeavor.

Intelligence, done right, also requires imagination. Analysts have to learn to think outside the box—to consider all possibilities and at times play devil's advocate not only to the theories of others, but also to your own.

~~~~~~~~~~~~~~~~~~~~~~~~~~~~

COMPETING CIRCLES OF ANALYSIS AND THE FAILURE OF IMAGINATION REGARDING PEARL HARBOR

When faced with issues of huge national importance, there is a deliberate effort in the Intelligence Community to foster competing circles of analysis—an A Team versus B Team approach to analyzing the same information. In setting up such an approach, it is important to make sure that the composition of the teams reflect different points of view. There is always room for dissenting views and, in fact, they are encouraged. The aim is not to achieve homogeneity but, rather, to capture those dissenting views and offer them along with the conclusions of the majority, in much the same way as the Supreme Court documents how the Justices in the minority came to a different conclusion than their majority-voting colleagues.

Analysts serve a vital role in spotting the significance, or lack thereof, of the information from the field and mission requirements. When analysis is missing or weak at this juncture, disasters can occur.

In her book *Pearl Harbor: Warning and Decision* (1962), Roberta Wohlstetter discusses the plethora of information that indicated that Japan was a threat and was within striking distance of the United States. She asserts that, despite having good intelligence, the United States took no action to avert the attack because of a "failure of imagination." That is, no one in power believed that Japan would actually bomb US territory.

Ron Kessler, in his book *Inside the CIA* (1992), actually went so far as to create a fictional President's Daily Brief (PDB) that would have been prepared for the President (if there had been an intelligence agency at the time to do so) that would read like this:

For the past two weeks, Japan has been warning its diplomats that war may be imminent . . . there have been these other signs that Japan may be preparing to go to war:

- On Nov. 22, Foreign Minister Tog informed Ambassador Numura that negotiations between Japan and the United States must be settled by November 29 because after that "things are going automatically to happen."

- For the past two weeks, the Japanese have been padding their radio messages with garbled or old messages to make decoding more difficult.

- Three days ago, the Japanese Imperial Navy changed its ship call signs. This is an unprecedented change, since they had just been changed. Normally they switch every six months.

- Two days ago, the Japanese Foreign Ministry ordered its consulates in six cities—including Washington—to destroy all but the most important codes, ciphers, and classified material.

- Three days ago, the U. S. became unable to locate previously tracked Japanese submarines.

- Scattered, unconfirmed reports indicate navel air units in southern Japan have been practicing simulated torpedo attacks against ships there.

This wasn't the only evidence by a long shot if you combine with it the personal reports of soldiers like William Sanchez on Corregidor in the Philippines, who reported to his commander that he saw Japanese vessels moving toward Hawaii. The point is, you can have all the facts you need to establish the truth, but if you don't have a mechanism for processing them and relating them to one another, and for delivering the intelligence to the key decision maker, then the information is worthless.

—Peter Earnest, *Business Confidential*, 139, 139–40, 141, 107–8

〰〰〰〰〰〰〰〰〰〰〰〰

Also of great interest is the actual President's Daily Brief about Bin Laden just thirty-six days before 9/11:

〰〰〰〰〰〰〰〰〰〰〰〰

THE PRESIDENT'S DAILY BRIEF TO PRESIDENT GEORGE W. BUSH AUGUST 6, 2001

Bin Ladin Determined to Strike in US

Clandestine, foreign government, and media reports indicate Bin Ladin since 1997 has wanted to conduct terrorist attacks in the U.S. Bin Ladin implied in U.S. television interviews in 1997 and 1998 that his followers would follow the example of the World Trade Center bomber Ramzi Yousef and "bring the fighting to America."

After U.S. missile strikes on his base in Afghanistan in 1998, Bin Ladin told followers he wanted to retaliate in Washington, according to (phrase redacted) service.

An Egyptian Islamic Jihad (EIJ) operative told an (phrase redacted) service at the same time that Bin Ladin was planning to export the operative's access to the U.S. to mount a terrorist strike.

The millennium plotting in Canada in 1999 may have been part of Bin Ladin's first serious attempt to implement a terrorist strike in the U.S. Convicted plotter Ahmed Ressam has told the FBI that he conceived the idea to attack Los Angeles International Airport himself, but that Bin Ladin lieutenant Abu Zubaydah encouraged him and helped facilitate the operation. Ressam also said that in 1998 Abu Zubaydah was planning his own U.S. attack.

Ressam says Bin Ladin was aware of the Los Angeles operation.

Although Bin Ladin has not succeeded, his attacks against the U.S. Embassies in Kenya and Tanzania in 1998 demonstrate that he prepares operations years in advance and is not deterred by setbacks. Bin Ladin associates surveilled our Embassies in Nairobi and Dar es Salaam as early as 1993, and some members of the Nairobi cell planning the bombings were arrested and deported in 1997.

Al-Qu'ida members—including some who are U.S. citizens— have resided in or traveled to the U.S. for years, and the group apparently maintains a support structure that could aid attacks. Two Al-Qu'ida members found guilty in the conspiracy to bomb the Embassies in East Africa were

U.S. citizens, and a senior EIJ member lived in California in the mid-1990s.

A clandestine source said in 1998 that a Bin Ladin cell in New York was recruiting Muslim-American youth for attacks.

We have not been able to corroborate some of the more sensational threat reporting, such as that from a (phrase redacted) service in 1998 saying that Bin Ladin wanted to hijack a U.S. aircraft to gain release of "Blind Shaykh" 'Umar' Abd al-Rahman and other U.S.-held extremists.

Nevertheless, FBI information since that time indicates patterns of suspicious activity in this country consistent with preparations for hijackings or other types of attacks, including recent surveillance of federal buildings in New York.

The FBI is conducting approximately 70 full field investigations throughout the U.S. that it considers Bin Ladin-related. CIA and the FBI are investigating a call to our Embassy in the UAE in May saying that a group of Bin Ladin supporters was in the U.S. planning attacks with explosives.

For the President's Eyes Only

6 August 2001

Declassified and Approved for Release, 10 April 2004.

—Peter Earnest, *Business Confidential*, 111–13

49

THE PRESS—AND HOW TO USE IT

- The *Daily Prophet*: The Government and Disinformation
- *The Quibbler*: Getting the Word out Any Way You Can

THE *DAILY PROPHET*: THE GOVERNMENT AND DISINFORMATION

The *Daily Prophet*, in a way, is an additional character in the Harry Potter series. The newspaper provides the entire Wizarding world with information about what's going on (or sometimes what's *not* going on). The *Daily Prophet* is an essential provider of open-source information throughout the series, particularly to our primary characters, Harry, Hermione, and Ron.

PART 2

〜〜〜〜〜〜〜〜〜〜〜〜〜〜〜〜〜〜〜〜〜〜〜

THE PRESS AS A NEUTRAL AND INDEPENDENT SEEKER OF THE TRUTH

At least *in theory*, the press is supposed to be a *neutral* and occasionally aggressive *independent* entity that keeps the government in check. There is a very good reason that the First Amendment to the United States Bill of Rights includes protection of the press. An independent press that truly serves as a watchdog on the government is an essential aspect of the concept of ordered liberty and protection of rights.

The Appendix at pages 556-66 provides an overview of the history of the press, the rights associated with the press, and some basic rules on how to deal with the press.

〜〜〜〜〜〜〜〜〜〜〜〜〜〜〜〜〜〜〜〜〜〜〜

The *Daily Prophet* demonstrates quite well what can happen when the government has control of the primary method of mass communication. As clearly shown throughout book 5 *Order of the Phoenix*, the Ministry of Magic uses the *Daily Prophet* to print any information it deems appropriate, *regardless of whether it is true or false*. Furthermore, although the articles in the *Daily Prophet* attempt to provide at least a veneer of equal and fair attention to both sides, it is obvious to anyone reading book 5 that the *Daily Prophet* prints whatever the powers that be want to print (*OP* 73).

There is an oft-stated maxim that truth is the first casualty of war. Perhaps, in regard to the Ministry's use and misuse of the *Daily Prophet*, truth is here the first casualty of Fudge's belief that there *is no war*!

〜〜〜〜〜〜〜〜〜〜〜〜〜〜〜〜〜〜〜〜〜〜〜

TRUTH IS THE FIRST CASUALTY OF WAR

Where did the phrase "Truth is the first casualty of war" come from? Even *this truth* is somewhat complicated.

CHAPTER 49

Although usually attributed in the United States to a statement made in 1918 by isolationist US Senator Hiram Warren Johnson of California (who served from 1917 until 1945, the day the first atomic bomb was dropped), the now famous saying has its true origins in Britain. Philip Snowden, a British politician, recorded in his introduction to E. D. Morel's book *Truth and the War* (1916), "'Truth,' it has been said, 'is the first casualty of war.'"

This quotation is almost certainly derived from Samuel Johnson, who wrote around 160 years earlier this much lengthier statement: "Among the calamities of war may be jointly numbered the diminution of the love of truth, by the falsehoods which interest dictates and credulity encourages."—Samuel Johnson, *The Idler* No. 30 (No. 11, 1758)

~~~~~~~~~~~~~~~~~~~~

We will now review the *Daily Prophet*'s appearances in all seven books and some of the most important articles mentioned in the series.

BOOK 1: THE *DAILY PROPHET* AND THE SORCERER'S STONE

The Attempted Theft of Gringott's Vault No. 713

Thanks to the *Daily Prophet*, Harry discovers—and relays to Hermione and Ron—that there had been a robbery attempt on vault number 713 *after* Hagrid had withdrawn whatever he obtained on Dumbledore's behalf (*SS* 141). Hagrid had already told Harry that he was on a mission for Professor Dumbledore and that it was top secret. Hagrid is definitely being a secret agent for Professor Dumbledore, though we wonder how secret an agent he is when he discloses so much of what he is doing to Harry (*SS* 63)!

BOOK 2: THE *DAILY PROPHET* AND THE CHAMBER OF SECRETS

Gilderoy Lockhart and the Making of a Celebrity

As we find out in book 2, Gilderoy Lockhart is *quite* the celebrity—in part thanks to all of the wonderful press that he receives from the *Daily Prophet,* and from the magazine *Witch Weekly,* which voted his the Most Charming Smile five times in a row (*CS* 91)!

Interestingly enough, no one on the *Daily Prophet* staff thought to investigate Lockhart's feats, so avidly detailed in all of his many books. Note also that the professors at Hogwarts determine—quite quickly—that Professor Lockhart is a fraud. You'd think that any newspaper with even a concept of *investigative reporting* could have found this out just as easily! But then again, any reporter who looked into Lockhart's alleged accomplishments would probably find himself or herself at the wrong end of a well-aimed Memory Charm—so perhaps the *Daily Prophet* would be unable to find out the truth after all (*CS* 297)!

BOOK 3: THE *DAILY PROPHET* AND THE PRISONER OF AZKABAN

The Hunt for Sirius Black—Supposed Death Eater and Escape Artist

As in the matter of Gilderoy Lockhart, the *Daily Prophet* seems unable to properly investigate the story of Sirius Black. Why was there no thorough and substantial investigation of how Sirius was able to escape Azkaban? Wouldn't his escape be a good opportunity to review the facts surrounding the murder of thirteen Muggles and determine whether there was any real proof that Sirius Black had committed the murders of which he had been found guilty? Of course, none of this is done, and the *Daily Prophet* rests instead in providing a "social benefit" to the Wizarding world by extolling the dangers of one Sirius Black, killer of Muggles, follower of Voldemort, and master escape artist. We also observe in this book that the Ministry of Magic is more than happy to use the *Daily Prophet* as a propaganda tool and purveyor of disinformation about Sirius Black— quite often as a cover-up for its own inadequacies, mistakes, and plain stupidity (*PA* 37).

BOOK 4: THE *DAILY PROPHET* AND THE GOBLET OF FIRE

The Tri-Wizard Tournament—Speak Slowly into My Acid Pen

In book 4, we find out through Rita Skeeter what damage an unethical reporter can do. It is obvious that her main focus is gossip and certainly not the truth. Rita Skeeter repeatedly fails to accurately document what people say, twisting it instead to her own ends and adding adjectives and adverbs to describe her "personal" observations—or, more accurately, her personal *slant* on her observations (*GF* 147, 202–3, 314–15, 437–40, 611–13)!

We eventually find out how Rita Skeeter gets so much juicy information: she is "bugging" everyone's secure areas—*by being a bug* (*GF* 727)! Obviously, she obtains her information without the permission of the person she is "interviewing"—which is in itself quite unethical. Reporters are supposed to identify themselves and request an interview. Rita Skeeter is instead using what we would consider spy craft to eavesdrop on people and gather information. Although spies are able to do this, it is unethical for the press to use such means—as certain members of the press in London found out in 2011 when it was revealed that reporters were illegally intercepting and taping phone calls of famous people (including royalty) to get juicy stories.

PART 2

BOOK 5: THE *DAILY PROPHET* AND THE ORDER OF THE PHOENIX

The Ministry Becomes the Ministry of Lies—Its Slogan, "We Fudge the Truth"

In the book that we have already spent so much time discussing and dissecting, we find out that the *Daily Prophet* has spent the entire summer (following the murder of Cedric Diggory and Harry's escape from Voldemort) denouncing Harry's story and publishing articles denigrating and attacking Harry Potter (*OP* 73).

When the ten Death Eaters escape from Azkaban, the Ministry of Magic uses the *Daily Prophet* to present its conclusion—based solely on the fact that Black had previously escaped from Azkaban—that the Death Eaters were assisted in their escape by Sirius Black (*OP* 544–45). Dumbledore repeatedly tells Fudge and the others the truth, but they refuse to have any part of it. Only at the end, when Fudge sees Voldemort with his own eyes (and in the presence of other witnesses!) does the paper *finally* print the truth about Voldemort's return—as well as Harry Potter's redemption as the lone voice of truth in the wilderness of lies (*OP* 817).

Notice how the *Daily Prophet* is also used to extol Professor Umbridge's values as a Professor of Defense Against the Dark Arts and as Hogwarts's first High Inquisitor (*OP* 306–8). In the process of describing what a wonderful headmistress Dolores Umbridge is, the *Daily Prophet* obtains a single countervailing view from one Professor Marchbanks—and then immediately attacks her credibility via a separate article providing "a full account of Madam Marchbanks's alleged links to subversive goblin groups" (*OP* 308). Talk about argument ad hominem!

Near the end book 5, an alternative newspaper, *The Quibbler*, prints an exclusive interview with Harry conducted by none other than Rita Skeeter. This game-changing piece is eventually reprinted in its entirety by the *Daily Profit*—er, we mean *Prophet*—once the return of Voldemort is *finally* acknowledged.

CHAPTER 49

BOOK 6: THE *DAILY PROPHET* AND THE HALF-BLOOD PRINCE

The Return of Voldemort—The Truth (and Fear) Will Set You Free (to Sell More Papers!)

In the next book—following Voldemort's return—the *Daily Prophet* spends much of its time warning the Wizarding world about the return of Voldemort (*HBP* 39–41). Finally! The *Daily Prophet* also informs the public that Fudge has been sacked, offers a description of the events at the Department of Mysteries (but not details of the prophecy), and covers almost daily stories of disappearances, odd accidents, and deaths (*HBP* 60, 77–78, 105). As time goes on, the *Daily Prophet* informs the public about Dementor attacks and the arrest of Stan Shunpike (*HBP* 221).

The Wizarding newspaper also reports an argument between Dumbledore and the new Minister of Magic, Rufus Scrimgeour, which we find out later was the result of Scrimgeour's request to meet with Harry (*HBP* 61, 357). Dumbledore tells Harry, "The *Prophet* is bound to report the truth occasionally, if only by accident" (*HBP* 357). (This reminds us of a saying: Even a broken clock is right two times a day!)

Importantly, when Hermione wants to do research on the Half-Blood Prince, she goes through the old *Daily Prophets* and discovers an announcement of one Eileen Prince marrying a Tobias Snape (*HBP* 637), thus confirming that Severus Snape was the Prince all along.

By the way, did you know that there is an evening edition of the *Daily Prophet* called the *Evening Prophet*? We learn about the *Evening Prophet* when Professor Snape confronts Harry and Ron about being seen flying in Mr. Weasley's Ford Anglia (*CS* 79) and also reference to an article about Arthur Weasley's search of Malfoy Manor book 6 (*HBP* 234, 635).

BOOK 7: THE *DAILY PROPHET* AND THE DEATHLY HALLOWS

Going Underground—the Daily Prophet under Ministry (and Death Eater) control, Potterwatch Begins, and The Quibbler *Quibbles*

In the final book, the *Daily Prophet* serves many uses, depending on who is in control of the paper at the time. Professor Charity Burbage publishes a spirited defense of half-bloods, resulting in her capture, torture, and murder at Voldemort's hands in the Malfoys' home (*DH* 12). The paper also contains a positive obituary of Dumbledore written by a longtime friend (*DH* 15–20) and an interview with Rita Skeeter about her forthcoming *negative* book on Dumbledore (*DH* 22–28).

While Bill and Fleur are getting married, the Death Eaters take over the Ministry (*DH* 206). We learn from the *Daily Prophet* that Harry is now "sought for questioning" about Dumbledore's death (*DH* 207). The *Daily Prophet* announces the "Muggle-born Register" (*DH* 208) and that Professor Snape has been selected as Hogwarts's new Headmaster (*DH* 225). In addition, the *Daily Prophet* informs our three good friends, who are on the run, that Hermione is "on the list of Muggle-borns who didn't present themselves for interrogation" (*DH* 231).

Harry is once again personally attacked as "Undesirable Number One" (*DH* 252, 315, 525), complete with wanted posters bearing his picture. Once Voldemort is in control of the Ministry of Magic, nothing in the *Daily Prophet* can be considered credible. Once again, the alternative newspaper *The Quibbler* attempts to describe what is really going on (*DH* 299). But once Luna is taken by a group of Death Eaters, Mr. Lovegood is forced to attack Harry publicly in his paper (*DH* 419). So another means is adopted to get the truth out— and *Potterwatch*, a radio program, is born (*DH* 437).

A picture from the *Daily Prophet* of Harry, Ron, and Hermione escaping from Gringotts on the back of a dragon is later used by the Snatchers to determine that they have just captured Hermione and Harry (*DH* 451).

CHAPTER 49

THE QUIBBLER: GETTING THE WORD OUT ANY WAY YOU CAN

In book 5, Hermione has the wonderful idea of blackmailing or extorting Rita Skeeter to write an article telling the truth about what happened to Harry the previous year. Rita Skeeter states that the *Daily Prophet* would certainly not publish it—which is why Hermione brought Luna Lovegood to the meeting and arranged to have the entire interview published in *The Quibbler* (*OP* 567–68). The magazine does not initially have a respected reputation or huge following, but circulation increases substantially once Harry's interview is published (*OP* 583). And, as we have already noted, at the end of book 5, Mr. Lovegood sells reprint rights for the interview to the *Daily Prophet*—no doubt resulting in a very good financial return— proving, perhaps, that the *Prophet* knew it would never get its own interview after the way it had treated Harry (*OP* 848).

~~~~~~~~~~~~~~~~~~~~~~~~~~~

THE CIA COMES IN FROM THE COLD AND ENGAGES THE PRESS

Although I give great weight to success stories to show what the CIA has done well over the years, I also note some of the Agency's failures that gave rise to "lessons learned," which you may find useful. For the first three decades of its existence, the CIA did not have an executive whose exclusive job it was to deal with the media or handle public relations. The CIA made a major policy shift after issuing a denial of *New York Times* reporter Stephen Engelberg's September 1985 story about defector Vitaly Yurchenko's identifying a few CIA employees as Soviet agents. Engelberg was essentially correct, and the ineffective denial made it clear that the CIA needed a better program for communicating with journalists. Following the post-Engelberg fiasco, a fiasco caused by policies reflecting an adversarial relationship with the media, the Agency's new director, William Webster, departed radically from his predecessor. He brought in a public affairs officer who saw the media as allies in speaking truth to power—the "power" including the American people.

—Peter Earnest, *Business Confidential*, 12, 159

50

POLITICS AND OTHER NEFARIOUS THINGS

- **The Need to Understand Politics and the Political System**

- **Organizational Structure: Who Has the Power and Why?**

- **Truth Serum, Interrogation, and Torture**

Throughout the Harry Potter series characters deal with and analyze politics, politicians, political organizations, the passage of laws and decrees, and many political manipulations. In our experience, many hard-working, well-intentioned people serve as leaders or government employees. It's just that politics often gets in the way of progress. The trouble with politics is that it *matters*. Otherwise, it is a lively parlor game of rumormongering, snide remarks, nasty accusations, nefarious characters, and the occasional attempt by the government to do something to assist the people it supposedly serves.

The power of the state evolved from politics. People must be elected, organizations must be formed, governments must act, and bureaucracy exists. One must understand politics in order to know how to use it, as well as how to change it.

PART 2

THE NEED TO UNDERSTAND POLITICS AND THE POLITICAL SYSTEM

The importance of politics increases with each of the Harry Potter books. In book 1, politics comes into play merely as an existing framework. Harry discovers the various laws and statutes relating to the use of magic, such as the Statute of Secrecy, which keeps witches and wizards disclosing that they still exist and from performing magic in front of Muggles (*SS* 65), and the Decree on the Reasonable Restriction of Underage Sorcery, which keeps students from using magic outside of Hogwarts (*SS* 309; *CS* 7, 69, 81; *PA* 26). Of equal importance is the fact that Albus Dumbledore has been appointed Headmaster of Hogwarts by the powers that be (*SS* 51).

In book 2, we find out about the power of politics in the Wizarding world, specifically the control the Ministry of Magic exerts over Hogwarts through the various discussions about whether Hogwarts would be forced to close after the reopening of the Chamber of Secrets (*CS* 261).

In book 3, we find out about the Wizarding justice system and the use of Azkaban as its correctional facility. We also witness the Ministry's attempts to apprehend Sirius Black and its use of the Wizarding press to alert the public to danger and ask it for assistance in locating Black (*PA* 40). Harry also learns how to avoid and circumvent the public authorities when he and Hermione save Buckbeak and engineer Sirius's escape (*PA* 393).

In book 4, the political focus deals more with the Triwizard Tournament diplomacy and interactions between wizards from different nations than anything else (*GF* 62, 187).

In book 5, we watch as Harry is subjected to a trial within the Wizarding judicial system, see his persecution via the Ministry's improper use of the press, and observe Umbridge's politically motivated assignment to Hogwarts, the issuance of many educational decrees, and the eventual removal of Dumbledore as Headmaster (*OP* 138–51, 211, 307, 351–52, 416, 551, 581, 624).

In book 6, politics shape interactions between Harry and the new Minister of Magic, Rufus Scrimgeour. Scrimgeour wants Harry to "stand alongside the Ministry" or, as Harry sees it, become a political mascot (*HBP* 345–46). Let's just say that didn't go well.

In book 7, we are dealing with an entirely new set of politics created by Voldemort's assumption of control of the Ministry of Magic. All the rules have changed, and the primary focus of the Ministry of Magic is finding Harry Potter (*DH* 206–9).

ORGANIZATIONAL STRUCTURE: WHO HAS THE POWER AND WHY?

In the Wizarding world, the Ministry of Magic controls the creation and enforcement of Wizarding laws, with an extensive bureaucracy supporting decisions made by the Ministry. Fudge serves as the Minister of Magic throughout most of the series, but we never learn whether this is an appointed or elected position, or even whether the Ministry of Magic has a legislative body that passes laws or makes decisions. It is clear, however, that the Ministry of Magic has the power to issue certain decrees—such as Educational Decree Number 24 restricting organizations at Hogwarts (*OP* 351-52).

We readers are very familiar with the judicial branch of Wizarding government, the Wizengamot. Judicial systems exists to resolve conflicts within society, whether they concern enforcement of contracts or enforcement of criminal law. The difficulty with the judicial system in the series is that the Ministry of Magic can use it to silence individuals—and indeed to send offenders to Azkaban. Fear of being sent to Azkaban is itself a tool used by the Ministry to keep witches and wizards in line. The clear intent of Harry's trial was to silence him and show that the Ministry of Magic's assertion that Voldemort had not returned was correct.

We note that the Wizengamot process consists of three individuals who ask the questions (like the old French inquisitors) and that the jury consists of the entire body, about fifty witches and wizards (*OP* 138). It is clear that there are certain rules and regulations that apply to trials, as well as certain rights that must be provided to defendants, such as the right to have an attorney or council to assist them (in Harry's case, Professor Dumbledore), the right to call witnesses (such as Mrs. Figg), and the right to cross-examine any witnesses that may be called (*OP* 142–43).

The foundation of the Wizarding correctional system is Azkaban prison. The prison is run by the Dementors, which live off of negative human emotions such as fear or sadness (*PA* 187). At the beginning of the series the Dementors are under the authority and control of the Ministry of Magic (and thus follow Umbridge's order to attack Harry and Dudley). But by book 5, the Death Eaters have escaped and it seems likely that the Dementors are no longer under the Ministry's control (*OP* 545). We wonder, who guards the guards—and when the Dementors left Azkaban (assuming they did), where did they go?

The mere fact of Azkaban's existence is reason enough for witches and wizards to follow whatever orders or rules are issued by the Ministry of Magic.

TRUTH SERUM, INTERROGATION, AND TORTURE

Although in the Muggle world there is such a thing as truth serum, it is very rarely employed. Use of such a serum violates the subject's right to autonomy and right against self-incrimination. We wonder whether Professor Umbridge had the right to use Veritaserum on students, but since Snape provided her with it, we assume that there is no rule or law against its use on the students (*OP* 744).

By the same token, the Ministry of Magic and two other inquisitors are allowed to interrogate and question individuals at trials before the Wizengamot. During Harry's trial, Fudge conducts the initial interrogation and succeeds in obtaining from Harry numerous statements about performing magic outside of school while underage that would be considered admissions of guilt (*OP* 140). However, there are limits to interrogation in the Wizarding world, as was clearly shown when Professor Dumbledore stepped in to prevent Umbridge from "manhandling" Marietta to elicit information about meetings of Dumbledore's Army after such gatherings had been banned by educational decree (*OP* 616).

It is also clear throughout the series that the use of torture—specifically the Cruciatus Curse—is not allowed (*GF* 214). Everyone who finds out about the punishment Professor Umbridge assigns to Harry during detention—writing "I will not tell lies" with a quill that magically cuts it into his hand—considers it to be torture and makes clear that such is not condoned in the Wizarding world (*OP* 272).

(For further reference, the Appendix at pages 566-88 includes an overview of the Muggle political system and some of the major tenets of that system.)

51

DIPLOMACY—BUILDING FRIENDSHIPS THAT MATTER

Case Studies of Diplomacy in the Wizarding World

- **Case Study 1: The Wizarding Tournament**

- **Case Study 2: Giants, House-Elves, and Centaurs**

- **Case Study 3: Shacklebolt at Number Ten, Downing Street**

Diplomacy is the art of using intellect to advance the interests of a nation, create good relations among nations, prevent war, and if possible advance the overall progress of humanity.

Diplomacy is the most sophisticated and subtle art of all social constructs. You must understand what you want, what the other nation is willing to provide, and how to make it happen. In order to be successful at diplomacy, you must understand the desires of those who have sent you, the culture and needs of those whom you are dealing with, and a way to find compromise between both sets of peoples.

CHAPTER 51

CASE STUDIES OF DIPLOMACY IN THE WIZARDING WORLD

CASE STUDY 1: THE WIZARDING TOURNAMENT

Book 4 focuses on bringing three different schools—and three different cultures—together at Hogwarts for the Triwizard Tournament.

The book begins with a weakened Voldemort living in his father's family's house, now empty but cared for by the longtime gardener, Frank Bryce (*GF* 1–2, 7). Bryce sees a light in the house and investigates, overhearing a man talking to someone named Wormtail and a plan involving the Quidditch World Cup (*GF* 7). Going to the Riddle House was Bryce's last mistake, as Voldemort soon kills him (*GF* 15).

We learn that Britain hasn't hosted the World Cup in thirty years; it is—as Molly Weasley states in her letter to the Dursleys asking if Harry can attend with them—a once-in-a-lifetime opportunity (*GF* 30). Voldemort's plan is simple: although it is not yet time for Voldemort to show himself, it *is* time for the Death Eaters to reappear and sow fear among the masses.

As the children prepare to attend the Word Cup, the adults drop numerous hints about something that will be happening at Hogwarts this term (*GF* 62, 91–92). We eventually find out that Hogwarts will be hosting the Triwizard Tournament, an event that hasn't been held for more than a century (*GF* 186). One cannot help but see Dumbledore's fingerprints all over this decision; no doubt Dumbledore himself had suggested it and offered to host it at Hogwarts.

ANALYSIS: *Why would Dumbledore want to host the Triwizard Tournament?* Because Dumbledore realizes that Voldemort will soon return and it is time for all the Wizarding world to prepare. Dumbledore hopes that by connecting the Wizarding world through friendly competition, he will make it easier for everyone to come together later and fight Voldemort whenever and wherever he begins his renewed attempt to take over the world. That is, Dumbledore undoubtedly plans to use it as a means of uniting the Wizarding world against Voldemort. Dumbledore explains to the Hogwarts students the history of the Triwizard Tournament:

"The Triwizard Tournament was first established some seven hundred years ago as a friendly competition between the three largest European schools of wizardry: Hogwarts, Beauxbatons, and Durmstrang. A champion was selected to represent each school, and the three champions competed in three magical tasks. The schools took it in turns to host the tournament once every five years, and it was generally agreed to be a most excellent way of establishing ties between young witches and wizards of different nationalities—until, that is, the death toll mounted so high that the tournament was discontinued.

"There have been several attempts over the centuries to reinstate the tournament," Dumbledore continued, "none of which has been very successful. However, our own Departments of International Magical Cooperation and Magical Games and Sports have decided the time is ripe for another attempt. We have worked hard over the summer to ensure that this time, no champion will find himself or herself in mortal danger" (*GF* 187).

The other three schools arrive, and the Triwizard Tournament commences, igniting many friendships that result in further connections with foreign witches and wizards. Dumbledore's plan succeeds at least in part, as the friendships forged during the tournament do make a difference in the upcoming fight against Voldemort, including Fleur Delacour's marriage to Bill Weasley (*DH* 145) and Madam Maxime's agreement to assist Hagrid on Dumbledore's delegation to the giants (*OP* 424–34)!

CASE STUDY 2: GIANTS, HOUSE-ELVES, AND CENTAURS

At different times in the Harry Potter series we find out that giants, house-elves, and centaurs exist. Through diplomacy and concessions from the Wizarding world, each of these groups is recruited to join against Voldemort.

The Giants: At first we think that giants are the same size as Hagrid. Throughout the first book, Harry repeatedly refers to Hagrid as a giant (*SS* 46–49). But Ron and Harry find out in book 4, when they happen upon Hagrid and Madame Maxime talking, that Hagrid is really only a *half*-giant (*GF* 428).

Ron tells Harry that giants aren't very nice—in fact, they're actually vicious (*GF* 430). Although giants used to live in Britain, Ron tells Harry, loads of them were killed by Aurors, and the remaining population is thought to be abroad, hiding out in the mountains (*GF* 430).

Hermione, always the smartest witch of her age, knew all along that Hagrid couldn't be a pureblooded giant because pure giants are about twenty feet tall (*GF* 433). Rita Skeeter's scoop tells the Wizarding world not only that Hagrid is a half-giant, but also that the giants had joined Voldemort's ranks during his first reign of terror and committed mass Muggle killings (*GF* 439). Voldemort himself confirms at the cemetery his plan to recruit the giants now that he has returned to human form: "The Dementors will join us . . . they are our natural allies . . . we will recall the banished giants . . . I shall have all my devoted servants returned to me, and an army of creatures whom all fear. . . ." (*GF* 651).

Upon Harry's return (bearing the body of Cedric Diggory), he tells Dumbledore precisely what had happened at the cemetery. Dumbledore takes action immediately—basically ordering the Minister of Magic, Cornelius Fudge, to "send envoys to the giants" and "Extend them the hand of friendship, now, before it is too late"

(*GF* 708). But of course Fudge refuses to believe that Voldemort is back and does not take Dumbledore's advice (*GF* 710)—so it is left to Dumbledore to send Hagrid and Madame Maxime on a very dangerous diplomatic mission to the mountains of Europe where the giants dwell (*GF* 719, *OP* 424-27).

We will not reiterate the in-depth discussion of Hagrid and Madame Maxime's trip (discussed in detail in chapter 20). It is enough to say that this attempt to get the giants on Dumbledore's side fails and other than Gawp, the giants once again decide to assist Voldemort in the final battle (*DH* 626, 648).

The House-Elves: The house-elves—thanks at least in part to Kreacher—join the final battle on the side of Hogwarts:

> The house-elves of Hogwarts swarmed into the
> entrance hall, screaming and waving carving knives and
> cleavers, and at their head, the locket of Regulus Black
> bouncing on his chest, was Kreacher, his bullfrog's voice
> audible even above this din: "Fight! Fight! Fight for my
> Master, defender of house-elves! Fight the Dark Lord, in
> the name of brave Regulus! Fight!" (*DH* 734).

No doubt Harry's affection for Dobby and his acceptance by Kreacher did much to convince the other house-elves to join the fight.

The Centaurs: As we learned from Firenze (and through Bane's comments) in book 5, the centaurs are unwilling to take sides, claiming "Our ways are not yours, nor are our laws" (*OP* 698). In addition, the centaurs are no fans of the Ministry of Magic or the Wizarding world's laws, which treat them as half-breeds deemed to have only "near-human intelligence," as rather tactlessly noted by Umbridge in the forest (*OP* 754). But upon seeing Harry's seemingly lifeless body carried in Hagrid's arms, the centaurs are apparently shamed into joining the fight:

> "BANE!" Hagrid's unexpected bellow nearly forced
> Harry's eyes open. "Happy now, are yeh, that yeh didn'

fight, yeh cowardly bunch o' nags? Are yeh happy Harry Potter's—d-dead . . . ?" (*DH* 728).

We know not the discussion that ensued among the centaurs or whether or not they knew that Firenze lay injured in the great hall (*DH* 661), but shortly thereafter—when the battle begins anew—the centaurs Bane, Ronan, and Magorian join Harry and the others in the final fight against Voldemort (*DH* 734)!

CASE STUDY 3: SHACKLEBOLT AT NUMBER TEN, DOWNING STREET

Our final foray into the use of diplomacy relates to the Wizarding world's relations with Muggles. As we all know, the Wizarding world is kept secret from the Muggles by the Statute of Secrecy. In our view, as we will discuss below in the realm of ethics, this law is in part a means to protect Muggles from less than ethical witches and wizards.

But there are times when the Wizarding world needs to inform the Muggle world of magical happenings, especially when there is a danger to Muggles themselves. The return of Lord Voldemort—who is more than willing to attack Muggles and, indeed, torture and kill them—must certainly be conveyed to the Muggles' leader.

And this is exactly what occurs in the very first chapter of book 6, when Fudge visits the "Other" Prime Minister and informs him of Voldemort's return (*HBP* 4, 10–11). Communications between the Prime Ministers are handled via a speaking portrait, just like those in the Headmaster's office (*HBP* 3).

We also find out that the British Prime Minister has had many discussions over the years with the Ministry of Magic, none of them particularly pleasant, given the pattern of hearing only bad news from its representatives:

- Upon the Prime Minister's election, Fudge drops by to introduce himself and to inform the shocked man about the Wizarding world, telling him not to worry, "odds-on you'll never see me again" (*HBP* 6).

- The Prime Minister sees Fudge again when the Minister of Magic comes to warn him that Sirius Black has escaped from Azkaban and he should put out a warning (*HBP* 7).

- Fudge next drops by to tell the Prime Minister about a spot of bother at the Quidditch World Cup match that involved some Muggles, but he should not worry about it; Fudge also informs the Prime Minister that they will be bringing three dragons into the country for something called a Triwizard Tournament (*HBP* 9).

- Less than two years later, Fudge informs the Prime Minister of a mass breakout from the Wizarding prison, Azkaban, but no need to worry—they'll be rounded up in no time, just thought he ought to know (*HBP* 9)!

- Fudge then informs the Prime Minister that He-Who-Must-Not-Be-Named is back, that he has been joined by his followers, that they are openly wreaking havoc, and that the Wizarding world is at war. (*HBP* 10, 12)

- At the same time, Fudge tells the Prime Minister that he suspects giant involvement in what the Muggles think was a hurricane, notes the murders of Amelia Bones and Emmeline Vance by Voldemort or his followers, and states that the Dementors have deserted the prison and joined Voldemort and are now swarming all over the place, attacking people (*HBP* 13–14).

- Fudge next admits that he is no longer the Minster of Magic and that the new Minister, Rufus Scrimgeour, will arrive shortly to bring the Prime Minister up to date on recent events (*HBP* 15–16).

When the new Minister of Magic Rufus Scrimgeour arrives, he

informs the British Prime Minister that his new assistant, Kingsley Shacklebolt, is actually a highly trained Auror who has been assigned to him for his protection and that one of his junior ministers had been the subject of an Imperius Curse (*HBP* 16–18).

The meeting ends with the British Prime Minister stating that the Minister of Magic do something, stating, "you're *wizards*! You can do *magic*! Surely you can sort out—well—*anything*!" (*HBP* 18).

To which Rufus Scrimgeour responds, kindly, "The trouble is, the other side can do magic too, Prime Minister" (*HBP* 18).

For further reading, we offer in the Appendix at pages 568-76 an introduction and overview of Muggle diplomacy and some of the major aspects of that discipline.

52

ETHICS IN HARRY POTTER

- **Positive Acts Based on Positive Values: Work Ethic, Loyalty, Duty, Bravery, and the Power of Love**

- **Finding a Moral Imperative: Fairness, Truth, and the Proper Use of Power**

- **Being Judged by How We Treat Those without Power: Peer Pressure, Taunting, Muggle Protection, Racism, and Charity to All**

- **The Nature of Good Versus Evil: Choosing Proper Means to a Laudable End**

POSITIVE ACTS BASED ON POSITIVE VALUES: WORK ETHIC, LOYALTY, DUTY, BRAVERY, AND THE POWER OF LOVE

If Dante can use Lucifer and visions of Hell as a tool to describe the battle between good and evil, why can't J. K. Rowling use witches and wizards and magic to teach some of the greatest values and virtues of mankind? The Harry Potter series is above all things a wonderful tale that models good morals—individuals struggling to determine the truth, to do good and defeat evil, and nasty villains who are, eventually, defeated.

It is great adventure, great storytelling, and great fun! But you already knew that or you wouldn't be reading this book!

So, what are the examples of positive values we find in the Harry Potter series?

From the very beginning of the very first book, we have *empathy* for young Harry Potter, a boy taken in by the Dursleys, the only family he has left, who treat him cruelly and with indifference—not to mention as a punching bag for his cousin, Dudley.

HARRY POTTER'S CHILDHOOD AND LES MISÉRABLES

Harry was not the first literary orphan to be abused, neglected, and relegated to a miserable "room" under a stairway! In the French novel *Les Misérables*—perhaps the GREATEST novel ever written by a man named Victor Hugo—the orphan girl Cosette sleeps on an old mattress in the cubbyhole beneath a staircase. Her guardians, the Thénardiers, make the Dursleys look positively *nice:* they beat and starve Cosette until she is rescued by the book's hero, Jean Valjean.

We find Harry in a house without love and a child relegated to growing up under the stairs, just as Cosette is found in *Les Misérables*:

> [Jean Valjean] came to a sort of triangular nook built under the stairs, or, rather, formed by the staircase itself. This hole was nothing but the space beneath the stairs. There, among all sorts of old baskets and old rubbish, in the dust and among the cobwebs, there

503

was a bed; if a mattress so full of holes as to show the straw, and a covering so full of holes as to show the mattress, can be called a bed. There were no sheets. This was placed on the floor immediately on the tiles. In this bed, Cossette was sleeping.

—*Les Misérables* (1862), Part II, Book 3, Chapter 8, page 249 (Barnes & Noble Classic ed. 2003)

Harry living under the stairs, in the dust and among the cobwebs?

Now let's return to the description of Harry's living arrangements in Book 1, *Harry Potter and the Sorcerer's Stone?*

Harry got slowly out of bed and started looking for socks. He found a pair under his bed and, after pulling a spider off one of them, put them on. Harry was used to spiders, because the cupboard under the stairs was full of them, and that was where he slept (*SS* 19).

~~~~~~~~~~~~~~~~~~~~~~~~~~~~~~~~~~~~

When Harry is first introduced to the reader, he has just awakened from a dream about a flying motorcycle, a green light, and pain from his scar—we learn that he sometimes thinks of someone, perhaps a relative, coming to rescue him from this terrible existence (*SS* 19, 30). But Harry realizes that this is impossible: he had no other family but the Dursleys (*SS* 30).

But, of course, someone *does* come to rescue Harry from the Dursleys—at first in the form of many, many letters inviting him to attend Hogwarts School of Witchcraft and Wizardry. Then a more forceful rescuer shows up during a storm on an island, in the form of the giant-sized Hagrid, who retrieves him from the Dursleys and begins Harry's introduction to the Wizarding world.

As Harry attempts to find platform nine and three-quarters and then travels on the Hogwarts Express, he meets many of those who will ultimately become his new family, including Hermione Granger, Neville Longbottom, and his new best friend, Ronald Weasley, whose parents will welcome Harry with open arms (*SS* 92–93, 94–95, 98). Thus, the series extols from its first pages the virtue and value of *family*—a *strong* and *supportive* family, as unlike the Dursleys as possible. And who needs family more than Harry Potter, the boy who lived, thanks to his mother's sacrifice and love?

With Ron and Hermione, Harry learns the value of *friendship*. As we see quite early in book 1, Harry already knows how to differentiate between friends he should accept and bullies he should reject. You can learn a lot from a cousin who regularly taunts you and finds joy in beating you up!

Harry's ability to choose his friends wisely is demonstrated—significantly—with Draco Malfoy. Harry first meets Draco while having his robes fitted, though at that point he does not know who the other boy is:

> "I really don't think they should let the other sort in, do you? They're just not the same, they've never been brought up to know our ways. Some of them have never even heard of Hogwarts until they get the letter, imagine. I think they should keep it in the old wizarding families" (*SS* 78).

Malfoy continues to promote this sordid agenda of racism and elitism when he comes to meet the famous Harry Potter and tries to befriend him, saying "You'll soon find out some wizarding families are much better than others, Potter. You don't want to go making friends with the wrong sort. I can help you there" (*SS* 108). Shortly later, Draco states, "You hang around with riffraff like the Weasleys and that Hagrid, and it'll rub off on you" (*SS* 109).

As Hagrid explains, "There are some wizards—like Malfoy's family—who think they're better than everyone else because they're what people call pure-blood" (*CS* 115–16). But Harry soon gathers demonstrative proof that being "pure" is meaningless, considering the examples of Neville Longbottom—who is pure-blood but not so capable—and Hermione, whose parents are Muggles but who is the brightest witch in her class (*CS* 116). Moreover, as Hagrid informs Harry, such purity is no longer practical or possible due to the inter-marrying that has occurred in the last thousand or so years (*CS* 116).

Harry also demonstrates the virtue of *loyalty* early in the series. Having just made friends with Ron, Harry considers Draco's comments that he shouldn't "go making friends with the wrong sort" and, when Draco then offers to help Harry select the "right" friends (*SS* 108), Harry doesn't even pause. He refuses to shake Draco's hand and tells him coolly, "I think I can tell who the wrong sort are for myself, thanks" (*SS* 108–9).

Harry, just a short while after meeting Ron, has already shown him true *loyalty*, and at the same time Rowling has shown her readers that we make choices every day: we should make good ones, rejecting those who berate others or claim superiority based on race, wealth, or any other trait or uncontrolled chance in life.

The Harry Potter series also champions the value of *hard work*. Harry and his friends work hard at school, try to do well in their classes, and truly want to learn and become better persons and better wizards and witches. While Harry and Ron occasionally slack off, they eventually come around (though they learn pretty quickly that last-minute cramming is much more painful than consistent study!). As an athlete, Harry trains hard without (much) complaint and, when he becomes team captain, tries to set high but reasonable expecta-tions for everyone. They don't always succeed, but the trio tries to study hard and aspires to become valuable members of their society.

The final value we will discuss is *duty*. Harry, even at the young age of eleven, understands duty—doing something for the good of others, even at great cost to yourself. Harry chooses duty over self-interest in book 1 when he decides to beat Snape to the Sorcerer's Stone, even though Ron says he's mad and Hermione tells him he will be expelled:

"SO WHAT?" Harry shouted. "Don't you

understand? If Snape gets hold of the Stone, Voldemort's coming back! Haven't you heard what it was like when he was trying to take over? There won't be any Hogwarts to get expelled from! He'll flatten it, or turn it into a school for the Dark Arts! Losing points doesn't matter anymore, can't you see? D'you think he'll leave you and your families alone if Gryffindor wins the House Cup? If I get caught before I can get to the Stone, well, I'll have to go back to the Dursleys and wait for Voldemort to find me there, it's only dying a bit later than I would have, because I'm never going over to the Dark Side!" (*SS* 270).

Harry fully understands duty and what is at stake. He gladly puts himself at risk for others. And that is exactly what spies do, every day.

But these values are just the tip of the iceberg in the Harry Potter series, because true evil lurks all too close to our good friends, and to survive they must be able to differentiate that which is good from that which is evil.

FINDING A MORAL IMPERATIVE: FAIRNESS, TRUTH, AND THE PROPER USE OF POWER

Harry understood from a very early age that the way he was being treated, compared to Dudley, was not fair (*SS* 18–20). We all develop a sense of *fairness* at a very early age.

Harry, living at the Dursleys, understood what it was like to be regularly beaten up (SS 20), treated as a servant (*SS* 21), subjected to ridicule (*SS* 22–23), and scorned by his classmates (who feared Dudley and his gang) (*SS* 30), and also the recipient of hand-me-down clothes (*SS* 20), tawdry birthday gifts (*SS* 43), and the barest semblance of love. Harry knew that he was being treated unfairly and knew all along what was right and wrong—perhaps because he experienced examples of unfairness every day.

PART 2

So it is no surprise at all that Harry immediately befriends Ron Weasley, a boy with worn-out clothes and no money to buy treats (*SS* 100, 101). By the time Harry *officially* meets Draco Malfoy (whom he overheard while being fitted with his first set of robes) and considers— after Draco publicly berates Harry's newfound friend—Draco's offer to help Harry select "proper" friends, Harry has no problem at all choosing good people above those who are not so good (*SS* 108–9).

By the same token, Harry's hatred for Professor Snape is easily and quickly ignited. From the moment Harry appears in Potions class, Snape taunts Harry and belittles him in front of the whole class, referring to Harry as "Our new—*celebrity*" (*SS* 136). Harry's hatred of and bias toward Snape understandably never wavers—at least, not until the final chapters of the final book. This is under-standable. Less understandable, in our view, is Snape's transference of his hatred for James Potter to James's eleven-year-old son, merely because Harry looks like James (except, of course, for his eyes) (*SS* 47) and because Snape still recalls, quite vividly, how badly James and his friends had treated him in school (*OP* 645–46).

Determining what is *fair* is much easier than determining that which is *true*. There are two types of truth. The first is an immutable truth, one that is easily determined and not subject to dispute, such as two plus two equaling four, or the blue color of a clear sky, or the roundness of the world. These types of truths can be easily deter-mined, and agreement upon them is practically unanimous.

The second type of truth is more opaque, subject to interpreta-tion and contrary views. Is the religion you believe in the correct one? Is the person running for election the best person for the job? Is what someone says true, or a brilliant lie? But be warned: the fact that the second type of truth is harder to determine does not mean that the truth does not exist—it does exist and must be found.

In book 1, Harry and his friends learn the truth about the Sorcerer's Stone and how Nicolas Flamel is using it (*SS* 220). Harry concludes—or, should we say, *assumes*—that Snape is going to steal it and give it to Voldemort (*SS* 268–70). Harry also learns the truth about the Mirror of Erised, how it works, what it shows, and how spending time before it yields nothing (*SS* 213–14). Later, Harry learns the truth about the Horcruxes, the truth behind Voldemort's actions, and the truth about Severus Snape and all the things he did to *help* Harry.

In the spy world, we deal with the second types of truth every day. Can the person I am dealing with be trusted? Is the information he or she is supplying true? Does this country have a secret weapon? Would they be willing to use it against us?

Which gets us to the *use of power.* Power can be individual—a person's physical strength or fortitude, for example. But it can also be a function of an entity or a government exercised through warships, the economy, or subtle pressures forcing others to yield.

Power itself is not bad. Good or bad depends upon how that *power is used.* A sword can be used to attack or defend, for good or ill: it can be used to attack the weak or defend the powerless. A weapon can be a protector or a destroyer, depending on who uses it and to what purposes.

The Elder Wand is a good example. Hermione reads the Story of the Three Brothers from *The Tales of Beedle the Bard* at Xenophilius Lovegood's house (*DH* 406–9). In it we find out that the wizard who possesses the Elder Wand cannot be defeated: the oldest brother asks for "a wand that must always win duels for its owner" (*DH* 407). Voldemort wants it (*DH* 431) so no one can ever defeat him, and he even kills Snape to get it (*DH* 656)—or what he *thinks* is it!

In his final battle against Voldemort, it is Harry who actually wields the Elder Wand—as he informs Voldemort, noting that *Draco* had it before Harry, having taken it from Dumbledore just before the Headmaster was killed by Snape (*HBP* 584; *DH* 742). Now Harry has it—and he does indeed defeat Voldemort. But Harry does not keep it: in the final book, he returns it to Dumbledore's mausoleum (*DH* 748), and in the movie version he destroys it by breaking it in half.

So the real issue of power is one of *how it is used* and *to what end.*

PART 2

THE BACKGROUND OF J. K. ROWLING

In order to understand J. K. Rowling's views on ethics and the proper use of power, it is helpful to review her background, particularly her prior work with Amnesty International. As you may already know, Joanne Kathleen Rowling—who was born on July 31, 1966 (which would be Harry's birthday, fourteen years later!)—attended Wyedean Comprehensive School, a middle school. She did quite well there; she was popular and outgoing and got good grades. In what we would call her eleventh year, at Stratford-upon-Avon, Rowling saw her very first play, Shakespeare's *King Lear*, and was "absolutely electrified by it"—her words. She also saw *The Winter's Tale*, featuring a character named Hermione! In her final year she was made Head Girl and graduated with high honors. Rowling next attended Exeter University, where she mastered French and spent one year abroad in Paris, working as an assistant teacher.

After graduating from Exeter with honors, Rowling spent six years working mostly secretarial jobs, including two years researching human rights violations for Amnesty International. In September 1990, she left England and took a position in Oporto, Portugal, teaching English as a second language. She married, had a child (Jessica), divorced, and returned to England in 1993. After spending a year working on the manuscript for the first Harry Potter book, Rowling took a job teaching French at the Leth Academy and later at Moray House Training College.

This information is derived from Marc Shapiro's *J.K. Rowling: The Wizard Behind Harry Potter* 17, 34, 38–39, 48, 64 (2007), and Lindsey Fraser's *Conversations with J. K. Rowling*, 31–32 (2000).

As discussed in earlier chapters, S.P.E.W. (the Society for the Promotion of Elfish Welfare) is *not* an accidental plot device. Rowling used to work for Amnesty International. Now her own philanthropic organization focuses on helping poor children. Rowling has chosen the side she wants to help—clearly the side of those in need—throughout her series as well as in her personal life.

BEING JUDGED BY HOW WE TREAT THOSE WITHOUT POWER: PEER PRESSURE, TAUNTING, MUGGLE PROTECTION, RACISM, AND CHARITY TO ALL

In our minds, how we treat others is the sine qua non of morality.

What is *sine qua non*? A wonderful Latin phrase that means an essential action, condition, or ingredient; as a legal term, it means a condition or preexisting ingredient without which that which follows cannot exist.

In other words, *how we treat those who are less powerful or disadvantaged in society is both a precondition and the measure of the worth and morality of that society.*

J. K. Rowling agrees. She introduces Harry Potter as a ten-year-old boy who is relegated to a cupboard under the stairs (*SS* 19), abused constantly by his cousin Dudley (*SS* 20, 25), and treated as a slave or worse by his guardians (*SS* 19, 21). We immediately have empathy for Harry, as we should.

In a similar vein, Hermione's moral compass directs her to defend the house-elves, the true slaves of the Wizarding world. To Harry's credit, even before Hermione creates S.P.E.W. (*GF* 224), he frees Dobby by tricking Lucius Malfoy into giving Dobby a piece of clothing, a sock (*CS* 338).

This moral view is not surprising. In the story of Christianity, Christ spends his time helping lepers and other people who are shunned by society and disparages—repeatedly—the rich, the tax collectors, and the powers that be.

Let us next discuss how the Harry Potter series deals with peer pressure. Our introduction to peer pressure occurs, as one would suspect, in the very first book where we find out that Harry is ostracized at school because his cousin hates him, and everyone is afraid of Dudley and his gang (*SS* 30). Harry recognizes that peer pressure makes other children think twice about reaching out.

But in book 5, the peer pressure *against* Harry is immense. After a whole summer of derogatory articles in the *Daily Prophet*, it is no surprise that some of his fellow students reject and even berate him (*OP* 184, 202, 215). Only after the Death Eaters escape from Azkaban and *The Quibbler* releases its interview with Harry (*OP* 578) do the others (not counting the members of Dumbledore's Army) come around, including Seamus Finnegan (*OP* 583).

The human proclivity to conform is both a positive and a negative force (just like a weapon). It is positive because through it we tend to reach a consensus and acclimate to general norms within the specific society to which we belong. But it can be negative for anyone who deviates from that norm and may therefore be rejected, scorned, and even physically harmed. And those in the majority are often *more* than willing to taunt those who seem different, claiming they do not belong.

The point in Harry Potter, we believe, is that we all belong, that we are all interconnected, and that rejecting those who are different (such as Luna Lovegood) who are doing no harm to others is just plain wrong.

Although taunting happens often in the Harry Potter series, Rowling makes it clear that taunting is not appropriate and often has an underlying taint of elitism, or just plain meanness—consider, for instance, that it is usually the unlikeable Draco who is doing the taunting. In book 1, Draco claims he feels sorry "for all those people who have to stay at Hogwarts for Christmas because they are not wanted at home" (*SS* 194–95). He pokes fun of Ron's lack of money often (*SS* 108, 197) and taunts Harry mercilessly after he faints when a Dementor enters the train on the way to Hogwarts (*PA* 87–88, 90, 96–97, 159, 184–85). Even worse, Draco gets into the habit of calling Hermione a Mudblood (*CS* 112, 223) and extolling the "fact" that the Heir of Slytherin will be killing all the Mudbloods (*CS* 139, 223,

224), which is both elitist and racist.

Which gets us to *defending those who need to be protected*.

The Wizarding laws relating to Muggles, we suggest, demonstrate a substantial moral imperative. Muggle baiting is outlawed. Using Muggles for your own ends is prevented by the Statute of Secrecy, which prohibits the Wizarding world from allowing Muggles to know of its existence—and at the same time prohibits the Wizarding world from *taking advantage* of Muggles! None other than Lucius Malfoy—overheard by Harry in Borgin and Burkes—notes rumors of a new Muggle Protection Act proposed, no doubt, by Mr. Weasley (*CS* 51).

Hagrid says it first and perhaps best in book 1:

> "But what does a Ministry of Magic do?"
> "Well, their main job is to keep it from the Muggles that there's still witches an' wizards up an' down the country."
> "Why?"
> "Why? Blimey, Harry, everyone'd be wantin' magic solutions to their problems. Nah, we're best left alone" (*SS* 65).

By the same token, racism is discussed openly throughout the series via the numerous discussions about pure-bloods and—sorry to have to say it out loud—Mudbloods.

There are those in the Wizarding world who believe in purity of a race, despite the fact that none is truly possible anymore—nor desired. As Draco laments to Harry about letting Muggle-borns into Hogwarts, "I really don't think they should let the other sort in, do you? . . . I think they should keep it in the old wizarding families" (*SS* 78).

In book 2, we find out about the founders of Hogwarts and how dissent developed due to Salazar Slytherin's views about racial purity: "Slytherin wished to be more selective about the students admitted to Hogwarts. He believed that magical learning should be kept within all-magic families. He disliked taking students of Muggle parentage, believing them to be untrustworthy. . . . Slytherin extolled such purity, but the other three founders rejected his view and Slytherin left the school" (*CS* 150).

As noted above, such purity is no longer possible as a practical matter due to intermarriage between Muggles and wizards and witches in the last thousand or so years. As Hagrid tells us in the very first book, "It's ridiculous. Most wizards these days are half-blood anyway. If we hadn't married Muggles we'd've died out" (*CS* 116).

And let us not forget that Voldemort—the primary proponent of *Wizarding purity*—himself has a Muggle father and is therefore a half-blood!

Unfortunately, claiming such superiority is a powerful method of obtaining converts. It is human nature to be proud of one's uniqueness and family background, but such pride of origin must be tempered by the realization that humanity is a large group of individuals. While all deserve to retain their uniqueness, they must also realize that they are part of a larger community of interconnections and commonality.

Elitism is also a method of *placing others below you*. But it is just plain wrong. History has shown us that; it is only the inferior who claim superiority, and the more organized they become, the more dangerous they are.

Charity for others is perhaps one of the greatest virtues extolled in the Harry Potter series. Hermione is concerned for the house-elves (*GF* 224), and Harry frees Dobby (*CS* 338) and literally adopts Kreacher (whom he now technically owns) by being kind to him (*DH* 199–200). Moreover, Harry befriends Luna Lovegood—in part due to the insistence of Ginny Weasley (*OP* 185)—and stands steadfast as her friend throughout the series.

CHARITY FOR ALL

The phrase comes from the Second Inaugural Address by President Abraham Lincoln in March of 1865, as the

American Civil War was drawing to a close. Lincoln said, "With malice toward none, with charity for all." A month later he was assassinated.

~~~~~~

Harry's concern for others is shown quite aptly in his concern for Luna Lovegood, such as when she is trying to find her personal belongings at the end of their fifth year (*OP* 862–63) or in the final book, when Harry observes the paintings on her wall depicting Harry, Ron, Hermione, Ginny, and Neville, all interlaced with the word *friends* (*DH* 417).

The ability to establish friendships is one of the most essential ingredients of human nature and social interaction. Indeed, we would argue that friendship is the sine quo non for society itself! Through the act of exporting this virtuous concept beyond family and close friends to a larger group of humanity, humans became capable of creating a society. It is, in our view, the virtue of *friendship* that begets positive social interactions and the development of society itself. And yet—significantly—it is Voldemort who has no friends (only servants) and no ability to love. People, to Voldemort, are only tools to be used and discarded when no longer useful to him.

Amazingly, Harry actually offers sympathy to Voldemort himself on several occasions, telling him that he is the one who does not understand redemption or love (*DH* 738). In the film series, Harry goes so far as to tell Voldemort that he pities him. And at one point in the final book, Harry offers him an opportunity to repent (*DH* 741)—which, of course, he does not take.

So, what virtues and vices are discussed in the Potter series?

Empathy. Family. Friendship. Loyalty. Hard work. Fairness. Truth. The proper use of power. Peer pressure, positive and negative. Not using people for your own ends. Helping people (and house-elves) who need help. The dangers of racism and elitism. The value of charity and compassion.

Strong stuff indeed!

PART 2

THE NATURE OF GOOD VERSUS EVIL: CHOOSING PROPER MEANS TO A LAUDABLE END

So, what then is the nature of good and evil as depicted in the Harry Potter series? Obviously Voldemort is evil, but *why* do we conclude that he is evil? Let's see: he tortures people, kills anyone in his way, is interested only in his own needs and in obtaining power, spreads lies—you'd think that is enough in itself!

But the point is, How do we determine who is good and who is bad?

Right or wrong, our country has associated itself with leaders of other countries that, quite frankly, do many of the things that Voldemort does. But are there indeed situations in which the end may justify the means?

This question is discussed in book 3, when the decision is made to protect Hogwarts with Dementors: "When you're dealing with a wizard like Black, you sometimes have to join forces with those you'd rather avoid" (*PA* 66).

By training agents to lie, use deceit, and even break laws—do we cross any ethical boundaries? Does *using*, though not rewarding, nefarious persons or countries make our country evil? Can we ever ethically associate with unethical leaders?

~~~~~~~~~~~~~~~~~~~~~~~~~~~~~~~~~~~~~

APPLYING ETHICS IN THE CIA

We take upstanding young and intelligent people whose motives are high-minded, and we ask them to maintain the highest standards of integrity with their colleagues while possibly acting in violation of the laws of another country in the course of carrying out their legitimate operational assignments. We teach them how to conduct unauthorized entries, plant bugs, steal secrets, and lie— and then to return to normal when it comes time to deal with their associates at the Agency. We test people for their honesty and do background checks to ensure their patriotism; and once we see that they are exactly what we want, we help them grasp the nature and purpose of their covert work, which may involve a deviation from their ethics. We help them develop a career that serves their country while on occasion doing things that may not be legal in the country where they are assigned.

—Peter Earnest, Business Confidential, 24

~~~~~~

To what extent should we engage in wars thousands of miles away? Is there a clear national interest that justifies the proposed action? Do we become the world's policeman, or avoid, to use the common phrase, "foreign entanglements"?

~~~~~~

GEORGE WASHINGTON'S WARNING AGAINST FOREIGN ENTANGLEMENTS

In 1793—at a time when the United States had an ocean and thousands of miles of sparsely populated lands protecting its borders—George Washington warned against "foreign entanglements" in his Second Inaugural Address. But the world has changed, dramatically. Distance no longer protects us from harm, and almost all countries have at least some interconnections with our country. And many of those countries do not inculcate the same freedoms that we hold dear.

On the other hand, more than a decade of wars in the Middle East has caused many of us to question whether these wars are worth the treasure and blood lost. This discussion encompasses not only our role in the world (as a policeman?), but also our moral obligation to prevent genocide, assist the poor, and create stability in countries that may fail and become a haven for those who would attack us or others. The decisions our leaders make on these matters affect us greatly. None of these issues are easy to discuss, but the discussion is essential and occurs every day.

~~~~~~

So where does all this leave us?

Just as Harry Potter refused to adopt Voldemort's methods to defeat him, we must strive to do the same.

It is possible to learn not only from history, but also from great works of literature that extol virtues and provide examples of morality in action, taking risks worth taking, and being true to your friends and what is right to believe in.

In our view, the Harry Potter series does exactly that.

53

SEVERUS SNAPE—THE ULTIMATE DOUBLE AGENT

Now let's take a really close look at Severus Snape and his role as the ultimate double agent!

SEVERUS SNAPE'S BACKGROUND AND HISTORY —IN CHRONOLOGICAL ORDER

Here is a review of what we know from the Harry Potter series— in chronological order—of Snape's background and personal history, relevant to his serving first as Voldemort's agent and then as a double agent to Albus Dumbledore:

- Snape as a young child, his father shouting at his cowering mother while Snape cries in a corner (*OP* 591)

- Snape meets Lily and Petunia Evans (*DH* 662–65)

- Snape tells Lily Evans about the Wizarding world (*DH* 665–67)

- Snape observes Lily at the train station talking to Petunia about her letter to Hogwarts and the letter from Dumbledore to Petunia (*DH* 668–70)

- Snape, on the Hogwarts Express with Lily Evans, meets James Potter and Sirius Black (*DH* 670–72)

- Snape, Lily, James, and the others are sorted into houses (*DH* 672)

- A girl laughs at Snape as he tries to mount a bucking broomstick (*OP* 591)

- Snape suspects that Lupin is a werewolf: he learns from Sirius how to get past the Whomping Willow and follows Lupin into the tunnel; James Potter rescues Snape and saves his life (*SS* 300; *PA* 356–57; *DH* 673-74)

CHAPTER 53

- Lily objects to Snape's choice of friends, while Snape objects to the behavior of James and his friends (*DH* 672–74)

- Snape, with greasy hair, shooting flies with his wand while sitting in his room (*OP* 591)

- Snape completes his O.W.L. in Defense Against the Dark Arts and wanders down by the lake, where he is bullied and taunted by James Potter but saved by Lily; Snape then calls Lily a Mudblood (*OP* 640–48, *DH* 674)

- Snape tries to apologize to Lily; Lily objects to Snape's Death Eater friends and claims he can't wait to join Voldemort (*DH* 675–76)

- Snape, now one of Voldemort's Death Eaters, serves as a messenger for Voldemort, delivering messages to Dumbledore (*DH* 676)

- Snape overhears the first part of the prophecy stating that the boy who can defeat the Dark Lord was born near the end of July to parents who had thrice defeated Voldemort and then relays what he heard to Voldemort (*OP* 843; *DH* 677)

- Snape meets with Dumbledore on top of a hill and asks Dumbledore to hide the Potters, hide them all, to keep them safe; in return, Snape promises Dumbledore "anything" (*DH* 677)

- Snape meets with Dumbledore after Lily and James's death and is told that the boy lived; Snape agrees to help protect Lily's son but insists that Dumbledore tell no one (*DH* 679)

PART 2

- Snape begins teaching at Hogwarts, though he is never allowed to teach the course he wants to teach, Defense Against the Dark Arts (*SS* 126; *OP* 363)

- Snape complains to Dumbledore about Harry during Harry's first year, and is asked by Dumbledore to keep an eye on Quirrell (*DH* 679)

- Snape's Dark Mark becomes darker during Harry's fourth year; Karkaroff intends to flee, but Snape will remain (*DH* 679)

- Snape ignores the Dark Mark when Voldemort returns, but goes to him two hours later on Dumbledore's orders, convinces Voldemort that he has remained faithful, and provides Voldemort sixteen years of information on Dumbledore (*GF* 709–10, 713; *HBP* 28–29)

- Snape does his best to save Dumbledore after the Headmaster is wounded by the Horcrux ring between Harry's fifth and sixth years; Dumbledore has maybe a year to live; Snape promises to do all he can to protect the students if the school falls into Voldemort's grasp; Dumbledore reveals that it is Snape who will have to kill him; Snape agrees to do so (*DH* 680–83)

- Snape objects to not being privy to all of Dumbledore's secrets; Dumbledore refuses to tell Snape everything because of the amount of time Snape spends with Voldemort—on Dumbledore's orders, Snape retorts (*DH* 683–84)

- That night Dumbledore tells Snape that a part of Voldemort's soul lives inside Harry; because of this, Harry must die, and Voldemort is the one who must kill him (*DH* 686-87)

- Snape keeps his promise and kills Dumbledore (*HBP* 596)

- Dumbledore, through his portrait, instructs Snape to tell Voldemort the correct date of Harry's departure from the Weasleys' home, have someone suggest decoys, and act his part well if he is part of the attempt to capture Harry (*DH* 688)

- Snape Confunds Mundungus to suggest using decoys (*DH* 688)

- During the chase after the decoys, Snape tries to hit the arm of a Death Eater who is aiming at Lupin's back, but misses, hitting George instead (*DH* 688)

- Once headquarters has been compromised, Snape searches Sirius's old room and finds the picture of Lily and a letter signed by her; he keeps the two items, after tearing her image only out of the picture (*DH* 688–89)

- Snape is appointed Headmaster of Hogwarts (*DH* 227)

- Snape gets the Sword of Gryffindor to Harry, using his Patronus to lure Harry to the lake where Snape has previously placed the sword (*DH* 365–66, 367–70, 689)

- During the battle of Hogwarts, Snape repeatedly asks Voldemort to let him find the Potter boy (*DH* 652, 654, 655)

- Snape is attacked by Voldemort's snake; Voldemort takes Snape's wand, thinking it is the Elder Wand; Voldemort leaves and before Snape dies he gives Harry his memories (*DH* 656-58)

Snape's Background and Psychological Assessment: A thin, scrawny kid, not well-liked by those who are well-liked; comes from a home filled with arguments; is in love with a young woman who rejects him, in part due to his beliefs and actions; a capable scholar, with a talent for and expertise in the use of potions and the Dark

Arts. As he comes of age, he becomes a young man who sees an unjust world that generally shuns him; he is an outsider who wants to be an insider; a young man with hatred for that which is and desire to be something different. And as a young adult who has just left Hogwarts, he is a man with little power or respect, who is willing to disregard the normal conventions or mores of "lesser" wizards and witches to obtain power and respect.

In short, the *perfect* **recruit** for Voldemort.

SNAPE AS A DEATH EATER—BEFORE LILY POTTER IS MARKED FOR DEATH

How he was recruited we are not told, but it is clear that Snape was a willing conscript: while still attending Hogwarts, Lily accuses Snape of having Death Eater friends and wanting to join Voldemort, and he does not deny it (*DH* 675–76). It is interesting from a psychological standpoint that Snape, like Voldemort, is willing to adopt a *philosophy of purity* relating to the Wizarding world. Yet Snape, like Voldemort, is not a pure-blood! *Both Snape and Voldemort have a Muggle parent.* But they nonetheless adopt a philosophy that is antithetical to their actual existence!

Snape tells Lily—before they begin at Hogwarts, and in an attempt to placate Lily's insecurities and worries—that it doesn't matter if she is Muggle-born:

> "Does it make a difference, being Muggle-born?"
> Snape hesitated. His black eyes, eager in the greenish gloom, moved over the pale face, the dark red hair.
> "No," he said. "It doesn't make any difference" (*DH* 666).

Are Voldemort and Snape drawn to this philosophy because they are embarrassed about the fact they are *not* pure-bloods? Or are they using this philosophy as a means to an end, a palatable viewpoint that the Wizarding community might accept, leading them to power over and control inferior people, including (and perhaps especially) Muggles? A person's insecurities can lead to inappropriate actions and the acceptance of objectionable beliefs; the desire to belong can supplant normal social mores; and an affront—personal or generic— can often lead to a strong desire for revenge.

***

THE DESIRE FOR FREEDOM AND THE NEED FOR CONFORMITY

Sigmund Freud tries to explain some of these aspects of human nature in *Civilization and Its Discontents* (1930), in which he asserts that human instincts remain even in modern society and that there is an inherent conflict between *the desire for freedom* (and the satisfaction of certain atavistic human desires) and *the need for conformity*, if civilization is to work.

***

So Snape, having been taunted by James Potter and saved by Lily Evans, calls Lily a Mudblood, showing his true colors (*OP* 640–48; *DH* 674). Lily refuses Snape's apology, telling him matter-of-factly, "You've chosen your way, I've chosen mine" (*DH* 676). Snape continues hanging around Death Eaters and plans on joining Voldemort when he leaves Hogwarts, no doubt envisioning regularly the revenge that he will be able to dole out to James Potter and his friends (*DH* 675–76). Once Snape leaves Hogwarts and becomes a Death Eater, he is assigned the task of being Voldemort's messenger, responsible for bringing messages to Dumbledore and returning any replies (*DH* 676).

THE AFTERMATH OF VOLDEMORT'S DECISION TO KILL LILY POTTER—TIME TO CHOOSE SIDES!

And then something happens that changes Snape's loyalties— forever. Voldemort, after hearing the portion of the prophecy that

PART 2

Snape overheard (naming the boy who was born at the end of July to parents who had thrice defeated Voldemort as his nemesis), decides to kill Harry Potter—and no doubt James and Lily Potter in the process.

Snape tries to convince Voldemort to just kill the boy and let Lily Potter live, asking for mercy only for the mother (*DH* 677). Voldemort refuses; he will hunt them down and kill them all (*DH* 677). So Snape meets with Dumbledore—"on his own account" (*DH* 677)—and asks Dumbledore to hide the Potter family, to keep them safe (*DH* 678).

And what will Snape provide Dumbledore in return? "Anything," he says (*DH* 678).

But Lily and James are betrayed by Peter Pettigrew, who had been spying for Voldemort for more than a year already (*PA* 374–75). Peter Pettigrew tells Voldemort the secret of their location, and Voldemort goes there to kill all three—succeeding in killing the parents, but not the boy.

Now that the Potters are dead, Snape goes to Dumbledore's office looking "like a man who had lived a hundred years of misery" (*DH* 678). Dumbledore tells Snape that the boy survived and, knowing his love of Lily, asks Snape if he remembers the shape and color of Lily Evans's eyes, that they are Harry's eyes too (*DH* 678). Dumbledore is using his knowledge of Snape and the love he had for Lily to *turn him*, to get Snape to agree to change sides permanently.

Snape wishes he was dead, but Dumbledore has a different plan for the broken man sitting before him: "If you loved Lily Evans, if you truly loved her, then your way forward is clear. . . . Help me protect Lily's son" (*DH* 678–79).

Snape asserts that the child needs no protection, for the Dark Lord has gone, but Dumbledore wisely claims that Voldemort will return and that Harry Potter will be in terrible danger when he does (*DH* 679). Snape agrees, but insists that Dumbledore tell no one (*DH* 679). Dumbledore agrees, noting that he has just agreed never to reveal the best of Snape (*DH* 679).

ANALYSIS: *Why would Snape trade sides, especially since Lily is dead?*

526

CHAPTER 53

Well, technically, Snape traded sides *before* Lily's death: as you will recall, once Snape had failed to convince Voldemort to let Lily live, he went to warn Dumbledore about Voldemort's plan and to ask that he keep Lily safe (*DH* 677–78). When asked what he would give Dumbledore in return, he answers, "Anything" (*DH* 678). *It is at this moment that Snape has been turned.*

The question remains, now that Lily is dead, *why would Snape remain on Dumbledore's side?* In our view, the answer is a bit more complex, not a simple matter of quid pro quo, where someone exchanges one thing for another. We see a couple of powerful reasons for Snape to permanently switch sides.

The first reason for Snape to permanently switch sides is that *Voldemort had killed someone he loved*—the *only* person he loved. Snape's reasoning could be an act of revenge, or just insight on the methods and ethics that Voldemort had adopted. The death of a loved one at the hands of a "friend" is powerful incentive indeed to transform friend into enemy. And, as described in the book, Snape was truly devastated by Lily's death: slumped forward on a chair, "making a terrible sound, like a wounded animal"; he "looked like a man who had lived a hundred years of misery" since he had begged Dumbledore to protect and save the Potters (*DH* 678).

The second reason for Snape to permanently switch sides is that *despite Snape's attempts to convince Voldemort not to kill Lily Potter,* Snape's master had killed her anyway. Voldemort's decision to kill Lily—despite Snape's protestations and fervent requests—demonstrated to Snape that his wishes and advice were of no consequence to his master: Voldemort is loyal only to Voldemort, and everyone else is expendable. In short, Snape's master showed that he had no *loyalty* to his followers; Voldemort's only interest is *his own* interest.

When Voldemort finally kills Snape, the Dark Lord says he regrets it. However, we believe that his regret was *not* for his servant and confidant of many years, but rather for no longer having Snape's services as an inside agent. After all, we are told that he says so "coldly" (*DH* 656).

The third reason for Snape to permanently switch sides is the fact that he is *fulfilling the promise* he made the first time he talked to Dumbledore "on his own account" and asked him to save the Potters (*DH* 677–78). Snape had promised in return to do "Anything," and Snape is a man of his word (*DH* 688).

The fourth reason for Snape to permanently switch sides *is so that Lily Potter did not die in vain*. Dumbledore tells Snape that if he really loved Lily, his way forward is clear:

> "If you loved Lily Evans, if you truly loved her, then your way forward is clear."
>
> Snape seemed to peer through a haze of pain, and Dumbledore's words appeared to take a long time to reach him.
>
> "What—what do you mean?"
>
> "You know how and why she died. Make sure it was not in vain. Help me protect Lily's son."
>
> "He does not need protection. The Dark Lord has gone—"
>
> "The Dark Lord will return, and Harry Potter will be in terrible danger when he does" (*DH* 678–79).

And fifth, we can surmise that Snape felt guilt for his part in causing the death of Lily Potter: It was Snape who overheard the first part of the prophecy and relayed that information to Voldemort.

Each of these reasons alone is sufficient to turn someone to your side, but all five combined certainly did the trick. Dumbledore recruits Snape as his most important agent—and, upon Voldemort's return, his most important double agent.

PROFESSOR SNAPE AT HOGWARTS—BEFORE THE RETURN OF LORD VOLDEMORT

Snape then begins teaching at Hogwarts, though he is never allowed to teach the course he wants to teach, Defense Against the

Dark Arts (*SS* 126; *OP* 363).

Ten years later, a young boy with no idea that he is a wizard, living underneath the stairs in a Muggle house, gets a letter inviting him to attend Hogwarts (SS 51).

Once Harry arrives at Hogwarts, Snape complains to Dumbledore about him, relaying a view of Harry that is, in reality, a mirror image of Snape's view of Harry's father, James (*DH* 679):

> "—mediocre, arrogant as his father, a determined rule-breaker, delighted to find himself famous, attention-seeking and impertinent—"
>
> "You see what you expect to see, Severus," said Dumbledore (*DH* 679).

Dumbledore asks Snape to keep an eye on Quirrell, which he does (*SS* 226; *DH* 679).

In Harry's fourth year, the year of the Triwizard' s Cup, Snape's Dark Mark is becoming darker—as is Karkaroff's (*DH* 680). But unlike Karkaroff, who "intends to flee if the Mark burns," Snape tells Dumbledore that he is not tempted to join him, stating that he is no coward (*DH* 680).

Dumbledore agrees, telling Snape, "You are a braver man by far than Igor Karkaroff," and mentions—to Snape's great horror—that perhaps they Sort too soon—meaning that because of his bravery *perhaps Snape should have been put in Gryffindor* (*DH* 680)!

At the beginning of book 6, Bellatrix Lestrange admits that she does not trust Snape and poses many important questions about his years at Hogwarts:

> "Where were you when the Dark Lord fell? Why did you never make any attempt to find him when he vanished? What have you been doing all these years that you've lived in Dumbledore's pocket? Why did you stop the Dark Lord procuring the Sorcerer's Stone? Why did you not return at once when the Dark Lord was reborn?

Where were you a few weeks ago when we battled to retrieve the prophecy for the Dark Lord? And why, Snape, is Harry Potter still alive, when you have had him at your mercy for five years?" (*HBP* 25).

Snape, importantly, asserts that Voldemort himself asked all the same questions—and was satisfied with his answers:

"Before I answer you, I say, let me ask a question in turn. Do you really think that the Dark Lord has not asked me each and every one of those questions? And do you really think that, had I not been able to give satisfactory answers, I would be sitting here talking to you?" (*HBP* 26).

Thus, Snape convinces Bellatrix that to question him is to question the infallibility of Voldemort himself.

And Snape provides the answers to Bellatrix Lestrange's questions:

- Where were you when the Dark Lord fell? Snape was at Hogwarts, where Voldemort had asked him to be in order to spy on Dumbledore; it was on Voldemort's orders that he took up the post of teaching at Hogwarts (*HBP* 26).

  Snape's cover story: *He was at Hogwarts because he was told by Voldemort to be there.*

- Why did you not attempt to find Voldemort? For the same reason his other followers did not do so: "I believed him finished" (*HBP* 26). While Bellatrix spent all those years in Azkaban, Snape continued at Hogwarts; when Voldemort resumed human shape after the Triwizard Tournament, Snape "had sixteen years of information on Dumbledore to give him when he returned" (*HBP*

27). Snape notes that it was only through Dumbledore's protection was he able to stay out of jail (*HBP* 27).

Snape's cover story: *He did not look for Voldemort because he thought the Dark Lord was finished, like everyone else.*

- Why did you not assist Voldemort in getting the Sorcerer's Stone? Because at that point Voldemort did not know whether to trust Snape and therefore did not confide in him that he had returned, using Quirrell instead (*HBP* 28).

  Snape's cover story: *He didn't assist in getting the Sorcerer's Stone because Voldemort hadn't revealed himself as behind the plan.*

PROFESSOR SNAPE AFTER THE RETURN OF LORD VOLDEMORT—SNAPE AS A DOUBLE AGENT

Once Voldemort had returned to human form and sent for his followers (*GF* 645, 709–10), Snape did *not* go immediately to the cemetery when the Dark Mark burned as the other Death Eaters had done (*HBP* 28). As Snape explained to Bellatrix—almost as to a schoolchild—he *did* return to the Dark Lord *two hours later.* By failing to heed the burning Dark Mark, Snape had demonstrated that he was no longer a follower of Voldemort, and then Dumbledore himself sent Snape to spy on Voldemort two hours later (*GF* 713; *HBP* 28):

> "Severus," said Dumbledore, turning to Snape, "you know what I must ask you to do. If you are ready . . . if you are prepared . . ."
> "I am," said Snape. He looked slightly paler than usual, and his cold, black eyes glittered strangely.
> "Then good luck," said Dumbledore, and he watched, with a trace of apprehension on his face, as Snape swept

PART 2

wordlessly after Sirius (*GF* 713).

Brave indeed, and well served by the cover story he had no doubt considered carefully as Voldemort's return grew more inevitable. Returning to Bellatrix Lestrange's questions:

- Why did you not return immediately when summoned by the Dark Lord, waiting for two hours before returning instead?

  Snape's cover story: *Because he realized it would be better to wait in order to convince Dumbledore that he was free of Voldemort's control.*

Snape convinces Voldemort that he had remained faithful—and is then sent back to Hogwarts to spy on Voldemort's behalf (*HBP* 29).

- Why did you *not* kill Harry Potter as soon as he began attending Hogwarts, even though you had the chance?

  Snape's cover story: *He did not do so because he thought Voldemort was gone, and killing Harry Potter would merely ensure that he would be sent to Azkaban (HBP 30).*

As it turned out, Snape explains to Bellatrix, it was good that he did not kill Harry, because the boy's blood was needed for Voldemort to regenerate (*HBP* 30).

Snape has provided satisfactory answers to Bellatrix—and, incidentally, sworn the Unbreakable Vow to protect Draco (*HBP* 36–37). And Snape continues in his role as double agent.

Upon Voldemort's return to human form, Dumbledore begins researching everything about Tom Riddle. Dumbledore talks to numerous people who had met Tom Riddle, especially in his early years, and if possible retrieves and saves their memories of Tom Riddle, storing them away like important reference books that can be reviewed repeatedly and—we note—shown to others as well.

Dumbledore eventually concludes through this thorough research that Voldemort has used Dark Magic to split his soul into at least seven parts, now contained in Horcruxes. This precaution allowed Voldemort to stay alive even after he was struck by the rebounding death curse when he tried to kill Harry, and to return to human form, using Harry's blood, in the cemetery at the end of book 4 following the Triwizard Tournament.

So the search for Horcruxes begins, and between Harry's fourth and fifth years, Dumbledore finds one: Marvolo Gaunt's ring. Harry first notices Dumbledore's injured hand when Dumbledore arrives at the Dursleys' to fetch Harry and to use him as an incentive to get Horace Slughorn to return to teaching at Hogwarts (*HBP* 48, 69).

Harry first "sees" both Marvolo's ring *and* the Slytherin locket thanks to the Pensieve and to Bob Ogden, the Ministry of Magic representative who went to the Gaunt house to discuss with Mr. Gaunt his son's improper use of magic against a Muggle (*HBP* 207–8). Dumbledore finds Mr. Gaunt's son, Morfin, at the Gaunt house and retrieves Morfin's memory of young Tom Riddle taking the ring and learning about the locket (*HBP* 365–66). Dumbledore finds the ring a few days before coming to fetch Harry to go see Slughorn (*HBP* 216) and foolishly puts it on (*DH* 680).

It is Snape who saves Dumbledore from the Marvolo ring's curse, trapping the curse in the injured hand. When asked how long the curse can be contained, Snape tells Dumbledore he has maybe a year to live. Dumbledore gets Snape to promise to do all he can to protect the students if the school falls into Voldemort's grasp. Dumbledore then asks Snape to offer Draco help and guidance so he can find out precisely what Draco is up to in his mission to kill Dumbledore. Dumbledore also states that Snape will have to be the one to kill him "when the moment presents itself." After some discussion, Snape agrees to do so (*DH* 680–83).

Sometime later—still during Harry's sixth year—Snape asks Dumbledore why he is spending so much time with Harry during the evenings; Dumbledore refuses to say, and Snape understandably objects to not knowing all of Dumbledore's secrets:

> "It is essential that I give the boy enough information
> for him to do what he needs to do."

PART 2

"And why may I not have the same information?"

"I prefer not to put all of my secrets in one basket, particularly not a basket that spends so much time dangling on the arm of Lord Voldemort."

"Which I do on your orders!"

"And you do it extremely well. Do not think that I underestimate the constant danger in which you place yourself, Severus. To give Voldemort what appears to be valuable information while withholding the essentials is a job I would entrust to nobody but you" (*DH* 684).

Dumbledore agrees to tell at least some of the secrets he has been holding back. That night Dumbledore tells Snape that a part of Voldemort's soul lives inside Harry, and as long as that piece of soul exists, Voldemort cannot die. Dumbledore goes on to say that once Voldemort takes special precautions to protect his snake, Harry must be told the truth. He must know that he must die, and that Voldemort is the one who must kill him (*DH* 684–87).

Snape is incredulous, considering Dumbledore more Machiavellian than even himself:

Snape looked horrified. "You have kept him alive so that he can die at the right moment? . . . I have spied for you and lied for you, put myself in mortal danger for you. Everything was supposed to be to keep Lily Potter's son safe. Now you tell me you have been raising him like a pig for slaughter—"

"But this is touching, Severus," said Dumbledore seriously. "Have you grown to care for the boy, after all?"

"For him?" shouted Snape. "Expecto Patronum!"
From the tip of his wand burst the silver doe (*DH* 687).

His love for Lily is so strong that his Patronus changed to take the same form as Lily's!

Next we "see" Dumbledore, through his portrait, instructing

Snape to tell Voldemort the correct date of Harry's departure from the Weasleys' home and to have someone suggest decoys. Dumbledore reminds Snape that he must act his part well if he is part of the attempt to capture Harry (*DH* 688). Next Snape Confunds Mundungus to suggest using decoys (*DH* 688).

During the chase after the decoys Snape tries to hit the arm of a Death Eater aiming at Lupin's back but misses, accidentally hitting George, cutting off one of his ears (*DH* 688).

We then observe Snape searching Sirius's old room at number twelve, Grimmauld Place—after the Death Eaters have gained access due to Yaxley holding on to Hermione when they tried to return to headquarters (*DH* 270)—and watch as Snape finds the picture of Lily and a letter signed by her; Snape keeps the second page of the letter with Lily's signature and the portion of the photograph showing just Lily (*DH* 688–89).

Snape continues his role as double agent and is in Dumbledore's office when Phineas Nigellus's portrait tells them that Harry and Hermione are at the Forest of Dean (*DH* 689). Snape withdraws the Sword of Gryffindor from its hiding place behind Dumbledore's portrait and is instructed by Dumbledore to make sure Harry gets it in conditions of need and valor—but still Dumbledore refuses to tell Snape why Harry needs the sword (*DH* 689).

Snape gets Harry to follow his Patronus to the sword, which Snape has placed in a frozen lake (*DH* 365–66, 367–70).

Snape undoubtedly observed Harry jumping into the forest pool, where he nearly drowns (*DH* 369–70). Given Snape's obligation to protect Harry, no doubt he continued watching as Ron rescued Harry and retrieved the sword (*DH* 370). Ron thought he had seen someone behind a tree as he rushed to save Harry, but when Harry investigates he observes no snow at that location and no footprints in the area (*DH* 372). As described in the book, the place where two oak trees stood close together was "an ideal place to see but not be seen" (*DH* 372).

PART 2

THE KILLING OF ALBUS DUMBLEDORE—OR HOW TO CONVINCE EVERYONE YOU'RE ON THE OTHER SIDE

At one point in the story, Snape reconsiders his grand bargain to kill Dumbledore when the moment is right:

> "After you have killed me, Severus—"
>
> "You refuse to tell me everything, yet you expect that small service of me!" snarled Snape, and real anger flared in the thin face now. "You take a great deal for granted, Dumbledore! Perhaps I have changed my mind!"
>
> "You gave me your word, Severus" (*DH* 685).

And then Dumbledore finally relents, telling Snape the strange truth: that Harry must die, and Voldemort must be the one to kill him (*DH* 685).

And so Snape, at the end of book 6, fulfills his promise. Dumbledore realizes that the moment has presented itself in due course and says, "Severus . . . please . . ." (*HBP* 595).

Significantly, Dumbledore's words can be taken two ways: Snape understands that Dumbledore is begging him to do what he promised—so that his death is quick and has meaning, in providing credence to Snape's cover story. To the others, it sounds like a man begging for his life. In other words, the two men are talking in code by using normal words, but words that have true meaning only for the two of them.

Snape steps forward, pushes Draco out of the way, and looks at Dumbledore with revulsion and hatred (*DH* 595). And Snape, as promised, executes the killing curse *Avada Kedavra*—which hits Dumbledore "squarely in the chest," blasting Dumbledore into the air and over the battlements of the Astronomy Tower to the ground far below (*HBP* 596).

And who witnesses Snape's purportedly evil act? Harry, Draco, and four Death Eaters: the werewolf Fenrir Greyback, Amycus Carrow, his sister Alecto Carrow, and one with a heavy, brutal-looking face (*DH* 593–94). Before Dumbledore is killed, Alecto comments that he looks close to death as it is: "He's not long for this world anyway, if you ask me!" (*HBP* 594). Snape has indeed done Dumbledore a favor by killing him at that moment—though no one knows it but Snape.

And now—following this act of murder—there can be no doubt among Voldemort or his followers that Snape is fully on the Dark Lord's side, for killing Dumbledore appeared to be the ultimate act of loyalty to Voldemort.

VOLDEMORT'S RIGHT·HAND MAN—OR HOW TO GIVE THE DARK LORD YOUR ALL

Following Dumbledore's death, Hogwarts does indeed fall into Voldemort's grasp (*DH* 682). Snape is appointed Headmaster, presumably in order to keep his promise to protect the students by limiting, to some extent, the malevolent actions of the Carrows (*DH* 225, 688).

Snape continues steadfastly on his mission, on behalf of Dumbledore and Harry Potter. During the Battle of Hogwarts, Snape repeatedly asks Voldemort to let him find the Potter boy (*DH* 652, 654, 655). To the end, Snape is trying to get to Harry first and tell him the information that Dumbledore had relayed to him.

But Snape's attempt to get to Harry fails because Voldemort—in furtherance of his goal to obtain the Elder Wand—orders Nagini to kill Snape (*DH* 656). As Snape lays dying, Voldemort takes Snape's wand—thinking it is the Elder Wand—and *claims* to regret what he has just done (*DH* 656).

Only as he lies dying is Snape able to give Harry his own memories and convey the critical information (*DH* 657–58). Snape dies, knowing that he has fulfilled his mission—and looking into the mirror image of Lily Evans's eyes.

The rest is silence (*Hamlet*, Act V, Scene ii, line 347).

Or is it?

PART 2

Thanks to the Pensieve, Snape still has quite a bit to tell, don't you think?

REFLECTIONS ON ONE MAN'S MOTIVES, BRAVERY, AND SACRIfiCE

So, what is left to say about Snape?

He was brilliant, brave, and a superb double agent.

Perhaps Harry says it best nineteen years later, when discussing with his son the possibility of ending up in Slytherin: "Albus Severus, . . . you were named for two headmasters of Hogwarts. One of them was a Slytherin, and he was probably the bravest man I ever knew" (*DH* 758).

Significantly, Snape tells Harry at one of his Occlumency lessons that Voldemort, when he was attacking Mr. Weasley, realized that Harry was there and that Harry was able to see the attack through the snake's eyes, as Voldemort himself did. When Harry asks how Snape knows this, Snape merely states, "It is enough that we know" (*OP* 533). Just as significantly, at one point during Occlumency lessons, Snape openly *admits* that he is the inside agent, the person who is spying for Dumbledore!

> "Perhaps," said Snape, his dark, cold eyes narrowing slightly, "perhaps you actually enjoy having these visions and dreams, Potter. Maybe they make you feel special—important?"
>
> "No, they don't," said Harry, his jaw set and his fingers clenched tightly around the handle of his wand.
>
> "That is just as well, Potter," said Snape coldly, "because you are neither special nor important, and it is not up to you to find out what the Dark Lord is saying to his Death Eaters."
>
> "No—that's your job, isn't it?" Harry shot at him.
>
> He had not meant to say it; it had burst out of him

in temper. For a long moment they stared at each other, Harry convinced he had gone too far. But there was a curious, almost satisfied expression on Snape's face when he answered.

"Yes, Potter," he said, his eyes glinting. "That is my job. Now, if you are ready, we will start again . . ." (*OP* 590–91).

Yes, Potter, that is my job. Wow! A clear revelation of the truth—that is *instantly* ignored. Harry fails to understand the significance of what Snape has told him (just as most if not all readers of the fifth book failed to understand the significance of these words as well)! Their full meaning is not clear until much later, when we know the truth about a *very good* double agent named Severus Snape!

By the last scene of book 7, Harry has had many years to contemplate the role of Severus Snape, the reasons for his actions, and the sacrifices he had made for a woman who—Snape probably knew—never loved him and was at most, for a time, his friend.

In our view, Snape stood steadfast in *the ideal* of the only real love he ever felt; steadfast in the memory of what it felt like to love someone and have the hope of that love being returned in kind; steadfast in his decision to try to protect her when she was placed in mortal danger by the man he called his master; steadfast in protecting her son, despite his inability to get past the hatred he felt for the boy, the inescapable visual reminder of the boy's father and the mother's eyes.

There are many types of loyalty, many of which we may never understand.

But above all things, Snape was loyal to the memory of the one woman he loved, and that was enough.

And thanks to Snape, the story ends well.

Indeed: "All is well" (*DH* 759).

54

THE VALUE OF SPIES AND SPYING:
A WORLD WORTH SAVING

In the 2012 film *Argo,* we follow a CIA operative to Iran in 1979, soon after the American embassy there was seized by militants, to conduct the exfiltration of six foreign service officers of the US State Department who had been working at the embassy but managed to escape capture. The six officers find refuge with the Canadians and eventually escape Iran by posing, with the operative, as a movie scouting crew.

This is all true, though there were in fact two CIA operatives that went to Iran to get the foreign service officers out.

Soon thereafter, the Canadians received all the credit for the escape (much of it deserved, for hiding the Americans in a dangerous situation), and all ended well for the six State Department employees. The heroism of the CIA operatives became known only in the late 1990s as part of the celebration of the fiftieth anniversary of the CIA, on the insistence of Director George Tenet.

We need spies. And really good analysts.

And we need to realize that our spies are out there every day, putting their lives at risk for our country and the greater good.

Not the greater good envisioned by Grindelwald, but rather that depicted by Professor Dumbledore. What did Dumbledore perceive?

An environment where children are protected, not assaulted (Take that Dolores Umbridge! Go away, you Carrows!), and where justice is served by the rule of law (No kangaroo courts, Cornelius Fudge!).

Severus Snape was perhaps the best spy ever portrayed in literature. But we must remember that there *are* real spies out there, spies who take all the risks, perhaps more than Snape did.

The world is full of risk. It is a very dangerous place. Only through information can our leaders make the right decisions.

And information is hard to come by.

Countries hide what they are doing. Leaders make statements that are intentionally false. And informants are often untrustworthy or just plain wrong.

It is spies—and intelligence analysts—who derive truth from a blurry world.

~~~~~~~~~~~~~~~~~~~~~~~~~~~~

"WILDERNESS OF MIRRORS"

The phrase "wilderness of mirrors" is generally attributed to James Jesus Angleton, a former senior CIA official, who expanded on it as a way to describe the difficulty and confusion of determining the truth in the realm of intelligence. He stated that the wilderness of mirrors "is that . . . myriad of stratagems, deceptions, artifices and all the other devices of disinformation which the Soviet bloc and its coordinated intelligence services use to confuse and split the West," thus producing "an ever-fluid landscape where fact and illusion merge. . . ."

However, the phrase "wilderness of mirrors" was first written by T. S. Eliot in his 1920 poem "Gerontion," line 65, where Eliot, at age thirty-two, describes himself as an old man who has lost his passion, lost his "sight, smell, hearing, taste and touch" and who smells pungent sauces that, in his chilled delirium, "multiply variety/In a wilderness of mirrors."

~~~~~~~~~~~~~~~~

~~~~~~~~~~~~~~~~

"RIDDLE WRAPPED AROUND AN ENIGMA"

Another wonderful phrase describing something difficult to discern is "a riddle wrapped around an enigma." The phrase is a compressed version of Winston Churchill's famous description of Russia, a country that was hiding just about everything it was doing, in a 1939 radio broadcast: "I cannot forecast to you the action of Russia. It is a riddle, wrapped in a mystery, inside an enigma; but perhaps there is a key. That key is Russian national interest." It is particularly hard to determine what is going on in secretive and authoritarian countries, such as North Korea is now, but spies today still seek out the same key: national interest.

~~~~~~~~~~~~~~~~

Our leaders cannot make decisions without credible information. It is the intelligence community that provides not only the basic information, but also the crucial analysis of that information.

In the real world, most spies in the field gather information through others—recruiting foreign nationals, reviewing open-source materials, and observing—ever so carefully—what is going on around them. Yes, there are spies who pick locks, seduce women (or men) to get information, and act like 007 in the movies. But most spies look normal, if not plain, existing quietly, surrounded by danger and opportunities to observe something important—and who relay that information back home without fanfare or a shot being fired.

Back home, there are literally thousands of intelligence professionals who organize, synthesize, and analyze every bit of information obtained, and produce from it a product or report that is given to the very highest levels of government.

And by the way: spying is fun.

But more significantly, spying is *important*. Real spies do this work every day, and our leaders receive the benefits of their work and use that information every day as well.

There is good and bad in the world, and spies provide the information essential to dealing with the bad and allowing the good to succeed. Some spies sit at desks as analysts; others delve into the world as operatives. But both are necessary, and the world needs more of both types of spies.

The best and the brightest serve our country as intelligence operatives, intelligence officers, and intelligence analysts.

They just can't talk about it.

APPENDIX

AN INTELLIGENCE PRIMER

You will have noted by now that we spent substantial time throughout this book working through the analytical steps toward each of our conclusions—that is, *applying and developing critical thinking.* Our goal was to allow you, the reader, to serve in the role of an intelligence analyst, working through all the possible and logical conclusions. We hope you have enjoyed this process as much as we have enjoyed creating these exercises.

We will now provide you with an overview of real-world intelligence analysis and topics, including dealing with the press and media and an introduction to diplomacy.

A. INTELLIGENCE AND THE INTELLIGENCE CYCLE

Intelligence in the spy world is information that is carefully gathered and evaluated. Some of this information is obtained by spies through espionage; other information is obtained through other means, such as **open-source** information. It is important to appreciate the fact that the gathering and receipt of such information is just the first phase of the intelligence cycle. Once the hard data is procured or gathered, it must be organized and analyzed by professional intelligence analysts before it can be forwarded as an intelligence **product**

to the appropriate decision-makers.

The intelligence cycle is a sophisticated and organized plan in which a country obtains and uses intelligence information. The gathering of specific intelligence generally must serve some important purpose. We do not just simply gather every bit of information we can, but instead organize ourselves in a way in which we can obtain important and essential information that can be used to determine policy.

Generally speaking, most intelligence entities employ the following intelligence cycle:

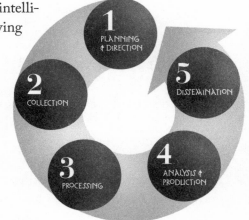

1. Planning & Direction

2. Collection

3. Processing

4. Analysis & Production

5. Dissemination

Planning and direction, the first step, is led by certain entities within the intelligence community that identify the primary issues and categorize the types of information that are most important to obtain. The person assigned the ultimate responsibility for intelligence collection and dissemination is the Director of National Intelligence (DNI). This position was created in the aftermath of the 9/11 terrorist attack on the United States, and the DNI was given the responsibility to "oversee and direct the implementation of the National Intelligence Program" (Intelligence Reform and Terrorism Prevention Act of 2004, codified at 50 U.S.C. 403(b)(3)).

More specifically, the new law directed the DNI to "determine requirements and priorities for, and manage and direct the tasking of, collection, analysis, production, and dissemination of national intelligence" (50 U.S.C. 403–1(f)(1)(A)(ii)). The DNI is advised on the production, review, and coordination of national intelligence by the National Intelligence Board, a group that includes the DNI, the Principal Deputy DNI, the Deputy DNI for Collection, the Chair of the National Intelligence Council, and the directors of most of the major intelligence organizations.

The next aspect of the intelligence cycle is **collection**, the aspects relating to gathering the information through spies, the use of open-source information, or other means, such as spy satellites, **surveillance**, wiretapping, interception of communications, and all other aspects of spying, including technological aspects.

The third intelligence cycle is **processing**. You can imagine how many intercepts and bits of data the National Security Agency alone obtains. Consider just the number of telephone calls that are intercepted and retrieved! Substantial foreign-language information is also gleaned from open sources, such as newspapers from other countries, and must be translated. In other words, the information *received* must be *organized* in a manner and language that can be used by the intelligence community.

The next intelligence cycle is **analysis**. As you can see from much of what we've done in this book, developing analytical skills is essential to both a **spy** and to the **intelligence analyst**. One must *do* something with the information beyond simply organizing it in a fashion that is understandable. It must be carefully *reviewed* and *analyzed* in a manner that results in *valid conclusions*. In addition, the information must be *compared with previous information* received or with *additional information* from some other source.

Oftentimes a different source is used for purposes of *collaboration*, sometimes resulting in the collection of contradictory information. Where lives or important policy decisions are at stake, the facts must be checked and double checked.

NOTE TO SELF: *Only through proper and careful analysis can information lead to a valid conclusion.*

One of the most important aspects of evaluating an enemy is determining the enemy's capabilities and intentions. This information is compiled by the National Intelligence Council in a document called an **intelligence estimate**. This can only be done through proper analytical study within the context of all information previously received and presently obtained.

The next aspect of the intelligence cycle is **production**. All the information obtained and received needs to be synthesized in a product that can be used by the person who makes the decisions, normally referred to as the policy maker. There are many types of products, everything from general reports on the chronology and history of a country, for example, to specific products describing the *capabilities* of a particular country or enemy. The person who creates the product must present the information not only concisely and accurately, but also in a manner that clarifies not only what *is* known, *but also what is not known*. In other words, the description of any weaknesses in the information or the conclusions provided is essential to any worthy intelligence product.

The next area of the intelligence cycle is **dissemination**, or distribution, to the correct person or persons so that proper decisions can be made. The best-known intelligence product is the President's Daily Brief, which is given to the president of the United States every day. This brief is also distributed to senior administration officials, including the vice president, the chairman of the Joint Chiefs of Staff, and several cabinet-level officials. The brief is prepared by the CIA and delivered to the president in person by a CIA briefer. An excellent history of the President's Daily Brief is contained in *For the President's Eyes Only* by Christopher Andrew (1995). According to Andrew, the precursor to the Daily Brief was a daily summary provided to President Harry Truman beginning in 1946 (Andrew 197). Following the 1961 Bay of Pigs disaster, the CIA attempted to regain President Kennedy's trust by supplying him with what they then called the President's Intelligence Checklist. This document was delivered by a CIA analyst every day just after 8:00 a.m. and contained an ultrasensitive operations report, which Kennedy loved to read. The analyst remained to answer any questions the president had (266).

President Johnson, however, had little interest in daily briefings (Andrew 309) and President Richard Nixon denounced the CIA en masse as a bunch of "Ivy League liberals" (350). Nonetheless, the daily briefings continued to be distributed, and Vice President Gerald Ford received a briefing regularly from William Colby, Deputy Director for Intelligence (398), and continued to take it throughout his presidency.

President Jimmy Carter found the President's Daily Brief very valuable and instructed that it be distributed to his vice president and the secretaries of state and defense. But he received the briefing not from the CIA, but instead solely from his national security advisor, Zbigniew Brzezinki, who had been briefed by the CIA earlier (430). President George H. W. Bush was very familiar with the President's Daily Brief, as he served as director of the CIA from January 1976 to January 1977 under President Ford. All presidents since then have received the briefing, some preferring to just read it and not be personally briefed by a CIA analyst, and others wanting the analyst present to answer questions.

One of the reasons for a *daily* briefing is providing *timely* information to the president. One of the most difficult tasks of an intelligence analyst is reaching a conclusion quickly—taking into account the limited information on hand—so that the policy maker has the most up-to-date information available when making the decision.

B. USES OF INTELLIGENCES

Obviously intelligence is used for many purposes. Intelligence can be used to analyze an enemy's **plans, capabilities, and intentions**, normally by means of a National Intelligence Estimate. Intelligence can also be used in the implementation of policy, or the planning or waging of a war. Intelligence can also be used *to prevent war*, defuse conflicts, or get through a particular crisis. From a budgeting or allocation standpoint, intelligence can be used to determine which research and development should be funded. For example, intelligence can serve as a basis not only for a *proactive* decision to fund a particular spy satellite, but also a *reactive* decision to counter or defeat a technology another nation is developing. And, of course, from a foreign affairs standpoint, intelligence can tell us about a country's human rights record and what type and amount of foreign aid should be offered. Lastly, intelligence can be used to verify important international issues, such as whether or not a country is complying with the terms of a treaty or is attempting to develop nuclear weapons.

C. TYPES OF INTELLIGENCE

There are numerous types of intelligence. As an overview, we provide this list of the most common types of intelligence:

political intelligence	information about a country or its leaders
military intelligence	information about the military powers and weaknesses of a particular country
scientific and technical intelligence	information about the technological aspects of a country and its military
sociological intelligence	information about the social aspects of a country or group within a country
economic intelligence	information about the economic situation of a country, or a business or other entity in that country

It is also important to realize that facts can be both static and dynamic. A *static fact* is a fact that tends not to change, such as the geography of a country, the country's history and culture, its political institutions, its economic resources, and its organizational structures. A *dynamic fact* is subject to change, such as the population of a country, the location of military troops, and the country's political leaders.

D. OBTAINING INTELLIGENCE

We have discussed numerous sources of intelligence in this book, especially open sources—documents that are public, such as newspapers, magazines, and political statements or pronouncements—and sources of **inside information**.

The intelligence community uses acronyms to designate the source or type of intelligence. The most common are HUMINT, ELINT, SIGINT, COMINT, GEOINT, IMINT or PHOTINT, MASINT, and OSINT.

Got all those?

Perhaps another table will help:

COMINT	Communications intelligence (part of SIGINT)
ELINT	Electronic intelligence (part of SIGINT)
GEOINT	Geospatial intelligence
HUMINT	Human intelligence
IMINT	Imagery intelligence (now GEOINT)
MASINT	Measures and signatures intelligence
OSINT	Open-source intelligence

PHOTINT	Photo intelligence (now GEOINT)
SIGINT	Signals intelligence
TELINT	Telemetry intelligence (part of SIGINT)

Human intelligence (HUMINT) is information obtained directly from individuals—either our own spies or some other person who is on the ground in a particular country and willing to provide us with important information. Such sources include anyone who may have official cover, persons who are in a country under **nonofficial cover**, **sleeper agents** (people undercover in the country for a long time), **walk-ins** (people who walk into an embassy and state their willingness to spy), and defectors (people who want to become citizens of another country against the wishes of their own). A **mole** is a person with a significant position in a governmental or spy agency who has **access** to essential information and is willing to relay it to another country.

There is also **communications intelligence (COMINT)**, **electronic intelligence (ELINT)**, and **telemetry intelligence (TELINT)**, all of which are now generally grouped into **signals intelligence (SIGINT)**. This realm of intelligence gathering involves everything from interception of phone calls to analysis of radar sites, sonar, and any information collected by electronic devices or technologies.

Other forms of intelligence include **photographic intelligence (PHOINT)** and satellite intelligence, which include photographs as well as standard radar or infrared imaging. Both are now generally grouped into geospatial intelligence (GEOINT). The National Geospatial-Intelligence Agency (formerly known as NIMA or the National Imagery and Mapping Agency) defines GEOINT as "information about any object—natural or man-made—that can be observed or referenced to the Earth, and has national security implications."

APPENDIX

Although undoubtedly offering an intentional oversimplification, one former director of the NSA once stated that IMINT tells you what *has* happened, while SIGINT tells you what *will* happen.

E. INTELLIGENCE ANALYSIS: POTENTIAL ERRORS AND BIASES

As you can imagine, despite our best efforts there have been many situations in which the conclusions reached by the analysts have been incorrect, occasionally resulting in incorrect policy decisions that resulted in misfortune, including loss of life. For all these reasons, it is important for the analyst to be aware of the weaknesses not only of the intelligence itself, but also of the analysis.

To that end we will now discuss six specific weaknesses or mistakes common to intelligence analysis:

1. Mirror Imaging

2. Stereotyping

3. Blindness

4. Overload

5. Timeliness

6. Politicization

Mirror imaging is when an analyst assumes that the enemy would act as if he or she would. In other words, instead of looking at the enemy objectively, the analyst looks at himself or herself *in the mirror* and analyzes what he or she would do under those circumstances. This is a major mistake because most enemies normally have not only different viewpoints and experiences, but also different ways of thinking and backgrounds in a different culture or mindset. In other words, when analyzing what another person or country would do, it is essential to take into account the specific differences and realities

553

of that particular person and country and *not* taint your analysis with personal views or biases.

The second weakness or mistake that can occur in intelligence analysis is *stereotyping*, a situation in which we automatically assume that all countries with shared characteristics or everybody within a country would act in the same way. As you can imagine, there are many different types of people, even in countries with the smallest populations. Moreover, people react differently to different things, even within one particular country. Stereotyping includes making a decision—intentional or otherwise—based on the analyst's preconceived notions, biases, and prejudices.

STEREOTYPING AND THE HARRY POTTER SERIES

A good example of a failure in analysis by stereotyping in the Harry Potter series is Professor Umbridge, who opens herself to manipulation by Hermione toward the end of book 5. When Harry and Hermione have been captured, Hermione convinces Umbridge that the "secret weapon" is not at Hagrid's hut but in the Forbidden Forest—using Umbridge's perception of Hagrid as an "oaf" and stating that Hagrid would not be given the weapon because he might accidentally set it off (*OP* 752).

The next intelligence weakness is *blindness*, which is simply looking through *the lens* of one's own narrow viewpoint as if through a telescope and deciding a particular issue only on that narrow view and not looking at the wider picture.

BLINDNESS AND THE HARRY POTTER SERIES

A good example of this in the Harry Potter series is the numerous times Harry and his friends assume Snape is a villain and not to be trusted. This continued bias prevented them from perceiving his true role.

~~~~~~

It is absolutely essential for an intelligence analyst to look beyond not only his or her own viewpoint, but his or her perceptions, to determine whether or not there are other areas that must be investigated and other points to be considered, and whether the analyst has correct **situational awareness** of the mistakes that he or she may be making.

The fourth intelligence weakness is *overload*, which is exactly what it sounds like: too much information to digest at one time. The amount of information that can be gathered, particularly electronically, is truly amazing. Luckily, thanks to computers that can sift through much of what is received, intelligence analysts have at least a chance of not being *totally* overwhelmed. But there is always more information than you'll ever need—somewhat like getting thousands of hits in a single Google search. The art and craft of intelligence analysis is seeing the big picture, determining which facts are really important, and applying all of the information received to the specific target or mission at hand.

Timeliness—or the lack of it—is the fifth weakness in intelligence analysis. If the information is late to the table or out of date, it often is of no value to the person requesting it. The information has little value if the decision has already been made, especially if it is too late to correct a bad decision. Thus, those who create intelligence must always take into account the needs of the person who will ultimately use that intelligence, including—quite significantly—*when* that information may be needed or *when* a decision needs to be made.

The last weakness or mistake in intelligence analysis is *politicization*. Intelligence analysis, including the content of the final product, should *not* take political sides. Even if the person receiving the intelligence has a political position or role, it is essential for the intelligence provider NOT to be influenced by the wants, needs, or desires of the person receiving the intelligence. A recent example of the alleged politicization of intelligence involved whether or not Iraq was attempting to make or actually developing weapons of mass destruction. A corollary of politicization occurs, by the way, when the intelligence is provided accurately and in an objective manner—to a person who then uses it for his or her *own* political aims, sometimes by selectively editing or cherry-picking information, or disclosing only selected portions of the information so as to reach the political result desired.

F. AN INTRODUCTION TO THE FIRST AMENDMENT AND THE PRESS

The Constitution was initially proposed without any Bill of Rights. The thirteen states, fearful of the power of a new federal government, refused to ratify or approve the new constitution without a Bill of Rights (similar to what the states already had in their respective constitutions), to be proposed immediately after ratification. The very first Congress did exactly that and, in 1791, proposed twelve amendments to the Constitution, ten of which were adopted and became our Bill of Rights.

The First Amendment includes rights relating to the freedom of the press, freedom of assembly, and freedom of association. The Bill of Rights was specifically intended to *limit* the powers of the federal government because the colonists—who had just thrown off the yoke of British rule—feared the power of the new governing body. An unfettered government can easily become tyrannical and, through the use of its courts and criminal laws, severely limit the freedoms expected in a free society.

The rights provided to the press through the First Amendment include the right to publish information *without prior restraint or government approval* and the right *not to be required to be licensed by the government*, particularly with regard to the *content* of what is published. This does not mean that the press has no limits. The press is held accountable through lawsuits for libel in the event that a newspaper or other publication distributes false information. However, such liability arises only if the person who has been wronged can *prove* that the newspaper or other entity printed the information *with a reckless disregard for the truth.*

This important balance of rights was articulated in *New York Times v. Sullivan*, a United States Supreme Court decision after the United States sued the *New York Times* to prevent it from publishing documents, known as the Pentagon Papers, many of them classified, showing the history of the Vietnam War. The Supreme Court refused to issue an injunction or "prior restraint" against that publication, despite the fact that publication would be detrimental to the interests of the US government. The court ruled that the government can limit the press from publishing information only if there is "a clear and present danger."

1. THE PRESS AND PUBLIC OPINION—"I'VE READ IT IN THE PAPER, SO IT MUST BE TRUE!"

It is important to realize that most people *believe* what they read in the papers, for better or ill. This fact alone explains many misperceptions and changes in **public opinion**—some warranted and some not. Particularly in a democracy, public opinion matters. The individuals reading the paper are the same individuals who decide who is going to be in power. As such, what the press says about an issue—or about a person—is very important indeed!

Another problem with the press and media is the fact that many people select a newspaper, magazine, or media outlet that parallels (if not parrots) their personal views. Thus, people who are fairly conservative and dislike President Obama and the Democratic Party tend to watch Fox News, where they receive positive reinforcement of their views, whether or not those views are factually correct. By the same token, these conservatives assert that certain newspapers, such as the *New York Times* and *Washington Post*, are bastions of the so-called liberal press and can't be trusted. Obviously, the best choice for the general population would be for individuals to gather infor-mation from at least three sources, one perceived as conservative, one perceived as liberal, and one perceived as neutral. Unfortunately, this seldom happens.

Another important press-related issue is that the number of owners of the media—that is, the number of people or entities in control of the press—has substantially *decreased* in the last decade or so. Thus, the "marketplace of ideas" shrinks in size and variety as the number of outlets drops.

There is an old saying that the truth shall set you free. We would assert that this is true—as long as the truth is actually disseminated and people have an opportunity to actually receive that information. The nice thing about lies is they tend to show themselves as lies even-tually, although that might take some time.

WHEN *THE QUIBBLER* SPEAKS THE TRUTH

As shown in book 5, *Harry Potter and the Order of the Phoenix*, many people came to Harry's side after *The Quibbler* published the truth specifically because *his version made more sense*—even though they did not want to believe that Voldemort had returned (*OP* 579, 583).

In our view, truth and lies are like snowballs rolling down a steep mountain in the winter. As a truth or a lie rolls down a hill, it gathers additional data points (more truths or untruths) that give it more weight or substance, as well as momentum. Distinguishing a truth from a lie is often quite difficult, and only by careful study and analysis can you determine the truth.

Only by thorough investigation and analysis can we get a chance at determining the truth. That is one reason this book focuses so much on critical thinking and the use of logic and common sense. Although it is easier to be spoon-fed whatever information the imme-diate outlet of choice provides, we assert that society—particularly a democratic society—is better served by an inquiring public, an inquiring press, and steadfast individuals who are willing to ask not only the right questions, but also the wrong ones!

2. REPORTERS: DEALING WITH RITA SKEETER AND THE LIKE

Both of the authors of this book have been interviewed by the press many times over the years, local and national, print and television. Getting the word out about an event or new exhibit—or better yet, getting the truth out about some important matter—is fun indeed, and is in some ways an art form. In the event that you have to deal with the press at some point, we provide you some basic guidelines to keep in mind when dealing with the press.

What reporters really want:

1. A good story

2. A good scoop

3. An opportunity to tell the story they envision

4. To relay the truth

What publishers and editors want:

1. Paper sales

2. Not to offend their readers

3. Sell papers

4. Have influence

5. Sell more papers

6. Appear all-knowing and powerful

HARRY POTTER AND THE ART OF SPYING

RULES TO FOLLOW:

1. Never lie

2. Only answer those questions you want to answer

3. Allow your answers, not the questions, to frame the discussion

4. Determine the reporter's slant or motive as soon as possible

5. Don't equivocate

6. If you don't know the answer, answer a different question or just say so (your choice)

7. Plan out and use pithy, understandable sound bytes

8. Remain calm and poised, no matter what

Number 7 is particularly important: you must select sound bytes and write out the most salient points *in advance* because most reporters are severely limited in the amount of space (or time) allotted to their article or segment. Although most interviews last a long time and delve into perhaps ten or twelve different issues or nuances, the portion of the interview actually used in the article or segment is necessarily abbreviated and focused primarily on the main issue under discussion. Does this mean that the rest of the interview is a waste of time? Absolutely not! The reporter is becoming educated on the other aspects of the main issue and may use this information in a subsequent story, or simply to better understand the entirety of the issue.

A good reporter will always identify himself or herself, the entity they work for, and the purpose of the interview. You should always assume that *anything said* to a reporter **AT ANY TIME UNLESS AGREED TO OTHERWISE** is **ON THE RECORD.**

What does "on the record" mean? On the record means that anything you say can and will be used by that paper and anyone who reads it!

APPENDIX

Unless you agree with the reporter *ahead of time*, everything you say can be used by that reporter for the intended article or segment. You cannot say something and have the option to suddenly withdraw that statement. Asserting that you didn't realize you were on the record doesn't count!

Four practical pointers:

1. Select a location for the interview where you are comfortable and, if possible, can have your notes in front of you.

2. Brush your hair and straighten your clothes *before* the camera starts to roll.

3. If you want to look like a pro at the beginning of an on-camera interview, hold up a blank sheet of white paper in front of you when the camera operator begins getting a focus on you; this allows the operator to adjust the camera's color balance.

4. Don't leave a reporter waiting past the assigned time for the meeting or press conference; reporters are always on a deadline, so start on time.

5. Be prepared to respond to (and perhaps provide) leaks.

6. For as long as there have been secrets, there have also been leaks. In the modern spy world, leaks are a fact of life. And quite often it is the press that publishes the leaks. It may also sometimes be your job to provide an (authorized) leak.

Leaks can be both positive and negative, intentional and accidental. Regardless of the origin or the intent behind the leak, it must be handled with the utmost care. Leaks often come from the top, not just some low-level person who happens to have access to the information.

SHIPS LEAK FROM THE BOTTOM, GOVERNMENTS FROM THE TOP

"The ship of state is the only known vessel that leaks from the top."

—James Reston, *New York Times*, November 9, 1946

Let us first discuss positive and intentional leaks. There are times when the government or a government official wants to get certain information out to the public, but without *officially* disclosing the information or having it attributed to the government or the person leaking the information. There are many ways to get such information out, and one of them is by a press interview in which you are "off the record" or merely providing *background* information. "Off the record" means that the information cannot be published, and most reporters will go to jail before revealing any of the information received.

The next steps removed from off-the-record status are *background* and *deep background*.

Background information can be used, but only in accordance with the agreement reached between the reporter and the source. Usually the source's main concern is that he or she not be named and any identifying factors not be revealed. Reporters can also be provided information off the record or as background *up to a certain date or time* when some act will become public. For example, there are situations in which reporters are provided with an advance copy of a speech, report, or other important document with the understanding that the reporter cannot report it until the date and time the document is made public by the person giving the speech, publishing the report, or otherwise distributing the information.

Another example of using background information is when a national security reporter finds out something that is highly classified and that the government does not want released at the time. Public officials have the option of inviting the reporter or publisher in and explaining exactly why the information should not be published. The press may withhold the information based on a duty to country, or may be offered a quid pro quo (something for something) agreement promising that reporter or news entity inside information when the matter can or does become public.

Deep background is information provided that can be used *without attribution* (in any way) to the person providing it.

THE ASSOCIATED PRESS'S DEFINITIONS

On the record: The information can be used with no caveats, quoting the source by name.

Off the record: The information cannot be used for publication.

Background: The information can be published, but only under conditions negotiated with the source. Generally, sources do not want their names published but will agree to a description of their position. AP reporters should object vigorously when a source wants to brief a group of reporters on background and try to persuade the source to put the briefing on the record. These background briefings have become routine in many venues, especially with government officials.

Deep background: The information can be used, but without attribution. The source does not want to be identified in any way, even on condition of anonymity.

In general, information obtained under any of these circumstances can be pursued with other sources to be placed on the record.

One historic example of giving the press prior access to top-secret information is when President Truman allowed William Laurence, a *New York Times* science reporter, months of access to various secret military locations used in the Manhattan Project before the dropping of the first atomic bomb. As a result, on August 10, 1945, the day after the first atomic bomb was dropped, the *New York Times* ran a large front-page story describing many of the details of the development of this new weapon of mass destruction. The public thus had immediate access to verified facts rather than wild and unsubstantiated speculation about the bomb and its development.

DEEP THROAT: THE SPY RUNNING HIS PRESS OFFICERS

Perhaps the most famous source in modern investigative reporting is Deep Throat, the individual who provided background information to Carl Bernstein and Bob Woodward of the *Washington Post* when they were investigating President Nixon's connections to the Watergate cover-up. In 1972, some of President Nixon's people broke into the Democratic National Committee headquarters in the Watergate office complex in Washington, DC, intending to photograph confidential documents and bug the office. (Ironically, the people were hired to conduct this **covert operation** by CREEP, the Committee to RE-Elect the President.) An alert security guard noticed black tape on a door latch and called the police. The burglars were caught and arrested, and several of them turned out to have been previously employed by the CIA.

Nixon and his cronies decided it would be necessary to pay these "employees" off so that they would remain silent and not disclose the fact that CREEP had hired them. Thus began the Watergate cover-up, which eventually resulted in President Nixon resigning from office in disgrace.

The press was somewhat interested in the story of five people breaking into the Democratic National Headquarters, but no one seemed to think it led anywhere and the story was dropped by almost everyone, except for Woodward and Bernstein.

These two reporters began receiving information from a confidential source that led them slowly and carefully in the right direction. They met their source, codenamed Deep Throat, in an unlit parking garage. Whenever they needed to meet, one of the reporters would signal by putting a flag in the flowerpot on his balcony. Thanks to the information from their source, the reporters discovered that the money used to pay the **operatives** came from donations to the president's reelection committee. This meant that the president's own people, including former Attorney General John Mitchell, were involved. Deep Throat told them that the conspiracy went much higher—and the two reporters finally discovered the truth.

In this situation, it was *not* the reporters running the spy, but rather the spy running *the reporters*. He told them what to do and what to look for, and they eventually found what they needed.

Thirty years later, Deep Throat revealed his identity as Mark Felt, a senior FBI executive. Up until that time, there were many discussions about who Deep Throat was—indeed, John Dean (who worked for Nixon at the White House and eventually told Congress about all of Nixon's illegal conduct) wrote a book examining every person who might possibly have been Deep Throat and selecting his best guess—which was wrong, by the way.

Think of the information you provide to the press as pieces of a puzzle. Some of these pieces are single, and a few have been fitted together. You might not give the reporter all of the pieces, and you might not even have them all yourself. When the issue comes to the public's notice, the reporter dumps the pieces on the table and figures out what each shows and how they fit together.

One point about interviews: Do not be upset if the information you provided to a member of the press is published with inaccuracies. Most newspaper articles and video segments contain minor mistakes or incorrect assumptions. Most reporters are on a deadline and have only enough time to address the most salient points and to briefly comment on the opposing side in a fair manner.

One other point about leaks: Given the increased use of computers in today's modern society, it is quite easy for someone to use a flash drive or some other device to quickly and efficiently download hundreds of thousands of documents and quietly—often anonymously—deliver those documents to a media outlet. The most famous example is the material provided to WikiLeaks by a young private stationed overseas who had access to hundreds of thousands of diplomatic cables, to the great embarrassment of the United States government.

Of course, one of the easiest ways to provide information is for somebody to make a copy of an important document, place it in an envelope without a return address, and send it to the press or the person who needs the information.

G. AN INTRODUCTION TO GOVERNMENT AND POLITICS

In the Muggle world, many governments are divided into three branches of government: legislative, executive, and judicial. The *legislative branch* is made up of individuals elected to represent groups or districts of people and comes together as a legislative body to pass laws. The *executive branch* consists of the leader of the country and the associated staff, who together implement (or *execute*) laws or decisions and manage the bureaucracy that underlies and administers the entire government. The *judicial branch* holds and decides trials and deals with both civil and criminal matters.

Most modern governments attempt to develop these three branches of government, with the intent that each branch will enforce

checks and balances on the other branch. For example, in the United States, the *legislative branch* at the national level consists of the House of Representatives and the Senate—the former with 435 members and the latter with 100 members. The House and Senate combined are called Congress. Congress passes all laws, which must then be presented to the executive, the president of the United States, for his or her approval. Thus, the legislative branch is checked and balanced by the executive branch, which can either sign the law or veto it. If the law is vetoed, the legislature can attempt to override the veto by a two-thirds majority vote of both houses.

By the same token, the legislature has a certain amount of control over the executive branch because it passes the budgets and appropriates money, in addition to passing laws that affect and sometimes direct the executive branch. In addition, many senior officials of the executive branch must be confirmed by the Senate in order to take their positions—which means that the Senate must vote to approve those selected by the president to assume office.

Lastly, the *judiciary branch* for the United States is the Supreme Court, which consists of nine judges who are appointed for life, but who must be confirmed and approved by the Senate before they can take office. The Supreme Court provides checks and balances on the legislature via its power to declare laws passed by Congress to be unconstitutional and therefore void. The Supreme Court also limits the powers of the executive branch through its decisions.

The framework of the US system is the Constitution, which creates in Article I the legislative branch, Article II the executive branch, and Article III the judicial branch. In theory, the powers of Congress are limited to those listed in the Constitution. However, these limits have not been entirely successful in limiting the power of the federal government, in part due to certain language in the Constitution that has been used to extend the power of Congress and the national government, such as the necessary and proper clause.

The British legal system, which Harry no doubt studied in his Muggle school, does *not* have a *written* constitution. Rather, it perceives itself as using a supreme law of the land based on the common law and the parliamentary system that evolved there over the centuries.

Moreover, the United States has not only the federal government, but also fifty separate state governments that have separate areas of control and lawmaking authority. This separation of powers into separate *federal* and *state* governments is called *federalism*.

Just as the Ministry of Magic passes certain decrees, the bureaucracy in the United States has the power to issue rules and regulations, and the president has the authority to issue executive orders. Many of the controls on the intelligence community, as well as the authorization for the CIA and other entities to take covert action, work through executive orders issued by the US president.

In the Muggle world, the use of torture to obtain information is a very divisive subject. After the 9/11 attacks on the World Trade Center and the Pentagon, the United States, under President George W. Bush, authorized the use of torture against individuals who had been captured and potentially had knowledge about Osama Bin Laden or terrorist organizations such as Al-Qu'ida. Many individuals, including Barack Obama while running for office, objected to this use of torture. Many nations consider the use of torture to be unconscionable and a violation of international human rights and international law.

H. AN INTRODUCTION TO DIPLOMACY

The primary system of international organization is nations. Nations are recognized through a formal process of diplomatic recognition. When one country recognizes another, the two countries establish that they are willing to negotiate with each other and to accept each other's ambassadors. An ambassador represents one country to another country. In order to protect individuals who will represent their own governments in a foreign country, ambassadors and other senior diplomatic officials receive *diplomatic immunity*. This status means that the host country cannot criminally prosecute the diplomat for any crimes whatsoever. Although this seems extreme, it is essential that diplomats be able to go to another country without fear of arrest or other restriction by that country. Although diplomats do commit crimes on occasion (and to which they are immune), it rarely happens. And when it does happen, that person is asked to leave.

There are several ways by which to communicate with another nation. One is *signaling*, in which you make statements or proposals that the other side is able to perceive and analyze. Once the other side is willing to communicate, we reach the next step: *negotiation*. Negotiation is, by definition, a formal discussion between two countries through the authorized representatives of each country.

1. LAWS, CUSTOMS, AND MORES

Laws are the formal decisions made by an entity authorized to act for a sovereign body or nation. *Customs* and *mores* are actions taken by a cohesive group of individuals: sometimes a complete nation, sometimes a group or portion of a nation (sect), and sometimes a group that has a particular common aspect, such as members of a specific organized religion. It is against the law in some countries for women to drive. It is a custom in some countries that women will wear a shawl or burka over their head so their faces will not be seen. Some countries allow a man to have many wives, and others state that a man or a woman can be married to one person only.

There is a saying: "When in Rome, do as the Romans do." This simply means that when you are in a particular country, you should abide by that country's laws, and its customs and mores.

In our view, diplomacy is a chess game in which both the pieces *and* the squares move.

The operational format is, in reality, the application of the basic concepts of contract law, in which the requirements for the creation of a contract apply equally well to the requirements to reach an accord, agreement, or treaty: there must be an offer, an acceptance, and a meeting of the minds. When this occurs, normally we have an agreement that can be enforced by either party. One exception is when a particular country must supply separate approval from the elected representatives of that country, such as ratification of the US Senate by a two-thirds vote.

There are both public negotiations and private negotiations. Most negotiations occur in private and are in that regard *covert*. It is often best for both countries to be able to discuss details in private and make them public only once a full agreement has been reached.

2. THE ORIGINS OF INTERNATIONAL LAW

In order to understand diplomacy, it is essential to understand the basics of international law. Unlike the laws that are passed by Congress, which are written down and become statutes, international law is fluid and based on the history of the decisions made by the international community.

International law is based, in a large part, on the very early laws of the Roman Empire, some of them defined as natural law. In Medieval Europe, the church—overwhelmingly the Roman Catholic Church—was a powerful political entity. Moreover, the church's structure and method of organization served as a basis for many nascent political systems. In the tenth century the Roman Catholic Church instituted a "Peace of God" by which it attempted to impose limits on war, violence, and plundering. A later decree entitled "The Truce of God," in 1041, attempted to limit the scope of violence in medieval Europe and actually prohibited fighting between Wednesday evening and Monday morning of each week!

The true father of international law, however, is Hugo Grotius (1583–1645), who attempted to codify international law in his 1625 treatise *On the Law of War and Peace*. Much of what Grotius developed was implemented in perhaps the most famous treaty of all, the 1648 Treaty of Westphalia, which formalized the concept of the nation-state and was the first attempt to develop international law among the new nation-states.

APPENDIX

There are five primary sources of international law:

1. International conventions (also known as treaties)

2. International custom

3. General principles of law recognized by civilized nations

4. Judicial decisions

5. Teachings of highly qualified jurors of various nations

In addition, international law is divided into two parts. The first is private international law, which focuses on such issues as application of international law to particular persons, including diplomatic immunity, extradition, sharing information, passports and visas, and other general issues. The second type is public international law, which relates to the nation-to-nation agreements dealing with everything from peace and trade to national security.

3. THE ETHICS OF WAR: "JUST" AND "UNJUST" WARS

There is a very specific area of international law relating to wars. The issue of war and nations has been around a long time, and indeed, in the fifth century, St. Augustine attempted to define the idea of a "just war" that was acceptable within Christian morality declaring that the commandment against killing did not prohibit the killing of "wicked men." In the 1200s, Thomas Aquinis added much to the concept of a "just war" and asserted certain rules for going to war, including that the war must be for a good purpose and the primary motive must be peace. In the seventeenth century, Grotius's famous treatise, mentioned above, delved into matters of defense of person and property, the right of conquest, and prisoners of war.

Concerning war, Grotius attempted to develop two major constructs: the justice of war (*jus ad bellum*), in which he described three just reasons for war (self-defense, reparation of injury, and punishment), and justice *in* war (*jus in bello*), describing the rules that apply in the conduct of war, whether or not the cause is just. In the first case, you must determine whether the war is just and moral; the second sets out the rules that would apply once the war has commenced.

These are all issues that continue up to today, including the issue of military necessity, the right of deterrence, and in what situations a country can "defend" itself even though it has not yet been formally attacked or its borders illegally crossed. There are additional issues relating to genocide and terrorism, among others.

4. THE CLASH OF CIVILIZATIONS VS. THE NATION-STATE

In 1992, political scientist Samuel Huntington presented a lecture entitled "The Clash of Civilizations." In it, Huntington argued that after the end of the Cold War, the traditional political boundaries of countries would have less and less significance as time passed, and future conflicts would thus be between *civilizations* (such as different religious groups) instead of between countries. (The lecture was adapted into an article for *Foreign Affairs* and later expanded into a book.)

You could argue that our modern war on terrorism is just that, a clash of civilizations. We would assert, however, that nations still have importance and meaning, that borders have significance, and at least the primary organizational structure creating political stability, distribution of goods, and social harmony remains the political institutions we call countries.

Though this organizational scheme does have faults—such as countries that refuse to allow political or intellectual freedom or liberty—it presently does more good than harm. Since few things remain constant, it is possible for the world to move toward one or the other extreme.

First, it is possible that Huntington's theory is absolutely correct and that the nation-states' reliance on borders will eventually fall apart and be replaced by smaller regions organized by the predominant religious or cultural aspects of their peoples. Our world would break into thousands of pieces, like hundreds of disjointed shards of a broken mirror still collected in the mirror's frame.

The second direction the world may possibly take is the opposite possibility, greater unification, with international treaties and covenants creating a unified system of laws and interconnections making borders basically irrelevant. To use a science-fictional example, the world might unite in a federation of countries, and then of worlds, a la Star Trek.

5. DEALING WITH WAR IN THE AGE OF TERRORISM

In the realm of foreign policy, we deal with issues of war and retribution every day. Some of the issues are relatively easy, such as what constitutes a clear act of war. Obviously if somebody attacks you—that is, if a particular *country* attacks you—then you have the right of *self-defense* to prevent the attack from succeeding, and the right of *retribution* for the attack.

In olden days, war was generally declared when one *country* attacked another *country*, and the decision of how to deal with such an attack was usually quite clear: defend, and then attack back. The best example of this is the bombing of Pearl Harbor, the declaration of war against Japan, and the subsequent entrance of the United States into World War II.

Things get a little more complicated when some *individuals* from one nation attack another nation. The issue then becomes, did those individuals have authority, explicit or implicit—or support, direct or indirect—in taking action against the country that was attacked? This becomes a very gray and messy area indeed!

A few modern examples of retribution against a government for the actions of its people come to mind immediately. In 1988, Pan Am Flight 103 blew up above Lockerbie, Scotland, killing all 259 people onboard and eleven people below. Through superb intelligence-gathering and analysis, the bombing was directly tied to the Libyan government, specifically several Libyan intelligence agents who assisted in planning this act of terrorism. As a result, numerous sanctions were placed on the Libyan government, punishing the government for an attack by individual citizens—individuals who should have been under the control of that country.

The more recent example occurred, of course on September 11, 2001, when four planes were hijacked by terrorists who had trained in Afghanistan and received direct support from its government. The terrorists crashed two planes into the towers of the World Trade Center in New York City and another into the Pentagon; the fourth was diverted from its intended Washington, DC, target and crashed in a field after passengers attempted to regain control. It was clear that the country of Afghanistan, which was then run by the Taliban, had supported these activities. As a result, the United States attacked Afghanistan.

Things become a little more complicated when you have not been attacked, but the opposing country is hostile to you. A recent example is the country of Iraq in the early 1990s, whose leader, Saddam Hussein, was vehemently anti-American. Although he did not attack the United States, he did attack Kuwait; the United States took action to protect Kuwait and began the Gulf War (or the First Iraq War). Kuwait was liberated and its borders secured.

The question then became whether or not it was appropriate to continue the battle onward, into the previously invading country. If borders are indeed sacred (our reason for protecting Kuwait), then shouldn't the sanctity of borders *prevent* the United States from invading Iraq? At what point are we justified in a preemptive attack? Whatever the proper analysis may be, the United States and its coalition did indeed invade Iraq, and we fought there for more than ten years.

6. FRIENDLY COMPETITION AND PING-PONG DIPLOMACY

Friendly competition is a very good means of getting two sides together, even two countries that are enemies—or at least antagonists. An excellent example is President Nixon and Mao Zedong's development of relations between the Western world and China by—you'd never believe it—Ping-Pong (also known as table tennis)!

In 1972, things were not looking good for President Nixon. Although he was on his way to reelection by a landslide, his domestic policies were in shambles and the Vietnam War continued unabated. Nixon, one of the nation's foremost anticommunists, decided to throw a Hail Mary and began trying to develop relations with China, which was then and still is ruled by the Communist Party. The catalyst for this amazing diplomatic about-face was an American table tennis player who missed his bus!

The US Table Tennis team was in Nagoya, Japan, in 1971 for the thirty-first World Table Tennis Championship. One of the American players, Glenn Cowan, and a Chinese player were playing a practice game when they were told that they had to leave, practice was over. Cowan, however, had missed his team bus, and the Chinese player waved him onto Chinese team's bus for a ride back to the hotel. Cowan did so, and through translators they did their best to communicate and give each other gifts. When Cowan arrived at the hotel and got off the bus, he was observed by a reporter who asked if he would like to visit China. Cowan said, "Of course!" The article was picked up by the international press, and Chairman Mao Zedong, leader of China, invited the American players and their wives to visit. They and their spouses visited China from April 11 through April 17, 1971.

This event opened the door to other exchanges, and a year later President Nixon himself visited China. Soon thereafter, the United States began trading with China. Indeed, the success using a sports event to thaw cold relations is now known as Ping-Pong diplomacy.

There is a saying: Only Nixon could go to China. The point is that Nixon, as a solid anticommunist, could get away with opening relations with China (a Communist country). And as a result, China today is our largest trading partner—and still a Communist country.

Much of the basic information shared here on the intelligence cycle, mistakes in the use of intelligence, and diplomacy is derived (with permission from the authors) from an excellent college textbook by Dean A. Minix and Sandra M. Hawley, Global Politics *(1998), which Lynn used in his course in International Relations. Unfortunately, this wonderful book is out of print.*

A GLOSSARY OF SPY TERMS

access—authorization to receive information that is limited to a select group of people who have the correct security clearance. *Example:* Members of the Order of the Phoenix attended the meetings at number twelve, Grimmauld Place, but Harry and his friends were not allowed to attend the meetings because of their age and not yet being members of the Order of the Phoenix.

accommodation address—a mailbox used as a drop point for mail. In the modern world, it applies not only to an actual mailbox, but also a person or business willing to accept the mail, or even a special email address that does not indicate the actual name of the address owner. *Example:* When Harry was staying at the Weasleys' home, before his second year at Hogwarts began, the Burrow served as his accommodation address.

administrative orders—orders or directives issued by an agency authorized to do so and directed at individuals or an entire group. *Example:* The educational decrees issued by the Ministry of Magic at the request of Professor Umbridge are administrative orders.

agent—an individual who is hired or employed by a country, or is acting on his or her own, to spy or obtain inside information; that information may be given or sold to a country or another entity. *Example:* Professor Quirrell and Peter Pettigrew both served as agents for Voldemort, assisting him in regaining his corporeal body.

agent in charge—The particular agent who is in charge of the details or operation of the mission. *Example:* On two occasions when Harry was moved from Privet Drive to another location, the agent in charge was Mad-Eye Moody.

agent-in-place (mole)—an individual who is "in place" and has access to information or knowledge, and who stays in that location in order to continue providing information or knowledge. *Example:* The Auror Kingsley Shacklebolt served as an agent-in-place at the Ministry, ostensibly looking for Sirius Black but in reality providing information to the Order of the Phoenix about not only the search for Sirius Black, but also about the Ministry's knowledge as to the actions of Lord Voldemort or his Death Eaters.

agent of influence—an agent with the ability to influence leaders of a country or the press by providing special information or insight that could result in a change of policy or public opinion. *Example:* Lucius Malfoy provided suggestions and opinions to Cornelius Fudge about what to do with Harry and his claims that Voldemort was back.

agent provocateur—an individual who is normally on site in a different country and attempts to serve as a catalyst to get others to take actions that are desired by the country or entity that employs that person. *Example:* Lee Jordan was trying to provoke (and generally bother) Professor Umbridge by secretly placing nifflers in her office.

alibi—an assertion by a person that he or she was somewhere else when something occurred, showing that the person could not have participated in that event. *Example:* When the Niffler was put into Professor Umbridge's office, Hagrid had what should have been a perfect alibi because he was seen teaching on the grounds at the time.

all-source intelligence—intelligence derived from every type of intelligence available, including covert or secret intelligence. *Example:* In book 7, when trying to figure out the locations of the Horcruxes, Harry uses every source of information available to him: the information Dumbledore shared with him, articles from the *Daily Prophet*, and even Rita Skeeter's tell-all book.

alternative explanation—a different explanation or reason for some occurrence or conclusion. *Example:* Harry went through many alternative explanations while trying to determine why he could see through the eyes of the snake, including being possessed by Voldemort.

analysis—the use of logic and observation to reach conclusions that are proper and based on fact. *Example:* Throughout book 7, Harry, Hermione, and Ron use analysis to determine where the Horcruxes are located.

appointment power—the authority of a high-ranking individual to select and appoint others to posts or positions in the organization. *Example:* Minister of Magic Fudge used his appointment power to install Professor Umbridge as the first Hogwarts High Inquisitor, and later as Headmistress of Hogwarts.

argument ad hominem—a fallacy in logic in which the position or viewpoint of a particular person is rejected based solely on a negative view of that person. *Example:* The *Daily Prophet* repeatedly rejected Harry's statements that Voldemort had returned by attacking him personally, making his credibility an issue, rather than by presenting hard evidence that Voldemort had not returned.

assessment—a formal review of the reliability or validity of information or intelligence, or the written version of such a review. *Example:* According to Fudge (who had just been sacked) there is going to be an inquiry about Sirius Black being murdered on Ministry of Magic premises; someone will be doing a formal assessment—and no doubt a written report will be

provided to the new Minister of Magic, Rufus Scrimgeour.

asset—something of value; in the spy world, an asset is an individual, technology, or other means to obtain intelligence. *Example:* Each time Harry was moved from number four, Privet Drive, members of the Order of the Phoenix formed a security team to protect Harry due to his being a high-value asset.

assumption of leadership—the act of taking over a particular position or leadership role. *Example:* Dolores Umbridge assumed leadership of Hogwarts after Dumbledore evaded capture and disappeared.

attaché—an expert assigned as a consultant to an embassy in a foreign country knowledgeable about a particular subject; if the person is an active duty military person, he or she is referred to as a *military attaché. Example:* Kingsley Shacklebolt, an expert on the Wizarding world and magical defense, is the Ministry of Magic's attaché to the Other Prime Minister.

Aunt Minnies—photographs taken to capture an item of interest *in the background* of what appears to be an innocent candid photo: for example, your "Aunt Minnie" poses in the foreground, with a building targeted for covert penetration in the background. It is a common pretext for photographing a target without *appearing* to be gathering information covertly. *Example:* In the picture of Ron and his family on holiday in Egypt you can see a Pyramid in the background, and of course Scabbers on Ron's shoulder. If the person taking the photo were really interested in something else (like the Pyramid, or even Scabbers!) and the use of the family was just an excuse to take the picture of something *other than* the family, then the photo would be an Aunt Minnie.

background—prior and historic information about an individual. *Example:* Throughout book 6, Dumbledore helps Harry research Voldemort's history in depth by examining the collected memories shared in the Pensieve.

background check—an exceedingly thorough review of a person's history; in the world of espionage, a background check usually involves an investigator meeting with hundreds of the subject's personal and professional contacts. *Example:* In book 6, Dumbledore does a thorough background check on Tom Riddle, researching and interviewing anyone who had contact with or information about Tom Riddle.

backstopping—the act of providing confirmation for a cover story so that it remains believable. *Example:* In book 7, Snape gives the real date and time for Harry's move from the Dursleys home, proving both that he has correct, inside information and is still loyal to Voldemort.

baiting the enemy—attempting, through words or actions, to provoke an opponent into a reaction, often an irrational reaction. *Example:* At the end of one of the Quidditch matches, Draco Malfoy baited Harry and the Weasley twins into attacking him, resulting in Professor Umbridge imposing a lifetime ban on Harry and the Weasley twins.

barium—a Russian term used for false information created for the purpose of catching a spy. False or nonessential information is provided to a suspected double agent; if that information shows up in enemy hands, it confirms the existence and usually the identity of the double agent.

basic intelligence—static or slow-changing information about a nation, such as its physical attributes, political structure, language, history, and culture. *Example:* Before Hagrid left on his recruiting mission, Professor Dumbledore provided him with basic intelligence on the giants, including their location, culture, and psychological attributes.

bias—an inclination, not necessarily based on facts or sound reasoning, toward or against a particular person or group. *Example:* Professor Umbridge has a bias against half-breeds, which came to light (much to her eventual dismay) in her discussions with the centaurs.

black bag job—a surreptitious or covert entry into a home, office, or other location without the knowledge of the owner. The term originates from the need to bring a black bag full of tools by which to gain entry, such as lock-picking tools. A black bag job is successful when the person gains entry, obtains the information desired or places surveillance devices, and leaves undetected and without the knowledge of the person who works or lives there. *Example:* Harry's first covert visit to Professor Umbridge's office to talk to Sirius is a successful (though not perfect) black bag job.

blackmail—using information about someone to force them to do something for you. *Example:* By threatening to disclose Rita Skeeter as an unregistered Animagus, Hermione blackmailed the reporter into writing a true article about what happened to Harry at the end

of the Triwizard Tournament, when Voldemort returned.

blind date—a meeting of a spy or agent with an unknown or untrusted contact at a time and place chosen by that contact; the meeting has high potential to be a trap. *Example:* Hagrid met with an unknown person or blind date and obtained a dragon's egg (after providing information on Fluffy).

blowback—negative consequences derived from an intelligence operation or false information distributed by an intelligence agency. *Example:* Voldemort's operation to get Harry to retrieve the prophecy resulted in the disclosure of Lucius Malfoy and the others as active Death Eaters.

bribe—an offer of money or other valuable inducement to convince the recipient to do what the offerer wants. *Example:* Although readers do not see an exchange of money, Mr. Weasley asserts that the money Lucius Malfoy gives to Cornelius Fudge and the Ministry of Magic is in exchange for information and influence.

brush contact—a brief, discreet transfer of information, documents, money, or other items in public between two agents, one of whom is presumed to be under surveillance. The agents do not speak or even acknowledge each other, so that the meeting appears to be no more than an accident. *Example:* Although not explicitly described in the book, we suspect that many students exchanged or transferred Harry's interview in *The Quibbler* to each other surreptitiously as they passed each other in the hallway.

bug—an electronic surveillance device that can intercept phone calls and other communications, or that can transmit auditory data from the bugged room. A common device consists of a microphone attached to a tiny radio frequency transmitter that broadcasts all noise in the room to the spy's receiver. *Example:* Animagus Rita Skeeter, in her beetle form, can sneak into a room and overhear private conversations—literally "bugging" a room!

burn—the act of a government, intelligence agency, or senior agent allowing the capture, disclosure, or death of one of its agents. *Example:* Voldemort burns his unwitting agent, Bode, by delivering a Devil's Snare plant to his hospital bedside so that he would be eliminated.

burn bag—a bag or device in which confidential documents are placed and then immediately destroyed to avoid capture or

exposure. Originally, a burn bag containing documents to be destroyed was sealed and then ignited, destroying all contents. As the amount of documents to be destroyed increased, small incinerators were placed on spy ships and other locations, allowing larger amounts of confidential material to be sealed into a larger compartment, in which the documents are quickly incinerated. With the advent of computers, more modern methods are employed, such as flash drives containing software that quickly and efficiently destroys all documents and traces of all documents on the target computer, if not the hard drive itself!

cell—a group, usually of three to seven persons, that is working together on a combined project or mission. Members often do not know of each other's existence, with only one individual serving as the common denominator (center spoke). Alternately, for security reasons, each person may know only *one* other person in the cell (a single spoke on the wheel). *Example:* Dumbledore's Army is a cell of students assembled to practice Defense Against the Dark Arts on their own.

character analysis—the act and art of evaluating a person's character and drawing conclusions about how that person will act in certain situations. *Example:* Hermione understands Professor Umbridge's weaknesses and biases and therefore concludes that the new Headmistress will insult the centaurs and possibly give her and Harry a chance to escape.

checks and balances—input and limitations applied by one branch of government to another. For example, in the United States, the Senate must confirm judges; judges determine the constitutionality of legislation; and courts can declare the acts of the president illegal or invalid. *Example:* During Harry's trial, the executive branch (Fudge) ran the trial, showing a lack of checks and balances in Wizarding government, thus demonstrating that the judicial branch is vulnerable to being used as a tool to enforce the policies of the central government, the Ministry of Magic.

chicken feed—confidential information intentionally supplied to an enemy by a double agent in order to convince the enemy that the double agent is working for that organization and providing valuable information. By definition, the amount of information

provided is only an amount necessary to convince the enemy that the agent is on its side. *Example:* Severus Snape provides Voldemort with substantial, but not exhaustive, information in order to convince Voldemort that Severus is on his side, including the correct day of Harry's departure from number four, Privet Drive.

CIA (Central Intelligence Agency)—the primary intelligence service of the United States, one of sixteen in the entire Intelligence Community, all of which are now under the Director of National Intelligence (DNI).

Classified—a low-level classification (higher than Confidential, but below Secret and Top Secret) of information, knowledge of which must be restricted to people who have the correct access or clearance to receive that information. *Example:* Hagrid mentions that his trip to Gringotts to retrieve an item from Vault No. 713 is "Hogwarts business." The information relates to Hogwarts and is restricted to those who have a need to know.

clean—a state in which no classified information on or in a document or location remains to be obtained. For instance, before classified documents can be released to the public, they are redacted: important words or names that must remain classified are blacked out, but the rest of the document may be seen by the public. *Example:* When Harry and his friends enter the kitchen after the Order of the Phoenix meeting, they see the building plans because the members had failed to insure that the room was clean.

clearance—the level of access available to confidential or secured information; levels include Confidential, Classified, Secret, Top Secret, and Sensitive Compartmented Information (code-word clearance required). *Example:* When asked what had been in Vault 713, Hagrid refuses to tell Harry and his friends because they don't have clearance for "Very secret, Hogwarts business" (*SS* 74).

code name—an alternative name for a person or thing that is known only to a limited number of people. *Example:* When Harry writes to his godfather, Sirius, he refers to him as Snuffles, the code name they had agreed upon. On the pirate radio show *Potterwatch,* the broadcasters use code names to hide their identities: Lee Jordan uses "River"; Kingsley Shacklebolt uses "Royal"; Lupin uses "Romulus"; and Fred

Weasley uses "Rapier" (instead of "Rodent").

code of ethics—a set of rules or norms that provide direction for ethical decisions in a profession. The intelligence community is developing a set of rules for analysts to provide direction in making independent judgments, not being swayed by political pressures, and other important ethical issues. *Example:* Throughout the series, Harry Potter develops his own code of ethics as he decides how to treat his friends (and his enemies), what methods he will use to achieve his desires, and how to determine right from wrong and then stand up for the right.

codes and code breaking—a code is method of disguising information so that the person or entity for whom that information is intended is the only person who can read or understand it. *Code breaking* is the art of taking a coded message and extrapolating its content. *Example:* The writing on the Mirror of Erised is written in code: the inscription, "Erised stra ehru oyt ube cafru oyt on wohsi" (*SS* 207), has been encoded by being written backwards and re-spaced. The true message reads, "I show not your face but your heart's desire."

A GLOSSARY OF SPY TERMS

Comint-Communications Intelligence—Any intelligence derived through interception of communications. *Example:* Harry's owl, Hedwig, had more than likely been intercepted and the message from Sirius read by the enemy. The message tied to Hedwig's foot is an example of communications intelligence.

communication device—any object that can be used to communicate; now usually an electronic device, such as a radio or a cell phone. *Example:* The mirror given to Harry by Sirius is a device that allows them to communicate, and later saves his life.

communication interception—the act of receiving a message, usually without the sender's permission or knowledge. *Example:* In book 5, Hedwig returns to Harry with an injury, suggesting that someone may have captured her for purposes of reading the letter she carried.

compromised—the state in which a secret, such as a person's role as a spy, has been exposed by the enemy, endangering the agent or the information. *Example:* Lucius Malfoy's secret status as a Death Eater is compromised when Harry escapes from the cemetery and identifies to Dumbledore the people who had answered Voldemort's summons once he returned to human form.

compromised communication—a message that has fallen into the hands of the enemy or third person. *Example:* The note that R.A.B. left in the replacement locket was compromised when it was retrieved and read by someone other than Voldemort.

concealment—the act of hiding something, often in plain sight. *Example:* Harry's Invisibility Cloak assists him on numerous occasions in concealing himself.

Confidential—a level of security classification below Secret and Top Secret. *Example:* The secret passages to and from Hogwarts are confidential and known to only a few people at Hogwarts.

consumer—the person or entity receiving intelligence information, such as a head of state or other senior official with decision-making authority. *Example:* Harry Potter, as the person destined to defeat Voldemort, is the ultimate consumer of the memories Dumbledore collected for the purpose of researching the history and nature of the Dark Lord.

Corona Project—one of the first spy satellite programs used to take photographic imagery of the Soviet Union in the 1960s, which ironically proved that the Russians were substantially behind the United States in nuclear weapons or intercontinental ballistic missiles (ICBMs).

counterintelligence—the use of intelligence or devices to prevent someone from spying on you. *Example:* In book 7, Hermione casts many spells and enchantments around their tent to prevent their discovery when they were on the run.

countermeasures—acts or devices that prevent someone from observing a spy's activities. *Example:* In order to prevent the children from listening in on the Order of the Phoenix's meetings with Extendable Ears, Mrs. Weasley employs countermeasures (an Imperturbable Charm) on the door.

counter surveillance—the practice of seeing whether you are being spied upon. *Example:* When Harry heads to the playground after being throttled by Uncle Dursley, he checks to see if someone is following him.

courier—a person who transfers a message from an agent to some other person or to headquarters. *Example:* Throughout the Harry Potter series, owls are used as couriers for information, a sometimes secure and sometimes not-so-secure method of communication.

cover, or **cover story**—a false story that provides an alternative for the truth, intended to conceal an agent's true reasons for being in a particular place. *Example:* The Dursleys tell their neighbors that Harry is gone during the school year because he is attending St. Brutus's Secure Center for Incurably Criminal Boys.

covert operation—an operation in which an agent or agents plan and complete a mission without anybody knowing the mission occurred. *Example:* When Harry uses Umbridge's office to talk to Sirius the first time, he leaves without being observed and makes sure to leave everything as it was when he entered so that Professor Umbridge would not know he had been there.

critical intelligence—intelligence of the highest level possible, normally distributed only to the most senior official in the government. *Example:* Fudge, after being relieved of his post as Ministry of Magic, provided critical intelligence to the "other" minister, the Prime Minister of the United Kingdom, about Voldemort's return and the actions of the Death Eaters within the Muggle world.

cryptography—the art and science of discerning messages from coded communications. *Example:* With the use of cryptography, Harry would have been able to read the coded message inscribed on the frame of the Mirror of Erised.

cultural sensitivity—the ability to understand, acknowledge, and, when appropriate, accept the ways of a different culture. *Example:* Although Hagrid used cultural sensitivity in his attempt to recruit the giants, the supposedly more sophisticated Dolores Umbridge totally failed to apply cultural sensitivity when talking with the centaurs, resulting in a rather knotty situation.

current intelligence—the most recent information on an enemy. *Example:* Whenever Harry "sees" what Voldemort is doing, he is receiving current intelligence on Voldemort, in real time.

cut out—a third person used as an intermediary between a spy and his or her handler so that the two main operatives are never seen together. *Example:* In book 7, Pius Thicknesse, the head of the Department of Magical Law Enforcement, is placed under an Imperius Curse and then used by Voldemort to communicate his orders to others in the Ministry of Magic.

dead drop—leaving an item at a preselected location. *Example:* Snape creates a dead drop by

leaving the Sword of Gryffindor in the pond for Harry to extract.

debriefing—a formal discussion and evaluation, after a mission is concluded, about how the mission went, both the positive and the negative, for the purpose of learning what can be done better next time. *Example:* At the end of many books in the series, Harry and Professor Dumbledore have a debriefing in which they discuss what happened, what it means, and often who is (not) to blame.

deep cover / deep cover agent—a mission or assignment so secret that only one or two people know of its existence; a deep cover agent usually stays put for many, many years, having little to no contact with his or her handlers. *Example:* Snape is a deep cover agent that no one knows about except Dumbledore.

Defense Intelligence Agency (DIA)—the US military intelligence agency, which is the largest intelligence agency for that country.

Directorate of Science and Technology—the CIA division that applies science and technology to trade craft. *Example:* The Weasley brothers use chemicals and magic to create jokes, diversions, and devices that can be used to hear others.

disguise—a change of apparel or appearance that makes a person unrecognizable. *Example:* Barty Crouch Jr., through the use of Polyjuice Potion, disguises himself as Professor Alastor Moody in order to manipulate the outcome of the Triwizard Tournament so that Harry will reach the Portkey first and be transported to the cemetery, where Voldemort awaits him. Many characters in the Harry Potter series use disguises: Professor McGonagall dresses like a Muggle, Professor Quirrell disguises himself as a frightened bumbler, Mundungus Fletcher wears a disguise when he is eavesdropping on the initial meeting of Dumbledore's Army at the Hog's Head, and Tonks is able to disguise herself merely by bespelling her looks!

disinformation—intentionally incorrect information, often provided to an enemy for the purpose of influencing the enemy's actions. *Example:* Hermione, when captured by Umbridge and the members of the Inquisitorial Squad, lies about hiding Dumbledore's secret weapon in the Forbidden Forest; as a result, Umbridge takes Harry and Hermione to the Forbidden Forest, where they

are able to escape, thanks to the centaurs and Grawp.

disinformation campaign—an intentional program of distributing false information. *Example:* After Harry asserts that Voldemort is back, the *Daily Prophet* produces a series of articles describing Harry as a show-off looking for attention, circulating disinformation in order to undermine his credibility.

diversion—an occurrence or idea that results in a person shifting attention away from the immediate situation, going elsewhere, or concluding something different than the truth. *Example:* In order to assist Harry in getting into Professor Umbridge's office the first time, the Weasley twins create a diversion that takes Umbridge away from her office.

double agent—an agent employed by one entity but working in reality for another entity or person. *Example:* Snape is a double agent who is working for Dumbledore and spying on Voldemort, who thinks Snape is *his* agent!

double back—the act of turning around and going past a spot where you have just been. *Example:* When Mad-Eye Moody leads the security team retrieving Harry from number four, Privet Drive, in book 5, he

A GLOSSARY OF SPY TERMS

considers doubling back to make sure no one is following them.

dry cleaning—actions taken to ensure you are not under surveillance. *Example:* One of the functions of a Sneakoscope is to determine whether anyone is near and observing you.

eavesdropping—surreptitiously listening to someone's conversation. *Example:* As a young Death Eater, Snape eavesdropped on Dumbledore as he met with Sybill Trelawney and overheard the first part of the prophecy, which he reported to Voldemort.

economic intelligence—information about a society's monetary system, financial power, and tools used to exchange goods and services. *Example:* The fact that Gringotts serves as the single bank and financial entity of the Wizarding world is a piece of economic intelligence.

egress—the act of leaving a particular place or country. *Example:* Every time Harry is "rescued" from the Dursleys', his rescuers are performing an egress.

electronic countermeasures—any electronic device that prevents an enemy from obtaining confidential information. *Example:* Although wizards do not seem to use electronics,

they do use magic to prevent being overheard, such as Mrs. Weasley's use of the Imperturbable Charm to defeat the twins' Extendable Ears during the meeting of the Order of the Phoenix.

electronic intelligence (ELINT)—the collection of any electronic signals or other information derived from such signals (such as the frequency used).

established source—any source that has been used regularly and found to be reliable. *Example:* While the *Daily Prophet* is considered an established source by the Wizarding world, *The Quibbler* is not.

executive order—an order issued by the president or another high-ranking official of the executive branch. *Example:* Throughout book 5, the Ministry of Magic issues educational decrees that give Dolores Umbridge extensive powers at Hogwarts; once Dumbledore leaves Hogwarts, the Ministry of Magic issues an order stating that Dolores Umbridge has replaced Dumbledore as the new head of Hogwarts.

exfiltrate—the act of getting an agent out of a certain location or country, often secretly. *Example:* Dobby assists in the exfiltration of Harry, Ron, Griphook, Hermione, and Luna from the

Malfoy dungeon, though at a great price: his own death.

eyes-only communication— information that is so important that it can only be shown to the recipient—usually the leader of a country—and not left in that person's possession in the form of a paper or electronic copy. *Example:* Dumbledore shows Harry the memories he has collected in the Pensieve; the memories have not been transcribed or copied, making them more secure.

family jewels—The term *family jewels* originally applied to the list, pulled together in 1973 by the CIA inspector general, of all illegal activities carried out by the CIA prior to Watergate. Disclosure of the *existence* of the list resulted in the creation of two different committees that investigated CIA activities and issued two reports: the Rockefeller Commission Report (1975) and the Church Committee Report (1976). In the aftermath of these investigations and press attention, essentially all of the agency's prior misdeeds had become public. The term *family jewels* is now used as a generic term for a nation's most important secrets. *Example:* If the Ministry of Magic, as part of its inquiry into the death of Sirius Black, were to document all of the mistakes, misuse of the press, and illegal activities that occurred while Cornelius Fudge was Minister of Magic (a lengthy list indeed!), the list could be considered part of the Wizarding world's "family jewels."

FBI (Federal Bureau of Investigation)—the primary domestic law enforcement agency of the United States government; it investigates all potentially illegal activities that occur in the United States, including acts of espionage by foreign governments on US soil. *Example:* The Ministry of Magic's Aurors and other departments enforce laws and investigate wrongdoing in the Wizarding world, such as the improper use of magic and the misuse of Muggle artifacts.

First Amendment—the first addition to the United States Constitution (part of the Bill of Rights, the first ten amendments, ratified in 1791) which stipulates in part that "Congress shall make no law . . . abridging the freedom of speech, or of the press; or the right of the people peaceably to assemble, and to petition the government for a redress of grievances." *Example:* The Ministry of Magic's use and misuse of the press presumably curtailed the *Daily Prophet's* normal function, and its educational decrees limit the rights of Hogwarts students to assemble in organized groups; both would be impermissible in the Muggle United States as violations of the First Amendment.

FISA (Foreign Intelligence Security Act)—a US law enacted in 1976 and effective in 1977 that deals primarily with obtaining search warrants or wiretaps of phones or other electronic devices against persons or entities that appear to be spying on the United States. The issuance of these search warrants remains secret unless necessary to a prosecution that takes place at a later time: to get such a warrant, the federal government must show a legal basis for its belief that a foreign agent or foreign country is operating in the United States.

floater—a person used by a spy agency only once or very rarely, such as a waiter who listens in on what certain diners are saying or a hotel clerk who delivers a message or item to a room to determine its occupants. *Example:* Willy Widdershins was a floater for the Ministry when he spied on Hogwarts students during their organizational meeting at the Hog's Head.

Foreign Intelligence Security Court—the "secret" court created by the FISA that actually receives applications for search warrants and issues those warrants at the request of the federal government.

gardening—a British term for tricking an agent into sending a message to his or her handlers. Because the person tricking the agent knows what information is being sent (such as the day of an upcoming activity), that person has a better chance of decoding the message and using that success to decode prior and subsequent messages sent by that particular spy. *Example:* Knowing that Harry was upset about what he saw in Snape's memories (his father being cruel to Snape) and that he would want to communicate with Sirius, both the Ministry and Voldemort (if they knew what Harry wanted to ask) would want to intercept his message to "Snuffles" in order to determine the code words used by Harry and, better yet, to follow Hedwig to Sirius's location at headquarters!

handler—a senior intelligence officer in charge of an agent. *Example:* Dumbledore was Snape's handler, giving him instructions and organizing his various assignments.

headquarters—the main location for the intelligence organization. *Example:* Number twelve, Grimmauld Place was the headquarters for the Order of the Phoenix.

heightened awareness—see **situational awareness**

high-security asset—a person or item that is actively sought after by the opposing side. *Example:* Harry Potter was treated as a high-security asset each time he was being retrieved from number four, Privet Drive.

historical analysis—the use of past events to understand a society's culture or probable actions in the future. *Example:* When determining how to convince the giants, centaurs, and goblins to join forces against Voldemort, the members of the Order of the Phoenix delve into the history and interests of each group to determine how best to recruit them.

human intelligence (HUMINT)—information derived directly from spies on the ground, acting covertly and often within the opposing side's organization. It is the primary and traditional means of gathering intelligence, although the development of modern communication and electronic-intelligence gathering has in some ways supplanted it. One of the lessons of 9/11 was that regardless of extent and sophistication of other means of gathering information, the traditional use of spies is not only relevant, but should in fact be expanded. *Example:* Dumbledore was able to know what Voldemort was doing and even thinking, thanks to the HUMINT provided by Severus Snape.

imagery intelligence (IMINT)—information obtained through means that allow you to "see" objects, most often through photography, infrared sensors, and other devices (including some forms of radar). *Example:* Although the picture of the Weasley family on vacation in Egypt that appeared in the *Daily Prophet* seemed like a standard family photo, to Sirius Black, who employed photographic interpretation and his own personal knowledge while sitting in his cell in Azkaban, it was demonstrative proof that Peter Pettigrew was alive and hiding in plain sight—as the rat that he was (PA 362-363)!

incommunicado—the status of being unable to communicate, either involuntary (while being held captive) or voluntary (not communicating in order to maintain cover). *Example:* When Harry and his friends were imprisoned in the Malfoy dungeon, they were initially held incommunicado; however, thanks to a fragment of Sirius's mirror, Harry was able to talk to a blue-eyed man, and soon Dobby arrived to rescue them!

infiltration—the act of entering a restricted area, usually by covert means. *Example:* In the final book, Harry, Ron, and Hermione infiltrated the Ministry of Magic by using Polyjuice to disguise themselves as Ministry of Magic employees.

informant—a person who provides inside information to someone else. *Example:* Marietta, Cho's friend, told Professor Umbridge about the secret meetings of Dumbledore's Army.

inside information—knowledge gleaned by a person already in place inside an organization for purposes of spying on that organization. *Example:* Kingsley Shacklebolt, while supposedly looking for Sirius, was actually keeping tabs on the Ministry and providing inside information to the Order of the Phoenix.

inspector general—a very senior position in many government agencies held by a person who has the authority to investigate any potential wrongdoing within that agency. *Example:* Professor Umbridge was assigned by the Ministry of Magic to investigate Hogwarts, initially as a professor

and then through her official appointment as Hogwarts's first High Inquisitor.

intelligence—information or communication that can be evaluated and used to determine facts, intentions, and capabilities of an enemy, generally organized within an intellectual framework capable of sophisticated analysis. *Example:* Arthur Weasley used his job at the Ministry of Magic to collect intelligence about Death Eaters' activities and the Ministry's own plans.

intelligence analysis—the act of organizing information in a way that can be used to determine facts, intentions, and capabilities of an enemy. *Example:* When Harry reports the attack on Mr. Weasley and describes seeing it happen through Nagini's eyes, Dumbledore performs an intelligence analysis and concludes that the connection between Harry and Voldemort is real—and potentially dangerous to both sides.

intelligence briefing—a presentation of facts, conclusions, evaluations, and often the plans, intentions, and capabilities of an enemy, normally delivered to a senior leader of the government. *Example:* Once sacked, former Ministry of Magic Cornelius Fudge is assigned to provide an intelligence briefing to the "other" Prime Minister, the one who lives at Number 10, Downing Street, London.

intelligence community—the sixteen separate US agencies that are responsible for providing intelligence, which is in theory consolidated, integrated, and forwarded to the separate office of the leading US intelligence officer, the Director of National Intelligence. These agencies are:

- Air Force Intelligence, Surveillance and Reconnaissance Agency (AF ISRA)
- Army Intelligence and Security Command (G-3)
- Central Intelligence Agency (CIA)
- Coast Guard Intelligence (CGI)
- Defense Intelligence Agency (DIA)
- Department of Energy's Office of Intelligence and Counterintelligence (DOE OIC)
- Department of Homeland Security's Office of Intelligence and Analysis (DHS OIA)
- Department of State's Bureau of Intelligence and Research (INR)
- Department of the Treasury's Office of Intelligence and Analysis (OIA)
- Drug Enforcement Administration's Office of National Security Intelligence (ONSI)
- Federal Bureau of Investigation (FBI)
- Marine Corps Intelligence (MCI)
- National Geospatial-Intelligence Agency (NGA)
- National Reconnaissance Office (NRO)
- National Security Agency/ Central Security Service (NSA)
- Office of Naval Intelligence (ONI)

intelligence estimate—a formal document, based on all known intelligence, describing in detail an enemy's capabilities and intentions; created by the National Intelligence Council.

intelligence oversight—a review performed by one branch of government (or appointed entity or individual) on the actions of another branch or of the government as a whole, particularly covert actions or use of the intelligence apparatus to spy on those within the territory of that government.

interception—the act of obtaining a communication, normally one that has been sent secretly to someone else. *Example:* Filch, most probably tipped off by Professor Umbridge, attempts to intercept the owl that Harry sent to Sirius, on the pretext that he had heard a rumor that Harry was ordering Dungbombs.

internal communication—messages sent within a confined or controlled area. *Example:* The paper airplanes used to deliver messages throughout the Ministry of Magic, which likely stay within the Ministry building in order to prevent anyone outside it from intercepting communications.

internal control—use of rules or selected persons to exercise authority or control over the larger group. *Example:* At Hogwarts, the Prefects, the Head Boy, and the Head Girl of each house assist and if necessary discipline the other students; Professor Umbridge takes this concept to a further level, assigning Draco Malfoy and other students to the Inquisitorial Squad to enforce her draconian policies and provide internal control.

interrogation—a lengthy questioning of a person, usually by an authoritarian figure, such as a police officer or detective. *Example:* At Harry's hearing, Cornelius Fudge interrogates

Harry, eliciting information to be used against him.

infrared intelligence (IRINT)—data and visually-enhanced information derived from the infrared spectrum, not visible to the normal sight or through normal photography.

Kryptos—Jim Sanborn's famous 1990 sculpture that is located at CIA headquarters in Langley, Virginia, that has four encrypted messages, three of which have been decoded.

laser intelligence (LASINT)—information derived by use of lasers, such as distance to objects.

layout—a geographic description or drawing of an area, usually the interior of a building. *Example:* In the kitchen of the Order's headquarters, Harry sees a parchment showing the layout of a building, probably the Ministry of Magic.

leading question—a question that contains its own answer. *Example:* Cornelius Fudge uses leading questions to elicit information from Harry to prove that he was guilty of the charge of using magic underage and in the presence of a Muggle.

left in the dark—the state of being intentionally denied what may be essential knowledge, even though that information is greatly desired or needed. *Example:* Dumbledore repeatedly, throughout the series, fails to share important bits of information with Harry.

legend—a detailed false history of a person under cover that is corroborated by documents or other forms of confirmation. *Example:* Peter Pettigrew, by killing a dozen Muggles and then escaping in rat form, leaves Sirius as the fall guy, creating his own legend of being killed by Sirius.

lookout—a person assigned to warn others if someone approaches during a covert operation. *Example:* Ginny and Luna serve as lookouts when Harry sneaks into Professor Umbridge's office the second time.

mail cover—a request by an intelligence agency to obtain information from a country's mail service (public or private) to examine the external aspects of an envelope or package, normally without opening the item (though some countries will allow the package to be opened and then carefully resealed so as to appear intact).

medical intelligence (MEDINT)—information about the physical or physiological aspects of a person of inquiry or someone presently under surveillance, most often the leader of a country or a group adverse to the entity obtaining the information.

microdot—extremely small lettering printed on a photo or a piece of paper that contains substantial information in what appears to be a dot (or period).

mole—a person stationed inside a government or spy agency who regularly provides information to another government or spy agency. *Example:* Unbeknownst to the "other" Prime Minister, his new assistant, Kingsley Shacklebolt, is actually a mole for the Ministry of Magic.

National Security Agency (NSA)—the US agency charged with intercepting and gathering phone and electronic communications from persons and countries of interest. Before its existence was declassified, this super-secret agency was known as No Such Agency.

need to know—a security standard in which only those persons who absolutely must know the information have access to it. *Example:* Only the members of the Order of the Phoenix are allowed to know the address of number twelve, Grimmauld Place, which is given to each person by the Secret Keeper, Albus Dumbledore.

nonofficial cover—a covert agent's putative "public" assignment or position used to justify his or her placement at an embassy or other overseas location. Due to the lack of legal status or any form of diplomatic immunity, if caught spying by the foreign government, that person will be subject to prosecution and prison.

nonviolent non-cooperation—a philosophical concept superbly employed by Mahatma Gandhi to force the British to give up control over India and used by many others afterwards, including Martin Luther King Jr. in the United States in the 1960s. Its primary moral tenet involves opposing the ruling authority and the oppression of the government in power by organizing the masses in nonviolent refusal to cooperate with the government, if possible shutting down the oppressive government entirely. *Example:* The Weasley twins oppose Professor Umbridge by using harmless distractions to create havoc and chaos throughout Hogwarts.

notional agent—an agent that does not exist but is invented for the sole purpose of providing false information to an enemy, sometimes used to find a mole. *Example:* Professor Umbridge, in order to get Filch to try to intercept Harry's mail, may have been the one to tell him that a student (who in reality does not exist) had told her that Harry was trying to order Dungbombs by Owl Post.

observation—the process of looking at a place, person, or situation and, importantly, remembering the information accurately. A skilled intelligence operative will have extensive training in gathering and remembering information. *Example:* When Harry and his friends enter the kitchen after the meeting of the Order of the Phoenix, Harry observes on the table plans for a building—and later correctly surmises that the plans are for the Ministry of Magic.

open source—a collection of information that is generally open to all, such as newspapers, articles, maps, or other publications or documents. *Example:* The *Daily Prophet* is an open source that provides Harry and his friends with substantial information, even when it is providing false facts or conclusions.

operative / operations officer / operations planner / operations team—Operatives or operations officers are people normally in the field and may be referred to as agents or officers; operations planners usually remain at headquarters or the regional station, but are sometimes deployed with or very near the agent conducting the spy mission. When more than one person is involved in an activity, those person are delineated as the operations team. As a whole, operations in an intelligence agency is the planned activity of agents and planners toward a specific goal, with specific actions planned. *Example:* When Harry uses his Invisibility Cloak to get into the restricted section of the Hogwarts library, he is acting alone and is an agent or operative. When Harry, Ron, and Hermione sneak past Fluffy to try to save the Philosopher's Stone, they are acting as an operations team. Before their mission to break into Gringotts with Griphook's assistance, our famous trio and Griphook conduct operations planning.

operations intelligence—any information that relates to or could affect any planned intelligence activity. *Example:* In order to get into the Ministry of Magic to retrieve the locket that Professor Umbridge had taken from Mundungus Fletcher, Harry, Ron, and Hermione select which persons to "become" through Polyjuice by observing the usual comings and goings of Ministry of Magic employees.

out in the cold—an agent left in the field with no communication from his or her handlers is said to be "out in the cold." When communication is restored, the agent has been "brought in from the cold." *Example:* Lucius Malfoy was in the cold for many years, awaiting the return of Voldemort.

outside influence—any attempt to alter the actions of a person, group, or country, made by someone from another country or group. *Example:* The Ministry of Magic, by sending Professor Umbridge to Hogwarts, is exerting outside influence to change Hogwarts and, better yet, get rid of Professor Dumbledore as Headmaster.

overflight—the use of any flight technology, whether it be an airplane or a broom, to observe a person, object, or area from above, usually in enemy airspace. For the most part, unmanned drones and satellites have taken over the role of spy planes, such as the SR-71 and U-2. *Example:* In order to get to Hogwarts after being denied entry to platform nine and three-quarters, Harry and Ron fly the Ford Anglia over the countryside and follow the Hogwart's Express back to school.

party line—the official or preferred view of a particular group in power. *Example:* Throughout *Harry Potter and the Order of the Phoenix*, the Ministry's party line is that Voldemort has not returned and that Harry is lying about this and many other things.

password—a word or number sequence that allows access to a building or information. *Example:* In order to get into Dumbledore's office, both the students and the teachers must use a password.

Pentagon Papers—a large group of documents showing the history of the Vietnam War, many of which were at the time classified documents, that were published by the *New York Times* during the Vietnam War. The US Supreme Court refused to issue an injunction or "prior restraint" to prevent the publication of the documents.

photographic intelligence (PHOINT)—information conveyed through photographs or the analysis of photographs. *Example:* In book 5, when Harry went up to Mr. Weasley's office to await his trial, he observed that Kingsley's office was literally covered with photographs of Sirius Black, the man he was ostensibly assigned to capture. In book 7, Harry, through *recollection* and proper *analysis* of a photo of the original

Order of the Phoenix, noted that Dumbledore's brother Aberforth had been a member of the Order and used that information to convince Aberforth to help him and his friends get into Hogwarts.

pianist—slang for radio operator. *Example:* In book 7, *Potterwatch* is a radio show, hosted by pianist Lee Jordan, that can be listened to only if you know the password.

pigeon post—messages carried by trained birds, specifically homing pigeons. Anyone who scoffed at J. K. Rowling's message-carrying owls should have realized that pigeons have be used to send messages since biblical times. Indeed, pigeons were used to relay the names of the winners of the early Greek Olympic games. Pigeons were also used during the Siege of Paris in the 1870s, and throughout World Wars I and II. Pigeons have carried cameras and electronic tracking devices. Some pigeons were even awarded medals for their work, including Cher Ami, a pigeon who saved an entire battalion and received the French Croix de Guerre with Palm. *Example:* In the first book, hundreds upon hundreds of persistent owls attempt to deliver Harry's invitation to attend Hogwarts.

plainclothed—an agent or officer wearing ordinary clothes instead of his or her normal uniform, thus preventing immediate identification with a uniformed group. Unlike a disguise, this technique involves only the exchange of a uniform for everyday clothing. *Example:* When the students head home from Hogwarts, they put away their robes and wands and dress in normal Muggle attire so as not to draw attention to themselves at the train station.

plans, capabilities, and intentions—the abilities, resources, and organized actions available to a person, group, or country, determined by a thorough analysis of all available intelligence. One of the most important aspects of evaluating an enemy is determining its capabilities and intentions. The best known final product of this information is a National Intelligence Estimate produced by the National Intelligence Council. *Example:* Severus Snape was assigned the very dangerous job of pretending to be on Voldemort's side in order to determine the Dark Lord's plans, capabilities, and intentions.

political intelligence—information about a political system, the leaders of a political party (normally the one in power), and any opposition groups, used primarily to determine what particular actions that leader or country might take. *Example:* In planning to circumvent Harry's security detail as he leaves Privet Drive in book 7, Voldemort discusses with his followers whether the Aurors will be used to protect Harry (they will not, because the Order believes that Voldemort's followers have infiltrated the Ministry) and whether the Ministry will "fall" by the time Harry is to be transported (it does not).

polygraph—a lie-detecting device used to measure extremely negligible physical reactions of a person while answering preplanned and exceedingly precise questions. It is used extensively in the security world, but not yet considered reliable enough to be admitted automatically into court proceedings. *Example:* Legilimency is used in the Wizarding world to determine if someone is lying, and Veritaserum is used to get someone to tell the truth.

potential agent—any person who could possibly be enticed to become an agent. *Example:* Draco, in book 6, is rightfully perceived by Voldemort as a potential agent, given his family's views about wizard purity and Draco's desire to seek revenge on behalf of his father, who has been exposed as a Death Eater and imprisoned.

pretext—an excuse to do something, often a pre-planned method to gain access to an item of interest or to remain at a location. *Example:* Harry and Ron, while walking slowly and pausing while Ron pretends to tie his shoes, had a pretext for listening as Professor Marchbanks, head of the Wizarding Examinations Authority, discussed Dumbledore's escape with Professor Umbridge.

Principal Agent—the agent in charge of other agents, sometimes referred to as the handler. *Example:* Voldemort is clearly the principal agent in charge of his Death Eaters.

product—the final form of intelligence, after it has been organized and analyzed by professional intelligence analysts, usually in the form of a report. *Example:* When Harry first arrives to Grimmauld Place, there is a meeting of the Order in progress and he is told by his friends that Snape is giving a "top secret" report, which is the product of his spying (though Snape, to keep his cover, would undoubtedly claim

that the information is from Dumbledore).

propaganda—false information, usually disseminated by the government. *Example:* The Ministry of Magic regularly distributed false information or innuendo about Harry Potter, which was printed in the *Daily Prophet* and used to discredit Harry and his assertion that Voldemort has returned.

provocation—an act made for the purpose of getting someone else to overreact and do something stupid. *Example:* Draco provokes Harry and the Weasley twins into attacking him after the Gryffindor team beat Slytherin, resulting in Harry receiving a lifetime ban from playing Quidditch.

psychic intelligence—information obtained by paranormal means, such as through a medium or fortune teller. *Example:* Of all the predictions Professor Trelawney made, only two had any substance: her original prophecy, given to Professor Dumbledore when she was being interviewed for a position at Hogwarts, and her prediction to Harry that Voldemort's servant would set out to return to him before midnight in book 3.

psychological assessment / psychological profiling—the use of information about a person's traits, characteristics, background, and psychological makeup to predict that person's reactions or future actions. *Example:* Voldemort, knowing Harry's heroic proclivities, lays a trap and convinces Harry (through information implanted in his dreams) that Sirius has been captured and is being tortured in the Department of Mysteries.

psychological operations (PSYOPS)—the use of psychological intelligence in an operation, normally intended to convince a person (an enemy agent or potential agent) of the need to act in a certain way or switch sides. *Example:* Professor Umbridge's use of detentions and torture on Harry was a psychological operation intended to break Harry; however, it had the opposite effect.

psychology of risk—the study or analysis of a person's aversion or proclivity to risk. *Example:* Throughout the series, Harry often disregards risk and continues to take action. He is definitely *not* risk averse. Hermione, on the other hand, has struck a more appropriate balance and is willing to take risks—but only after thinking them through and determining that there is no other option.

public opinion—the views or biases of a large group of people, usually a large geographical region or an entire country. *Example:* The Wizarding world's public opinion about Harry changed dramatically throughout the series, often as a result of the Ministry's use of propaganda and the later "discovery" of the truth.

Pyrrhic victory—a term drawn from two battles waged against the Romans by King Pyrrhus of Epirus in 280 and 279 bc. Although King Pyrrhus won both battles, he won them at a great cost, losing many soldiers and his best leaders. The Romans were able to replace the men they lost, but King Pyrrhus was unable to do so and was eventually defeated. *Example:* Even though Harry won the match against Slytherin, his and George Weasley's attack on Draco Malfoy afterward resulted in the ultimate loss to Harry and both twins in the form of Professor Umbridge's lifetime ban on playing Quidditch

radar intelligence (RADINT)—information received through radar.

reconnaissance—any observation or operation used or intended to obtain information covertly. *Example:* Our favorite trio regularly looks out their dorm windows at Hagrid's hut to see when he has returned from his mission to recruit the giants.

recruitment—the act of getting someone to join your side. *Example:* Professor Dumbledore recruits Slughorn to teach at Hogwarts at the beginning of book 6.

risk analysis / risk assessment—the intentional study of and reflection on whether the risk involved in an act is worth the price of failure. *Example:* Harry enters the Department of Mysteries because the risk to Sirius is so great that he believes he has no choice but to do so.

risk averse—unwilling to engage in risky behavior. *Example:* Hermione, unlike Harry, tends to be risk averse, thinking things through and acting only if absolutely necessary.

rogue agent—an agent who has gone out on his or her own, no longer under the control of the principal agent or country. *Example:* Fenrir Greyback, a werewolf, refuses to follow the orders of the Ministry, under Voldemort's control, and often acts on his own volition, as when he attempts to defy Bellatrix's demand that he give her the Sword of Gryffindor after Harry, Ron, and Hermione have been captured in book 7.

routine—tendency to do the same thing on a regular basis, intentionally or out of habit, such as taking the same route to work every day. *Example:* Harry, Ron, and Hermione study the routine of the Ministry employees as they go to work at the Ministry of Magic in order to determine how to get in to get the locket from Dolores Umbridge.

safe house—a place where agents or defectors can be safely hidden; often a place to debrief agents. *Example:* Number twelve, Grimmauld Place, is the Order of the Phoenix's safe house throughout the last half of the series—until it is compromised.

Sensitive Compartmented Information (SCI)—the highest level of security, which uses a code name for categorization, thus limiting access to the information to only those who have a need-to-know basis.

Sensitive Compartmented Information Facility (SCIF)—a secure facility in which people with the proper security clearance may retrieve and submit extremely sensitive information, often in a vault or location with limited access and proper security protection and countermeasures.

Secret—a level of security classification below Top

Secret and above Classified or Confidential.

secret agent—a person who is gathering information covertly, usually on behalf of a government.

Secret Service—the United States government agency, part of the Treasury Department, that holds responsibility for protecting the president of the United States, the First Family, and former presidents.

secure / secure area / secure communication / secure communication device / secure location / secure meeting place—a state of being safe from eavesdropping or observation; a communication device that prevents interception; any location in which one cannot be overheard or seen. *Example:* The Room of Requirement is a secure meeting place for the members of Dumbledore's Army to train in Defense Against the Dark Arts.

security clearance—a formal designation by a government, awarded after thorough investigation, that allows a person access to restricted information. *Example:* Hagrid refuses to tell Harry and his friends what Fluffy is guarding because it is "top secret" and cannot be revealed to anyone who does not have the proper

clearance to receive the information.

security detail—a group of people engaged in the protection of a high-ranking or otherwise important person, particularly when that person is going from one place to another and is at a higher risk than normal. *Example:* Harry, when he is taken from the Dursleys' home at the beginning of each school term, often has a security detail to protect and transport him.

security risk—a situation in which confidential information is or could be retrieved by an opponent; also a person who may intentionally or accidentally divulge sensitive information. *Example:* Hagrid is often a security risk because he carelessly divulges information that he is supposed to keep secret, such as how to get Fluffy to fall asleep.

shopworn goods—information (or even a person) that is no longer needed or no longer secret. *Example:* The information Avery supplies to Voldemort turns out to be incorrect and useless—to Avery's great misfortune.

signal—any subtle action conveying a covert message or indication to take a preplanned action. *Example:* When Harry is being taken from Privet Drive by his security team in book 5, someone has been assigned to a more distant location to send up an all-clear signal of sparks from a wand, confirming that it is safe to proceed.

signal intelligence (SIGINT)—intelligence derived from communications and electronic intelligence, generally the interception of radio and cell phone communications. *Example:* The *Potterwatch* broadcasters change the password for each broadcast to avoid interception of their signals by Voldemort and his Death Eaters, as such information would be considered valuable signals intelligence.

situational awareness—a person's intentional attentiveness to what is going around him or her, a term most often used in the military, as when a soldier or pilot must watch for danger from all directions. In the intelligence world, spies are trained to use this heightened state of awareness in denied areas. *Example:* When Harry, Ron, and Hermione sneak into the Ministry to get the locket from Umbridge, they are aware that they are in enemy territory and must use situational awareness to remain undetected.

sleeper agent—an agent left for an extended period, sometimes even years, awaiting a particular assignment or a signal indicating

that the time has come to execute a preplanned mission. *Example:* Mrs. Figg is a sleeper agent assigned by Dumbledore to watch over Harry and act only if the circumstances warrant it, such as when she intercedes after Harry and Dudley are attacked by Dementors.

source—any person who provides information to an intelligence officer. *Example:* Rookwood acts as a source when he informs Voldemort that he used to work at the Ministry of Magic's Department of Mysteries and reveals that Avery should have known that Bode could not have retrieved the prophecy.

sources and methods—*sources* are the individuals *providing* the information, or in some situations the technology being used to *obtain* information. *Methods* are the means by which the information is procured or relayed, including both technology and the manner in which a person gathered the information. *Example:* Snape is Dumbledore's most important source as to getting information on Voldemort, and Dumbledore's Pensieve (using slivers of memories) and the twins' extendable ears are both methods to getting information.

spy craft—all operational aspects and techniques used in spying, including the use of psychology, weapons, intelligence, analysis, secure locations, indirect communication, forgery, and disguises. *Example:* Harry, Ron, and Hermione's use of Polyjuice Potion is a great example of employing spy craft to gain access to people and places and obtain important information.

sterilize—removing any markings or components that can be used to trace an object back to the intelligence agent or entity that deployed it, such as scratching the serial number off a weapon.

stringer—a low-level agent who lives or works near an intelligence target and provides basic information about it, often sporadically, and usually without pay. *Example:* Mrs. Figg is most appropriately defined as a stringer, assigned to watch over Harry when he is at Privet Drive and provide updates to Dumbledore as information is received or observed.

subversive organization—a group of people who object to the present government or regime and organize themselves into a working group that acts in some way against the offending government or regime. *Example:* The Hogwarts students organize Dumbledore's Army to teach themselves what Professor Umbridge forbade them to learn;

later, the organization becomes more subversive and active, taking direct action against the Ministry and those it has placed in charge of Hogwarts.

Sun-Tzu—a famous Chinese general who lived in the fourth century BC and is the author of the earliest known writings on war and spying, including his most famous, *The Art of War*.

surveillance—the systematic observation of a person or preselected target. *Example:* When Harry, Ron, and Hermione are in hiding at number twelve, Grimmauld Place, they notice Death Eaters outside conducting surveillance (watching for a sign of anyone coming and going to and from a building they could not see).

sweeper—a person who checks an area or room to make sure that no one can eavesdrop. *Example:* When Harry and Hermione enter Umbridge's office to use the fire to communicate with Sirius, they immediately look around to determine whether there are any devices that will inform Umbridge that they are in her office.

talent spotter—a person who provides the names of potential recruits to an intelligence officer or entity. *Example:* Someone likely told Professor Dumbledore about a young orphan named

Tom Riddle who seemed to have very strange powers; that person would be considered a talent spotter for Hogwarts. (It is also possible that the Ministry discovered Riddle when he used magic underage.)

telemetry intelligence (TELINT)—part of SIGINT, telemetry intelligence is information about the speed, angle, and direction of objects, quite often missiles being test-fired or dummy warheads entering the atmosphere.

Top Secret—the highest security clearance in the US classification system. *Example:* Snape was providing a top-secret report to the Order of the Phoenix when Harry arrived at Grimmauld place for the first time.

turning—convincing an agent to switch sides. *Example:* Dumbledore turned Snape at the same meeting Snape asked Dumbledore to protect Lily Potter from Voldemort.

unwitting agent—a person who provides information without realizing that the information will be given to an intelligence agency or hostile government. *Example:* Hagrid, after receiving a dragon's egg from a stranger (Quirrell?), told the stranger how he was able to control Fluffy by putting him to sleep with music.

utilitarianism—originally proposed by philosopher Jeremy Bentham, the goal of utilitarianism is *to promote the greatest happiness for the greatest number.* *Example:* While a young man, Dumbledore accepted a form of utilitarianism, proposed by Gellert Grindelwald, in which those with magic powers would seize control of the world and dominate the Muggles—for their own good, of course.

walk-in—a person who voluntarily agrees to provide information to an intelligence officer or agency, usually after literally walking into an embassy and offering his or her services. *Example:* Snape, when he went to ask Dumbledore to protect and save Lily Potter, was a walk-in.

walking back the cat—a thorough review of an agent or mission—from the very beginning of that person's employment or the entire planning and execution of a mission—in order to determine what went wrong and why. *Example:* Through analysis and the Pensieve, Dumbledore was walking back the cat through the history of Tom Riddle and his development into Lord Voldemort, all in an attempt to find out not only what went wrong, but also how to defeat him.

watch list—a list of persons who are of interest to an intelligence entity. *Example:* In book 7, the snatchers have a list of persons whom the Ministry (now really Voldemort) wants captured.

weapons of mass destruction—weapons capable of inflicting mass casualties, including nuclear weapons and chemical weapons.

wilderness of mirrors—a phrase created by T. S. Eliot in his 1920 poem "Gerontion," line 65, and used by James Jesus Angleton, a former senior CIA official, to describe the difficulty and confusion of determining the truth in the realm of intelligence, "that . . . myriad of stratagems, deceptions, artifices and all the other devices of disinformation which the Soviet bloc and its coordinated intelligence services use to confuse and split the West," thus producing "an ever-fluid landscape where fact and illusion merge."

INDEX OF
MUGGLE-RELATED REFERENCES

INDEX OF MUGGLE·RELATED REFERENCES

INDEX OF MUGGLE·RELATED REFERENCES

ABOUT THE AUTHORS

LYNN BOUGHEY is North Dakota's first Truman Scholar (a Congressional Scholarship begun in 1977), graduating from Grinnell College in Grinnell, Iowa, in 1979 and from Hamline University School of Law in St. Paul, Minnesota, cum laude in 1983. Lynn has clerked for a federal trial judge and a state Supreme Court justice, and held a political post as Deputy Insurance Commissioner for the State of North Dakota. Lynn, who has been a trial litigator in North Dakota for more than twenty-five years, taught numerous college-level courses from 1985 through 2008, including Introduction to Political Science; International Studies; Terrorism; Law and Society; Criminal Law; and Criminal Procedure. Lynn is the author of *Mission to Chara*, a spy novel published in 2000. Lynn lives in Montana, practices law in North Dakota, and has two twin daughters, age eleven.

ALSO BY LYNN BOUGHEY

- *Mission to Chara* (2000 North American Heritage Press) available on the Kindle through amazon.com.

- *Using Shakespeare in Continuing Legal Education* (E-book 2014)

- *Shakespeare and Criminal Law: A Workbook for Criminal Law Students* (E-book 2014)

COMING SOON FROM BOTH AUTHORS:

- Boughey and Earnest, *Harry Potter and the Art of Spying Intelligence Studies Workbook* (E-book 2014)

- Boughey and Earnest, *Harry Potter and the Art of Spying— Children's Version* (forthcoming 2015)

PETER EARNEST is the Founding Executive Director of the International Spy Museum in Washington, DC. His thirty-six-year CIA career included more than twenty years in the agency's Clandestine Service. A member of the CIA's Senior Intelligence Service, he was awarded the agency's Intelligence Medal of Merit for "superior performance throughout his career." In his final posting, he served as the agency's principal spokesman, developing and implementing a strategy of greater openness with the media and the public. He also served as President and Chairman of the Board of the Association of Former Intelligence Officers (AFIO).

ALSO BY PETER EARNEST

- *Business Confidential: Lessons for Corporate Success from Inside the CIA,* coauthored with Maryann Karinch (2011 AMACOM)

- *The Real Spy's Guide to Becoming a Spy,* with Suzanne Harper (2009 Abrams Books for Young Readers)

- Introduction to *International Spy Museum Handbook of Practical Spying,* by Jack Barth, illustrated by Steven Guarnaccia (2004 National Geographic)

- Foreword to *The Dictionary of Espionage: Spyspeak in English,* by Joseph C. Goulden (2012 Dover Publications, Inc.)

- Principal researcher, *A Secret Life: The Polish Officer, His Covert Mission, and the Price He Paid to Save His Country,* by Benjamin Weiser (2004 Public Affairs/Perseus Group)